THE MEMOIR OF
JOSEPH PIERCE BRAUD, MD

HIS LIFE JOURNEY ON THE GRAVEL ROAD AND BEYOND

As Told to Dr. Lionel D. Lyles

JOSEPH PIERCE BRAUD

Copyright © 2022 Joseph Pierce Braud.

All rights reserved. No part of this book may be reproduced, stored, or transmitted by any means—whether auditory, graphic, mechanical, or electronic—without written permission of both publisher and author, except in the case of brief excerpts used in critical articles and reviews. Unauthorized reproduction of any part of this work is illegal and is punishable by law.

ISBN: 979-8-88640-556-9 (sc)
ISBN: 979-8-88640-557-6 (hc)
ISBN: 979-8-88640-558-3 (e)

Because of the dynamic nature of the Internet, any web addresses or links contained in this book may have changed since publication and may no longer be valid. The views expressed in this work are solely those of the author and do not necessarily reflect the views of the publisher, and the publisher hereby disclaims any responsibility for them.

One Galleria Blvd., Suite 1900, Metairie, LA 70001
1-888-421-2397

CONTENTS

Dedications xxiii
Preface xxvii
Acknowledgement xxxiii

I   Introduction 1

II   Geography Of The Louisiana River Road,
       Plantations, And The Mississippi River 17
       A. Origin of the Mississippi River 17
       B. River Road: From Baton Rouge, LA To New Orleans, LA ... 19
       C. Slavery Plantations That Operated Within The
           Louisiana River Road Parishes By 1858 And Into
           The Early Twentieth Century 21
       D. Names of Selected Slaveholders Who Owned
           African Slave Plantations In identified River
           Road Parishes By 1858 25
       E. Names Of Selected Slaveholder Families In St. James
           Parish By 1858 27

III   Selected Demographic Characteristics Of The
       White And African Slave Population For River Road
       Parishes-1850 To 1950 31
       A. Total White And African Slave Population, 1850 31
       B. Total Free White, Black, And Mulatto Populations
           On The River Road By 1860 34
       C. Total White And Free Colored Populations By 1870 35
       D. Total White And Free Colored Populations By 1880 38
       E. Total White And Colored Populations By 1890 41
       F. Total White And Negro Populations By 1900 41
       G. Total White And Negro Populations By 1910 42
       H. Total White And Negro Populations By 1930 46
       I. Total White And Negro Populations By 1940 47

IV   Thirteenth Amendment To The U. S. Constitution, Freedmen Bureau Bill, 1865, Sharecropping System And Out-Migration On The River Road 51
      A. Former African Slave Plantations and Villages and Cities Outgrowth During Post-Civil War Era...................51
      B. Thirteenth Amendment to the U.S. Constitution............ 53
      C. Freedmen Bureau Bill, 1865.. 56
      D. Sharecropping System After The American Civil War 58
      E. Sharecropping System And Practice On The Louisiana Gravel Road.. 59
          a. House Types... 59
          b. How The Sharecropping System Operated On The Gravel Road... 60
          c. Water Pumping System Used To Inundate The Rice Fields 62
          d. Cutting Rice At Harvest Time.................................... 65
          e. Sharecroppers And Other Workers' Catch Twenty-Two Bondage... 66

V   Domestic Terrorism, Ku Klux Klan, And Jim Crow Restrictions Put In Place To Stop Negro Progress From 1800 To The Present Day.. 68
      A. Rutherford B. Hayes And Samuel J. Tilden 1876 Presidential Election Fraud 68
      B. Post-Civil War Reconstruction Act, 1867 70
      C. End Of Reconstruction, 1877... 71
      D. Southern Democrats And Northern Republicans Unite Against Reconstruction By 1877 72
      E. Political And Social Disempowerment Of The Freed Negroes In The South After The American Civil War And Throughout The Twentieth Century.................... 73
          a. Dismantling Of President Abraham Lincoln's Reparation Reconstruction Program 74
          b. Fifteenth Amendment And The Right To Vote (Black Voter Suppression).. 75
          c. United States Supreme Court Cases, 1873, 1876, and 1896 76

		d. KU Klux Klan And The Post-Reconstruction Period: Enforcers' Use Of Violence To Maintain The White Status Quo 78

        d. KU Klux Klan And The Post-Reconstruction Period: Enforcers' Use Of Violence To Maintain The White Status Quo 78

        e. Out-Migration Of Freed Black People From Louisiana By 1940 80

    F. Braud Family Group: Twenty-Five Generations-1600 To 1950 82

VI   Origin Of The Pierce- Braud Family Group From Pre-Civil War To 1921 84

    A. Vincent Brault And The Immigration Of The White Brault Family Group To The "New World" Beginning in 1632 85

    B. Voyage Across The Atlantic Ocean 86

    C. L'Acadie or Acadia, 1605 to 1755 87

        a. Economic Life Of The Acadians In The Maritime Province Of Nova Scotia 88

        b. French And British Struggle For Domination Of L'Acadie 89

    D. Grand Derangement And Expulsion Of Acadians From L'Acadie In Nova Scotia In The Spring 1755 89

    E. White Brault Family Migration From Nova Scotia To St. Jacques de Cabannoce' Later Renamed St. James Parish 91

        a. Vincent Brault: Source Of All Of The Brauds (Breaux, Breaus, Braud, etc) Who Migrated To Louisiana After The Grand Derangement In 1755 92

        b. Origin Of The F. Braud Plantation In St. Jacques de Cabannoce' (Later Renamed St. James Parish) 93

    F. Crossover: Edouardo Breaux, Jr Marriage To The African Slave Woman Celestine And The Beginning Of The Black Braud Family Group On The Louisiana River Road 95

    G. Manifestation Of The Crossover And The Beginning Of The Braud Family Group Lineage On The Gravel Road 97

		H.	Braud Family Group And Selected Generations During The 19th And 20th Centuries 98
			a. Braud Family Group: First Generation On The Louisiana River Road In St. James Parish 100
			b. Braud Family Group: Second Generation On The Louisiana River Road In St. James Parish 101
		I.	Pierce Family Group And Selected Generations During The 19th and 20th Centuries 102
VII		Joe Braud And Lillian Luellen Pierce-Braud Household 103	
		A.	Joe Braud's Character Traits 103
		B.	Lillian Luellen Pierce's Character Traits 105
		C.	Joe Braud And Lillian Luellan Pierce Marry, September 11, 1921 105
			a. Joseph Pierce Braud: Second Born Child Of Joe Braud And Lillian Luellen Pierce Braud On September 11, 1926 107
			b. Home Delivery Assisted By Ms. Rose Williams-Midwife 107
		D.	Reflections Of Joe Braud's Character During My Early Childhood Years 109
		E.	Reflections Of Lillian Luellen Pierce Braud's Character During My Early Childhood Years 110
		F.	Brookstown: A Description Of My Home Village 111
		G.	Description Of Joe Braud And Lillian Luellen Pierce Braud's House In Brookstown 113
		H.	Farm Equipment And Barn Behind Our House 115
		I.	Rise Of Wide-Scale Sugarcane Production During My Childhood Years 116
		J.	Brookstown And Education Opportunity For Black People By The Early 1930s 118
VIII		Social Life In Brookstown And Surrounding Villages 121	
		A.	Getting To The One-Room School On Side Of A Ditch .. 121
		B.	Two men Walking In Opposite Directions 123
		C.	Christmas Gift Child And The Stepfather 123

	D.	Powerful Women And Collection Day On The Gravel Road 124
	E.	Jitney Bus Ride Up And Down The Gravel Road To Donaldsonville, LA 125
	F.	"Big Sunday" Baptism Process Day And The March To The Mississippi River 126
	G.	Joseph Pierce Braud's Unlikely Early Inspiration To Become A Medical Doctor ? 130
	H.	Danneel Elementary School Years In New Orleans, LA School District, 1931 To 1936 132
	I.	St. Louis School Given To Black People Due To White Flight, 1935 134
	J.	J. W. Hoffman Junior High School Affectionately Known As The "Chicken Coup", 1938 To 1939 135
	K.	Lowery Training School In Donaldsonville, LA Located In Ascension Parish, 1940 To 1943 138
IX		Joseph Pierce Braud's Childhood World Turned Upside Down In 1936 141
	A.	Untimely And Sudden Death Of Joe Braud In 1936 141
	B.	The 1929 Great Depression 143
	C.	Pierce-Braud Family Safety Net Before And After Joe Braud's Death In August 1936 144
	D.	Lillian Luellen Pierce Braud's Strategic Family Development Plan 144
		a. Sustainability 145
		b. Food Acquisition And Evariste "Fray" Washington Commitment 145
		c. Aid To Families With Dependent Children (AFDC) Recipient In 1936 146
	E.	Five Components Of The Strategic Family Development Plan In 1936 147
	F.	Scrapping Rice And Irish Potatoes During 1936 And Thereafter 148
	G.	Shoe Shine Boy On Carrollton Street And Tulane Avenue In New Orleans, LA In 1938 149

	H. Stevedore Work Removing Mud From The Hole Of Cargo Ships In New Orleans, LA During The Summer 1943 150
X	Southern University Education Temporarily Put On Hold To Join The Military To Advance The Pierce-Braud Strategic Family Development Plan............................. 152
	A. Joined The Navy To Help Lillian Luellen Pierce Braud To Financially Support My Six Siblings.................. 153
	B. Years Of Service In The Navy, 1945 To 1948..................... 154
	a. Boot Camp And Company #311 154
	b. Port Chicago, San Francisco, California Preparations For Overseas Station In Japan, 1945........ 155
	c. From Port Chicago, San Francisco, CA To Okinawa, Japan In 1944 156
	d. Saipan And Tinian Island In 1946 157
	C. Davis Street Incident In 1946 160
	D. Transferred To The National Naval Medical Center In Washington, DC, 1946 161
	E. Transferred To Treasure Island, California And Unexpected Reunion With Edward Turner In 1947 162
	F. Discharged From The Navy After Four Years Of Service Was Over In 1948... 162
	G. Hollywood And Dreams Of Being Discovered By Metro Goldwyn Meyers (MGM) In 1948........................ 163
XI	Returned To Southern University To Complete My Undergraduate Degree In The Fall 1948 165
	A. Southern University Football Powerhouse And My Attempted Tryout.. 165
	B. Academic Curriculum Change From Agriculture To Biology And Sciences... 166
	C. College Dating In 1948 167
	D. Biology Project Lesson And Personal Growth 168
	E. Mrs. Patrick, President J.S. Clark's Administrative Secretary And The Reading Lessons 169
	F. Medical Aptitude Test Taken At Louisiana State University In 1950 170

	G.	Lillian Luellen Pierce Braud Strategic Family Development Plan Reached a New Crossroad Between 1945 And 1950 171
		a. Education Status Of The Pierce-Braud Family Group . 171
		b. Part-Time Employment As A Laboratory Assistant In The Biology Department 172
XII		Post-Southern University And The Beginning Of My Professional Career In 1951… 173
	A.	Charles H. Brown High School Science Teaching Position In 1951 173
		a. Science Classroom Facility 173
		b. Industrial Arts Teacher Ask To Build Biology Style Tables 174
		c. Southern University Thirteen In 1956 175
	B.	Reunited With Swedie Weary Brown At Charles H. Brown High School In 1951 176
XIII		Marriage To Swedie Weary Brown In 1952 186
	A.	Home Economics Teacher 186
	B.	Description Of Swedie Weary Brown's Character 187
	C.	Double Ring Wedding Of Joseph Pierce Braud To Swedie Weary Brown And Alphonse Jackson To Ruby Helen McClure In Shreveport, LA In 1952 187
		a. Family Life In Springhill, LA In 1952 To 1955 188
		b. Social Network Of Friends In Springhill, LA And Surrounding Area... 188
	D.	Adoption Of Children Problem Emerged In 1953 189
	E.	Swedie Weary Braud's Siblings In-Laws Interference In Our Marriage 190
	F.	Dream Of Attending Medical School And The Lillian Luellen Pierce Braud Strategic Family Development Plan In 1953..192
	G.	No Respect For "Authority" Revelation In 1954 194
		a. Post-Howard University Medical School Interview And Exit From Charles H. Brown High School In The Summer 1954 195

        b. Stay In My Place And Don't Rock The Boat Syndrome 196

XIV Howard University Medical School In Washington, DC From 1954 To 1958 198
    A. Howard University Medical School Mystery Letter 198
    B. Howard University Medical School Interview Day In August 1954 199
    C. Joseph L. Johnson, MD And Dean Of The Howard University Medical School Conduct Interview 200
        a. Medical School Tuition Payment Question 202
        b. Louisiana "Out Of State" Tuition Program 203
        c. Grass Cutting Business During Medical School Study From Fall1954 To 1958 204
    D. Howard University Medical School First Year From Fall 1954 To Spring 1954 205
        a. 11th Street Apartment 206
        b. Fall Semester 1954 Medical School Coursework 207
        c. Professor Moses Young And Neuro-Anatomy Coursework 208
        d. Anacostia High School And The 11th Street Riot And The 13th-16th Street Riots In 1954 209
    E. Completion Of First Year Of Medical School And Navy Reserve, Fall 1954 To Spring 1955 And Summers 1955 To 1958 211
    F. Swedie Braud Came to Washington, DC To Stay In May 1956 To 1958 213
        a. Third And Senior Years In Medical School From 1956 To 1958 214
        b. Areas Of Specialization In Medical School From 1954 To 1958 215
    G. Graduation From Howard University Medical School And Passage Of The Maryland Medical Board Examination In The Spring 1958 216

XV Post-Howard University Medical School Internship Decision And Family Matters 219

  A. Howard University Medical School Hospital Internship Program, Fall 1958 To Spring 1959 219
  B. Youngstown, Ohio Hospital Association Fall 1958 To Spring 1959 220
   a. Rotating Internship Program Fall 1958 To Spring 1959... 221
   b. Internship Experience Today......................... 221
  C. Adoption Problem Resurfaced As An Elephant In The Room By 1959... 222
  D. Bank Meeting Coincidence In Early 1960 223
   a. Swedie Braud Moved Out Of Apartment................... 224
   b. Decision To Reunite Amidst Unspoken Internal Dialogue.. 225
   c. Decision Made To Return To Louisiana After Internship And General Practice Residency Successfully Completed In Early 1960 225

XVI Louisiana Homecoming And Returned As A Medical Doctor...227
  A. Triumphant Return To Louisiana As A Medical Doctor.. 227
  B. Return To Springhill, LA In Early 1960 230
  C. New Orleans, LA: A Virgin Territory To Set Up A Medical Practice In 1960..231
   a. Dr. Anthony Hackett Breakthrough In 1960 232
   b. Medical Practice Setup At St. Bernard Avenue And North Claiborne Avenue In 1960 233
   c. Circle Food Store And Available Office Space Use For Free In 1960.. 234
  D. Flint-Goodridge Hospital Of Dillard University: A Light Post For Black Physicians In New Orleans, LA By 1960 235

XVII Flint-Goodridge Hospital Of Dillard University Glory Years From 1959 To 1982 237
  A. Phyllis Wheatley Sanitarium And Training School For Nurses 238
  B. Flint-Goodridge Hospital Of Dillard University And Dillard University Established, 1911 To 1932................. 239

C. Dedication Of Flint-Goodridge Hospital Of Dillard University In 1932 241
D. Mr. A. W. Dent Superintendent Of Flint-Goodridge Hospital Of Dillard University And President Of Dillard University 242
E. Flint-Goodridge Hospital Of Dillard University Expansion During Mr. Albert Walter (A.W.) Dent's Presidency Of Dillard University From 1941 To 1969...... 244
F. Flint-Goodridge Hospital Of Dillard University Glory Years, Including Black Physicians And Nurse Anesthetists-1960 To 1982... 247
    a. Began Employment at Flint-Goodridge Hospital Of Dillard University In 1960...................................... 247
    b. The Glory Years Of Flint-Goodridge Hospital Of Dillard University And Black Physicians-1960 To 1982.. 248
    c. Nurse Anesthetist Training Program And The Dr. John Adriani Policy In 1960 249
    d. Nurse Anesthetist Training In The Charity Hospital Anesthesia Training Program By 1958 252
G. Private Medical Practice And Family Life Between 1960 and 1963 254
H. First Black Physician Admitted To The Charity Hospital Residency Program In Anesthesia In 1965 256
I. Silent Revolution At Charity Hospital In New Orleans, LA In 1965 To 1967 259
J. Marriage To Swedie Weary Braud Comes To An End In 1966... 262
K. Named Chief Of Flint-Goodridge Hospital Of Dillard University's Department Of Anesthesia And Phase-out Of The Nurse Anesthetist Program By1968..... 263
    a. Black Physicians Became Department Heads At Flint-Goodridge Hospital Of Dillard University In 1968 264
    b. American Medical Association Denial Of Membership And Phase-out OF Flint-Goodridge

          Hospital Of Dillard University's Nurse
          Anesthetist Program By 1968 265
    L. Flint-Goodridge Hospital OF Dillard University
       And Its Surgery And Anesthesia Groups From 1968
       To 1982 267
    M. Family Life-Work Life Balance From 1960 To 1982......... 269
    N. Medical Practice Incorporation In 1972............................ 273

XVIII Flint-Goodridge Hospital of Dillard University Rise And
Untimely Fall From 1960 To 1982 275
    A. Surgery And Anesthesia Department At Flint-
       Goodridge Hospital Of Dillard University During
       The 1970s.. 276
    B. Angela Dixon And Our Children During The Flint-
       Goodridge Hospital Of Dillard University Glory
       Years Of The 1970s... 277
    C. Brownsyn Braud Graduation From Meharry Medical
       School And Outpouring Of Brookstown Appreciation 280
    D. Hill-Burton Act Of 1946 281
       a. Federal Government Restrictions On Hospitals
          That Received Federal Funds By 1963......................... 282
       b. Low Income And Underinsured Population 283
    E. Hill-Burton Act Impacts On The Flint-Goodridge
       Hospital Of Dillard University From 1970 to 1982.......... 284
       a. Anesthesia Associates Of Flint-Goodridge
          Hospital Of Dillard University Established In 1981 ... 285
       b. Black Medical Politicians And Flint-Goodridge
          Hospital Of Dillard University Board Of
          Management 287
    F. Out As Flint-Goodridge Hospital of Dillard
       University's Chief Of Its Anesthesia Department In
       Early 1981.. 288
       a. Terminated As Chief Of The Department Of
          Anesthesia At Flint-Goodridge Hospital Of
          Dillard University In Early1981................................... 288
       b. Absence Of Data To Support Medical Staff
          Politicians' Decision 289

  G. Picking Up The Pieces And Moving Forward With
Medical Practice In 1982 And Thereafter 289
    a. Landscape Therapy And Refocus 290
    b. Mind, Body, And Soul Gradually Deprogrammed 292
  H. Flint-Goodridge Hospital Of Dillard University And
Its "Last Rites" In 1982 293
    a. Hill-Burton Act Of 1946 Impact On Flint-
Goodridge Hospital Of Dillard University By 1982 ... 294
    b. Medicare And Medicaid By 1982 295
  I. Flint-Goodridge Hospital Of Dillard University On
"Life Support" By Early 1982 296
  J. Flint-Goodridge Hospital Of Dillard University
Closed In Early 1982 296
    a. Financial Downfall Of Flint-Goodridge Hospital
Of Dillard University In 1982 298
    b. Flint-Goodridge Hospital Of Dillard University
Sold In Early March 1983 299
  K. Local White Hospitals Absorbed Beds And Available
Equipment In Obstetrics, Gynecology, And
Pediatrics Among Others In 1983 301
  L. Afro-American Hospital Closures Nationwide 301

XIX Black Physicians Reorganization Of Their Medical Practices . 303
  A. Re-Organization Of Medical Practice Response
To Flint-Goodridge Hospital of Dillard University
Closure In Early 1982 303
    a. Medical Practice Incorporated in 1972 304
    b. Strategic Downsizing Steps Taken To Save
Medical Practice 305
  B. Turmoil In The Internal Organization Of Medical
Practice By 1988 305
  C. Change In Marital Status In 1997 306
  D. Re-Organization Of Medical Practice By 2000 308

XX Hurricane Katrina Struck New Orleans, LA And
Changed The City Forever 310

    A. Hurricane Katrina Turned New Orleans, LA Upside Down On August 29, 2005 310
    B. Modular Building That Housed The Corporation Flooded On August 29, 2005 313
    C. Return To New Orleans, LA After Hurricane Katrina Moved North..315
        a. Tudor Court Home Heavily Damaged By Katrina's Wind And Water......................................316
        b. New Orleans East Became A Ghost Town After Hurricane Katrina Wreaked Havoc In the City...........317
        c. Mental Toll Caused By Katrina's Power Packed "One-Two" Punch..319
        d. No Work In The City In Late 2005 320
    D. Recovery And Rebuilding Process-Ordeal Of A Lifetime..321
    E. Household Repairs, Chemical Treatments, And Home Insurance Struggles 324
        a. Removing Mold And Mildew From My House.......... 324
        b. House Repair Stage 325
    F. Finished Product House More Elegant Than Before Hurricane Katrina And Rita 327
    G. "The Jackie Robinson Affect:" Brief Overview Of The Drug Enforcement Administration (DEA) Payback For Breaking Down The Closed Door Of The Charity Hospital Residency Anesthesia Training Program In 1966.. 328

XXI Drug Enforcement Administration (DEA) Case Based On "Allegations" And Would A Trial By Jury Reach A Guilty Or Innocent Verdict?... 330
    A. Racial Climate Of The Time 330
    B. Climate Change.. 332
    C. Work Climate Change... 333
    D. Drug Enforcement Administration (DEA's) Unproven Allegations 335
        a. Non-Participation In A Conspiracy To Develop A Secret Plan To Organize And Manage Maximum Urgent Care LLC In Lafayette, LA-2005 336

		b. What Did I Know About The Organization Of The Two Entities?	336
	E.	DEA's Unproven Claims And Allegations	337
	F.	Maximum Urgent Care LLC Top Level Management	341
	G.	Motion To Sever Filed On November 18, 2008	342
	H.	Drug Enforcement Administration (DEA) Knockout	343
	I.	Final Solution To The DEA Allegation Ordeal Designed To Silence	343
XXII		Character Impressions Remembered By Medical Colleagues, Relatives, And Friends	345
XXIII		Conclusion	350

APPENDIX

Appendix A:	Braud Family Tree	359
Appendix B:	Pierce Family Tree	361
Appendix C:	Black Physicians At Flint-Goodridge Hospital of Dillard University	366
Appendix D:	Black Nurse Anesthetists At Flint-Goodridge Hospital of Dillard University	368
Appendix E:	Assessment Of Dr. Joseph Pierce Braud's Character From A Physician And Medical Colleague's Perspective Survey	369
Appendix F:	Assessment Of Dr. Joseph Pierce Braud's Character From A Relative's Perspective Survey	372
Appendix G:	Assessment Of Dr. Joseph Pierce Braud's Character From A Friend's Perspective Survey	375
Bibliography		379

LIST OF TABLES

Table 1.0	Land Area Of The Louisiana River Road Parishes	20
Table 1.1	Names of Slaveholders And The Plantations They Owned In Selected River Road Parishes By 1858	27
Table 1.2	Total Population For Selected Louisiana Parishes, Including Whites And African Slaves By 1850	31
Table 1.3	Improved Land In Farms, Value of Farms And Implements, And Deaths By Selected Louisiana Parishes, 1850	32
Table 1.4	Free White, Black, And Mulatto Populations For Selected Louisiana Parishes, 1860	34
Table 1.5	White And Free Colored Population In Selected Louisiana Parishes-Post Emancipation Proclamation, 1870	35
Table 1.6	School Attendance And *Illiteracy In Selected Louisiana Parishes, 1870	37
Table 1.7	Population By Race And Selected Parishes In Louisiana, 1880	38
Table 1.8	Total White And Colored Population By Selected Louisiana Parishes, 1890	41
Table 1.9	White And Negro Population For Selected Louisiana Parishes, 1900	42
Table 1.10	White And Negro Population By Sex For Selected Parishes, 1910	42
Table 1.11	White and Negro Illiterate Population By Selected Louisiana Parishes, 1910	43
Table 1.12	White And Negro Population By Selected Louisiana Parishes, 1930	46
Table 1.13	Total White And Negro Population In Selected Louisiana Parishes by 1940	47
Table 1.14	School Attendance and Years of School Completed For Selected Louisiana Parishes By 1940	48
Table 1.15	Former African Slave Plantations And Village Or Cities Built On Them Between 1865 and 1930	52

Table 1.16 Total Negro Population Arrested For Vagrancy And Drunkeness And Disorderly Conduct Per 100,000 By 1910 54

Table 1.17 Total Negro Prisoners Arrested For Selected Slave States And By Race Per 100,000 Population 55

Table 1.18 Freed Negroes Lynched In The Louisiana River Road Parishes By Date, Name, And Alleged Offense 79

Table 1.19 Danneel Elementary School Years From 1931 To 1936 ... 133

Table 1.20 J.W. Hoffman Junior High In New Orleans, LA From 1938 To 1939 136

Table 1.21 Lowery Training School In Donaldsonville, LA 138

Table 1.22 Drug Enforcement Administration Allegations Related To Count 1 Unlawful Actions Purportedly Performed At The Maximum Urgent Care LLC, From 2005 To 2007 338

Table 1.23 Character Survey Results 346

Table 1.24 New Generation of Educational Achievement In St. James Parish 354

LIST OF MAPS

Map 1.0 Louisiana Parish Map 19

Map 1.1 African Slave Plantations Along The Louisiana River Road By 1858 23

Map. 1.2 African Slave Plantations Along The Louisiana River Road In St. Charles Parish By 1858 24

Map 1.3 Illiteracy Along Louisiana River Road By 1870 36

Map. 1.4 Density Of The Louisiana River Road Population By 1880 39

Map 1.5 Pie Graph Showing Proportion Of White and Colored Populations In Louisiana By 1880 40

Map 1.6 Percent Illiterate Negro Population 10 Years Of Age And Over In Louisiana, 1910 and 1920 45

LIST OF IMAGES

Image 1.0 Joe Braud And Lillian Luellen Pierce Braud's Marriage License Dated September 15, 1921 In Ascension Parish 106

Image 1.1 Flint-Goodridge Hospital In 1916 240

Image 1.2 Flint-Goodridge Hospital Of Dillard University Dedication Ceremony In January 1932 242

Image 1.3 Black Physicians And Postgraduate Course In 1944 243

Image 1.4 New Wing Addition To The Flint-Goodridge Hospital Of Dillard University In 1960 246

Image 1.5 Charity Hospital Physical Plant And Its Racially Divided Healthcare Practice In New Orleans, LA By 1931 258

Image 1.6 Certificate Of Completion Of The Charity Hospital Residency Anesthesia Program, From June 1, 1965 To June 30, 1967 261

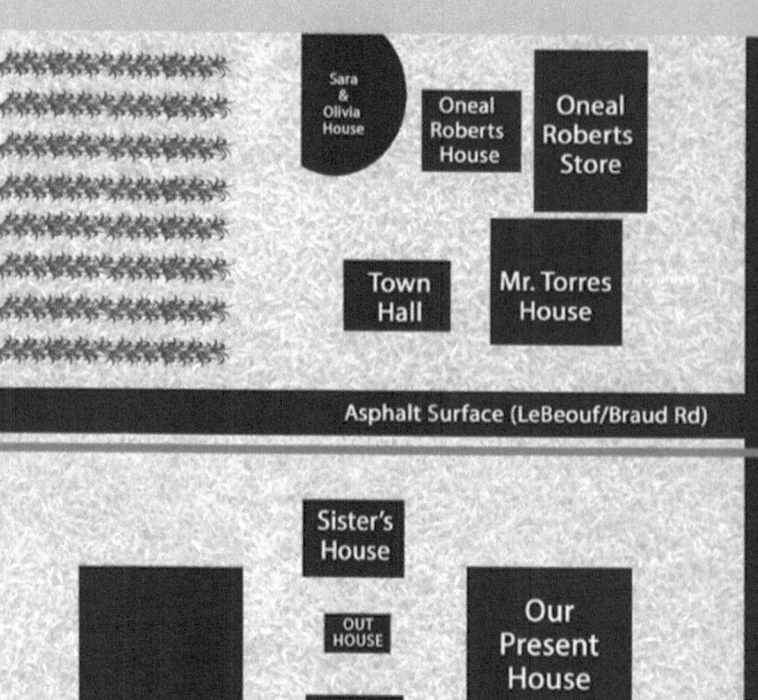

BROOKSTOWN
1930 - 2020

BETWEEN 1943-1947, THE MISSISSIPPI RIVER WAS EXPANDED TO INCREASE WATERWAYS FOR LARGE SHIPS AND BUSINESS TRANSIT. THIS ILLUSTRATION SHOWS THE GROWTH OF THE MS RIVER AND HOW THE COMMUNUNITY STRUCTURES WERE SHIFTED WEST AFTER THE NEW LEVEE WAS CONSTRUCTED.

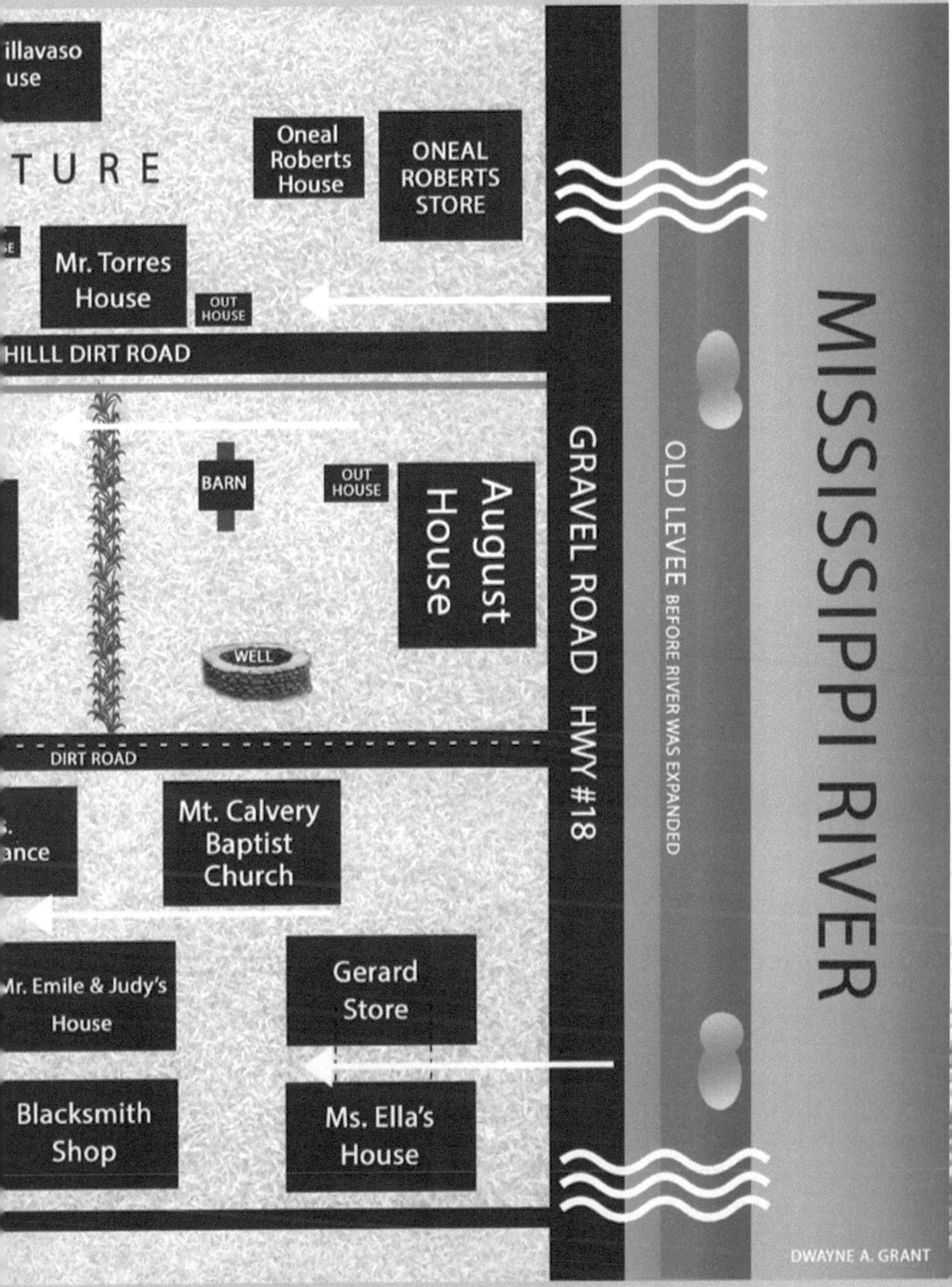

illavaso use

...TURE

Oneal Roberts House

ONEAL ROBERTS STORE

Mr. Torres House

OUT HOUSE

...HILLL DIRT ROAD

BARN

OUT HOUSE

August House

WELL

DIRT ROAD

Mt. Calvery Baptist Church

Mr. Emile & Judy's House

Gerard Store

Blacksmith Shop

Ms. Ella's House

GRAVEL ROAD   HWY #18

OLD LEVEE BEFORE RIVER WAS EXPANDED

MISSISSIPPI RIVER

DWAYNE A. GRANT

DEDICATIONS

Throughout my childhood and adult life, there have been many people who have assisted me when I needed their timely help. When My father- Joe Braud- made his transition in 1936, I was 10 years old, and as you can imagine, this lost left a huge hole in my Pierce-Braud Family Group. By 1936, my household consisted of seven siblings, who formerly depended on my father for our daily survival as I did also. The mid-1930s were Great Depression Years, and it was also a time when Jim Crow carried out acts of domestic terrorism against Black People without impunity.

Regarding food security, a basic need for survival, Evariste "Fray" Washington committed he would provide my Pierce-Braud Family Group with a wagon load of corn and potatoes to get us through the winter months every year during my childhood. By the time I was old enough to attend high school, namely, Lowery Training School, Mr. Jackson took me under his wings, and he taught me Biology in such a way that I learned everything about anatomy, tissues, nervous system, circulatory systems, and the respiratory system among many others.

By the time I graduated and enrolled at Southern University in Baton Rouge, LA, I already knew nearly everything my Biology Professors taught in their classes. I was so far advanced, and ahead of the curve, that Dr. J. Warren Lee, Chair of the Biology Department, became my mentor and prepared me to go to Graduate School to earn a Doctor of Philosophy Degree, and return to Southern University to teach in its Biology Department. While I studied at Southern University, Mrs. Sarah Netterville Phillips, sister of Dr. G. Leon Netterville, who later became President of the educational institution, befriended me and gave me a job working in the Café on campus. I needed the money to help my Pierce-Braud Family Group at home on the Gravel Road. These are a few of the people who were instrumental in helping me to move along my journey early in my life.

However, there is one person who has been more consistently impactful in my life from birth, and throughout my childhood and adult life, and that person is to whom I dedicate my Memoir.

This person is Mrs. Lillian Luellen Pierce Braud, my mother and Matriarch of the Pierce-Braud Family Group.

Lillian Luellen Pierce Braud was my "Rock." Although the winds of Jim Crow and Separate But Equal were blowing with gale force during her young adult life, which paralleled my childhood years; and, no doubt, I needed protection from these adverse racial conditions, my mother's determination did not waver, regarding the educational goals she lovingly outlined for me and my siblings. My mother's sister, Aunt Leah Pierce Argierard, told her education was the key to my protection. Many of Lillian's peers on the Gravel Road in St. James Parish could not stand up against the troubles too many Black People had seen for generations; however, while the news oftentimes was not the best, my mother's demeanor was never one of depression or confusion. Her outlook remained positive through the good and bad times.

The only time in my entire life I ever witnessed Lillian Luellen Pierce Braud "down" was when she lost her man-Joe Braud-at such a young age. My father was 38 years old when he made his transition. And, as beautiful a woman as my mother was then, her sadness was not that she did not know what she was going to do with herself anymore, it was primarily caused by the fact my mother felt she had so much more love left in her to give her man. I was moved by her feelings! Can you imagine how my mother felt? It causes me to tear-up every time I think about this beautiful woman going through this trial. My mother was 41 years old when Joe Braud died.

She was so young but Lillian decided against remarrying because she wanted to protect her children. During the mid-1930s, slavery practices were still a traumatic "sore spot" in the memory of many of the descendants of African Slaves. Only five generations before were African Slave Women considered the property of the slave master. His thought and practice directly conditioned the minds of all African Slave Men and Women. Their descendants, generally speaking, still patterned their default behavior accordingly. In order to avoid the risk of predisposing her children to the residuals of women being the property of a man, Lillian Luellen Pierce Braud chose not to involve herself with another man to protect them from any possible fall-out behavior.

In face of this decision and drastic change in her life, Lillian Luellen Pierce Braud developed a Strategic Family Development Plan for us. The heart of her plan was love, and she taught me, and my other siblings, that "not one of us would be left behind" because everyone of us would, without any reservations, provide whatever means of support necessary so everyone of her children would get the education we desired. The Louisiana Department of Social Services gave my mother $18 per month to raise her seven children. Unbowed by the gross inadequacy of this miniscule amount, Lillian put her own plan to work. She was determined not to allow Jim Crow to take her mind or those of her children.

My mother was so powerful that I could not stop looking at her every chance I got during my childhood and adult life. For this reason, whenever I was in Lillian Luellen Pierce Braud's presence, and like on a cloudy day, the clouds miraculously evaporated, and blue skies and sunshine suddenly appeared in her eyes when she looked at me. My mother always was glad to see me, and it was as if "I made her day!" Not taking anything away from my siblings because our mother loved us all equally, there was an indescribable change in her eyes that warmed her soul when she saw me. After many years of pondering what this indescribable change was, it dawned on me recently that Lillian Luellen Pierce Braud saw Joe Braud, embodied within Joseph Pierce Braud, either sitting or standing talking to her in real life. She was transformed and transfixed because she loved that man! I reminded her of him every time she saw me.

Lillian Luellen Pierce Braud lived 99 years, and to the very last day of her life, she was my/our "Rock." Though time has a way of slowly changing our physical beauty, her century of living was a beautiful storehouse of wisdom that still lives in me today. Through these years, my mother altered the course of the Pierce-Braud Family Group similar to the way the Mississippi River, slowly and assuredly, meanders and alters its course through time. By the time she married Joe Braud in 1921, the tiny village of Brookstown, and on any given day, could boast of having maybe 300 residents. Regardless, my mother passed an educational heritage to me, and my siblings, that generated six Medical Doctors, and a host of other college-educated professionals such as Doctors of Philosophy, Jurist Doctors (Lawyers), schoolteachers, social workers, and nurses among others, whose source is Brookstown, St. James Parish. No one would suspect these highly skilled people came out of such a tiny village like Brookstown. Lillian Luellen Pierce Braud and her sisters, especially Leah Pierce Argieard, laid the educational foundation upon which we all proudly stand today. It will likely take another century before such educational excellence is seen again flowing like "Ole Man River" through a single family like it flowed through my Pierce-Braud Family Group in Brookstown during the Twentieth Century.

It is for these special and heartfelt reasons that I dedicate my Memoir to my mother-Lillian Luellen Pierce Braud.

PREFACE

Usually, but not always, a person comes along, during a particular generation, and makes a unique contribution to either the social, economic, political, or judicial aspects of American Life, and, by using the available resources in the immediate, external environment, the individual forges an example that demonstrates to the people in a particular area, and elsewhere, that their long overdue need for change, which they have hoped for-and dreamed about-for centuries of living a better life, is possible. One such individual, namely, Joseph Pierce Braud, came along during the early 20th Century, and using the resources and tools available to him during the Jim Crow and Separate But Equal Era, he endeavored to transform himself into an educated man, which became a landmark example for the African-American People, and others, in St. James Parish, the larger Louisiana River Road, and elsewhere, to see and feel they-too-could change the illiteracy legacy that was handed down to them by the American Slavery Institution.

By 1850, 33.0 percent, or one-third of the African Slave Population were illiterate in St. James Parish; by 1870 for example, 95.3 percent of the Negro Descendants of African Slaves could not write; and by 1910, a decade before Dr. Joseph Pierce Braud was born in A-Bend in Ascension Parish, 55.1 percent of the Negro Descendants of African Slaves there were classified as illiterate by the Thirteenth Census of the United States in 1900. For St. James Parish, 50.0 percent of its Negro Descendants were illiterate. This was the by-product of several centuries of existence of the American Slavery Institution, which by 1860, made it possible for two-thirds of the millionaires in the United States to develop on the Louisiana River Road.

Using education as a weapon to combat illiteracy, Dr. Joseph P. Braud, while standing on the giant shoulders of his Pierce-Braud Family Group, defied the illiteracy status quo for Negroes, and gave his life, as an example, for others to see that illiteracy could be defeated through a pedagogy of sustained and systematic educational training. How Dr. Joseph Pierce Braud proved illiteracy could be defeated is captured in his Memoir that spans the course of his 95 years journey thus far, which began in Western France 289 years before he was born in A-Bend in Ascension Parish.

During the mid-17th Century, the social, economic, and political situation in Western France had a most oppressive impact on the lives of the French People in Western France in particular. In 1632, Vincent Brault was born in Loudun, France, and by 21 years old, along with the support of the French Government, Vincent Brault, his family, and 300 other Acadians journeyed across the Atlantic Ocean to Nova Scotia, which is one of thirteen provinces of Canada. By the mid-17th Century, there were between 12,000 and 15,000 Acadians living in Nova Scotia. However, this group was caught in the middle of a brewing political feud between Britain and France, which eventually broke out into a Seven Years War. Because the Acadians refused to publicly support Britain's claims to the Nova Scotia Province, by 1755, 10,000 were deported. Some of Vincent Brault's offsprings were deported elsewhere. According to statistical records, 1,000 migrated to the Louisiana Territory located on the west bank of the Mississippi River by 1765. Because the Acadians were rooted in Agriculture, they obtained large tracts of land from the Spain located in St. James Parish and other River Road Parishes.

It was in St. James Parish where Alexis Breaux established the F. Braud Plantation. By 1770, African Slaves were introduced in this parish and others, along the Louisiana River Road. One of the descendants of Vincent Brault, namely, Honore Breaux had six children of whom one was Edouardo Breaux, Sr. The latter had two children, and one was name Edouardo Breaux, Jr.

Edouardo Breaux, Jr is the direct link that created a new branch on the White Breaux Family Tree that dated back to Vincent Brault, who was born in Loudun, France mentioned earlier. As it happened, Edouardo Breaux, Jr broke family tradition, and the generalized slavery custom of the day, and, by doing so, he publicly dated an African Slave Woman name Celestine, who he married after the American Civil War. Before that time, Edouardo Breaux, Jr and the African Slave Woman had three children, who were Leontine Breaux, Theophile Breaux, and Marie Leontine Breaux. Theophile Breaux was born in 1842 and his wife Louisa (Lise) Mulberry in 1851. By Theophile Breaux's eighteenth birthday, the United States Census reported the spelling of his surname as Braud.

Together, they produced the First Generation of the Black Braud Family Group shortly after the American Civil War. They had ten children, and among them was Albert Israel Braud, aka, Joe Braud. At the same time, the Pierce Family Lineage was active, and Phillip Pierce and Suky Chatman Pierce produced 12 children. One of them was Lillian Luellen Pierce born in 1895, who Joe Braud married on September 21, 1921. Joe Braud was born in 1896.

Joe Braud and Lillian Luellen Pierce Braud produced seven children. Joseph Pierce Braud was the second child born in their family. Unexpectedly, Joe Braud Passed away in 1936, and this involuntarily thrusted Joseph Pierce Braud into taking on a man's responsibility(s) at the tender age of 10 years old.

Although Joseph Pierce Braud did not know it yet, but he was already Standing On The Shoulders Of Giants; that is, Celestine Breaux, Theophile Braud, Louisa (Lise) Mulberry Braud, Phillip Pierce, Suky Chapman, Joe Braud, Lillian Luellan Pierce Braud, Leah Pierce Argieard, and many others unknown. They were the invisible "Wind under His Wings."

Taking the education teaching he received from his Aunt Leah Pierce Argieard, Joseph Pierce Braud set in his mind at five years old that he would become a Medical Doctor. By 1958, he graduated from the prestigious Howard University Medical School in Washington, DC. Afterwards, he and his wife, Swedie Weary Braud, returned to Louisiana to work. Dr. Joseph P. Braud came to New Orleans, LA and successfully setup his medical practice. While doing his internship in Youngstown, Ohio, he became interested in Anesthesiology as his specialty. Pursuing this specialty, he took a staff position at Flint-Goodridge Hospital of Dillard University, and with the help of Drs. Roy Boggs and John Adriani, he became the first Black Physician admitted to the Charity Hospital Residency Anesthesia Training Program in 1965. Two years later, he received his certificate. Similar to Rosa Parks, who refused to give up her seat on the city bus, Dr. Joseph P. Braud broke down the Segregation Door at Charity Hospital, which had barred Black Physicians from its Residency and Internship Programs since its inception. His little-known achievement in the Civil and Human Rights Struggle subsequently made it possible for an increase in the number of African-Americans, and other Peoples of Color, who were accepted to do their medical training in these programs at other local White Hospitals as well as those located elsewhere in the South and so forth. Dr. Joseph P. Braud worked his entire Professional Medical Career at Flint-Goodridge Hospital of Dillard University where he served in the capacity as its Chief of the Department of Anesthesia. He held this position, from 1968 until the hospital was forced to close its doors as a result of a combination of factors, one of which was the mandates of the Hill-Burton Act. Though challenged emotionally by the hospital's closure, Dr. Braud continued to work in his medical practice until Hurricane Katrina and Rita shutdown the Healthcare Industry in New Orleans, LA in 2005.

Amid the devastation of these Acts of Nature, Dr. Braud sought employment at the Maximum Urgent Care LLC Clinic located in Lafayette, LA. He ran into some unexpected difficulties with the Drug Enforcement Administration (DEA) in 2008-2009. A full accounting of this struggle awaits your attention.

Every step Dr. Joseph P. Braud took on his life journey, during the course of the 95 years of his life, which are related to family, education, and work, are systematically outlined and explained in detail in his Memoir by him. Of all the action-steps he took, there is one educational achievement he made that stands-out far above all of the others considered herein.

That is, he grew up in Brookstown, St. James Parish in the midst of all of the day-to-day survival humbug, and unbeknownst to the White Power Structure Class in St. James Parish, an imminent change was about to occur, which was predestined to set Brookstown on a different trajectory that was hitherto unknown to Black People on the Louisiana River Road since its coming into existence during the 18th Century.

Specifically, all of the African Slaves through the generations, both individually, and collectively, "prayed for a change," namely, the possibility that there would come a time when their children and others would be able to live in Freedom and experience the promise of a better life that is written in the American Constitution. Their prayers were long overdue, and the hoped for a change they prayed to God for was sung about every day in the fields and on Sundays. Their energies swirled about them, like an invisible Spirit, through the generations, and similar to a snowball rolling down the side of a hill, it continued to grow stronger and stronger until the exact point was reached when two family lineages made an intersection, and the "prayed for change," by numerous generations of African Slaves, Freed Negroes, and African-Americans manifested in real, physical life in the form of the birth of a child.

The Pierce and Braud Lineages carried the seed of the "prayed for change" for several centuries. Lillian Luellen Pierce Braud and Joe Braud were born on the Louisiana River Road, and on September 21, 1926, Lillian Luellen Pierce Braud gave birth to her second child, namely, Joseph Pierce Braud. His birth was unusual because, during the time of his birth, illiteracy was a predominant demographic among Black People, and Joseph Pierce Braud, therefore, came into the world to demonstrate to the Black People of Brookstown, the larger Louisiana River Road, or Gravel Road, and the World that education is the key to opening the door to the better life that generations of African Slaves, Freed Negroes, and African-Americans had dreamed about, and prayed for, for so long.

Unlike before, Dr. Joseph Pierce Braud created an educational template when he became a Medical Doctor in 1958. All of his work since has contributed to the subsequent production of six Medical Doctors, one Juris Doctor, one Doctor of Philosophy, four Masters Degrees, and fourteen Bachelor Degrees in his lifetime. No doubt, more educational achievement will come through the next generations of the Pierce-Braud Family Group. It is worth mentioning here that all of this groundbreaking educational change began in a tiny village known as Brookstown, St. James Parish. On a sunny day, the total population of the village usually did not exceed 300 people.

What awaits everyone in Dr. Joseph Pierce Braud's Memoir is a systematic and detailed account of how a young boy "shined shoes," "scrapped rice and potatoes with his siblings," and overcame many indignities, including some of the toughest odds, to break through the walls of misunderstanding that were placed before him on his path, and like what happens in a dark room when the light is turned-on, understanding pushes back the darkness of fear, anger, and doubt. Then, *love* prevails and triumphs similar to the lifting of a dense fog, and the sunlight shines forth.

Dr. Joseph Pierce Braud has taken his place among the Giants in the Pierce and Braud's Lineage, and the current generation of the Pierce-Braud Family Group clearly stands on his shoulders.

What a Blessing he is to his Pierce-Braud Family Group, Brookstown, St. James Parish, Louisiana, United States, and the World. Dr. Joseph Pierce Braud encourages you to become a witness to his personal and family history(s), Louisiana History, and American History. This history is perfectly and intentionally interwoven into his Memoir for your consideration and contemplation.

From A-Bend to Amen.

Lionel D. Lyles, PhD
Baltimore, Maryland
December 16, 2021

ACKNOWLEDGEMENT

Spirits are born into the world as human souls, and they choose to take various forms, for the sole purpose of assisting other human beings as they move along their journey toward the fulfillment of their goals, during the allotted time they have on Earth. Many times, after reflecting on my life thus far, I have wondered how everything I have attempted to do, through the years, always turned out right, or, for example, if there was something I needed, my needs were mysteriously met at each stage of my journey, from my childhood to adulthood. By no means am I suggesting my life did not have its ups and downs, learning curves, or times when I felt fear, doubt, afraid, and misunderstood among other emotions and feelings that make an individual a human being. I had my share of human experiences; yet, when times looked like they would get the best of me, seemingly out of nowhere, a solution was provided to me so I could move forward on my journey. During my reflection, over the course of my life journey, some Spirits had already chosen a human form, and unbeknownst to me, the Spirit embodied in these human beings, whom I acknowledge here for helping me to reach the highest mountain peak I set for myself as a five year old, when I first decided I wanted to become a Medical Doctor when I grow up.

Their intervention in my life as "helpers" started 90 years ago on the Gravel Road, in Baton Rouge, LA, and in New Orleans, LA.

Two of my mother's sisters, namely, Mrs. Leah Pierce Argieard and Ms. Evelyn W. Pierce, were the two relatives that taught me the importance of education, and the significant role it can play in my life. Aunt Leah was an Adult Education Teacher and Aunt Evelyn was a Public School Teacher in the A-Bend Community in Donaldsonville, LA in Ascension Parish. On many occasions, Aunt Leah, who was an African Griot, had me seated at her feet, and as I listened to her, I always wondered "How does Aunt Leah know what is going to happen in American Society 70 years in the future?" For example, she told me education would make it possible for men and women to move around in "space." This was 29 years before President John Kennedy set going to the moon as a goal in 1960. I was fascinated by Aunt Leah's insight and intuition, which launched me on an educational course that helped me to fulfill my dream of becoming a Medical Doctor. I became one in 1958, two years before the goal was set to go to the moon.

Food Security is necessary because a hungry child will not be able to concentrate on achieving one's educational goal. My father, Joe Braud, passed away when I was ten years old, and Food Insecurity was a threat to my survival, and with the loss of the former, I could have easily given up on my educational goal to become a Medical Doctor. However, when the food need arose in my life, the Spirit in Mr. Evariste "Fray" Washington came to the rescue. I cannot thank and acknowledge "Fray" enough for selflessly providing my Pierce-Braud Family with a wagon load of potatoes and corn for ten years until I completed high school. His generosity was more than I could imagine, given the fact "Fray" had a wife and twelve children of his own to feed. Nevertheless, his intervention is still remembered by me, and it is priceless, regarding how it helped me to stay focused on the educational goal I set for myself when I was five years old. Because I had sufficient nourishment every day, I was able to earn high academic marks throughout my school years, from Danneel Elementary School to Lowery Training School.

By the time I enrolled at the Lowery Training School, one of my teachers, namely Mr. Charles Jackson, who was my Science Teacher, taught me everything I needed to know about Anatomy and Biology. Besides being an outstanding Science Teacher, the reason I enjoyed Mr. Jackson Biology Lectures so much is I wanted to become a Medical Doctor. Mr. Jackson taught his Biology Class so thoroughly that what I learned made the rest of my Biology and Science Studies, after I graduated from high school, so much easier. I acknowledge Mr. Charles Jackson for being the Science Teacher I needed because he so thoroughly prepared me for the next level of my educational journey toward becoming a Medical Doctor.

In fact, by the time I enrolled at Southern University in the Fall 1943, I was well-prepared to succeed in my chosen field of Biology. My Biology Professors introduced me to new ways of understanding the subject matter with my exposure to laboratory experiments. This added hands-on work significantly expanded my awareness because it gave me an opportunity to gain a richer insight related to the connections between Anatomy Theory and Practice, for example. Given this opportunity to improve my Biology Work, my performance caught the attention of Dr. J. Warren Lee, who was Chair of the Southern University Biology Department at the time. Recognizing my potential, Dr. Lee took me under his wings and he groomed me for Graduate School because he wanted me to return to Southern University and become a Professor in the Biology Department. Dr. Lee was so encouraging, and I learned from him that I had what it takes to become a Medical Doctor. I acknowledge his mentorship because he saw deep down on the inside of me my potential, and he was not shy about letting me know I had a promising future in the Medical Science Field.

In addition, another cornerstone in my undergraduate life at Southern University was Mrs. Sarah Netterville Phillips. She was the Director of the Café, which was located in the center of the campus. Mrs. Phillips gave me a job at a time when I needed some money to help my Braud Family back home, and I also needed some cash to buy a few things I needed for school. Mrs. Phillips introduced me to every big-name faculty member and administrator, who worked for Southern University. They would invariably come to the Café for coffee or lunch, and many times, I found myself sitting down talking to influential people who could help me along my way in some manner or other. Mrs. Phillips was in my corner, and I needed all of the positive support I could get, and she gave me more than enough. I would not become who I am today without her attention to my development. I was a "Diamond In The Rough;" and, Mrs. Phillips pointed-out to me I just needed to continue shining my "Diamond.".

Through it all, I became a Medical Doctor with these individuals' help in 1958. Once I passed my Medical Board Exam in Maryland, I could setup my medical practice in any state due its Reciprocity Clause. That is, Maryland's Medical Board Exam was more difficult than those of any other state, and if one passed it, he or she could setup a medical practice wherever one chose to do so. I passed the Maryland Medical Board Exam with a high score. My passage of this Exam qualified me to setup my medical practice in most states. Therefore, I chose to setup my medical practice in New Orleans, LA in 1960.

That year, I traveled to New Orleans, LA, and I found it to be an ideal location for my medical practice. Not long after I was in New Orleans, LA, I was steered to visit Flint-Goodridge Hospital of Dillard University. Upon my arrival, and with no prior notice or communication, I met Dr. Anthony Hackett, who held a Staff Position at the hospital and he had his own medical practice in the city. Dr. Hackett and I became instant friends; our relationship was solid after our first meeting. During the discussion, Dr. Hackett told me he was going on vacation for at least six weeks, and he would like to know if I wanted to manage his medical practice in his absence? I wanted to shout out "Yes Indeed!" But, I controlled my excitement, and I answered favorably. Dr. Hackett told me what I needed to know about his medical practice, and this chance meeting is how I began my Professional Medical Doctor Career in New Orleans, LA. I cannot thank Dr. Anthony Hackett enough for his help and assistance in helping me to break into the medical practice world in the "Big Easy." Without this jumpstart, my transition into setting up my own medical practice in New Orleans, LA would have been much more difficult. I acknowledge Dr. Anthony Hackett for making this part of my journey's path smoother, and my load significantly lighter.

CHAPTER I

INTRODUCTION

For many centuries, during the timeless geological development of the Mississippi River, it has meandered, slowly but certainly, on its way to the Gulf of Mexico, where it deposited its successive loads of sediments. As the muscles of the Mississippi River carried-out its ageless task of building the Louisiana Coast and Delta Region, a stretch of the river's channel, from Baton Rouge, LA to New Orleans, LA has famously become known to many as the River Road. Before modern times, the latter was referred to by the older generations, or by many residents in Brookstown in St. James Parish, as the *Gravel Road*. The latter holds a special place in my heart because I-Joseph Pierce Braud-lived out a majority of my childhood days growing up there. I had my ups and downs as you will learn about later, and as anyone who is familiar with Charles Dickens Classical Writing might fittingly say-*"It was the best of times and it was the worse of times."*

    Owing to the importance of the River Road to community life through the generations, this geographic feature is examined further in Chapter Two, regarding its spatial dimensions and locations. A brief history of the Mississippi River is also provided. As we know, most highways we travel every day, to get where we are going, usually have a few winding curves along the route. Sometimes our Apple Smartphone's "Siri" feature warns us of a coming deep curve along our route. These are more prevalent along secondary roads inside cities, towns, and villages relative to the interstate. Oftentimes, the curves, or bends in the road, are caused by some obstacle, mostly a naturally occurring one, that force the highway to curve around them. During my days growing up on the Gravel Road, I-too-have had to make adjustments to get around both man and woman-made obstacles, including a few natural ones I had to face in my everyday environment such as walking and running several miles, down the Gravel Road, to get to and from school every day.

Similarly, the Mississippi River carved its meandering channel, from Baton Rouge, LA to New Orleans, LA, during the past several millenniums. As we shall see, an engineered highway was eventually built, which parallels some of the winding bends and curves in the Mississippi River Channel today. It began as a secondary Gravel Road, and it was later paved with Asphalt. Today, most people, who grew up along the River Road know it as Highway 18. Anyone who has driven along the River Road, from New Orleans, LA to Baton Rouge, LA, or versa, has experienced the unusual quiet, occasional appearance of wildlife, and scenic beauty, which fills up the traveller's senses. For those, who have not had this experience, Highway 18 is located on the West Side of the Mississippi River, where, in our fast-paced world outside of the River Road, time still moves today as slowly as the river flowed several millenniums ago-1.5 mph.

By 1858, most of the land area on either side of the Mississippi River was divided into Arpent-Shaped Slave Plantations, which intersected the river, and radiated away from it horizontally. I will provide the names of all of the Slave Plantations that operated along the River Road by this time. Interestingly, I discovered there was a Braud Plantation that operated on land where Welcome, LA stands today. Some of the plantation owners are identified also.

Moreover, the land area west of the River Road, or Highway 18, particularly the land in the Welcome, LA Community, which includes my Brookstown Neighborhood and surrounding region, All-exist on land today where slave plantations operated by 1858. The economic sustainability of St. James Parish, and other River Road Parishes such as Ascension, St. Charles, and St. John the Baptist-All-depended on African Slave Labor before the Civil War, and sharecropper labor afterwards.

The extent to which African Slave Labor fueled the economy of the River Road is demonstrated using demographic Data in the form of Tables and Maps in Chapter Three. Using appropriate census data, beginning in 1850, the latter enabled me to show, for each River Road Parish identified earlier, there were two to three times more African Slaves in each one, relative to the Native White Population in them. This disproportionate number of African Slaves clearly indicates that their labor power was the driving force of economic sustainability for the Slaveholder Class that owned the vast majority of plantations along the River Road. This is a very important fact because the life chances of a vast majority of "freed" African Slaves, after the Emancipation Proclamation, were greatly diminished, and for too many others, their opportunities to survive were nearly extinguished.

Moreover, this information is included because I felt it timely and necessary to emphasize just how significant an undertaking it was for the Pierce-Braud Family Group to excel in face of the "lingering traumas" of the American Slavery Institution and Systemic Racism. Many African-American Families did not prosper because the mentioned traumas were just too much for them to overcome.

Brookstown, within walking distance to Welcome, LA, is the focus of my interest for a number of key reasons. The most important one is this is the place where the Pierce-Braud Family began its journey. Welcome, LA was the hub in the River Road Wheel for this family, which in time, its influence radiated out, like spokes in a wheel, which, unlike any other family, gave Louisiana and America and unsurpassed Medical Doctor Heritage. This does not include those family members, who earned Doctor of Philosophy, Masters, Law, Education, and Engineering Degrees. More details will be mentioned about how this educational achievement was accomplished, during a time when the vast majority of African-Americans struggled to survive the inhuman legacy of the American Slavery Institution and Systemic Racism. In spite of the many struggles and roadblocks thrown on its path, the Pierce-Braud Family continued to excel in the education field at the highest level.

Given the predominant influence of the American Slavery Institution, and the Systemic Racism it produced, the slave plantations that operated west of the Mississippi River, along River Road, or Highway 18, have already been identified. In Chapter Four I will identify those where Brookstown and Welcome, LA exist today. The implications, regarding the social, economic, and political well-being of Welcome, LA, and Brooktown Residents, are significant. Emphasis is placed on the Thirteenth Amendment to the United States Constitution, Freedmen Bureau Bill of 1865, Sharecropping System, and out-migration. After the collapse of the Freedman Bureau, sharecropping became a pseudo-slavery form on the Gravel Road. Some details related to how rice was produced is addressed to point-out many freed Negroes were still caught in a "Catch 22" Bondage on the Gravel Road during my childhood years. To some degree, sharecropping remained a major way many African-Americans earned their living in this village and town after the Civil War, and during the early Twentieth Century? No doubt, the residual effects of slavery carried-over well into this century. As such, and as we shall see later, what the Pierce-Braud Family accomplished, in view of these dicey odds, makes its story of standing up against them that much more of a compelling and timely consideration.

Moreover, I will make it very clear, in Chapter V, exactly how unusual the Pierce-Braud Family Group is, regarding the restraints and obstacles the American Slavery Institution placed on African Slave Family Development, and later on African-American Family Development after the Civil War, and by the time of the 1929 Great Depression. I will highlight some of the difficulties faced by a vast majority of families, during and after slavery, regarding their survival. In particular, beginning immediately after the end of Reconstruction in the mid-1870s, a *Reign of Domestic Terrorism* was unleashed on Black People by the Southern Slaveholder Democrats and Northern Republicans. It swept across the Deep South and Northern States like a raging California Wildfire. The plight of a vast majority of African-Americans was so bad that by the late 1940s and early 1950s, Billy Holiday sung her iconic song, namely, *Strange Fruit*, in protest against this inhumanity of man and woman against man and woman. The Reign of Domestic Terrorism was allowed by the Rutherford B. Hayes Administration as a compromise for Southern White Democrat support of his well-known fraudulent Presidential Election in 1876; when President Rutherford B. Hayes turned a blind eye to all kinds of attacks against African-Americans, he gave the greenlight for them to be carried-out more broadly by the Ku Klux Klan, whose membership, generally speaking, consisted of prominent men in the River Road Parishes' Communities such as lawyers, doctors, teachers, and policemen among others. No one really knew who these men were because they wore White Robes to conceal their identities. The United States Supreme Court approved the Plessey v. Ferguson Law on May 18, 1896, which made *Separate but Equal Accomodations* the law of the land for most of the Twentieth Century. The end of Reconstruction meant, therefore, the end of President Abraham Lincoln's Reconstruction Reparation Program for "freed" Negroes. He was assassinated to pave the way for a century or more of "Domestic Terrorism" intentionally acted-out against them. Its legacy can still be observed today through any discerning eyesight.

Therefore, in order to get through the *Eye of this Survival Needle*, I will share with you later the intimate details of Lillian Luellen Pierce Braud's-my biological mother- *Strategic Family Development Plan*. The tactics she taught my siblings and I instilled in us a Family Value System that enabled us to withstand the powerful winds of this Systemic Racism; we learned how to bend in face of adversity without being *broken by it*. Her teachings continue to influence the direction and development of the Pierce and Braud Family Groups today.

Without the employment of a large number of African Slaves needed to produce increasingly larger rice and sugarcane output, along with the to protect it, the massive wealth that each White Slaveholder Family in St. James Parish used to establish and sustain itself would have been impossible. Collectively, these slaveholder families were a part of what is known as the Southern Slaveholder Oligarchy. Without the exploitation of the African Slaves' Labor overtime, the Southern Slaveholder Oligarchy lifestyle, including its political and economic power, would not have been possible to develop, or maintain, as a ruling class form, along the River Road in St. James Parish, and Welcome, LA in particular.

To maintain its social, economic, and political power, the Southern Slaveholder Oligarchy, including its influence in the River Road Parishes, did everything in its power to control and limit the development of African-American Families on the Gravel Road.

Chapter VI deals with the African-American Population in St. James Parish and Welcome, LA. Specifically, the emergence of two-family groups in Brookstown and Welcome, LA were destined to *unite,* and, go on, during later years, to have an unprecedent impact on these two communities and the state, especially in the areas of Public Education and the Medical Profession.

Particularly, by the beginning of the 20th Century, the two-family groups that joined together were the Braud's and Pierce's. Their family origin is explored in some detail within the context of their respective family trees. The historical development of the Braud Family Groups is traced back to the 19th Century and earlier in France. The patriarch and matriarch of each family group is established as far back in time as possible. And, as time moved forward within a generational context, each family group's Family Tree grew through an addition of new family members. By the time the 19th Century came to a close, one of the females, during the early Pierce Group's Family Tree evolution married into the early Braud Group's Family Tree Lineage.

I give special attention to the White Breault Family Group that initially migrated to the River Road Parishes from Nova Scotia. The White Breault Family Group is traced from Western France beginning in 1632. Vincent Breault was the Patriarch, who led his families, and roughly 15 others, to Nova Scotia, Canada. As time passed, the Grand Derangement and Expulsion occurred, and the White Breaults were scattered to the South, along the Atlantic Seaboard of the United States. Some ended up in the Carolinas, and others found their way farther southward into the Lower Mississippi River Valley. Many died of starvation along the way, and of those who survived, some the White Breaults made it to Natchez, MS and farther south to St. James Parish.

The White Breault Family Group is the thread off of which the Black Braud Group evolved a new branch during the march of time. A crossover occurred, which involved the marriage of Edouardo Breaux, Jr (Once the White Breault Family Group made its way to St. James Parish, and to the South Louisiana Region, they changed their name to Breaux) to an African Slave Woman, whose name was Celestine. This union produced the beginning of the Black Braud Family Group in St. James Parish (The Black Braud Family Group name was spelled as shown to distinguish it from the White Breaux Family Group). The Pierce and Braud Groups' Family Trees are examined in some detail. It was the merging of the Pierce and Braud Family Groups that set the table for the significant contributions it made in the Education Field.

As we shall see in more detail later, the Pierce-Braud Marriage laid the foundation upon which the Braud Family Group produced a number of offsprings that would later make a *unique* contribution to the Brookstown and Welcome, LA Community, Louisiana, and America. Before May 2021, the single factor that set the Braud family Group apart is the unknown fact this family group, native to such a small village, produced more medical doctors per capita than any other Louisiana Family. This outstanding contribution to society may also exceed Medical Doctor Production by American Families nationwide. This monumental achievement has gone unrecognized, for many decades, until now.

That is to say, from 1900 to 2022, more than a century ago, no other family, African-American, White, or others of color, has duplicated the Braud-Pierce Family production of medical doctors, along the River Road, or anywhere else, USA. Quietly and purposely, like the Mississippi River, this family group produced six medical doctors, whose origin began in Brookstown near Welcome, LA. By itself, this is a remarkable achievement! In addition, if those members of the Pierce-Braud Family Group, who became lawyers, engineers, and schoolteachers are added to this ledger of human achievement, the total number of highly skilled professionals would be even more compelling and fascinating. In an appropriate place in my Memoir, I will present all of them to you.

To gain a deeper understanding of exactly how this educational achievement occurred in Brookstown, against some of the most formidable odds, ranging from the United States Supreme Court, Federal Government, State legislatures, local governments, and other organizations' resistance to African-American Progress, I have the unique opportunity of taking the reader inside of the Braud Household where one will get a living room view of my biological parents' character, and the household in which they lived and raised their seven children. I will discuss this information in Chapter VII. The primary agricultural crop grown at the time my parents got married in 1921was Rice. I did not know it, but as I grew older, this crop would play a central role in the Braud Family survival. The farm equipment owned by my parents is revealed; its barn for produce storage is identified; and the rise of sugarcane production is highlighted.

Chapter VIII is one in which I spend some time discussing the social life that went on in Brookstown when I was a young boy about 10 years. Many of the social situations I remember were observed by me before I was ten years old, and some during my teen years. By the late 1920s and early 1930s, the Native White Population in St. James Parish, and those who lived in other River Road Parishes, did not go out of their way to champion the educational needs of the majority of African-Americans at this time. One of the real legacies of the American Slavery Institution is, African-Americans were not allowed to learn how to read or write. Illiteracy was high among this group. Early in my life, I remember there was only a one-room building on the side of a ditch located on Gerald Roberts Property; it was set up as an elementary school for Black People. The one-room school building next a ditch in Brookstown. There were many other strange family behaviors, which I call oddities.

For example, I will discuss Two Men Walking in Opposite Directions on River Road; Children of the Railroad Worker, and Christmas Gift Child to name a few of them. On Saturdays there was a Jitney Bus Ride Brookstown Residents would take to Donaldsonville, LA, where they would shop for items they could not get at the corner grocery store in Brookstown. How I became interested in becoming a Medical Doctor is also addressed? And, my years enrolled in the Daneel School in New Orleans, LA provided me an opportunity to receive a better quality elementary education relative to the kind my peers received in the one-room building, which was located by a ditch in Brookstown. I also had the good fortune of living with two of my mother's sisters while enrolled in the Daneel Elementary School. One of them was named Leah Pierce; she was so wise, and I sat down at her feet, and she would tell me what life would be like for me 70 years later, if I would be serious about getting my education. Everything Leah Pierce Argieard told me sounded so true, but it is still a mystery to me where she got her intuition and foresight from. She must have been a part of a lineage of African Priestesses or Griots, stretching back to West Africa. Interestingly, after living more than half a century, I am a personal witness that everything Leah Pierce Argieard told me about what life would be like 70 years from the day she told me what it would be like actually is true, and came to pass in my own personal life experience. Both of my Aunts were schoolteachers at the time, including Ms. Evelyn W. Pierce.

By the time I reached 10 years old, and beginning to enjoy my biological father's company inasmuch as Joe Braud took me just about everywhere he went, something completely unexpected happened that turned my entire inner world upside down. In Chapter IX, I explain this non-ordinary occurrence as the day my father-Joe Braud-died! On that day, unlike all others I had lived beforehand, I quickly saddled up the Braud Family's horse, and with my adrenaline flowing through my body at what felt like its maximum level, I rode my horse, for four miles in a wide-open gallop, to the home of the only medical doctor in the Brookstown Welcome area of St. James Parish. By the time Dr. Stephen Campbell drove to my house, he had already pronounced Joe Braud dead. Without the benefit of the guidance of Joe Braud, it was Lillian Luellen Pierce Braud-my biological mother-who called her Braud Family together, at which time, she laid-out her Strategic Family Development Plan. Although she had just lost the love of her life, namely Joe Braud, she summoned, from somewhere deep on the inside of her, the strength her seven children needed to feel and hear related to how we would survive and thrive in the absence of our father's leadership.

With all of the obstacles being thrown in our way by Systemic Racism and the KKK, it is no doubt in my mind that the Braud Family persevered due to the Lillian Luellen Pierce Braud Strategic Family Development Plan. Its details are revealed here. I share what Mr. Evariste "Fray" Washington provided us in the form of food, and I explain how my siblings and I "Scrapped Rice and Irish Potatoes." I also mention how I worked as a "Shoe Shine Boy" in New Orleans, LA. I worked hard because acquiring an education was my indispensable goal.

After my graduation from the Lowery Training School in Donaldsonville, LA, I enrolled at Southern University located in Baton Rouge, LA. Because Joe Braud passed away in 1936, and by the time I matriculated at Southern University, there was a shortfall in the cash-flow of money coming into the Braud Family Household. Chapter X outlines what action I took after a meeting Lillian Luellen Pierce Braud called to discuss the matter with her children. Her Strategic Family Development Plan was fluid and changeable as required to meet the new realities our Braud Family Group faced. Because money, in some form, was needed to come into the Braud Family Household, I decided, after lengthy discussions with my siblings and mother, that I would temporarily withdraw from Southern University and join the Navy. This decision was taken in 1944-45, which was the middle of World War II. The purpose of my leaving Southern University and joining the military was far larger in scope than the war; it was solely and singularly motivated by *my deep love for my Braud Family Group*. With this being my over-arching vision, that is, the survival of the Braud Family Group, I knew I would be protected from any harm, although World War II was raging, and I had just enlisted in the Navy.

My journey in the Navy, which took me to exotic places around the world, is outlined in detail in this Chapter. In addition, I sent a financial allotment, or a portion of my Military Pay, home so Lillian Luellen Pierce Braud would have the finances required to continue to nurture her children.

After my four year hitch in the Navy came to an end in 1948, I re-enrolled at Southern University in Baton Rouge, LA. At the time, Southern University had a powerhouse football team, and I believed I could play well enough to be selected by legendary Coach Mumford as a member of the squad. I attempted to try-out for the team, but I quickly learned there is a big difference between cheering for your home team in the stands and actually making a tackle, or being tackled by an opposing football player, who might be 50 to 100 pounds heavier than myself. So, I quickly regrouped myself and placed all of my attention on my science classroom work and related homework. This was a better fit for me I quickly realized. Chapter XI provides insight regarding my undergraduate Biology Studies. Because I had learned so much about anatomy, tissues, bones, cells, and much more from Mr. Jackson, who was my Science Teacher at the Lowery Training School, I excelled in my Biology Studies at Southern University. I entered the latter with a solid background in Biology. In short, my adjustment to university academic life went smoothly.

When I was not studying Biology and other subjects, I did my share of socializing with the friends I met, who were a part of my Freshman Class. One female co-ed I met was a young lady from Columbia, MS whose name was Swedie Weary. Although I did not know it at the time we met, circumstances would bring us back together after our graduation from Southern University. As my journey unfolds, Swedie Weary and I would get married a few years later. While at Southern University, I took the Medical Aptitude Test at LSU and passed it. Because my Braud Family Group needed more funds, I took a job as a Laboratory Assistant in the Biology Department.

Toward the end of my Senior Year at Southern University, I worked part-time in the Biology Department as a Laboratory Assistant. As I explain in Chapter XII, this job came to an abrupt end when I applied for a Science Teaching Position at Charles H. Brown High School in

Webster Parish located in North Louisiana. During my adjustment to teaching science at the high school level, and getting use to the culture of living in North Louisiana, and within the mix of these changes, I had also previously contacted Howard University Medical School about seeing if I could get an interview to discuss the possibility of me getting into medical school there. Strangely, I received a letter from the Howard University Medical School, but with all the commotion going-on in my life at the time, somehow the letter from this medical school, which offered me an interview, got lost in the shuffle. Though the Letter got lost somehow, but my idea of going to medical school, which I planted in my mind when I was five years old growing up on the Gravel Road, remained alive and well.

My teaching job provided me a steady source of income, and it coincidentally brought Swedie Weary back into my life. Chapter XIII explains how my unexpected reunion with her occurred, and, for first time in my life, I setup a household, and I learned it is not until one actually lives in an intimate setting with another person that they learn there is a difference between one's spoken words and actual behavior. This was a good time in my life, but at a subconscious, or subliminal level, certain things such as adoption of a child would remain troublesome, which challenged my marriage to Swedie Weary from the outset. I also learned firsthand that racism was very much alive at Charles H. Brown High School. During my Exit Interview, I was told I had "No Respect For Authority."

Chapter XIV explain how I translated my boyhood dream of becoming a Medical Doctor into reality. I eventually reset an interview with the Howard University Medical School while teaching my Science Class Lesson Plans every day at Charles H. Brown High School. I enjoyed working with students; we had many successes and there were a few regrettable moments. However, my successes in the classroom far outweighed any regrets I may have had during my brief high school teaching career. I explain in detail the circumstances under which I left the classroom, and made my transition to becoming accepted as a student at the Howard University Medical School. I started to see a glimmer of light at the end of the tunnel as I progressed ever closer to fulfilling my biggest childhood dream of becoming a medical doctor. No matter how hard anything tried to stop me now, nothing could because I was well-armed with the Braud

Family Strategic Development Plan; it had worked perfectly throughout my life to this point; and, on my first day of class in medical school, I could clearly hear in my mind the valuable teachings of my mother-Lillian Luellen Pierce Braud-echoing clearly, in her loving voice, urging me closer to educational excellence. Swedie Braud came to Washington, DC in May 1956 to stay until I completed Medical School.

Throughout the trials of medical school, I reached my Childhood Dream of becoming a Medical Doctor in 1958!

What remained for me to do, regarding my medical school training, was to decide where I would do my Internship. This period in my life was as one might characterize as *"It was the best of times, and it was the worst of times."* Chapter XV captures this feeling because on one hand, I was steadily advancing in the art of my medical training, and, on the other, Lillian Luellen Pierce Braud had taught me so much about the value of Family Love, that is, how I should love myself and my siblings unconditionally; yet, my own family had a subconscious level contradiction in it related to my wife's-Swedie Weary Braud-Resistance to Adoption of my two children-Brownsyn Braud and Glenn Braud. This contradiction would not go away, and it starred me in my mind's face constantly. But, I persevered forward with my life, thinking optimistically that one day it would, somehow dissolve on its own, like snow does on a warm, sunny day.

Regardless, I set-aside my surfacing doubts in my private married life, and I completed my internship tenure at the Yougstown, Ohio Hospital Association with the latter's seal of approval. It seems I had to make so many major decisions in my life in what seemed to me like a short period of time. Yet, here I was faced with another big decision of what to do now that I had finished my Internship work.

In Chapter XVI, Swedie and I decided to return to Louisiana to pursue employment. This was a good decision because we did not sell the new house we purchased shortly after we got married. Having a place to stay help me decide what to do. So, given the fact Swedie refused to adopt my two children, although I voluntarily adopted her child, namely, Brenda Brown, I had a *gut feeling* it was best for me to bring Brownsyn and Glenn to live with my mother in Brookstown in St. James Parish. Upon arrival at my mother's home, I unpacked Brownsyn and Glenn's belongings, from the rented U-Hual Truck; Swedie and I visited with my mother a few days;

and then we drove back to Springhill, LA in Websters Parish. Swedie got her former teaching job in Home Economics back at Charles H. Brown High School. I attempted to setup a medical practice in the city, by taking over the medical practice of Dr. Jewell Phillips, who had recently passed away. When negoiations broke down with his widow, I decided to travel to New Orleans, LA to explore what opportunities might exist in the Big Easy that would be advantageous for me to setup my first medical practice?

To my surprise and liking, I concluded the New Orleans, LA Environment, from a medical need standpoint, was what I called *Virgin Territory*. I knew this was the place for me to get into my medical practice, and in the meantime, I would periodically travel back to Springhill, LA to visit with Swedie, but I knew my time was up in the marriage.

It appeared amid the hard times I had gone through during my life thus far, things that needed to fall in place did so effortlessly, and, upon self-reflection, I could not figure-out why things were falling into place for me so easily. Don't get me wrong for one minute; I was not in the business of tempting fate. I took advantage of the opportunity, and moved forward with my life work. For example, I was able to set up my medical practice without having any money to do so. I mean one of the basic things I needed to start my practice was a building to setup my office. The owners of the Circle Food Store allowed me to use office space in one of their buildings *free*.

Moreover, I met some of the best Black Doctors and Nurses in New Orleans, LA, and they extended a helping hand to me when I needed one the most, especially since I needed to make some money, at the outset, to startup and develop my medical practice. One of the first ones to befriend me was Dr. Anthony Hackett. Just when I thought to myself, "things can't any better, they did!" I landed employment at the only Black Hospital in New Orleans, LA, namely Flint-Goodridge Hospital of Dillard University. My *Glory Years* had begun!

In Chapter XVII, I go into details about my medical practice at this prestigious hospital. I spent more than a decade working at Flint Goodridge Hospital. It was, in the words of Charles Dickens, "The Best Of times." However, as it was, the 1960s through the early 1980s was a time when Jim Crow, and its modern-day version, which I call James Crow Esquire, was constantly at work, sometimes overtly, and at others-covertly. In Chapter XVIII, I spend time explaining how Flint-Goodridge

Hospital of Dillard University eventually was forced to close its doors. There were some internal factors that combined with a Congressional Bill, namely, the Hill-Burton Act, that eventually made it impossible for the Flint-Goodridge Hospital of Dillard University to continue to serve the healthcare needs of the African-American Community in New Orleans, LA in particular. The closure of the latter played out quietly beneath the daily news reported by the social media. In fact, many of Louisiana's life-long, African-American Residents never heard of Flint Goodridge Hospital of Dillard University. Its doors closed as quietly as the Mississippi River's Waters flow pass New Orleans, LA to the Gulf of Mexico. As you might imagine, for the Black Physicians and Nurses, who were directly and indirectly impacted by the hospital closure, everyone had to make adjustments, including myself. I was unceremoniously removed as Chair of the Department of Anesthesia in early 1981. I was also married and raising a young family at the time. To survive this blow to my "gut," like the ones Heavyweight Champion Joe Frazier delivered to the Abdomen of Heavyweight Champion Muhammad Ali, I took time off and engaged in Landscape Therapy to refocus myself and deprogram.

Chapter XIX includes information that demonstrates what the loss of Flint Goodridge meant, regarding the challenges I had to deal with. In many instances, Black Physician were forced to give up their private practices, and begin working for private clinics and Hospital Corporations. By the early 1980s, large Hospital Corporations were buying up smaller hospitals in an attempt to gain a larger market share of the Healthcare Industry. In my case, the fallout of the closure of Flint Goodridge Hospital of Dillard University caused me to make some major internal changes in my private medical practice. My staff and marriage were eventually adversely affected by the internal structural changes I had to make in order for my medical practice to survive. The stress caused by the re-structuring took a psychological toll on me, and I had to seek professional medical help. And, if you think, "Wow, things had hit rock bottom for me!" No, I found out there were several more levels below the bottom caused by the closure of Flint-Goodridge Hospital of Dillard University.

Namely, Hurricane Katrina made her powerful presence known everywhere in New Orleans, LA, and she shutdown the local economy, including the Healthcare Industry in the City. It was simple: There was no work in the medical field! I explain in detail in Chapter XX how Hurricane Katrina turned my life, and the life of New Orleans, LA, upside down. It would take several years for me to recover from the devastating impact Hurricane Katrina had on my medical Practice, and her impact on my residence. At one point, I had 10 feet of water inside the first floor of my home. This was unimaginable, but it happened in real life, and in my own. I hadn't felt turned upside down since my father died in 1936. I felt that feeling again by 2005 when Hurricane Katrina made her unwanted house call. I go into details to show just how life-changing Hurricane Katrina was, regarding Recovery and Repair of my Soul and Property. Many New Orleanians gave up, and others disappeared and died anonymously. There was an X mark placed on every door of every house left standing, and a number was placed on it to alert city and health inspectors, if there was someone(s) deceased on the inside of them.

And, in an effort to earn some money to pay for all of the devastation caused by Hurricane Katrina, and the financial and human cost caused by the earlier closure of Flint Goodridge Hospital of Dillard University compounded on top of it, I, in keeping with my Hippocratic Oath, whose goal is to serve the healthcare needs of the people, inadvertently allowed myself to become involved with Maximum Pain Clinic in New Orleans, LA before 2005. Chapter XXI outlines how I was swept up in the Drug Enforcement Administration's (DEA) takedown of this clinic, namely, Maximum Urgent Care, LLC, which was located in Lafayette, LA, based on charges that I was completely unaware of, but I was forced to plea bargain to them, as if I was the motive force underlying them. Eventually, this was, at the end of the day, a legal assault on my medical professionalism, and on my Navy Military Service during World War II. During this time, I risked my personal life to protect the liberty of the American People and the world's, from Adolph Hitler's, and his supporters' attack on Democracy and human life. I ended up being sentenced to serve one year in the Oakdale, LA Penitentiary, and ordered to pay restitution, which exceeded $500,000.

For the first time in my life, I took the opportunity to set the record straight in my Memoir. I carefully examined the Drug Enforcement Administration's Case it made against me, and with much relief, I discovered that the DEA only presented a set of unproven allegations against me. I thoroughly deconstructed them in Chapter XXI, and reconstructed the istorical record related to what actually happened, and my role in it, based on the Truth. The relevant details are provided in this Chapter.

Chapter XXII, or the Conclusion, and after all things I considered during my long and productive life, one fact emerges that is indisputable, that is, as a 95 years old Black Man today, I am proud of my Braud Family and friends I have made everywhere I traveled, all of whom got to know me as loving, sensitive, and creative human being. Many know there were times when I was hit hard but I got up off of the canvass of life; wiped my forehead and brow; and met the next challenge with more determination than I confronted the previous ones I faced. Frankly speaking, this is the Pierce-Braud determination to excel in the face of any adversity, both real, or imaginary that tries to takedown another African-American Role Model.

The final Chapter XXIII provides some detailed information related to how my family, friends, and medical colleagues feel about my Character. The information here indicates how each person, who completed a Character Survey, remembers me when I was either raising my family; or, when we shared a friendship; in addition to those I worked together with as a Medical Doctor Colleague. This information is valuable because it gives one a multi-dimensional view of the manner in which I treated the people who were the closest to me in my life.

Every man and woman aim to leave behind a legacy of "Goodwill" as one lives their life, from day-to-day during a lifetime. I have endeavored to love people, regardless of the situation I was in, at the time we were in this or that relationship. *Anthrapas Estin Kalos*, or my Memoir demonstrates the happy and good place I am in today, 77 years after I embarked on my life journey from the Gravel Road in St. James Parish. I am stronger today, and my Memoir explains how I have accumulated my strength in the form of wisdom. Much of it has come from the people who have given back to me with an abundance of kind words, which affirm my Character being love. This is my gift to the Pierce-Braud Family Group, River Road Family Groups, and the World Family.

CHAPTER II

GEOGRAPHY OF THE LOUISIANA RIVER ROAD, PLANTATIONS, AND THE MISSISSIPPI RIVER

Sam Cooke, the famous Rhythm and Blues Singer must have had Joseph Pierce Braud in mind when he wrote his iconic song *Change is Gonna Come*. Similarly, Sam Cooke told us he was "born by the river in a little tent." Joseph Pierce Braud was born on September 21, 1926 by the sharpest bend in the Mississippi River in a little house in the village called A-Bend, which is also known as Point Houma, in Ascension Parish. I was born in my grandparents' house located on the west bank of the Mississippi River. The latter is an old river according to geological history. Since this water body played a significant role in the economy and social life of St. James Parish where I grew up, it is only fitting that I mention a few words about the origin of the Mississippi River, which was ever present in my early life, and remains present in my mind today.

A. Origin of the Mississippi River

The word Mississippi is derived from "…*(Misi-ziibi)* actually mean "long river,"[1] and this name was given to the river by the Anishinaabe People, a Native American Tribe, that currently live in southern Canada and the northern Midwestern United States. It is not commonly known that that a mountain chain spanned the entire portion of the North American Continent. This geographic feature caused water to flow to the Western Interior Sea, and northward to Canada's Hudson Bay. Klinkenberg added

---

[1] Klinkenberg, Dean, "The 70 Million-Year-Old History of the Mississippi River," Smithsonian Magazine, smithsonianmag.com, September 2020.

"in the late Cretaceous, around 80 million years ago, a mountain chain spanned the southern portion of the continent, blocking southbound water flows, so most North American rivers flowed to the Western Interior Sea or north to Canada's Hudson Bay."[2] As water is perennially known to do, it seeks the shortest distance between two points, and as it occurred roughly 80 million years ago, "…a gap in those mountains formed, opening a path for the river we now know as the Mississippi to flow to the Gulf of Mexico. Scientists call that gap the Mississippi Embayment, but the rest of us know it as the Mississippi Delta…"[3] In short, water began flowing through the Mississippi River Delta "…some 70 million years ago…"[4] -a time when Dinosaurs roamed the North American Continent.

The source of the Mississippi River is in Minnesota. On a good sunny day, and riding in a motor boat, one could easily go across its 20 to 30 feet wide channel located at Lake Itasca, MN without any difficulty. You wouldn't want to attempt this crossing in a motor boat at the Port of Baton Rouge or New Orleans, LA much farther down river. It's simply too dangerous for a small boat to navigate its width at these locations or others. As it is, "at Lake Itasca, the river is between 20 and 30 feet wide, the narrowest stretch for its entire length…At Lake Itasca, the average flow rate is 6 cubic feet per second…At New Orleans, the average flow rate is 600,000 cubic feet per second."[5] A crossing of the Mighty Mississippi River at New Orleans, LA would, no doubt, end in disaster. Regarding its length, "the Mississippi River is the second longest river in North America, flowing 2,350 miles from its source at Lake Itasca through the center of the continental United States to the Gulf of Mexico. The Missouri River, a tributary of the Mississippi River, is about 100 miles longer."[6] Of particular interest to me is that portion of the length of the Mississippi River, which formed the region where I grew up, namely, River Road.

---

[2] Ibid.
[3] Ibid.
[4] Ibid.
[5] Mississippi River Facts, National Park Service, nps.gov.
[6] Ibid.

B. River Road: From Baton Rouge, LA To New Orleans, LA

According to the National Park Service, the most famous River Road in America is located in Louisiana. "… none is more evocative or famous than…Louisiana's fabled Great Mississippi River Road [which] consists of a corridor approximately 70 miles in length located on each side of the river between Baton Rouge and New Orleans."[7] Actually, the spatial distance is between 70 and 78 miles. Map 1.0 below is a Louisiana Parish Map. It is used, as a reference point, to indicate the miles that the Mississippi River meanders through the River Road Parishes where I grew up.

Map 1.0 Louisiana Parish Map

---

[7] Louisiana Division of Historic Preservation, The River Road, National Park Service, U.S. Department of the Interior, nps.gov.

The Louisiana Parishes that makeup the River Road are as follows: (1) Ascension (2) St. James (3) St. John the Baptist, and (4) St. Charles. As I mentioned earlier, the Mississippi River flows through each one of these Parishes: 25 miles, 10 miles, 18 miles, and 25 miles respectively.[8] I grew up in St. James Parish. Table 1.0 shows the land area of the River Road Parishes. This information is important to make note of here because shortly, I will provide more data, which indicates how it was utilized by 1858.

Table 1.0 Land Area Of The Louisiana River Road Parishes

Parish	Total Area/Sq. Miles	Land/Sq. Miles
Ascension	303	290
St. James	258	242
St. John the Baptist	348	213
St. Charles	411	279

Source: www.en.m.wikapedia.org

The American Slavery Institution did not bypass the River Road; rather, it left its footprint on the way this land area was utilized by 1858. *It was primarily organized as plantations throughout the Louisiana Road.* Even after the American Civil War, which took the lives of at least 650,000 people, the land area of the Louisiana River Road Parishes was still, to a large degree, organized in the form of plantations. This is significant to me for two reasons. First, I later grew up here where these plantations formerly operated, and in some subtle ways, both overt and covert, my family life was impacted. And, second, the vast majority of the families I grew up around, and love, also continued to suffer from many of the ill-effects of slavery that their ancestors endured only a few generations before the turn of the Twentieth Century. While it is true the plantation economy, in the Louisiana River Road Parishes affected everyone, everything, and present everywhere within them, later, I will share something *special* with you that will demonstrate how the Pierce-Braud Family I grew up in was able to move through the eye of the slavery needle, and go on to succeed at the

---

[8] Road Atlas, Large Scale, Rand Mcnally, 2021.

highest level of educational excellence. When you discover how and what was achieved, no doubt, you-too-will be amazed.

Meantime, I will turn my attention to the plantations that operated within the Louisiana River Road Parishes by 1858, and to those which still remained active during my childhood days during the 1920s and 1930s.

C. Slavery Plantations That Operated Within The Louisiana River Road Parishes By 1858 And Into The Early Twentieth Century

Throughout the complete expanse of the River Road Land Area shown in Table 1.0 above, every available parcel of land was divided into a series of African Slave Plantations, which were located on either side of the Mississippi River's West and East Banks, stretching downriver, from Ascension, St. James, St. John the Baptist, to St. Charles Parishes. Every available square mile of land area was organized in the form of a plantation by 1858. According to Jordan Brewington's article titled "Dismantling the Master's House: Reparations on the American Plantation," "in southeastern Louisiana, many plantations still stand along River Road, a route along the Mississippi River that connects former slave ports with the present-day cities of New Orleans and Baton Rouge. During the era of slavery, nearly every inch of land between these two cities was claimed by slave owners for the production of sugarcane, indigo, rice, tobacco, and cotton."[9] Map 1.1 and 1.2 below shows the spatial distribution of African Slave Plantations that were active, along the Louisiana River Road, by 1858.

As we see, every available acre of land was consumed by this or that African Slave Plantation. The plantations colored green were classified as a cotton plantation, and those with a beige color were designated as a sugar plantation. One of the unexpected discoveries revealed by Map 1.1 is of all the plantations shown along the Louisiana River Road, I did not expect to find one called Braud Plantation in St. James Parish where I grew up. It was owned by F. Braud; I do not know who this person was other than the fact the White Breauxs had located in this region after being deported from Nova Scotia. It should be pointed-out here that the White Breauxs

---

[9] Brewington, Jordan, "Dismantling the Master's House: Reparations on the American Plantation," The Yale Law Journal, Vol. 130: 2160, yalelawjournal.org, 2021, p. 2167.

spelled their surname as shown, and the Black Brauds as noted. Thus, on the 1858 Plantation, the surname is F. Braud, which suggest this plantation was owned by Black Brauds. More research is required that could shed more light on the ownership question. More details related to the White Breauxs and Black Braud's cultural interconnection will be discussed later. Before I mention a few words about the Plantations, which were still around during my childhood during the late 1920s and 1930s, Map 1.2 is included to show the land tenure in St. Charles Parish was, similar to the other River Road Parishes shown in Map 1.1 upriver, was, generally speaking, dominated by African Slave plantations.

Map 1.1 African Slave Plantations Along The Louisiana River Road By 1858[10]

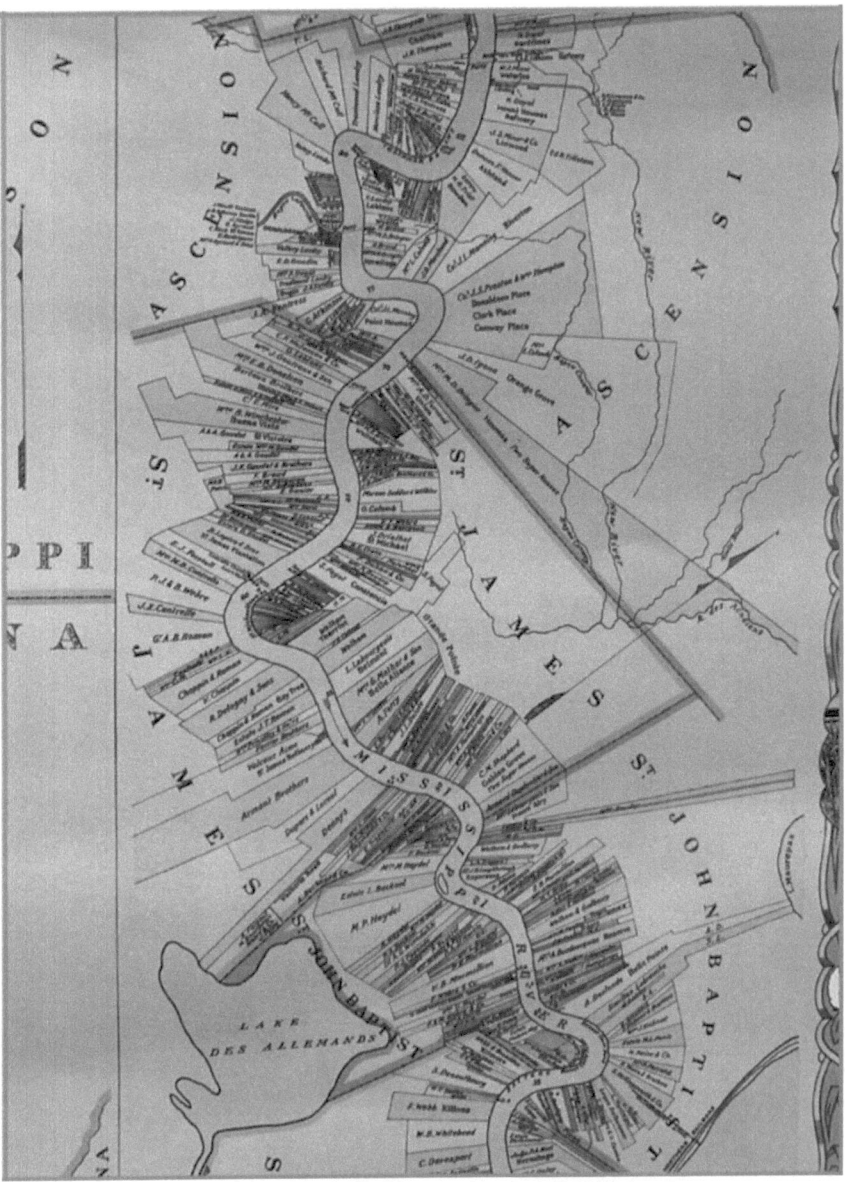

[10] "Plantations of the Mississippi River from Natchez to New Orleans, 1858," 1931, TSLA Map Collection, 42389, Tennessee State Library and Archives, Tennessee Virtual Archive, https://teva.contentdm.oclc.org/digital/collection/p15138accessed 2021-07-11.

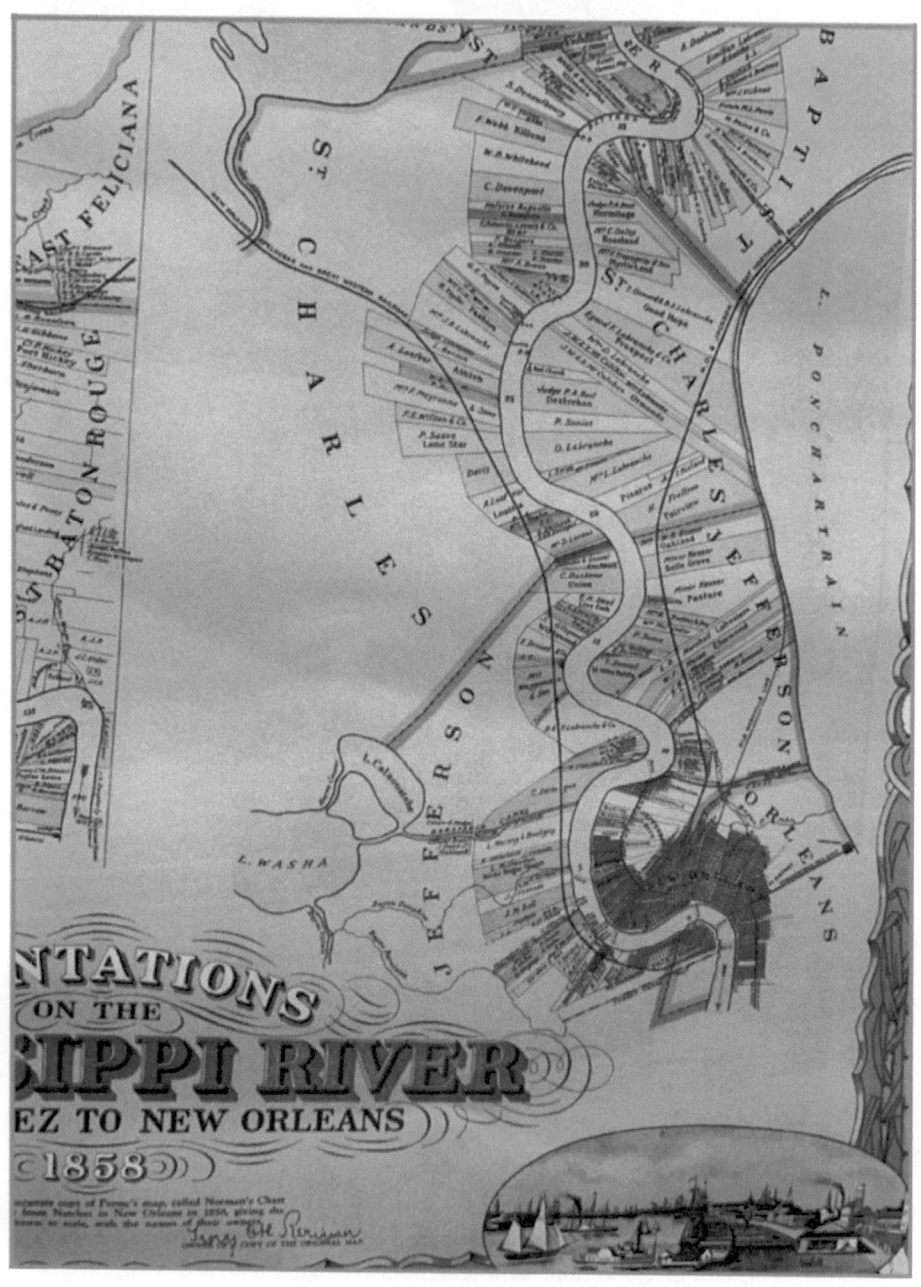

Map. 1.2 African Slave Plantations Along The Louisiana River Road In St. Charles Parish By 1858

St. Charles Parish's African Slave Plantation distribution has one thing that stands-out. That is, if you look closely, and adjacent to the "n" letter spelling of L. Ponchartrain, there was a plantation called Judge P. A. Rest Destrahan, and another one located between the 30 and 35 Mississippi River Marker called Judge P. A. Rest Hermilage. This is interesting because two Judges names are attached to these plantations! This is an indication that Justice throughout the Louisiana River Road was totally non-existent for African Slaves, and likely highly marginalized for Free People of Color. In addition, although African Slave Plantations in Jefferson Parish are not my concern, it is noteworthy to point-out here that a large number was operated on the West Bank across the Mississippi River from New Orleans, LA. In 2021, such cities as Marerro, Harvey, Westwego, Gretna, and Algiers-ALL-evolved on land that was formerly organized as African Slave Plantations by 1858. By 1850, less than a decade earlier, the African Slave Population on Louisiana River Road was more than 50.0 percent.

When I was a young boy growing up in Brookstown in St. James Parish, some of the largest African Slave Plantations, which were in existence by 1858, still maintained their presence by the mid-1930s.

D. Names of Selected Slaveholders Who Owned African Slave Plantations In identified River Road Parishes By 1858

In Ascension Parish, the J.A. Ventress, Point Houma, E.D. Gaudin, and G. Atkinson's Plantations were active by 1858, and I remember, or heard of them, when I was a young boy. That year, every available acre of land in St. James Parish was organized as an African Slave Plantation. Map 1.1 identifies the C. R. Melancon & Co, J. Geutreaux & Son, C. E. Mire, F. Braud, B. Lapice & Bros St. James Plantation, E.J. Ferstell, M.B. Cantrelle, J. & B. Webre, J.K. Cantrelle, Gov. A. B. Roman, and Armant Brothers among many others. The exhaustive list of African Slave Plantations, which were in operation by 1858, can be found in Maps 1.1 and 1.2 above.

Based on my recollection of what my parents told me about the tiny village where I grew up, in 1926, there was a little settlement, on the West Bank of the Mississippi River, call Brookstown. Though I have tried to figure-out where the name Brookstown originated, I have been unable to obtain information related to the origin of name. It had a population of approximately 300 people, including adults and children. Based on Map 1.1, Brookstown likely evolved on land connected to the B. Lapice & Bros' St. James Plantation. There were other small settlements along the River Road (Gravel Road).

As we already know, going north, there were many former African Slave Plantations around during my childhood. Most notable were the Lapice, Salsburg (Sugar Mill) Plantation, Lemonville, Pedescleaux, Point Houma Plantation, A-Bend, Petivan Plantation, Cofield Plantation, and the Town of Donaldsonville. Going South of Brookstown, there was the Jones Yard, a settlement of all relatives (Jones and Geasons), Jamestown, Old Barton Plantation, Freetown, Chatmantown, and Burton Lane. Oddly speaking, in the midst of these predominantly Black Settlements, there was one that consisted mainly of White People. They were all tall and skinny, both women and men. The children were also tall and skinny. Their hair was blond, and it was thought they had migrated to that area from one of the Scandinavian Countries. There was a Catholic Church nearby. In short, as one continued on his or her route, along the Gravel Road, there was one plantation after the next, for many miles, from Ascension Parish to St. Charles Parish near New Orleans, LA. Each Plantation was referred to by the of the family that owned it.

There was another settlement called Moonshine. In that settlement, there was a Baptist Church that sat between the Mississippi River Levee and the Gravel Road in a deep curve. If one continued down the Gravel Road, there was another plantation called Pikes Peak. All plantations had houses where African Slaves use to live. The typical house had a porch, and one room with a kitchen. Generally, the houses were arranged in rows, and they all looked just alike. They had dirt floors. Other plantations of noteworthy attention were Vacherie Road, Baitry, Bay Tree, and the Oak Alley Plantation. The latter had an Antebellum Mansion whose entrance was lined with large Oak trees, which, today, is now a famous tourist attraction. Some of the families that owned African Slave Plantations by 1858 are briefly examined below.

E. Names Of Selected Slaveholder Families In St. James Parish By 1858

As Maps 1.1 and 1.2 show, the vast majority of available, arable land located in Louisiana River Road Parishes by 1858, were predominantly organized in the form of African Slave Plantations. The enslaved population on each plantation, throughout the Gravel Road, accounted for-ALL-of the plantation owners' profit. He could not successfully operate a plantation otherwise, especially if his own family had to clear the land, plant the rice and sugarcane, and harvest it annually for centuries. According to the National Park Service, the African Slave Population "...made profits possible..."[11] Table 1.1 below shows the names of some of the Slaveholding Families, who singularly benefited from the centuries of profits extracted from the labor power of the African Slave Population each held in bondage during the 18th and 19th centuries, along the River Road.

Table 1.1 Names of Slaveholders And The Plantations They Owned In Selected River Road Parishes By 1858

Name	Plantation	Parish
Fernand Armant	Armant Brothers	St. James
Earnest H. Barton	St. Emma	Ascension
Peter M. Lapice De Bergondy	B. Lapice & Bros St. James Plantation	St. James
Jerome Louis Gaudet	A. &A. Gaudet	St. James
F. Braud	Braud	St. James
Jerome Evariste Poche & Prosper Ganier	Pikes Peak	St. James
Nelson P. Himel	M. B. Cantrelle	St. James
Alfred Roman (6th and 8th Governor of Louisiana)	Gov. A. B. Roman	St. James
Antoine M. Sobral	Oak Alley	St. James

Source: http://genealogytrails.com/lou/st.james/bios.html

---

[11] Louisiana Division of Historic Preservation, The River Road, National Park Service, U.S. Department of the Interior, nps.org.

In his research, regarding this period, Greg Timmons wrote "…a near-feudal society emerged in the South. At the top was the aristocratic landowning elite, who wielded much of the economic and political power. Their plantations spanned upward of a thousand acres, controlling hundreds—and, in some cases, thousands—of enslaved people. A culture of gentility and high-minded codes of honor emerged."[12] As we have already seen, Louisiana's River Road, where I grew up, was no exception. The slaveholding families shown above are evidence of this fact. Moreover, Timmons added "slavery was so profitable, it sprouted more millionaires per capita in the Mississippi River valley than anywhere in the nation."[13] These individuals did not become millionaires off of the sweat of their own brow, but, accurately, their enormous wealth was obtained from the ancestors of the descendants of the African-Americans I grew up with during the 1920s and 1930s in Brookstown, and other surrounding nearby villages. In fact, Timmons also stated "by the start of the [Civil War]war, the South…creat[ed]more millionaires per capita in the Mississippi River valley than anywhere in the nation. Enslaved workers represented Southern planters' most significant investment—and the bulk of their wealth."[14] The slaveholding families that owned Oak Alley was Antoine M. Sobral; the B. Lapice & Bros' St. James Plantation fit this description very well also.

In order to dispel anyone's lingering disbelief, regarding how much profit was extracted from the labor power of African Slaves held in bondage throughout the Louisiana River Road, or Gravel Road, which I chose to call it during my childhood, Maria Clark quoted New Orleans, LA Attorney John Cummings, who has owned the Whitney Plantation since 1998, saying "in 1860, two-thirds of all the millionaires in the United States were here on River Road."[15] This was true as early as 1850. According to Peter Bingham Mires, In 1850, the greatest concentration of millionaires in this country was along the Mississippi River between

---

[12] Timmons, Greg, "How Slavery Became the Economic Engine of the South," History, https://www.history.com/.amp/news/slavery-profitable-southern-economy, September 2, 2020, (Original: March 6, 2018).

[13] Ibid.

[14] Ibid.

[15] Clark, Maria, "River Road plantations wrestle with selling slavery," New Orleans City Business, https://neworleanscitybusiness.com/blog/2014/12/11/river-road-plantations-wrestle-with-selling-slavery/, December 11, 2014.

Natchez and New Orleans. This opulence resulted from the plantation system of agriculture… In sum, Louisiana in 1850 can be fairly described as "The Golden Age of the Plantation."[16]

By 1858, the main crops produced on the River Road Plantations previously identified, was cotton and sugarcane. Mires, in support of this fact, wrote "prior to 1850 a number of cash crops had their period of popularity; among these were indigo, rice, and tobacco. Sugarcane and cotton came to dominate the plantation scene in Louisiana…"[17] River Road. Those plantations, once again, that are colored green produced cotton; and, those colored beige produced sugarcane. Rice became popular by the turn of the early Twentieth Century, which coincided with my early childhood days in Brookstown.

Having established how the vast majority of the land area, along the Louisiana River Road, was organized in the form of plantations, and given the fact we also are now aware that-ALL-of the available arable land was utilized this way; in addition, every African Man, Woman, son, and daughter, albeit a grandmother, grandfather, aunt, uncle, niece, and nephew were likewise caught-up in the net of the American Slavery Institution practices, from Baton Rouge, LA to New Orleans, LA. No one could escape the reach of the plantation's impact of working for a lifetime without any allotment, or compensation, from sun up-can see-to sundown-can't see. Even on full moon lit nights, employment of slave labor continued well into the midnight hours! It is only fitting to show how many African Slaves were caught-up in the net of the practice of slavery, along the Louisiana River Road. A series of Tables and Maps are forthcoming that consistently shows that, regardless of the River Road Parish focused on, each one similarly had a 3 to 1 ratio of African Slaves to Free, Native White Population. The purpose of this ratio is made clear at the appropriate time.

One last thing I must say here, and that is, any African-American Family, which is a descendant of this wide slavery network, including all

---

[16] Mires, Peter Bingham, "Predicting the Past: The Geography of Settlement in Louisiana, 1699-1890, and Its Application to Historic Preservation." (1988). LSU Historical Dissertation and Theses. 4661. Https://digitalcommons.lsu.edu/gradschool disstheses/4661

[17] Ibid., p. 153.

of its debilitating influences, no doubt, had to put in play a *Herculean Determination* to overcome its anger and wraths to survive! I grew up a part of one such family, and although I did not know it at the time, I, along with my siblings, was set on a trajectory course toward achieving high educational excellence in spite of any perceived hardships, which to me, as a young boy at the time, was unimaginable. But, I did have my dream of becoming a Medical Doctor one day. As far away as it seemed to me, the Pierce-Braud Family I grew up in talked about the future in such a way I felt becoming a medical doctor was possible. During my lowest moments, my dream would always bring a smile to my face. I knew I would come through everything just fine. For me, survival was not a choice. I had a voice in me, and I was determined to discover it.

Nevertheless, the task was definitely challenging. For a majority of the Black People, who lived through the toils and strife of the daily practice of slavery, along the Gravel Road before the beginning of the Twentieth Century, their children's opportunities for a better life one day remained merely a vision. Nearly all Black People were slaves before 1860; the following data shows many of our people were born into slavery, and they died a slave, but their *dreams for their children did not die.* I plucked one of their dreams out of the air, and made it my own. How I made it my reality is forthcoming. Presently, a few words related to the extent Black People were entangled in the Slaveholding Families' System of Slavery is a valuable plank I used to build my life-story, which would not begin until the early Twentieth Century.

CHAPTER III

SELECTED DEMOGRAPHIC CHARACTERISTICS OF THE WHITE AND AFRICAN SLAVE POPULATION FOR RIVER ROAD PARISHES-1850 TO 1950

A. Total White And African Slave Population, 1850

To begin, the total population of Whites and African Slaves is shown in Table 1.2 below. The disproportionate number of the latter can quickly be observed, regarding their presence on the Louisiana River Road by 1850.

Table 1.2 Total Population For Selected Louisiana Parishes, Including Whites And African Slaves By 1850

Parish	White		Total	Slaves		Total	Free Colored		Total
	M	F		M	F		M	F	
St. James	1,696	1,589	3,285	4,378	3,373	7,751	26	36	62
St. Charles	463	404	867	2,397	1,735	4,132	59	62	121
St. John the Baptist	1,302	1,284	2,586	2,615	1,925	4,540	74	117	191
Ascension	1,725	1,615	3,340	3,718	3,548	7,266	70	76	146
Total White Population			6,738						
Total Slave Population						23,689			

Source: U.S. Census of Population, 1850 Census: Population of the United States, Statistics of Louisiana, Population By Parishes-Ages, Color, And Condition-Aggregates, p. 473

Interestingly, the African Slave Total Population far outnumbered the total for the White Population. What other reason can be imagined why so many of the former were present on the Louisiana River Road relative to the White Population. That is, the African Slave Population was the means of production for the creation of all wealth. As wise as the Slaveholder made himself out to be, while standing in his glory, "he knew the "mother of-ALL-of his wealth was the labor of the African Slaves he held in servitude." Notably, St. James Parish had more African Slaves than any of the others. Aggregately, there were 23,689 African Slaves held in forced servitude on the Louisiana River Road by 1850. Of the 30,427 Whites and African Slaves, the latter accounted for 78.0 percent of the total population. The pattern was set by 1850, largely, because the Slaveholding Families depended on the African Slaves labor power to survive. For the latter enslaved people, they received zero compensation for their work.

For many in my Pierce-Braud Family Group, the Gravel Road was not paved with gold as it was for the Slaveholding Families, who extracted it from the labor power of the African Slaves. As early as 1850, the practice of slavery on the River Road was widespread, and it would not reach its peak until 1860. Table 1.3 shows the amount of land still in an unimproved condition, and the cash value of farms, or plantations.

Table 1.3 Improved Land In Farms, Value of Farms And Implements, And Deaths By Selected Louisiana Parishes, 1850

Parish	Acres of Land In Farms		Value of Farms and Implements		Deaths	
	Improved	Unimproved	Cash Value of Farms	Value of Farming Implements & Machinery	Whites & Free Colored	Slaves
Ascension	28,346	65,138	$6,335,270	$780,425	37	103
St. James	41,905	49,164	2,505,235	590,920	24	194
St. John the Baptist	22,285	33,412	1,703,500	663,800	26	129
St. Charles	20,596	66,746	1,801950	560,050	14	111

Source: U. S. Census of Population, 1850: Population of the United States, Statistics of Louisiana, Agriculture-Farms and Equipment, And Deaths, pp. 475 and 482.

Accordingly, there were 214,460 unimproved acres of land waiting for African Slaves to improve and make productive. Those African Slave Plantations already in production had a cash value of $12,345,955. In St. James Parish where I would later grow up, it was 20.3 percent of the identified total. If we read behind the hidden meaning of the cash value of farms in the Louisiana River Road Parishes, one will have to conclude that the value of the African Slaves is accounted for in the sum totals per parish. In addition, the most painful thing, which certainly overrides what I have mentioned thus far, is found in the death column.

Since African Slaves were the primary mode of production, and the main motive force used to create wealth for the Slaveholding Families shown earlier, including those not identified, unfortunately, deaths of African Slaves far outpaced those of Whites and Free Colored. For example, in St. James Parish, the former accounted for 89.0 percent of all deaths! Of the factors that could cause an early death such as poor medical care, malnutrition, and infant mortality among many others, working from sunup to sundown, in the sweltering sun daily, while doing many backbreaking tasks to improve unimproved land, notwithstanding the other labor intensive work related to planting, grassing, and harvesting crops,-ALL-combined to lead an African Slave to a premature death. The other hidden point in these statistics is the low number of deaths of White and Free Colored People can be attributed to the fact African Slaves did the heavy lifting work while they did less life-threatening tasks. Mires research corroborates the fact that the Louisiana River Road Economy rested squarely on the shoulders of the African Slaves. No millionaire Slaveholding Families would have ever existed without *slave labor*. And, their descendants know it today.

For example, Mires added "a [defining] component of plantation agriculture of the Antebellum South was slavery. The production of sugarcane and cotton were both labor intensive activities that relied almost exclusively on the labor of black slaves…a shipload of 500 slaves arrived in 1719 just as New Orleans was being built…By 1850, half of the population of the State of Louisiana was black and most of them were slaves."[18]

---

[18] Ibid., p. 157.

B. Total Free White, Black, And Mulatto Populations On The River Road By 1860

There were 23,689 African Slaves on the Louisiana River Road by 1850, and 6,738 White People. Of the 23,689 African Slaves, by 1860, 111, or 0.5 percent were Free Colored. This means on the eve of the American Civil War, less than a handful of Black People was free. Table 1.4 shows the total White Population relative to the total free Black Population. Nothing had changed; if anything did, the 0.5 percent Free Colored Population likely decreased by 1860!

Table 1.4 Free White, Black, And Mulatto Populations
For Selected Louisiana Parishes, 1860

Parish	White		Total	Black		Total	Mulatto		Total
	M	F		M	F		M	F	
Ascension	1,767	1,820	3,587	23	33	56	53	56	109
St. James	1,548	1,543	3,091	11	14	25	17	17	34
St. Charles	450	406	856	14	16	30	62	82	144
St. John the Baptist	1,384	1,325	2,709	18	53	71	98	128	226

Source: 1860 Census: Population of the United States, Eighth Census, pp. 195 and 196.

There were 10,252 White People living in these parishes by 1860. And, only 182 free Black People, which suggests, since there was no mass outmigration from the area, the vast majority were still held in bondage. In other words, only 1.8 percent of the Black People were free; the overwhelming vast majority were still African Slaves! Regarding Mulattoes, which refer to people who are of mixed-race ancestry that includes White Europeans and Black African roots, there were only 500, or 5.0 percent, on the River Road in the selected parishes. In either case, the slavery trend remained intact right up to the day the first cannons were fired by the Southern Confederacy in their desperate attempt to keep the Slaveholding Families' American Slavery Institution alive on the Gravel Road. How much changed, if anything, regarding slavery, is shown in Table 1.5 below.

C. Total White And Free Colored Populations By 1870

Table 1.5 White And Free Colored Population In Selected Louisiana Parishes-Post Emancipation Proclamation, 1870

Parish	White	Free Colored	Total	Free Colored % of Total
Ascension	4,265	7,310	11,575	63.2
St. James	3,275	6,877	10,152	67.7
St. Charles	897	3,963	4,860	81.5
St. John the Baptist	2,715	4,044	6,759	59.8

Source: United States Census of 1870: Volume 1. The Statistics of the Population of the United States, Population By Counties-1790 to 1870, p. 34.

By 1870, five years after the American Civil War, and based on the resounding military defeat suffered by the Southern Confederacy, at the hands of the Union Army, everything, momentarily, changed for the former African Slaves. They were *freed* when President Abraham Lincoln signed his Emancipation Proclamation. Although the former slaves on River Road were emancipated by this act, the former slaves had nothing, nor did they have anywhere to go.

The Free Colored Column shows the disproportionate number of African-Americans, who were formerly slave labor ten years earlier by 1860. As I pointed-out earlier, the larger number of Free Colored represent the people, who did all of the work on the plantations for centuries. In each case, 60.0 percent of the total Population were former African Slaves. As I mentioned earlier, not only did the vast majority of Free Colored People came out of slavery *penniless*, most of them *could not read or write*.

Map 1.3 below indicates that illiteracy, along the River Road, was 60.0 percent and higher by 1870. Remember, the primary goal of the Slaveholding Family was to maintain an ignorant, docile slave at all times. He or she was only valuable as a physical worker and reproducer of children; there was no need for anyone to think; everyone was told what to do; when to do a task; how to do a task; and what was considered a finished product. No slave had a say in important matters when any decision, large or small, had to be made. Looking at Map 1.3 (Source: 1870 United States Census), it perfectly parallels the ones which shows the spatial distribution of plantations along the Mississippi River, from Natchez, MS to New Orleans, LA. The Slaveholding Families, who owned these plantations, set in place a system aimed at keeping every African Slave ignorant and docile for the duration of his or her life, both presently and through the coming generations during the time the American Slavery Institution was in existence and thereafter. The data in Table 1.6 corroborates this chilling reality.

Map 1.3 Illiteracy Along Louisiana River Road By 1870

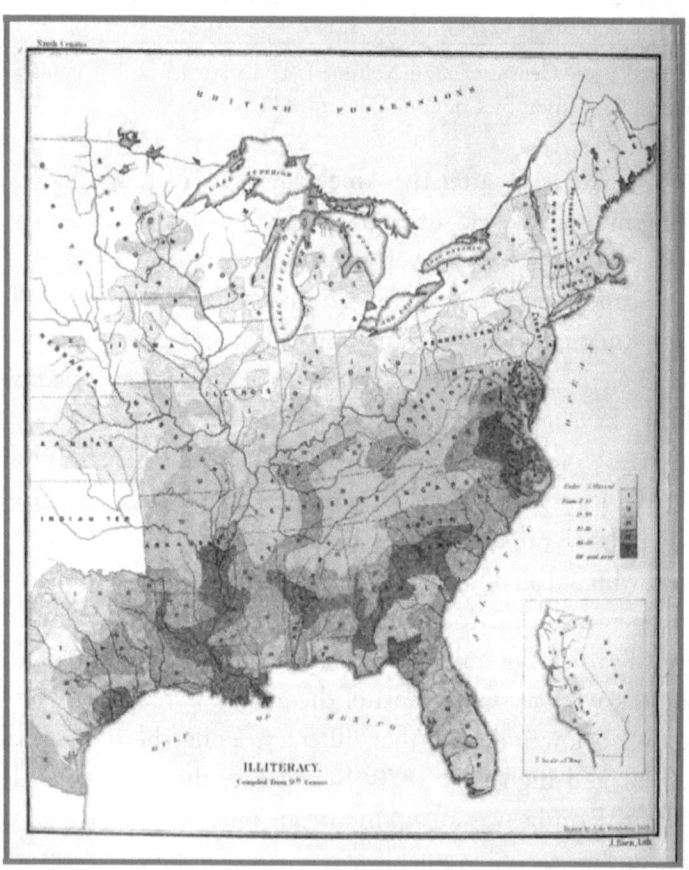

By 1870, hardly any recently freed African Slaves, or their children, attended public school. The data in Table 1.6 below supports this fact.

Table 1.6 School Attendance And *Illiteracy In
Selected Louisiana Parishes, 1870

Parish	Attended Sch		T	Attended Sch		T	Can't Write		T	Can't Write		T
	WM	WF		CM	CF		WM	WF		CM	CF	
Ascension	41	32	73	18	12	30	201	258	459	1,955	1,854	3,809
St. James	162	212	374	30	43	73	87	86	173	1,923	1,591	3,514
St. Charles	105	80	185	271	269	540	25	17	42	1,111	1,020	2,131
St. John the Baptist	108	96	204	30	43	73	307	278	585	705	620	1,325

Source: United States Census of 1870, School Attendance And Illiteracy In Each State And Territory, State of Louisiana, p. 414.

*60 percent or more of the people, who lived along River Road by 1870, were illiterate. CM is Colored Males and CF is Colored Females; WM and WF represents White Males and White Females.

As we see, with the exception of St. Charles Parish, (This total for Free Colored is influenced by school attendance in New Orleans, LA) school attendance, for recently freed Black People, was generally low throughout the River Road Parishes. Simultaneously, those who can't write quadrupled the same for the White Population. For example, of the 3,687 White and Black People in St. James Parish, who could not write, the latter accounted for 95.3 percent! This enormous percentage is a reflection of what the educational attainment level was for Black People in St. James Parish, where I was born 56 years later. The prospects for a high level of educational achievement were low, and having maximum compassion for the Black People who were barred from obtaining a good education due to Systemic Racism, Jim Crow Laws, KKK Domestic Terrorism, and the U.S. Supreme Court's Ruling that Separate But Equal Educational Facilities were legal, ALL of these barriers, and many unnamed ones, crushed many Black People's American Dreams half a century before I was born in 1926. Would the Pierce-Braud Family Groups fall victims to this Unholy Trend? I could answer this question presently, but I do not desire to deflate the suspense related to how the Pierce-Braud Family Group strategically managed to set my feet upon a different path, or the "road less traveled" at the time.

D. Total White And Free Colored Populations By 1880

The Free Colored Population did not decrease, but it continued to increase by 1880. Table 1.7 substantiates this trend.

Table 1.7 Population By Race And Selected Parishes In Louisiana, 1880

Parish	White	Colored	Percent Colored
Ascension	5,908	10,855	65
St. James	4,850	9,802	67
St. Charles	1,041	5,746	85
St. John the Baptist	3,855	5,792	60

Source: United States Census of 1880, pp. 393 and 394.

Throughout the Gravel Road, the Free Colored Population, in each River Road Parish, increased significantly. This population accounted for 60.0 percent or more of the people, including Whites. Between 1870 and 1880, the Freed Colored Total Population in St. James Parish increased 179.0 percent. Having been forced to reproduce a large number of children to work in the fields during the 244 years of existence of the American Slavery Institution, Freed Colored People, by 1880, were still trapped in "slavery by another name," namely, sharecropping. Later, I will show this system only sunk Freed Colored People deeper in debt to their former slave masters.

The main point to grasp here is Freed Colored People total population numbers steadily rose, and this fact, as I will show shortly, became a worrisome question, in the minds of White People, of how to control their formerly enslaved workers, who, by 1880, outnumbered them, on average, 3 to 1! Map 1.4 below shows the Louisiana River Road's population density was one of the highest in America by 1880 (Source: United States Census, 1880). Given the fact the American Slavery Institution was known to thrive financially off of plenty of African Slaves' labor power, after the former came to an end by 1860, there was a large number of Freed Colored People living along the Louisiana River Road. In fact, more than half of the Louisiana Total Population by 1880 consisted of Freed Colored People. Map 1.5 consists of a series of Pie Graphs, which shows the proportion of Freed Colored People in the total population of the states.

Map. 1.4 Density Of The Louisiana River Road Population By 1880

Map 1.5 Pie Graph Showing Proportion Of White and Colored Populations In Louisiana By 1880

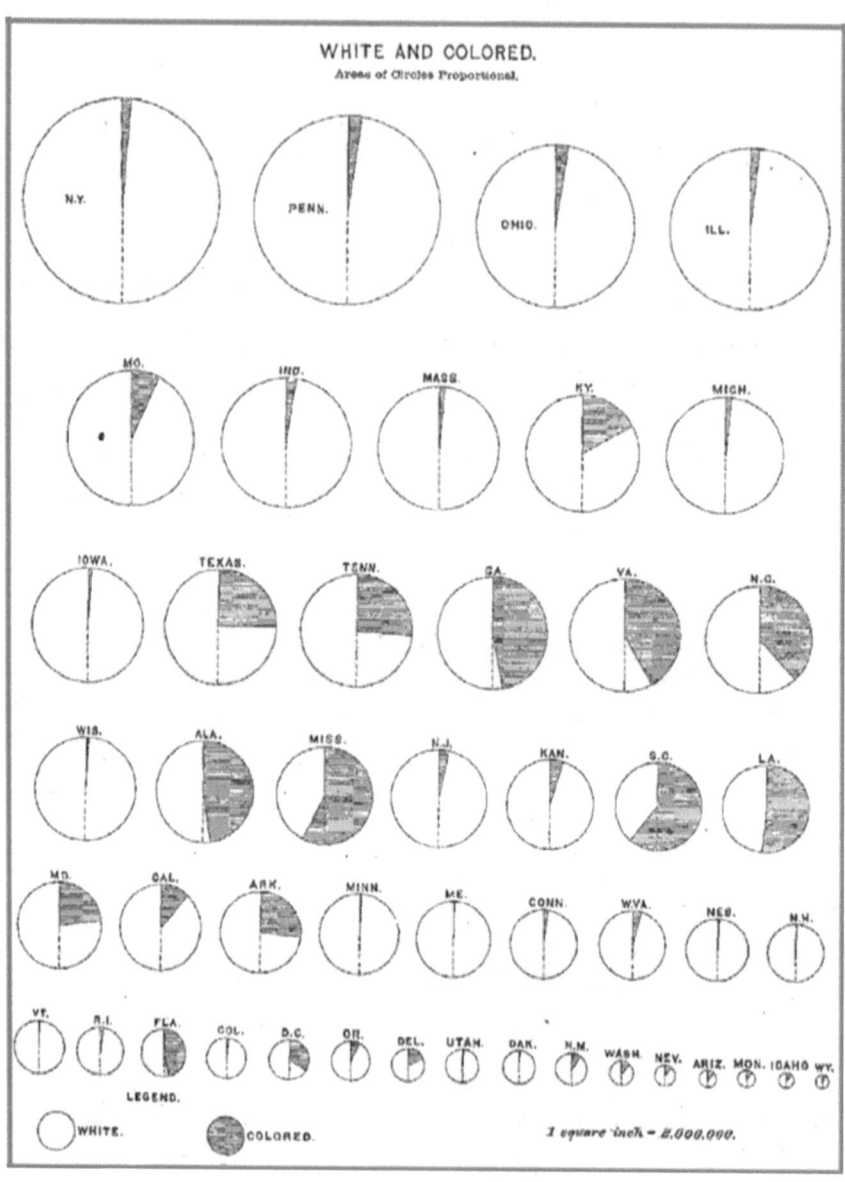

Source: United States Census of 1880.

E. Total White And Colored Populations By 1890

Louisiana is surpassed only by Mississippi, regarding the proportion of Free Colored People in its total population. This trend continued during the 1880s. The data in Table 1.8 substantiates my claim.

Table 1.8 Total White And Colored Population By Selected Louisiana Parishes, 1890

Parish	White		Colored		Percent Colored
	M	F	M	F	
Ascension	3,720	3,769	5,636	5,676	60.2
St. James	2,606	2,572	5,151	4,873	66.0
St. Charles	831	742	3,016	2,735	78.5
St. John the Baptist	2,095	2,181	3,346	3,333	61.0

Source: United States Census of 1890, Eleventh Census, Sex, General Nativity, And Color, 1890, p. 501.

Again, Freed Colored People (This is the term used by the U.S. Census to classify African-Americans by ethnicity by 1890) significantly outnumbered the White Population in the River Road Parishes by 1890. In fact, the former made up 60.0 percent or more of the total population. Keep this trend in mind as I move forward with my life story, and also keep in mind, that my Pierce-Braud Ancestors had to endure some hard times due to Systemic Racism, KKK Activity, and generalized inequality, which were all supported by the U.S. Government at the time.

F. Total White And Negro Populations By 1900

By 1900, which was the beginning of the Twentieth Century, the U.S. Census stopped classifying African-Americans as Freed Colored, and began referring to us as *Negro*, and I am sure the *N-Word* followed this new classification. Table 1.9 shows the trend in which Negroes outnumbered the White Population was unbroken.

Table 1.9 White And Negro Population For Selected Louisiana Parishes, 1900

Parish	White		Negro		Total	% Negro
	M	F	M	F		
Ascension	4,772	4,680	5,995	6,086	21,533	56.1
St. James	3,331	3,269	5,966	5,390	17,956	63.2
St. Charles	199	189	3,227	2,875	6,490	94.0
St. John the Baptist	2,110	2,059	3,745	3,439	11,353	63.3

Source: United States Census of 1900. Twelfth Census, Sex, General Nativity, And Color, pp. 585 and 586.

In St. James Parish, 63.2 percent of the total population was Negro by 1900. Although my birth was still more than a generation in the future, I was destined to be born into a parish and nation in which the White Population felt comfortable referring to any Negro, including those who were unborn, by using the N-Word to do so. This practice should not surprise anyone because throughout the duration of the American Slavery Institution and thereafter, White People followed the lead of the Slaveholding Families along River Road, who called African Slaves, and later Free Colored and Negroes, every derogatory name under the heavens but a child of God.

G. Total White And Negro Populations By 1910

Table 1.10 includes data that shows Negroes continued to outnumber the White Population with the exception of Ascension Parish.

Table 1.10 White And Negro Population By Sex For Selected Parishes, 1910

Parish	Total		White		Negro		% Negro
	M	F	M	F	M	F	
Ascension	11,942	11,945	6,370	6,258	5,568	5,687	47.1
St. James	11,828	11,181	5,032	4,812	6,795	6,369	57.2
St. Charles	6,139	5,068	2,454	2,033	3,685	3,035	60.0
St. John the Baptist	7,508	6,830	3,176	3,032	4,328	3,798	56.7

United States Census of 1910, Thirteenth Census, Population For The State And For Parishes, 1910, pp. 779 and 787.

There was a noticeable decrease in the Total Negro Population in Ascension Parish. It fell below 50.0 percent for the first time! Other River Road Parishes also experienced a decline in their Total Negro Population. Several factors can explain these drop-offs. First, as I will explain, in some detail shortly, KKK Activity, Jim Crowism, Systemic Racism, and the U.S. Government's unwillingness to stop this domestic terrorism, caused many Negroes to bundle up their few items and belongings, and migrate to the North in search of a better life. Times were harder than hard for many! And, Second, large numbers of Negroes were lynched and forced into the Convict Labor System where many simply *disappeared* forever. In the midst of so much racial turmoil and antagonism, Negro Women likely curtailed the number of children born into the prevailing Domestic Terrorism Environment. Infant Mortality took a toll on babies; too many did not live to see their first birthday. This was the state of play a generation before my birth in St. James Parish.

While the Total Negro Population decreased by 1910, those who remained in the River Road Parishes had a starkly contrasting and higher rate of Illiteracy, relative to the percent of White Illiterates. Table 1.11 established this fact.

Table 1.11 White and Negro Illiterate Population By Selected Louisiana Parishes, 1910

Parish	White	% Illiterate	Negro	% Illiterate
Ascension	453	18.5	1,603	55.1
St. James	404	21.3	1,793	50.0
St. Charles	220	25.7	960	50.7
St. John the Baptist	262	18.5	1,275	54.5

Source: United States Census of 1900, Thirteenth Census, Population For The State And For Parish, 1900, pp. 779, 787.

Amazingly, but not surprising, the incidence of illiteracy among Negroes was astronomical by 1910. For instance, the percent illiterate figure merely means, half of the Negroes in Brookstown were illiterate 16 years before my birth! This is beyond hearth-breaking, given the fact Negro School Attendance was simultaneously low, and do not forget in 1896, the U.S. Supreme Court ruled, in the Plessey v. Ferguson Case, that Separate but Equal Educational Facilities, among others, were *Constitutional*. Also, this was the year my mother was born! She could not have imagined the roadblocks that were already placed on her path, which, collectively, were screaming-*Turnaround and bury your family dreams!* More on how Lillian Luellen Pierce Braud and Joe Braud handled the situation later. Map 1.6 below shows Louisiana led the nation in illiteracy for all classes in both 1910 and 1920, and the state led the nation, regarding the Percent of Illiterate Negroes at the same time.

Map 1.6 Percent Illiterate Negro Population 10 Years
Of Age And Over In Louisiana, 1910 and 1920

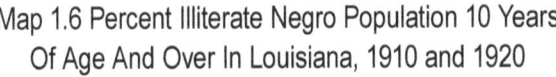

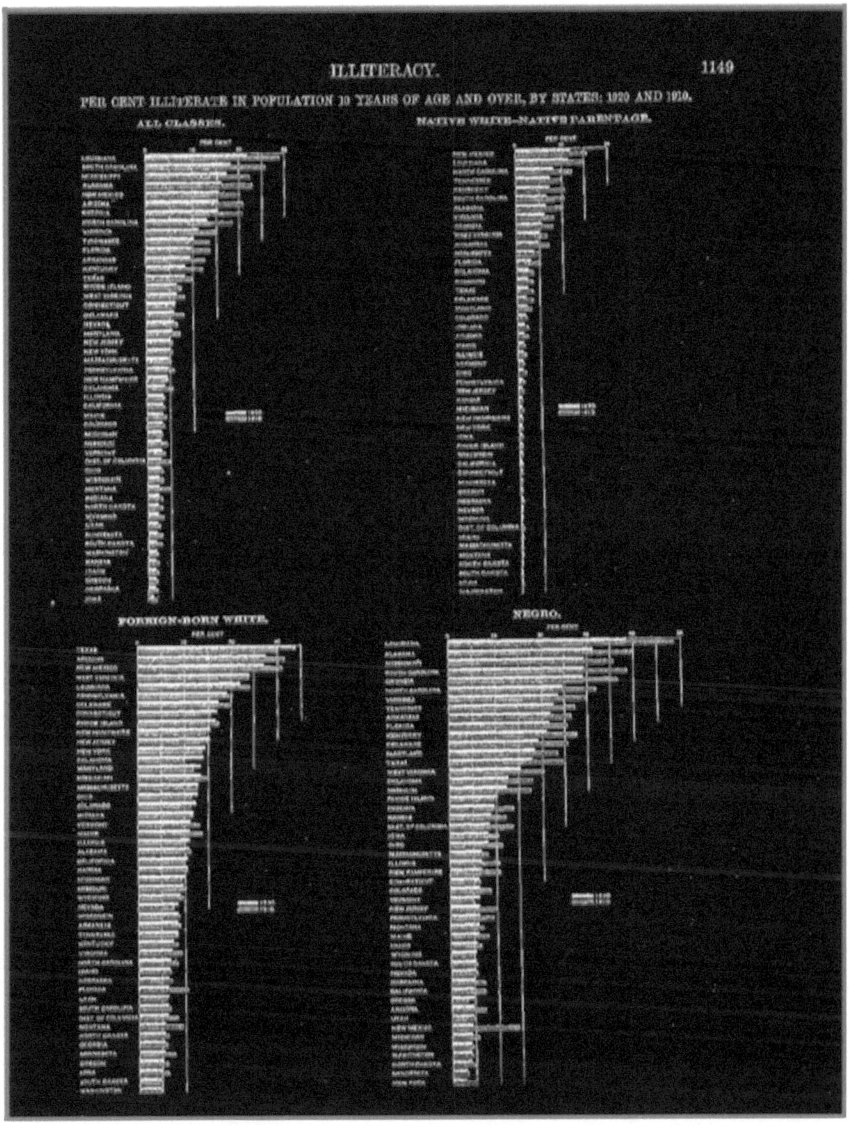

This is the educational achievement environment, or put more accurately-the lack thereof, that I was destined to be born into by 1926. With so many illiterate Negroes living on the Gravel Road, would my prospects for living a better life be any different than it was for so many during previous generations? If I would have any chance of avoiding the illiteracy trap, which was widely set against Negro Educational Achievement at the time, something *special and different* would have to occur inside the Pierce-Braud Family I was destined to be born into a half decade later. Stated another way, I mean would my parents put a plan in place that would break me free of the path of this inertia, which has held so many Negroes on River Road in a State of Illiteracy, similar to the way the sun's gravity holds the Earth in its orbit? Rather than prematurely unpack the plan here, which would deflate the suspense in my life story, I defer, and instead, provide more demographic information related to the River Road's White and Negro Populations by 1930. Before I do so, a Catholic Priest, namely Father McKnight, from Opelousas, LA, once remarked "If you want something that you never had, you must do something that you never did." This thought captures the challenge my parent's faced by the time I was born in 1926.

H. Total White And Negro Populations By 1930

Table 1.12 shows a declining Negro Population trend on River Road, which was underway by 1920, and it continued by 1930.

Table 1.12 White And Negro Population By Selected Louisiana Parishes, 1930

Parish	White		Negro		% Negro
	M	F	M	F	
Ascension	5,587	5,604	3,457	3,020	36.7
St. James	3,810	3,800	3,706	3,754	49.5
St. Charles	3,048	3,698	2,208	1,091	32.8
St. John the Baptist	3,531	3,471	3,597	3,360	49.8

Source: United States Census of 1930, Fourteenth Census, Population By Age, Color, Nativity, And Sex, For Parishes: 1930, pp. 974 and 997.

As it was, by 1930, Negro Labor was no longer needed the way their African Slave Ancestors' Labor was heavily depended upon by the Slaveholding Families, which owned-All-of the plantations on River Road by 1860. In short, Free Negroes were expendable! If a White person could not get a dollar out of the pocket of a Negro, he or she was of no value to him whatsoever. Negroes, though considered free on paper, they were still valuable to the former Slaveholding Families who owned them before the American Civil War. As I will explain shortly, they used the Thirteenth Amendment to the U.S. Constitution to legally re-enslave thousands of Negroes in their Convict Labor and Sharecropping Systems.

I was four years old by the time the Census of 1930 was recorded, and rather than the vast majority of Negroes being wealthy by this time, they were, on the contrary, *Quasi-Free, Illiterate, mostly Landless, and Poor.* Survival, for many, was a day-to-day struggle, and a moment-to-moment life or death prospect. The 1929 Great Depression added even more uncertainty, regarding their chances to succeed. Hope, for many, was hanging by the size of a single strand of hair. Negroes, in large numbers, were simply disappearing, relative to their once large concentration on the River Road several decades earlier.

I. Total White And Negro Populations By 1940

The continuation of the downward trend in the number of Negroes on the River Road by 1940 is documented in Table 1.13.

Table 1.13 Total White And Negro Population In
Selected Louisiana Parishes by 1940

Parish	White	Negro	Percent White	Percent Negro
Ascension	13, 064	7,948	59.8	38.4
St. James	8,313	8,228	50.1	49.6
St. Charles	8, 265	3, 909	67.1	31.7
St. John the Baptist	7,778	6,875	52.7	46.6

Source: United States Census, Characteristics Of The Population, Composition Of The Population, By Parishes: 1940, pp. 362 and 364.

The primary finding is the Total Negro Population continued to noticeably decline. In each case, the percent White Population increased, and the percent Negro Population fell. By 1940, I was 14 years old, and frankly, I didn't notice the fall-off in the Total Negro Population because Brookstown, the place where I grew up, was a tiny village. Maybe, the reason my hometown remained a village during my childhood is due to the recognized declining trend in the Total Negro Population in St. James Parish and others. In 1900, as I have already shown, 63.2 percent of the Total Population in this parish were classified as Negro. Nevertheless, and regardless of the total number of Negroes, by 1940, their educational achievement was far below the White Population. The School Attendance and Years of School Completed information shown in Table 1.14 proves this point.

Table 1.14 School Attendance and Years of School Completed For Selected Louisiana Parishes By 1940

Parish	Age7-13	Age14-15	Age16-17	HS Completed M F		Med Sch Yrs Comp.	
Ascension	2,787	777	519	101	65	M/4.7	F/5.2
St. James	214	735	363	87	54	4.6	4.9
St. Charles	2,118	592	342	86	252	5.5	5.8
St. John the Baptist	2,275	665	295	215	255	4.2	4.7

Source: United States Census, 1940, Characteristics Of The Population, Composition Of The Population, BY Parishes: 1940, pp. 362 and 364.

Interestingly, as the age of the students, who attended school increased, the total number decreased. The U. S. Census for 1940 did not distinguish ethnicity for school attendance; however, based on the previous information shown for percent of Negro Illiteracy, no doubt, Negro School Attendance lagged far behind Whites.' If White School Attendance declined with age, it is safe to say on one hand, not many Negroes attended school, and on the other, even fewer continued their schooling as they got older. Systemic Racism and Separate But Equal School Facilities were responsible for low Negro Educational Achievement by 1940. In short, the idea of *No Child Left Behind* did not apply to the Negroes, who lived on the Gravel Road; many were left behind when they were born, and educational opportunities were few. Every Negro Child was suppose to be intentionally left behind insofar as White People were concerned. Given this fact, it adds to the growing suspense surrounding why I was not left behind, including my siblings. All of the factors that were in play during my childhood pointed to the fact we could easily be left behind, like generations of African-Americans before me, regarding my educational achievement, if something miraculous, but, nevertheless, as real as the air we breathe, did not intervene in the Pierce-Braud Group that overrode the real possibility of my educational failure. The latter had happened to-too- many good African-American People before I was born in 1926.

When Median Years of School Completed is taken into consideration, overall, those who attended school during the 1930s, and the former was recorded for them, the number was less than 6 years in the River Road Parishes by 1940! And, this figure, for the most part, applies to the White Population too.

Moreover, of the 21,012 total population in Ascension Parish by 1940, 101 males and 65 females completed 4 years of college or more; of the 16,541 in St. James Parish, 87 males completed 4 years or more of college and 97 females completed 4 years of college or more; for St. Charles Parish, its total population was 12,174, and 86 males completed 4 years of college or more and 27 females completed 4 years of college or more; of the 14,653 total population for St. John the Baptist Parish, 77 males completed 4 years of college and 49 females completed 4 years of college or more by 1940.[19] These figures suggests only a handful or less of Negroes had completed 4 years or more of college.

And, having laid down the social and economic foundation of the Gravel Road, from 1850 to 1940, it is clear and reasonable to conclude that the educational opportunities for the descendants of former African Slaves were very few. This is the situation I inherited; would going to college be possible for me? yet, as everyone will learn, my Pierce-Braud Family Group devised a plan that allowed its member to excel in the education field in spite of the fact-ALL of the social and economic indicators heavily leaned toward the opposite. One of those social indicators is the domestic terrorism that came into being during the mid-1870s, or, more specifically, during the so-called Reconstruction Era following the American Civil War. It continued unabated throughout most of the Twentieth Century.

As we shall see shortly, it was purposely set into action to maintain control over the former slaves similar to the way they were micro-managed

---

[19] United States Census of Population, 1940, Sixteenth Census, Characteristics Of The Population, Composition Of The Population, By Parishes: 1940, pp. 362 and 364.

with violence during the 244 years of the American Slavery Institution. The suspense in my life story continues to build because while domestic terrorism and violence put an end to many African-American Dreams at the time, my Pierce-Braud Family Group continued to surface stronger and more determined to excel in the education field, although my family group also faced many hardships and challenges; but, fortunately, the plan it put in place provided my siblings and I a way to move forward productively.

Presently, I will provide information that identifies the Pre-Civil War Plantations on the Louisiana River Road where the villages and towns evolved in which I spent much of my childhood years working and playing. This is a necessary connection to make because the land area of the villages and towns on the Gravel Road, only a few decades earlier, was where African Slaves were born, worked all of their lives, and laid to rest after many hard years of work without any compensation! Many were buried without a headstone, and, as a young boy, I probably played baseball, or someone may have planted a garden, under which a former African Slave may have been buried in an unmarked grave.

CHAPTER IV

THIRTEENTH AMENDMENT TO THE U. S. CONSTITUTION, FREEDMEN BUREAU BILL, 1865, SHARECROPPING SYSTEM AND OUT-MIGRATION ON THE RIVER ROAD

Thus far, I have shown every parcel of arable land was organized in the form of an African Slave Plantation before 1860. In addition, two-thirds of all of the millionaires in the United States resided on the Louisiana River Road then, and they owned the vast majority of African Slave Plantations there. *African Slave Labor was the source of their fortunes.* After the Union Army defeated the Southern Confederate Army by1865, some of the land formerly organized as African Slave Plantations, along the River Road, became the site where various villages, towns, and cities were constructed during the Post-Civil War Reconstruction. Those villages and cities I call home are linked to several former African Slave Plantations. Table 1.15 shows the former African Slave Plantations, and the names of the villages and cities that were built on former agricultural land.

A. Former African Slave Plantations and Villages and Cities Outgrowth During Post-Civil War Era

Those former African Slave Plantations connected to village and city development in Ascension and St. James Parishes are shown below.

Table 1.15 Former African Slave Plantations And Village Or Cities Built On Them Between 1865 and 1930

Parish	Former Slave Plantation	Village Or City Built
Ascension	J. Delgo, C. Argread, Clark St. Emma, E. Rodrigues, Ryewood & Sons	Donaldsonville, LA
St. James	F. Braud	Welcome, LA and Brookstown
St. James	M. J. & B. Webre	St. James, LA
	J. B. Cantrelle	
St. James	Cantrelle	Plattenville, LA

Source: "Plantations of the Mississippi River from Natchez to New Orleans, 1858," 1931, TSLA Map Collection, 42389, Tennessee State Library and Archives, Tennessee Virtual Archive, https://teva.contentdm.oclc.org/digital/ collection/p15138accessed 2021-07-11.

Before I was born in 1926, and during my childhood, I did know that the identified villages and cities were built on former African Slave Plantations. Later, I will describe the village I grew up in, which is known to those who know about the Gravel Road, as Brookstown. Right after the American Civil War, ALL-of the former African Slave Plantations were temporarily faced with *impending ruin* because their free labor supply was no longer available to their former millionaire Slaveholding families under the same *terms and conditions* that existed during the rein of their American Slavery Institution, namely, *free labor.* Knowing that the former African Slaves, who were called Free Colored when the American Civil War came to an end, had no place to go, and the plantation they worked on was known as home for generations, the former Slaveholding Families quickly reorganized their plantations by using the Thirteenth Amendment to the U. S. Constitution.

This Amendment was enacted to "theoretically" free African Slaves after the Civil War. By carefully examining the Thirteenth Amendment's legal language, I am able to demonstrate how thousands of so-called Freed Colored were actually returned to the kind of slavery life they had lived before 1860.

B. Thirteenth Amendment to the U.S. Constitution

With so many Free Colored People on River Road with no means of income by 1865, the Southern Slaveholding Families, in cooperation with others in each state that had practiced slavery for 244 years or more, influenced the American Government to include language in this Amendment that would open the door for the *re-enslavement of the Free Negro*. I did not know the Thirteenth Amendment served this purpose for the former Slaveholding Families, who owned plantations along the Louisiana River Road. Obviously, they did not desire to have their millionaire status degraded by the loss of their former free African Labor. So, they conspired with political sympathizers, at the highest levels of the federal government, to enact the Thirteenth Amendment, which, on one hand, seemed to be one step forward, by freeing the former African Slaves, and on the other, it also meant two steps backward for many, inasmuch as any former African Slave, or Free Colored, who was later referred to as a Negro, could be re-enslaved, if he or she was convicted of a misdemeanor crime such as vagrancy, or a more serious offense. According to Dr. Lionel D. Lyles' research, "...millions of African-Americans today are unaware of the fact that the Thirteenth Amendment to the U.S. Constitution contains language that permits involuntary servitude as a punishment for a convicted criminal. By 1865, vagrancy was made a crime, and thousands of so-called freed African Slaves were convicted of this crime; sent to prison; and then leased to private businesses to work for "nothing" like they did during the centuries of slavery itself."[20] Some of the language of the Thirteenth Amendment is written as follows: "Neither slavery nor involuntary servitude, except as a punishment for crime whereof the party shall have been duly convicted, shall exist within the United States, or any place subject to their jurisdiction."[21]

When the Emancipation Proclamation was signed by President Abraham Lincoln, and before the ink on the paper dried, thousands of Free Colored, who lived on the Gravel Road, did not own a home; they

---

[20] Lyles, Lionel D., Ph. D., <u>Neoliberalism Economic Policy And The Collapse Of The Public Sector: How the Jindal Administration Allowed It to Happen-2008 to 2016</u>, iUniverse, Bloomington, IN, 2018, p. 309.
[21] Ibid., p. 310.

did not have a job from which they received a regular salary; a majority could neither read nor write; and most, on a daily basis, moved from one place to another aimlessly. Taken together, this was the perfect gumbo, which placed thousands of Free Colored at-risk for being picked-up by the local police for vagrancy. According to Douglas A. Blackmon's book titled Slavery By Another Name, 2008, soon after the U.S. Congress adopted the Thirteenth Amendment in 1865, and by the time White Slaveholding Families returned to political control in 1877, "...every southern state enacted an array of interlocking laws essentially intended to criminalize black life...Every southern state...had passed laws by the end of 1865 outlawing vagrancy and so vaguely defining it that virtually any freed slave not under the protection of a white man could be arrested for the crime."[22] The Free Colored Population, who lived in the Louisiana River Road Parishes, were not exempt from the laws that outlawed vagrancy. In other words, after the African Slave Male and Female, and ALL of his or families and friends, worked for the Slaveholding Families on the Louisiana River Road for several centuries, and by 1865, they still could not move about freely without running the risk of being arrested as a vagrant, and subsequently reintroduced into slavery.

Fifteen years before I was born in 1926, hundreds of Negroes were still being arrested; charged with the crime of vagrancy, and many, were re-enslaved-oftentimes-on the same plantations where they were held captives by 1860. Table 1.16 shows a disproportionate number of Negroes were charged with vagrancy relative to White People by 1910.

Table 1.16 Total Negro Population Arrested For Vagrancy And Drunkeness And Disorderly Conduct Per 100,000 By 1910

U.S. Total	Negro		South	Negro	Vagrancy/100,000		Drunk & Disorderly/100,000	
50,302	Total	%	8,399	4,794	**Negro**	**White**	**Negro**	**White**
	8,250	16.4			54.8	17.5	336.3	135.9
Percent				57.1				

Source: United States Census of 1880, Black Population 1790-1915, Part V-Educational And Social Statistics, The Delinquent, Defective, And Independent Classes, 1880, pp. 438 and 439.

---

[22] Blackmon, Douglas, A., *Slavery By Another Name,* Doubleday, 2008, p. 53.

In fact, 57.1 percent of the individuals charged with vagrancy that year resided in the South, or in those states classified as slave states by 1860. What is equally interesting is when I took a look at the ratio Negro and White persons charged with vagrancy and drunkenness and disorderly conduct, Negroes were charged three times more frequently than White People with vagrancy per 100,000 population. And, to make matters even worse, they were arrested for drunkenness and disorderly conduct at least two-and-a half times more frequently than White People at the same time. Should this be a surprise to anyone inasmuch as the average African Slave, including those who resided on the Louisiana River Road, experienced a life of physical and emotional traumas from birth, and notwithstanding the grinding hard work one was forced to do daily, monthly, and yearly, without any compensation or therapy, which, no doubt, ended many of their lives prematurely. This trend was played-out over and over again in the slave states where the African Slaves were held captives. Table 1.17 shows the number of Negro Prisoners arrested in the former slave states by 1910.

Table 1.17 Total Negro Prisoners Arrested For Selected Slave States And By Race Per 100,000 Population

Slave States	Negro	White	Negro/100,000	White/100,000
Virginia	8,069	4,624	1,202.4	332.7
West Virginia	1,255	4,974	1,955.7	430.0
North Carolina	2,050	657	293.8	43.8
South Carolina	4,397	1,090	526.1	160.5
Georgia	9,717	2,084	825.6	187.5
Florida	5,817	4,017	1,884.5	905.5
Kentucky	7,228	7,157	2,762.4	352.9
Tennessee	6,525	3,443	1,379.2	201.2
Mississippi	3,063	568	303.4	72.3
Arkansas	2,938	2,052	663.4	181.4
Louisiana	**3,376**	**1,642**	**472.9**	**174.5**

Source: United States Census of 1880, Black Population 1790-1915, Part V-Educational And Social Statistics, The Delinquent, Defective, And Independent Classes, 1880, p. 437.

Overall, more Negroes per 100,000 Population were arrested for vagrancy, disorderly conduct, or some other crime; then, they were convicted by a local court; and they were usually forced to serve out their sentence on a plantation, or private business. Most free Negroes were forced to work the same way they did when they were slaves. Once the older generation died, their children and relatives, in many instances, were enslaved by the beginning of the Twentieth Century or before. The Convict Labor System was introduced as means of re-enslavement of Free Negroes by the Sixth Governor of Louisiana, namely, Governor Alexandre Mouton.

He served as governor from 1843 to 1846. Governor Alexandre Mouton was one of the largest plantation owners in the state while he was governor. He owned the Ille Copal Plantation in St. Martin Parish, which was a 20,000 plus acre Sugarcane Plantation. As governor, Alexandre Mouton "…initiated the leasing of convicted prison population labor by 1846."[23]

The Slaveholding Families, who owned the vast majority of plantations along the Louisiana River Road, benefited from this system. Acting as a Ruling Class, its members realized in order to regain the economic power they enjoyed before the American Civil War, a way had to be found, and implemented by them, to re-capture as much of their loss African Slave Labor as possible. The foregoing data I shared in Tables 1.16 and 1.17 are a direct product of this class' Convict Leasing Labor System. With its implementation, the Slaveholding Families were back in business, and it did not hurt their continued accumulation of wealth, by having one of its own in the Governors Office. The Freedmen Bureau Bill enacted by the United States Congress in 1865 also contributed greatly toward the goal of re-enslavement of Free Negroes after 1865.

C. Freedmen Bureau Bill, 1865

Cotton was King at the time. Free Colored, Negroes, or by another name anyone choose to call them, the fact is, if cotton was to maintain its title as King, then, the former had to be re-enslaved to plant, cultivate, and pick

---

[23] Lyles, op. cit., p. 309.

cotton. President Abraham Lincoln wanted to punish the Slaveholding Families in Louisiana, and those in other slave states located throughout the South for seceding and rebelling against the Union. Their crime was sedition.

Meantime, on March 3rd, 1865, the U.S. Congress, acting on the leadership of President Lincoln, passed the above legislation, which established a Bureau for the Relief of Freedmen and Refugees; its objective was to empower the Free Colored by providing them with food, shelter, clothing, medical services, and land to the landless. This was Reparations! With this kind of help, Free Colored People would have no reason to go back and work on the oppressive slave plantations along Louisiana River Road, and other places throughout the South. The Slaveholding Class knew what this would mean to them-economic *ruin*. Therefore, on April 15, 1865, only 1.5 months after the Freedmen Bureau for the Relief of Freedmen and Refugees was established, President Abraham Lincoln was assassinated! With this major political obstacle no longer standing in their way as a formidable roadblock, the road was now cleared, for the Slaveholding Class to overthrow the Freedmen Bureau, and re-enslave as many Free Colored again as possible.

Contrary to popular belief, the Freedmen Bureau Bill, which was passed for humanitarian purposes devolved into a bureau of oppression. According to Dr. Lionel D. Lyles' research, "...it was passed to *revitalize raw cotton production to its pre-Civil War level of output*. To realize this goal, the labor of the masses of so-called "Freed Negro Slaves" (Black people would suffer another 100 years of oppression before the passage of the Civil Rights Bill of 1964) had to be systematically reorganized and reintroduced into agrarian life...the Negro found himself [and herself] after the Civil War, in a position that resembled the slave system of a few years earlier."[24] Many Free Colored, or Negroes, in my Pierce-Braud Family Group, and many other family groups, who lived along the Gravel Road after the Civil War, were likely impacted by the slave masters' reorganization of their free labor in his newly formed Sharecropper System.

---

[24] Lyles, Lionel D., PhD, <u>Historical Development of Capitalism In The United States And Its Affects On The American Family: From Colonial Times to 1920</u>, Volume One, iUniverse, Inc., New York, 2003, p. 107.

They were some clever old Foxes because the Prefix-Share-was merely an empty word; the former Slaveholding Families owned everything during slavery, and they would still own the Free Colored Negro Man and Woman via his personally devised *credit system*. The Slaveholding Families, along the Louisiana River Road, were intoxicated by the thought of making their families' more wealthy off of the uncompensated labor of the Negro.

D. Sharecropping System After The American Civil War

This was a brutal system! It was similar to slavery, in many ways, because the affected Negroes caught in its sharp teeth, worked, from one year to the next, without ever breaking even. They just sunk deeper in debt because, literally speaking, *every sharecropper family truly owed their soul to the Slaveholding Families' company store*. Matthew Reonas stated "sharecropping was a labor that came out of the Civil War and lasted until the 1950s."[25] When I was born in 1926, the Sharecropping System was still being practiced on the Gravel Road. I will share what I observed shortly.

Meantime, Reonas captured the feelings of the oppression of the families caught up in the Sharecropping System. He wrote "of all the images of economic backwardness, racial oppression, and social stagnation associated with Louisiana and the South in the post-Civil War decades, that of sharecropping has persisted most vividly as a defining symbol of a region held captive by the chains of poverty and tradition."[26] Underlying the chains of poverty called forth by the Sharecropping System was the plantation owners, like before, controlled the product produced by the sharecroppers. They settled all accounts at the end of the season, and the sharecroppers had no input. Reonas added "the landlord, however, retained control of the crop's marketing as well as the settlement of accounts. This final reckoning of the plantation books rarely favored the cropper, who often cleared only $50 to $150 in a good season, and dipped further into debt during a bad one."[27] According to Public Broadcasting Station's American Experience, "although blacks outnumbered whites, the sharecropping system that replaced slavery helped ensure they remained

---

[25] Reonas, Matthew, "Sharecropping," 64parishes.org, February 15, 2019.
[26] Ibid.
[27] Ibid.

poor and virtually locked out of any opportunity for land ownership or basic human right."[28] How the Sharecropping System normally worked insured the sharecropper family would not prosper.

For instance, a sharecropper family usually rented a plot of land on a plantation, and it was paid for with a 30% to 50% lien on the sharecroppers' harvest. The plantation owners would provide the sharecroppers with seed, fertilizer, tools, and animals, and the latter would have to pay him back at an exorbitantly high interest rate. PBS' American Experience stated "at the end of the year, sharecroppers settled accounts by paying what they owed from any earnings made in the field. Since the plantation owners kept track of the calculations, rarely would sharecroppers see a profit."[29] As it was, the sharecropper started the planting season in a hole, and by the time came for harvesting, the hole was five or six times deeper in debt. Keep in mind, I mentioned earlier two thirds of the millionaires lived on their plantations, along the Louisiana River Road, by 1860; even though the Slaveholding Families remained extremely wealthy after the Civil War, they, nevertheless, drained as much additional money out of the *souls, bones, and marrow* of the sharecroppers indebted to them.

As a young boy growing up on the Gravel Road during the 1930s, I witnessed the great hardship many Negro Sharecroppers endured.

E. Sharecropping System And Practice On The Louisiana Gravel Road

The River Road covered some seventy-five miles, from the Huey P. Long Bridge to Donaldsonville, LA, ending in New Orleans, LA. There were multiple settlements, villages, plantations, and so forth along the way. I will start with Brookstown. After my birth in 1926, I will go into more detail about the village I grew in during the late 1920s and early 1940s.

a. House Types

Presently, in this settlement (village), there was a church, a one room school (Given the pervasiveness of illiteracy on the Gravel Road, from Ascension Parish to St. Charles, certainly, a one-room school was far less than what

---

[28] "Sharecropping in Mississippi," American Experience, pbs.org
[29] Ibid.

was required to begin to make a slight dent in it among Negroes), post office, two grocery stores, and houses. Most of the houses had the same cookie-cut similarity. That is, they were slave quarters by 1860. Generally speaking, each house had a pitched A-framed roof at the center; the roof sloped noticeably to the rear of the house; and, the roof's slope in the front of the house was interrupted by a porch, which extended all the way across the front of the house. I do not know for sure, but with every house constructed the same way, this probably was done to create a *psychological effect* in the mind of every African Slave, Free Colored, and Negroes thereafter so their occupants would not feel special, or any different from every other person who lived in houses constructed this way.

To access the houses in Brookstown and elsewhere, there were no streets but there were lanes. Some of the lanes had names and others did not have any. There were three to four houses in the average lane. Some lanes were farther from the Gravel Road than other lanes, or some of the houses in the lanes were farther from the Gravel Road than other houses. Some of the families owned the properties where they stayed, and some did not. Other families lived or had houses on properties owned by non-family members. Still others lived on plantations, which was more the norm.

b. How The Sharecropping System Operated On The Gravel Road

In addition, other families lived on property owned by White Farmers, who also owned the local stores and operated the post office in Brookstown. Oneal Roberts, owned and operated one of the local grocery stores. His brother-Gerald Roberts, who was called Gerra' by most local residents, owned and operated a second grocery store. Both were located about one block apart separated by the Mt. Calvary Baptist Church. Gerald Roberts operated his farm. The Negro Families depended on these farmers to take care of their love ones. That is, the major work tasks involved raising rice, sugarcane, and vegetables and so forth. The Roberts farmed rice and sugarcane. There were no plantation houses but they operated on the same system as plantation workers did who worked on their farm, and they were paid by the White Farmers between fifty cents and seventy-five cents a day! This was not enough money to last anyone through the winter. Many Brookstown Residents were forced to buy on credit from the Roberts Grocery Stores.

When I would go to Gerra's Grocery Store to purchase something for my family, he would always pull out an old notebook that I remember had some rumpled pages near their edges that seemed to me had been used by Gerra for ten years or more. When I was at the counter, I tried to get a closer look at his old and worn notebook, but Gerra knew I was trying to see what he had written down in his notebook, which had stain smears on it here and there, but he would cover part of a page with his hand to keep me from seeing what he had written on those rumpled pages. I would take the items I bought and leave Gerra's Grocery Store, and on my way home, I would have a good "belly laugh" at Gerra and his old notebook.

During the spring, summer, and fall months, the people-workers-would pay for their food, clothes, and others as they worked. However, during the winter and early spring months, there were few jobs, or no jobs on the farm, and the people had to get food, clothes, and other basic necessities on *credit*. Therefore, the Sharecropping System kept the working people in debt all year. It was a "catch twenty-two" operation. They were constantly owing someone because they could never "catch up." A similar situation occurred with the Plantation Sharecropping System.

During the late spring, summer, and fall, the Negroes, who lived in the plantation houses, would work and were able to get their basic needs met. However, in late fall and winter, there was no work on the plantation, or at best a precious few jobs, and the families had to get, or borrow money, from the millionaire plantation owners to take care of their families. Although these Negroes, and their ancestor African Slaves, worked themselves down to the bone for centuries, the former slave owners did not have any sympathy, or empathy, for the working people who made them millionaires all along the Gravel Road. *They squeezed blood out of the Turnip Greens!* Again, this was a "catch twenty-two" situation. The Negroes were rarely able to catch up with what they owed the former Slaveholding Families.

In spite of this life and death struggle, there were some families that were able to grow a small crop of rice, or sugarcane on their land, and sometimes on the big farmers land. That is, they would let them have areas way in the back lands among trees and so forth. Though this was true in some cases, I often wonder whether the big farmers allowed the Brookstown Families to use their unimproved lands as a direct way to leverage the use of such families labor when a situation arose? Not much benevolence was shown to the Negroes on the Gravel Road by the big farmers and former Slaveholding Families. The big White Farmers may have been given some land by the former Slaveholding Families, and it would not be a surprise, if some Negro Families were allowed to use the unimproved portions of it that were located among the trees. At any moment, without any prior notice, the big White Farmers could demand that the Negro Families leave his property, if this or that work task was not done for free. In addition, there were also the people that grew gardens; a few chickens, a few hogs; and a few cattle and so on, in order to subsidize themselves. Those groups, unlike many others, were able to weather the storm, and lived with small debts, or none at all.

The only way the poor people, who lived on the Gravel Road, were able to get themselves from under the Sharecropping Bondage, the older members of the family would continue to operate on the "Catch Twenty-Two" System, and as the children grew up, and were able to contribute to the workforce, they relocated to other Louisiana Cities and other states. In order to counteract the Negro Survival Problem, which made the free use of their labor uncertain during the Sharecropping System Era (1865 to 1970) uncertain, the big White Farmers gradually mechanized the planting, tilling, cutting, and harvesting of crops they grew on their farms. That is, they developed the rice planter, rice cutter, rice cranes, tractors, and wagons among others. The only thing the big White Farmers were unable to mechanize was *Grassing Rice*. They did have a trial on poisoning the grass, and preserving the rice. However, that weed control system was not economically feasible, and it was eventually cancelled. Thus, the big White Farmers stopped raising rice in the Brookstown/Welcome, LA area, which was located very close to where the F. Braud Plantation use to operate by 1858, and during my childhood years during the 1930s, they switched from growing rice to sugarcane. It is worthwhile to explain here how Rice was grown near the Brookstown Village before I was born and during several years of my childhood.

c.   Water Pumping System Used To Inundate The Rice Fields

During those years, the landowners-Former Slaveholding Families-or plantation owners raised rice and sugarcane. Others would have truck gardens in which they raised beans, corn, green vegetables, peas, squash, White Irish Potatoes and Sweet Potatoes among others. The Sharecropper's Labor was used to grow and harvest these cash crops. Because of mounting annual debt owed to the former Slaveholding Families, the Sharecroppers were seldom able to escape their imposed "Catch Twenty-two" Mountain of Debt. Unlike the mentioned cash crops, Rice Production was different inasmuch as a large volume of water was needed to successfully produced it. Before I go into more details related to Rice Production, it is timely here to indicate how many acres of land were used to produce this crop by March 1942.

According to Boonstra, in Ascension Parish, there were 2,737 acres devoted to Rice Production; St. James had 8,446, St. John the Baptist had 732, and St. Charles only had one or two farms engaged in this activity.[30] This was a sizable area to flood with water. How the task was accomplished is explained below.

Raising rice required a simple irrigation system; the water required was acquired from the Mississippi River, or from large ponds. There were large pipes called Syphons leading from the river and connected to generators. The large pipes were submerged in the water of the Mississippi River, and the generators caused a suction device to start after it was primed, to cause water from the river to flow into the pipes that ran over the back side of the levee; over the top of the levee; then down the front of the levee; and, it continued under the Gravel Road into a large irrigation ditch. From the large irrigation ditches, the water flowed into the Rice Fields via tributaries, or smaller ditches and combinations of dams and small levees were built to direct the water where it was needed to go.

Large plots of land, acres as a matter of fact, were first cultivated, then ditches, dams, and small levees were constructed. Then the Rice Seeds were planted with the hands of sharecropper; some companies used Rice Planters. Then, the irrigation of the Rice Fields followed; ditches, dams, and small levee systems came into play because Rice Fields needed large amounts of water in order to grow until it was near time for harvest. As the water level rose, there were individuals-sharecroppers-who would go

---

[30] Boonstra, C A., "Rough rice marketing in Louisiana" (1942). *LSU Agricultural Experiment Station Reports*. 595. http://digitalcommons.lsu.edu/agexp/595, March, 1942, p. 3.

around the Rice Fields to see that the small ditches and levees were open well enough to enable the water to cover the acres evenly and so forth.

There was an art in how the White Farmers gauged the water in the development of the Rice Plants. Planting rice occurred from late February to April of each year. A certain level of water had to be maintained throughout the rice growing season. When the rice was well on its way to maturity, the White Farmers had to hire people to pull unwanted grass out of the Rice Fields. In the meantime, the human footsteps would indirectly cultivate the rice. Specifically, Sharecroppers, oftentimes called gangs, were formed. That is, twelve to fifteen people were put in a row-nearly shoulder to shoulder-and they walked through the Rice Fields pulling unwanted grass. There were also people that collected the bundles of pulled grass from the Rice Grassers, and the grass bundles were taken to a designated areas that were called headlands. Sharecroppers worked from six to eight hours per day for a very small amount of money. This miniscule wage was barely more than the *zero compensation* African Slaves received before the American Civil War. In order to assemble a work crew, trucks were sent out in the early morning to transport the waiting workers to the Rice Fields.

As it was, there were trucks, busses, and wagons that transported the workers in the early morning. The trucks, busses, and wagons traveled along the Gravel Road, and made stops to pick up waiting workers. Some of them were foremen, grass pickers, grass carriers, and occasionally water boys. These tasks were carried-out during the early months of the Rice growing season mentioned earlier. As the Rice matured, there were smaller groups of workers that went through the Rice Fields and took out, or pulled any grass that had escaped the initial pulling. The irrigation waters were gradually decreased, and then discontinued.

By the time the rice was almost ready to harvest, the plants had grown to about four feet tall. It was always an amazing sight to see miles and miles of acres of dark green Rice Plants stretching across the country side as far as the eyes could see. Then came the time when the Rice Seeds would grow out the center of the plants. The sprouts grew straight up and as the Rice Seeds matured, they became heavier and heavier, and eventually toppled over. As the year progressed, it would be late in July or August when there would be miles and miles of acres of Rice Plants whose seeded area had turned shades of orange. This was harvest time.

During those days, the time of the harvest for rice was referred to as "Cutting Rice."

d. Cutting Rice At Harvest Time

The White Farmers would pay workers, many of whom were Sharecroppers, three or four dollars per acre to *Cut Rice*. According to Science Trends, "an acre is a unit of area that historically has been used to measure tracts of land. 1 acre of land is approximately equal to 43,560 sq. ft. So, if the plot of land is a perfect square, then one side of that square would have a length of 208.71 feet."[31] Imagine being asked to cut one acre of rice for $3 or $4 per acre. The odor of slavery in this wage arrangement is, if the sharecropper, or other working person, did not complete cutting one acre of rice in one day, and if it took three days, for example, to complete cutting one acre of rice, he or she would be paid $3 or $4 for three days work by the former Slaveholding Family(s)!!! This truly is the core of how the "Catch Twenty-Two" stranglehold on the Negro worked.

During the actual Cutting Rice Process, the stalk of the rice was cut between knee high and waist length, and then, it was placed in a row behind the workers knees. Rice was always placed in a row and remained there until it was time to make *bundles*. The Rice Pods had to dry out and that took approximately one week. When the Rice dried-out, the workers had to tie the Rice Plants in bundles. The secured bundles were then put in stacks with the pods upright. Each stack was constructed in a cone-shape. This enabled the Rice Pods to continue to dry. Being in the upright position enabled the water from the rain to drain off of it to the ground. Again, there would be miles and miles of acres of rice sitting in stacks that were knee high. To add to that beauty was the miles and miles of acres of Conical Stacks of rice waiting for the next stage of harvest.

At the appropriate time, the White Farmers then had to hire crews to transport the Rice Bundles using tractors with partially enclosed wagons. The tractors and wagons were driven to the *Rice Thrasher*. Wagon loads were put in a special area where another crew of workers could feed the "Conveyor Belt of the Thrasher," which took the Rice Bundles to the

---

[31] Bolano, Alex, "How Many Feet Are In 1 Acre?" Science Trends, https://sciencetrends.com, January 5, 2019.

machine where the Rice Seeds and Stalks were separated. The Rice Seeds were eventually passed through a "Hopper;" separated from the Stalk; and finally deposited in sacks. The sacks were filled, and the top of it was sown closed to prevent spillage. Finally, the Rice Sacks were stacked in an enclosed shed, or warehouse, etc., while arrangements were made by the former Slaveholding Families to sell them on the general market. The true loss of the value of the worker can be seen strikingly clear at this point.

e. Sharecroppers And Other Workers' Catch Twenty-Two Bondage

As it was, the Sharecropper, for example, earned $3 or $4 dollars to cut one acre of rice per day. Although the number of sacks of rice varied, from acre to acre and from one Rice Field to another due to such variables as soil type, fertilizer, grass competition, insects, rodents and so forth, I feel accurate saying, on average, the plantation owners, using Negro Labor, produced roughly 7 Rice Sacks per acre. Boonstra stated "in Louisiana, Rough Rice quantities are measured in terms of a barrel of 162 pounds… Rice in Louisiana is generally stored in bags weighing from 180 to 200 pounds, while milled rice is handled in bags, or "pockets," weighing 100 pounds…"[32] During the time I was engaged in Cutting Rice, around 1937, the White Plantation Owners in St. James Parish received $3 for one barrel of rice. If his Rice Field yielded 7 barrels of rice per acre, this meant he received $21 per acre. And, if 900 hundred acres of his plantation was devoted to growing Rice, the former Slaveholding Family would receive $18,900 in the marketplace. Without having access to the former Slaveholding Family's accounting books, once he paid his Sharecropper Workforce $1,200 for one Rice Harvest Season, and once his overhead cost for tractor maintenance, gasoline, transportation to the Rice Mill, Rice Thrashing, and transportation to the marketplace were added into the sum total, this may have cost him another $2,000.

Therefore, once the former Slaveholding Family paid his Sharecropper Labor Cost and Overhead Expenses, which together may have come to $3,200, and when he deducted this cost from his cumulative Rice Value of $18,900, he was left with a profit of $15,700. If 10 Sharecropper Workers worked 30 days during the Rice Cutting Season, and if each was paid $4,

---

[32] Boonstra, op. cit., p. 4.

this means their pay for the Rice Cutting Season came to $120. The "Catch Twenty-Two" is clear. For the rest of the year, including the winter months, the Sharecropper Family would have only $120 to survive. Inevitably, he or she would have to go to the former Slaveholding Family's Plantation Store, and purchase food and other basic needs on *credit*. From one Rice Cutting Season to the next, the Sharecropper Family sunk deeper into debt to the former Slaveholding Family. The Sharecroppers' dependence on the latter was nearly the same as it was during the Slavery Era before the Civil War Era. In his famous song, Sam Cooke sung these words: "Sixteen tunnels and what do you get, another day older and deeper in debt. Oh boy don't you worry cause I owe my soul to the company store (Paraphrase Mine).

As you can imagine, not too many Brookstown Working People were happy about giving so much of their labor, and receiving so little compensation for it in return. The former Slaveholding Families were also aware of the people's growing dissatisfaction with the way things were going for them. They knew the Sharecroppers could not make ends meet because they made sure there would be no end in sight where the former would be paid an equal wage for an equal days work. That had never happened, and, to insure it did not, the former Slaveholding Families used their political influence and money to get the United States Government to abandon the Negro during the 1870s, by bringing the so-called Reconstruction Era to an abrupt and tragic end. In its place, the former Slaveholding Families, on the Gravel Road, and elsewhere in the South, unleashed a *Reign of Terror* on the Negroes, or African-American and other people of color, for the purpose of keeping him or her in their place due to an on-going State of De facto Slavery.

CHAPTER V

DOMESTIC TERRORISM, KU KLUX KLAN, AND JIM CROW RESTRICTIONS PUT IN PLACE TO STOP NEGRO PROGRESS FROM 1800 TO THE PRESENT DAY

A. Rutherford B. Hayes And Samuel J. Tilden 1876 Presidential Election Fraud

When the 2000 Presidential Election between George W. Bush and Al Gore ended in a U. S. Supreme Court legal challenge, and the democratic will of the American People was ignored, and democracy was trumped by political partisan intrigue, the affair was not without a political precedent. Roy Morris, Jr wrote a book titled <u>Fraud Of The Century</u> in 2003 in which he skillfully established how the 1876 Presidential Election between Rutherford B. Hayes and Samuel J. Tilden replayed itself again in 2000, when Presidential Candidate Al Gore's election, by the American People, was set aside by the U.S. Supreme Court in favor of George W. Bush's, which overrode the democratic will of the American People. According to Morris, "the American presidential election of 2000, with its hanging chads, butterfly ballots, flummoxed oldsters, and pop-eyed Florida election officials, certainly qualifies as farcical...its parallels to another disputed presidential election, one that took place on the same date 124 years earlier...The 1876 contest between Republican nominee Rutherford B. Hayes and Democratic nominee Samuel J. Tilden also involved the state of Florida, and it, too, ultimately was decided by the vote of a single Republican member of the U. S. Supreme Court."³³ After four months of wrangling and Voting Ballot Audits conducted by a flood of lawyers and other political officials, who had a stake in the outcome of the 2000 Presidential Election, in the end, while the American People waited breathlessly, "...the candidate [George W. Bush] who probably had lost the election in Florida and definitely had lost the popular vote nationwide nevertheless was declared the winner, not just of Florida's electoral votes but of the presidency itself."³⁴ There was "Moby Dick" size fish on the line, and nothing would stand in the way of it being caught.

Likewise, Rutherford B. Hayes was selected President in 1876 because there was a big fish on the line that had to be caught also. That is, the former Southern Slaveholding Oligarchy I have spoken about repeatedly, thus far, needed to put an end to *Reconstruction* so that its members could reinstate themselves once again as the sole political and economic power in the South. And, this would simultaneously mean delaying the human rights of the Free Negro for another century or more. It would also mean they would regain control over the labor of the latter. In short, the U. S. Supreme Court installed Rutherford B. Hayes in the White House, and the former Southern Slave Holding Oligarchy pledged its political support of President Rutherford B. Hayes National Agenda. This compromise was the big Moby Dick size fish at stake in 1876!

Accordingly, Morris stated "...modern historian Paul Johnson has aptly termed [the Tilden-Hayes Affair]... "a legalized fraud"...The election and its aftermath gave rise in the South to the infamous Jim Crow laws that officially sanctioned the social and political disenfranchisement of millions of southern blacks. The Republican Party there was overthrown, and the unprecedented experiment in social engineering known as Reconstruction came to an abrupt, if largely predetermined end. It would be another ninety years before southern blacks stepped free from the shackles of legalized segregation...The election itself, in many ways, was the last battle of the Civil War."³⁵ This was the centerpiece, or cornerstone, of the foundation of the former Slaveholding Oligarchy's, Domestic Terrorism Plan.

---

[33] Morris, Jr, Roy, Fraud Of The Century: Rutherford B. Hayes, Samuel Tilden, and the Stolen Election of 1876, Simon & Schuster, New York, 2003, p. 1.
[34] Ibid., p. 1.
[35] Ibid., p. 3.

B. Post-Civil War Reconstruction Act, 1867

Two years after the Civil War came to an end, the former Southern Slaveholding Class, and its Democratic Party, with the exception of Tennessee, ALL rejected the 14th Amendment, which gave former African Slaves equal citizenship. The majority of former slave states, including Louisiana, chose to "...remain unrepresented in Congress rather than accept blacks as equal citizens..."[36] To realize this aim, President Abraham Lincoln had already been assassinated. And, holding out hope, that it was not too late to get the Southern Democratic Party to change its mind about the citizenship question for Black People, the U.S. Congress passed the Reconstruction Act in 1867.

Theoretically, this Congressional Act, according to Morris, "...repudiated the new southern state governments, divided the South into military districts, called for widespread disenfranchisement of former confederates, and required the states to draft constitutions embracing universal suffrage and the ratification of the Fourteenth Amendment before being readmitted to the Union."[37] In essence, on paper, the former Slaveholding Oligarchy control of southern states seem to be placed in a checkmate situation. Their old Pre-Civil War State Constitutions, based on the requirements of the Reconstruction Act passed by the U.S. Congress in 1867, had to be discarded, and a new constitution had to be written, which included a Loyalty Clause to the United States, and it must contain provisions that safeguard the *Voting Rights* of Free Black People. Moreover, the United States Military would be stationed in each former slave state until this process was satisfactorily complete. Given the extreme importance of Negro Labor to the continued financial stability of the former Slaveholding Families on the Gravel Road, and throughout the southern slave states, the latter, as I have already shown, struck a *Behinds the Scene Political Deal* with Presidential Candidate Rutherford B. Hayes in 1876, which stole the Presidential Election from Samuel J. Tilden. The consequence of this political deal would intentionally bring an abrupt end to Reconstruction, and return thousands of Free Negroes to a quasi-slavery status.

---

[36] Ibid., p. 63.
[37] Ibid., p. 63.

C. End Of Reconstruction, 1877

As I already indicated, the Reconstruction Act of 1867 was, theoretically speaking, a strong set of rehabilitation requirements that were suppose to hold the former Slaveholding Oligarchy control of southern slave states accountable for their Civil War Crimes. The teeth in this Act was the presence of Military Districts stationed in each Former Slave State. Without Military Reinforcement, the Reconstruction Experiment was destined to fail before it carried-out its stated mission.

So, as a *quid pro quo*, the former Slaveholding Oligarchy, or plantation owners, along the Louisiana River Road and elsewhere in the South, made a political bargain with Rutherford B. Hayes, which essentially ignored the American People's Choice of Samuel J. Tilden for President in 1876, and, through coordinated political manipulation, altered the Popular Vote in favor of Rutherford B. Hayes. This was the Death of Reconstruction, and it created a political model that would be used again when it becomes politically necessary to *override the Collective political Will of the American People*.

Morris wrote "By The SPRING of 1876, [the] mission [of Reconstruction] was largely finished…for …other likeminded Republicans in the South. With the Democrats' recapture of Mississippi, only South Carolina, Florida, and Louisiana were still unredeemed. Congressional Reconstruction in the South was as good as over…"[38] Before the 1876 Presidential Election, "Ulysses S. Grant…had clearly begun the psychological, if not physical, withdrawal of troops from the South as early as 1875, when he refused to intervene in the violent state election in Mississippi. Furthermore, the House of Representatives already had acted in March 1877 to forestall future troop deployments by blocking the annual military appropriations bill, and there was no money available to pay the troops."[39] By the time Presidential Candidate Rutherford B. Hayes was selected to serve as President in 1876, he had no army to enforce the Reconstruction Bill Congress passed in 1867; he did not have any money to pay the troops! The Southern Democrats-Slaveholding Oligarchy-and the northern Republicans, who were once deadly enemies during the Civil

---

[38] Ibid., p. 44.
[39] Ibid., p. 249.

War, united against Reconstruction, and they served as the Pallbearers for the Reparation Program that was set up by President Abraham Lincoln to help the so-called Freed Negroes commonly known as the Freedmen Bureau.

D. Southern Democrats And Northern Republicans Unite Against Reconstruction By 1877

By 1877, the "die was cast" against the survival of Black People on the Gravel Road, and throughout the former slaveholding states in the South. The sting of the death of Lincoln's Reconstruction Program was felt by ALL Black People everywhere. No place, North or South was exempt! Morris added "…decentralization was one way to rein in the [Federal] government…that Thomas Jefferson had foreseen by diffusing that power among the individual states. If that meant returning control of the southern states to the white Democrats who made up their social and political elites, then so be it…Reconstruction must end so that reunion might begin."[40] *States' Rights* was born, and the nightmare for the people, who lived on Louisiana River Road and elsewhere, was not far away. Selected President Rutherford B. Hayes understood "…*local government*…was a code phrase for states' rights, and he [sent] a signal to the growing numbers of northern voters, who were heartily sick of Reconstruction that he, too, was ready to move on with his life and leave the South to its own devices."[41] Those devices, for many Freed Negroes, eventually ended in physical death and emotional traumas for numerous others. Selected President Rutherford B. Hayes' critics "…were far outnumbered by the thousands of southern Democrats and northern Republicans who fully supported the end of Reconstruction."[42] It was advantageous for the Slaveholding Families on the Gravel Road to support its end as well.

All-in-all, for the former southern Slaveholder Oligarchy to regain control of the South, several factors are worth a brief review. First, President Abraham Lincoln had to be removed permanently from the political scene. Second, the Presidential Election of 1876 had to be reversed, and

---

[40] Ibid., p. 119.
[41] Ibid., p. 133.
[42] Ibid., p. 247.

Rutherford B. Hayes was selected President against the American People's Will. And, Third, the Federal Troops were withdrawn from the South, which opened the door for the southern Slaveholder Oligarchy to reinstitute slavery practices everywhere, including the sharecropper and convict Labor System. Morris wrote "THE WITHDRAWAL OF federal troops from the statehouses in South Carolina and Louisiana represented the symbolic end of Reconstruction."[43] Finally, the Union was preserved by the Unholy Union of the southern Democrats and northern Republicans. The Freed Negroes were disenfranchised, marginalized, dehumanized, ostracized, demonized, and delivered back into the hands of their former slaveholders.

E. Political And Social Disempowerment Of The Freed Negroes In The South After The American Civil War And Throughout The Twentieth Century

During the American Slavery Institution, the life of every African Slave, and his or her family, dangled precariously, from day-to-day-on a thread. On any day, the shoe could drop. This pattern continued after 1865, and it was greatly strengthened by the intentional death of President Lincoln's Reparation Program, namely, Reconstruction. All of the Freed Negroes on the Gravel Road were at-risk. Living was still hard, in many ways, as it was during the American Slavery Institution itself. I am not talking about a few hundred Freed Negroes, but the large numbers that lived along the Louisiana Gravel Road after the American Civil War, and before I was born in 1926. The foregoing demographic data shows how many Negro lives were directly impacted, regarding education, employment, health, and many other social indices.

In fact, Morris stated "…the end of Reconstruction would prove to have catastrophic and far-reaching effects on the four million black Americans living in the South…The *Nation*, which fancied itself the journalistic conscience of the country, ventured the confident prediction that "the negro will disappear from the field of national politics. Henceforth, the nation as a nation, will have nothing more to do with him. Even [President Ulysses S.] Grant allowed that the Fifteenth Amendment giving blacks

---

[43] Ibid., p. 246.

the right to vote had been a mistake, one that "had done the Negro no good, and had been a hindrance to the South, and by no means a political advantage to the North."[44] Imagine the statements made by the Nation and President Ulysess S. Grant, given the fact Black People provided ALL of the labor power that was used, and uncompensated, to build America! Where is their heart and soul? Deconstruction could only be done by those who have an *abandoned and malignant heart*. At the American Constitutional Convention, which convened on May 25, 1787 to September 17, 1787, at the Pennsylvania state House, the "Founding Fathers" refused to disallow slavery. In fact, the latter was written into the American Constitution that pertains to the Three-Fifth Compromise and Fugitive Slave Laws. Thus, for the next 90 years, or by 1877, Systemic Racism prevailed, and it would continue to have debilitating effects on African-Americans into the Twenty-First Century.

a. Dismantling Of President Abraham Lincoln's Reparation Reconstruction Program

Morris wrote "the dismantling of Reconstruction, and the consequent political and social disempowerment of the region's sizable black minority, set the stage for nearly a century of de facto and legalized segregation, culminating in the notorious Jim Crow Laws of the early 1900s that formalized the social, political, and economic marginalization of southern Blacks begun in earnest three decades earlier."[45] Black People may have been a minority group on the national scale; however, on the Gravel Road, African Slaves outnumbered the White Population by a ratio of 3 to 1. For a decade after the Civil War, this trend continued. This legalized segregation was aimed at weakening the Thirteenth Amendment, which *freed* the African Slaves. The Jim Crow Laws essentially monitored the movement of Freed Negroes similar to the way their movements on the plantation were highly restricted. They were considered as second class citizens, which was an attack on their Fourteenth Amendment Rights, which gave Freed Negroes American Citizenship. How does one go from

---

[44] Ibid., pp. 247 and 248.
[45] Ibid., p. 248.

being a citizen at birth to a second-class citizen after he or she takes their first breath outside of a Mother's Womb?

b. Fifteenth Amendment And The Right To Vote (Black Voter Suppression)

Of all of the catastrophic effects of the dismantling of the Reconstruction Program, the denial, or suppression of the Freed Negroes right to vote, is at the top of the list. For more than two centuries, they were slaves without an identity or voice, regarding self-determination. With the defeat of the South by the North's Army, the U.S. Congress passed several amendments to the American Constitution, which gave the newly Freed Colored-Negroes-the right to vote. However, southern Democrats had another idea of its own, which was to bar them from participation in the political life of American Democracy. And, they did using States Rights.

As it turned out, Morris stated "the right to vote, so recently received, was abruptly snatched away again…from the former slaves. Redeemer governments across the South quickly wrote new laws into the books, similar to the infamous Black Codes of the late 1860s, that severely curtailed black's ability to vote in sufficient numbers to measurably influence elections on the local, state, or national level."[46] Such tactics as gerrymandering, poll taxes, literacy tests, and complicated registration laws-ALL-were implemented to significantly weaken the Freed Negroes' Political Voice, or worse, prevent them from ever acquiring one. These tactics are being used today. A southern newspaper wrote a column, which openly and shamelessly boasted that while the Fourteenth and Fifteenth Amendments "may stand forever…we intend to make them dead letters on the statue-book."[47] Today, the same mentality, generally speaking, still prevails inasmuch as at least 47 states have proposed voter suppression legislation aimed at making it harder for African-Americans, and other People of Color, to cast their vote. At least 17 states' Legislatures have already passed Voter Suppression Legislation.

In addition, the South placed further restrictions on Black People, which further limited their participation in civic life. The Gravel Road was no exception. Morris added "the reduction of black voting power was

---

[46] Ibid., p. 248.
[47] Ibid., p. 248.

reinforced by restrictive new laws diminishing their rights to own and sell property, obtain credit, serve on juries, become policemen, or educate their children. Almost overnight, the Republican party in the Deep South disappeared as an effective political force."[48] The Republican Party was buried at President Abraham Lincoln's Funeral.

In short, the Freed Negroes no longer could depend on President Abraham Lincoln's Republican Party for any assistance; it was a dead letter like the 13th, 14th, and 15th Amendments. There was virtually "no place in the sun" for the Freed Negroes except "under the sun" that beamed down on them on the plantation. They were checkmated by the Solid South. Morris stated "the Solid South, which for the next century would mean the solidly Democratic South, was the ironic…result of [President] Hayes's conciliatory policy toward the region…That policy proved to be a grievous political mistake…as Hayes himself conceded in 1878…"[49] This was no unintended, or unforeseen mistake.

It was a *quid pro quo*. A bargain with the Devil was made, and the Freed Negroes paid the price in every egregious, unconscionable, and inconceivable way. For the former southern Slaveholding Oligarchy, which re-emerged as masters of the Solid South, threw its political support behind its selected President Rutherford B. Hayes, and in return for its favors, the latter allowed President Abraham Lincoln's Reparation Reconstruction Program to wither and die like a grape in the hot sun. Black People continued to suffer one tragedy after another in the Solid Democratic South. No one was suppose to ever escape its racial vice grip-ever! If this was not depressing enough, the United States Supreme Court added its mortar and bricks to the Systemic Racism's Brick Wall.

c. United States Supreme Court Cases, 1873, 1876, and 1896

These U.S. Supreme Court Cases put salt on the wounds and injuries so many on the Gravel Road and elsewhere had previously suffered for generations during the 244 years of the American Slavery Institution. Black People had nowhere to go to get its voice heard, either legally or otherwise. Morris wrote "the Supreme Court, in such landmark decisions

---

[48] Ibid., p. 248.
[49] Ibid., p. 248.

as the Slaugtherhouse Cases (1873) and U.S. v. Cruikshank (1876), had rolled back the authority of the federal government to intervene in state and local civil rights cases, and state courts in the South increasingly arrogated to themselves the power, if not necessarily the need, to rule on such matters in the foreseeable future."[50] The federal government was handcuffed by these U.S. Supreme Court Rulings; and, therefore, no matter what injury any Freed Negro suffered at the hands of a White Person, or other, there was nothing that could be done, for him or her, as far as seeking *justice* was concerned, at the federal, state, and local levels of government.

Making matters even worse, "then, on May 18, 1896, the Supreme Court delivered its verdict in *Plessy v. Ferguson*. In declaring separate-but-equal facilities constitutional on intrastate railroads, the Court ruled that the protections of 14th Amendment applied only to political and civil rights (like voting and jury service), not "social rights" (sitting in the railroad car of your choice)… In its ruling, the Court denied that segregated railroad cars for Black people were necessarily inferior."[51] The greatest fallacy of this decision is it is impossible to separate a human being, who is a social creature, from political, civil rights, and so-called "social rights." The latter is human rights. As Thomas Jefferson wrote in the Declaration of Independence, these are inalienable rights. Therefore, this decision was apparently based on a clumsy, unmerited foundation; surprisingly, few, if any, social scientists took the seemingly faulty argument serious enough to challenge it. Some social scientists, or others, may have recognized the weakness in the argument, but indifference overrode their ability to raise any questions.

What else is interesting about this decision, which ordered American Race Behavior for a century or more, Justice Henry Brown blamed the inferior status attached to ALL Black People on Plessey and not the U.S. Supreme Court. He stated "…to consist in the assumption that the enforced separation of the two races stamps the colored race with a badge of inferiority. If this be so, it is not by reason of anything found in the act, but solely because the colored race chooses to put that construction upon it."[52] In short, no one I know on the Gravel Road believes his or her social

---

[50] Ibid., p. 250.
[51] History.com Editors, "Plessey v. Ferguson, https://www.history.com/.amp/topics/black-history/plessy-v-ferguson, January 20, 2021.
[52] Ibid.

plight was caused by their own inferiority. If anything, it was likely the result of slavery in their lineage.

With President Abraham Lincoln's Reparation Reconstruction Program laid to rest, the former southern Slaveholding Oligarchy Class needed an organization to carry-out domestic terrorists acts against the Freed Negroes, for the single purpose of "keeping them in their place."

d. KU Klux Klan And The Post-Reconstruction Period: Enforcers' Use Of Violence To Maintain The White Status Quo

After several centuries of the American Slavery Experience on the Gravel Road, and elsewhere in the Solid South, hardly any Freed Negroes were happy about what they had gone through; their descendants were anxious for a better life, and the overthrow of the Reparations Reconstruction Program made many even more frustrated and angry. The former Slaveholding Oligarchy Class knew this very well, and therefore, not leaving their own survival to chance, it needed a new type of overseer. One or two was not enough to do the job of maintaining law and order among the Freed Negroes. An organization was required, and its members were subtly conditioned to believe that their own survival was dependent on *keeping their knees on the neck of the Freed Negroes*. The former Slaveholding Oligarchy Class had to keep its hands clean. The dirty work was left to its followers

Accordingly, Morris stated "southern whites soon began a violent and determined struggle to regain political power within their own states. Led by such shadowy organizations as the Knights of the White Camelia, the Black Calvary, the Red Shirts, the Men of Justice, the White Brotherhood, the Knights of the Rising sun, the White Line, the constitutional Union Guard, and most notorious of all, the Ku Klux Klan, disgruntled southerners commenced a...brutally effective campaign of physical force and psychological intimidation aimed at reversing the process of Reconstruction."[53] Today, these are the "Proud Boys" and the "Oath Keepers" among others. Anyone who showed the least support for the Republican Party, especially politically active Blacks, were bullied, intimidated, and many cases, murdered. Their reign of terror was relentless and sustained, and local, state, and federal

---

[53] Morris, op. cit., p. 33.

governments did little, if anything, to bring the abusers to justice. Morris added "no one knows how many victims, black and white, were assaulted during the peak years of Klan activity between 1868 and 1871, but the numbers certainly totaled in the thousands."[54]

Though the KKK was active during these years, their first priority was to gain control over the reconstructed governments in their states, and then turn back the hands of times to the days of slavery. Toward this end, Morris added "one newly organized paramilitary force, the White League, fought pitched battles with black Republicans in several rural Louisiana towns and wantonly murdered white officials in their homes."[55] No Freed Negroes could move about freely, and if some did, they did so at their own risk and peril. Therefore, St. James Parish, and other River Road Parishes, were not an exception to the rule. A relatively large number of Freed Negroes were lynched by the turn of the Twentieth Century. Table 1.18 shows the number of Freed Negroes who were lynched in the River Road Parishes between 1877 and 1900.

Table 1.18 Freed Negroes Lynched In The Louisiana River Road Parishes By Date, Name, And Alleged Offense

Parish	Date	Name	Alledged Offense	Race
St. James	1-20-1893	Chicken George	Murder, Robbery	Negro
St. James	1-20-1893	Richard Davis	Murder, Robbery	Negro
St. James	2-28-1896	Gilbert Francis	Rape, Burglary	Negro
St. James	2-28-1893	Paul Francis	Rape, Burglary	Negro
Ascension	11-13-1888	Unidentified Man	Rape	Negro
St. John the Baptist	6-14-1899	Edward Gray	Burglary	Negro
St. Charles	12-28-1892	Adam Gripson	Murder. Robbery	Negro
St. Charles	7-11-1899	George Jones	Horse Theft	Negro
St. Charles	8-8-1896	Decino Sorcorro	Murder, Robbery	Italian
St. Charles	8-8-1896	Angelo Marcuso	Murder, Robbery	Italian
St. Charles	10-10-1899	Basile LaPlace	Political Causes, Illicit Laison	White

Source: Lynching in Louisiana, 1877-1900.

---

[54] Ibid. p. 33.
[55] Ibid., p. 37.

The Equal Justice Initiative (EJI) reported there were 15 Lynchings[56] in the Louisiana River Road Parishes during this period. The former Slaveholding Oligarchy did not stop at any point short of its re-establishment of White Supremacy in the Solid South. The creation of an atmosphere of violence in the minds of Freed Negroes was foremost a necessary step toward achieving this end. According to the EJI, "lynchings were violent and public acts of torture that traumatized black people throughout the country and were largely tolerated by state and federal officials. These lynchings were terrorism...Lynching created a fearful environment where racial subordination and segregation was maintained with limited resistance for decades."[57] The latter was a fear tactic aimed at promoting White Supremacy.

No Black Man or Woman would deny a White Person's greatness based on moral grounds; to take another person's life to prove White Supremacy is superior, is an action that grows out of one's inferiority complex projected onto someone else.

The former Slaveholding Oligarchy's fear tactic worked! Thousands of Freed Negroes migrated out of Louisiana to other states outside of the Deep South. They had had enough by 1940.

e. Out-Migration Of Freed Black People From Louisiana By 1940

When the Emancipation Proclamation "Freed" the African Slaves by 1865, they were penniless, and their clothing was in tatters. All they had was a *hair-size, slim hope* of a better day ahead? Their hopes were dashed, for more than a century, when the former Southern Slaveholding Class negotiated a compromise with the 1876 Presidential Candidate, namely, Rutherford B. Hayes. As part of the compromise, a quid pro quo was reached between the two sides: The legitimate election of Presidential Candidate Samuel J. Tilden was overturned and fraudulently handed to Rutherford B. Hayes, and the latter simultaneously brought President Abraham Lincoln's Reparation Reconstruction Program, for the newly Colored Freedmen and Women, to an end. The result was the former

---

[56] "Lynching in America: Confronting the Legacy of Racial Terror, Supplement: Lynchings by County," www.eji.org, 1877-1950, p. 3.
[57] Ibid., Report Summary, pp. 2 and 3.

Slaveholding Oligarchy regained political, economic, and judicial power in the South, while the Freedman and Women faced another century or more of quasi-slavery, which was characterized by the Sharecropper and Convict Labor System. The Ku Klux Klan was sanctioned to protect the former Slaveholding Oligarchy's power by carrying-out a domestic terrorism practice that physically and mentally traumatized Freed Black People, who lived on the Louisiana River Road, and elsewhere throughout the Deep and Solid South.

That being so, millions of Black People, of whom many were burdened with large debts owed to the plantation owners' stores and so forth, reasoned they had no way out of their "Catch Twenty-Two Dilemma" but to migrate out of the Deep South. Between 1865 and 1940, Black People, largely, had to struggle to survive every day during this time. The Equal Justice Initiative stated "terror lynchings fueled the mass migration of millions of black people from the South into urban ghettos in the North and West during the first half of the twentieth century."[58] With this real threat to their personal well-being, and the financial debt hanging around their necks like an Albatross, they were left with no choice but to migrate. Many eventually did. Without going into any details, there was no *Pot of Gold* waiting for the Black Migrants at the other end of their destinations. Malcolm X once mentioned in a speech if you live south of the Canadian Border, you are still in the South.

Nevertheless, driven by fear and a desperation to survive, by 1940, of Louisiana's 842,817[59] residents 14 years old and over, 39,526 Black People were forced to migrate to another state outside of the Deep South. 5.0 percent of the Black Population left the state. Of the 39,526, 13,176, or 33.3 Percent migrated to Texas. In addition, 24,005 or 61.0 percent migrated to an urban area within a non-contiguous state.

According to these Black Migration Statistics, 95.0 percent of the Black Population remained in Louisiana, and many of the people I grew up with in Brookstown did not migrate. Staying home on the Gravel Road did not mean socio-economic, political, and judicial life was easy; it was not!

---

[58] Ibid., p. 3.
[59] United States Census of 1940, Sixteenth Census of Population: Internal Migration, 1935 to 1940, p. 98. This was the first census to compile statistics on the subject.

Survival was a constant, daily reminder for every Brookstown Resident. The Pierce-Braud Family Group was not an exception.

F. Braud Family Group: Twenty-Five Generations-1600 To 1950

Of everything I have mentioned thus far, it is difficult to imagine how any family on the Gravel Road could actually find a way through the traumas of the American Slavery Institution and the untimely end of President Abraham Lincoln's Reparation Reconstruction Program. The "Way Out" was the needle in the "Catch Twenty-Two" Haystack. As I mentioned earlier, the troubles faced by many Black People on the Louisiana River Road were too great for them to handle, and many, unfortunately, never found that seemingly elusive Needle in the Haystack. There was no technology with a ringtone that could guide a Brookstown Family, or individual, through the harmful maze of closed opportunities and related doors. Systemic Racism dating back to Thomas Jefferson's Declaration of Independence, and its legalized doorkeeper, namely, legalized segregation, barred just about every avenue of upward mobility. There were not many, few, if none at all, government programs available that took up the cause of Black People's survival. In truth, their lives did not matter; however, only their labor mattered to White People, if they could squeeze it out of a working man or woman without paying them anything, as was the case for 244 years of the American Slavery Institution; or, by paying a sharecropper only enough money to keep him or her alive for the next growing season and harvest and so forth.

Humpty Dumpty had been shattered in a thousand pieces. Therefore, as far as the former Slaveholding Families, and the Oligarchy Class they belong were concerned, every avenue open to Black Progress had been thoughtfully and systematically closed. Yet, in the midst of all the barriers placed on the path of African Slaves, and later Freed Colored and their descendants, who lived along the Louisiana River Road for several centuries before I was born, the Pierce-Braud Family Group navigated successfully through the fear, minimal opportunities, and reign of terror. And, surprisingly, it did not just survive, but, in face of all of the negative odds hitherto mentioned, my Pierce-Braud Family Group advanced, from the tiny village of Brookstown, and proceeded to distinguish itself in a way only a few, if any, Louisiana Families had previously done before. Seemingly out of nothing, my Pierce-Braud Family Group eventually created a Strategic Family Development Plan (SFDP), which, in due time, generated more Medical Doctors and highly trained educational professionals, which most Louisianians are still unaware. Until now, no one, from the Louisiana Governor's Office to the people in all walks of life, have ever thought such a giant educational step was possible; or, more importantly, that my Pierce-Braud Family would have the *audacity to feel and think* it could excel in spite of the fact the Gravel Road, where I grew up during the late 1920s and 1930s, was once dominated by many of the legacies of the American Slavery Institution, and it was overtly, and covertly, supported by the U. S. Supreme Court, including federal, state, and local governments in the form of various Jim Crow Laws among many others.

With this background and social environment established, which was primarily aimed at halting my educational development, and Black People Progress in general, including others of color, I have reached this point where it is now appropriate for me to begin my discussion of the origin of my Braud Family Group, which dates back to the 1600s-twenty-five generations ago-in Western France. The Pierce Family Group united with Braud's after the American Civil War. Some emphasis is placed on the former during this time.

CHAPTER VI

ORIGIN OF THE PIERCE- BRAUD FAMILY GROUP FROM PRE-CIVIL WAR TO 1921

The White Brault (This is how Brault was spelled during the Feudalism Period in France before the French Revolution in 1790) Lineage, of which my Black Braud Group is a direct derivative, or branch, originated in the western region of France in its Vienne Province not far from the Atlantic Ocean. This province is located in the Poitou-Charente Region. Historically, the majority of the French People were the subjects of Feudalism, from 1500 to 1850. The Feudalism System consisted of four levels, namely, Monarchs, Lords/Ladies (Nobles), Knights, and Peasants/Serfs. In this hierarchy, the King, or Queen, was the most powerful person, and every level beneath the King and Queen, depended on the labor of the Peasants/Serfs. This class did the majority of the work; its members received less income for their workday; and the Peasants/Serfs paid, not surprisingly, the majority of taxes. The Feudalism System can be visualized as a triangle, where the wealthiest people at the Apex, who were non-producers, received the lion-share of revenues from the producer Peasant/Serf Class locked at the bottom of its social structure. Feudalism was an early form of quasi-slavery, which would eventually, dialectically speaking, change into a new qualitative form commonly known as slavery in America.

That being so, the White Brault Family(s) were part of the Peasant/Serfs Class; and, they struggled to survive under the Tyranny of Feudalism for more than three centuries. However, as it is inevitable it will rain somewhere on the Earth every day, social change was similarly inevitable inasmuch as by the Mid-17th Century, the Peasant/Serfs Class became politically disillusioned and discontented with the Feudalism System in the Poitou-Charente Region, and across others nationwide. This discontent reached its boiling point by the beginning of the French Revolution, which eventually contributed to its outbreak on May 5, 1789. Like so many others, the White Brault Group was tired of the Feudalism System, and some of its members were ready for a change. They had a dream, which burned deep inside of their souls, of creating a better family life. Uprooting oneself from his or her homeland is not an easy thing to do. Someone, among the White Brault Group, had a vision of building such a better life in another world totally different from the one he or she had become accustomed to, during several centuries of cultural experience. That person was Vincent Brault,[60] whose written Brault Surname in France would change in the New World to-*Breaux*.

A. Vincent Brault And The Immigration Of The White Brault Family Group To The "New World" Beginning in 1632

According to the archive records titled *On The Shoulders Of Giants: A History Of The Breaux Family-Addendum To The Allendom Papers*, "the search for the origins of the Breaux in North America leads us back more than a hundred years beyond the American Revolution to the Maritime Provinces of what is now Canada. Our story begins in feudal France where, in 1632, some 300 members of the peasant class, weary of the rising prices levied by the landlords and a class system that kept them forever chained to someone else's land for life set sail for the New World."[61] Vincent Brault was born one year before this Peasant/Serfs Uprising. He "…was born ca 1631…"[62] in Loudun, France. This city is located in the Department of Vienne in the west-central province of Poitou. Vincent Brault's "…grandfathers had probably experienced feudalism."[63] Motivated by the

---

[60] "The family name comes from either an ancient Gaulish word, "Brolii" meaning small woods surrounded by a wall; or a town named Broilum, about year 1142 in Department of Seine-et-Marne…Brault, a word derived from Gallo-Germanic Beroaldus, is a very old name borne by many French families in and around France." Breauxfamily.files.wordpress.com/2017/03/vincentbreaux article.pdf, p. 1.

[61] Duncan, Janet Wood and Duncan, Stephen Joseph, "On The Shoulders Of Giants: Addendum To The Allendom Papers," www.safero.org, Acadia, June 1995.

[62] Op. cit., See Footnote 61.

[63] Ibid., See Footnote 61, p. 2.

possibility of obtaining wealth from the New World, "from 1535 to 1650 Charles de Menou de Charnisay, Sieigneur d'Aulnay, was Governor and Lieutenant General for the King [Louis XIII] in all the Acadian Coast of New France. Many colonists for Acadie were recruited from his lands, the Siegneury of Aulnay...all near Loudun, in the Department of Vienne, France..."[64] Vincent Brault arrived in this area in 1652 when he was 21 years old. Stirred by his hope for a life better than his grandfathers/mothers during the generations of the existence of the Feudalism System, Vincent Brault was recruited from the village of Aulnay near his birthplace in Loudun, France as one of the colonists enroute to the Maritime Province of Canada. At least fifteen Brault Families made the journey across the Atlantic Ocean with him.

B. Voyage Across The Atlantic Ocean

Being 21 years old at the time, Vincent Brault likely had no prior experience aboard an ocean-going vessel; it is safe to say he did not know what lay ahead of him; pilots of large ships know from their personal experiences that the ocean can be calm one day, and the next, it can be a raging, angry sea with 12 feet or higher waves. According to the Vincent Breaux Article, "he probably left France from LaRochelle. It was the chief western port for voyages to the New World...The ship would leave LaRochelle, travel northwest along the coast of France, maybe as far as the Isle of Sein, off the tip of Brittany, then head west for Newfoundland. Ships going to Acadia, would have rounded Cape Able, sailed up the Bay of Fundy, and into Annapolis Basin."[65] If everything went as planned, it typically took a ship two months to navigate across the Atlantic Ocean.

But, everything rarely went 100% as planned. There were storms and raging seas to contend with; and, from a health standpoint, some of the passengers suffered with such illness as yellow fever, scurvy, and sea sickness. Scurvy is caused by a severe deficiency of Vitamin C. In spite of the challenges the Atlantic Ocean presented, Vincent Brault, and his fellow Acadian Travelers, made it to their destination, namely, Acadia or Acadie. The latter was derived from the ancient Greece's Arcadia, and the French

---

[64] Ibid., p. 2.
[65] Ibid., p.2.

called it L'Acadie, which grew over time to comprise the whole province of Nova Scotia.

C. L'Acadie or Acadia, 1605 to 1755

"Acadia's first permanent settlement was in 1605, which was two years before the English settled Jamestown, Virginia and 15 years before the Pilgrims arrived at Plymouth Rock, Massachusetts."[66] During the next 100 years, and by 1710, and in spite of a 50% infant mortality rate, the total population had grown to "…2,500 [; by] 1755…it is estimated that there were 12,000 to 15,000 Acadians living in 10 different towns scattered around the Bay of Fundy and the Gulf of St. Lawrence."[67] Upon his arrival in Acadie, "Vincent Brault settled at Port Royal (now Annapolis Royal, Nova Scotia), along the south bank of the Riviere Dauphin, now called the Annapolis River…[which] flows into the Annapolis Basin [and] empties into the Bay of Fundy."[68] For the better part of the Seventeenth Century, the Acadians worked and developed a community with the family as its centerpiece.

Vincent Brault, and his fellow Acadians, brought with them a very intense family value system from France. A belief in maintaining their family integrity was paramount, and it overrode political and economic factors. The latter to the Acadians were means to build strong families in their community. According to Janet Wood and Stephen Joseph Duncan, "although superficially united by their common language and a desire for a better life, their ties to each other ran much deeper; virtually all were from the same west central provinces in France and all shared a history of intensely strong family ties and a love of working the land that was already generations old. These elements provided a foundation and bond that would hold their society together through the rigors of a new and hostile environment and help them to survive and attempt on the part of a mighty nation to obliterate their culture entirely—an effort at one point would include placing a bounty on their scalps."[69] With this

---

[66] Op. cit., See Footnote 62.
[67] Ibid., See Footnote 62.
[68] Op. cit., See Footnote 61, p. 2.
[69] Ibid. Part 2.

sentiment flowing through his veins, Vincent Brault "about 1661, at Port Royal, Acadie...married Marie Bourg. She was the daughter of Antoine Bourg and Antoinette Landry. Marie's parents were born in France but had moved to Acadie. Her father was from Martaize and her mother from La Chaussee. Marie Bourg was born about 1645 in Port Royal, Acadie."[70] Marie Bourg embodied the same fierce family values as her husband-Vincent Brault.

a. Economic Life Of The Acadians In The Maritime Province Of Nova Scotia

The 1671 Census reported Vincent Brault was a farmer, fisherman, levee builder, and owner of 9 cattle and 7 sheep. It also listed him as owner of four arpents of arable land. Vincent Brault and Marie Bourg Brault had four sons and two daughters reported in the 1678 Census. They were born in Nova Scotia: Antoine Brault, Pierre Brault, Francois Brault, Jean Brault, Marie Brault, and Marguerite Brault. Vincent and Marie Bourg Brault lived in Port Royal, Acadie for another[71] years before the Acadians were expelled from this area. Other Acadians, during this time, engaged in various economic pursuits. Jordan Marsh wrote about the elaborate infrastructure the Acadians built to support their agricultural pursuits. He stated "the Acadians had lived on Nova Scotia's territory since the founding of Port-Royal in 1604. They established a small, vibrant colony around the Bay of Fundy, building dykes to tame the high tides and to irrigate the rich fields of hay."[72]

As payment for their voyage across the Atlantic Ocean, Janet Wood Duncan and Stephen Joseph Duncan stated "bound to the fur-trading companies for a period of five years after their arrival in the New World, they initially earned their way by trapping and shipping furs to France and trading furs for other goods with French and English colonies to the south."[73] Meantime, the Acadians worked on clearing the forest "... [so they could]return to their first love—tilling the soil. The area around Pisiquid—the settlement where our Breaux ancestors lives—became

---

[70] Op. cit., see Footnote 61, p. 2.
[71] Marsh, Jordan H., "Acadian Expulsion (the Great Upheaval)," the canadianencyclopedia.ca, July 15, 2015.
[72] Op. cit., See Footnote 61, Part 1.
[73] Ibid.

known as the breadbasket of the colonies and surplus Acadian apples, vegetables, oats, rye and wheat made their way into the grateful New England colonies..."[74] All-in-all, the Acadians were well on the way to developing a diversified and prosperous economy. They made great strides toward this end; however, because of competition between the French and British for resources in the L'Acadie Region, a political struggle broke-out over which nation would enjoy dominant control over the natural and human resources, namely, Acadians.

b. French And British Struggle For Domination Of L'Acadie

The fight between these two European Powers was not a complex one; rather, it was a struggle over who would control the L'Acadie Colony? In the political squabble leading up to the Franco-English Colonial Wars, and based on the propensity of one side or the other to break a treaty, the Acadians made a demand to the British Government for neutrality in the nation-states struggle. Unfortunately, their demand for neutrality was a verbal one! The Provincial Governor, Richard Phillips, who served as England's caretaker of the L'Acadie Colony in Nova Scotia, abruptly ceased negotiations with the Acadians after six years of talks about their demand for neutrality. Governor Phillips "...sailed back to England and announced to the Lords of Trade that his mission had been a complete success and that the Acadians had abandoned their claims to neutrality."[75] This was not true, but a *big lie*! The Acadians, including Vincent Brault and Marie Bourg and their family, had been duped; and, in the spring of 1755, the Grand Derangement and Expulsion of Acadians from L'Acadie began.

D. Grand Derangement And Expulsion Of Acadians From L'Acadie In Nova Scotia In The Spring 1755

As the political tension between France and England continued to escalate during the early1720s, each side was looking for a way to gain a stronger foothold over the L'Acadie Colony. Although the Acadians pledged their neutrality to England, the latter knew it could strike a blow against France

---

[74] Ibid., See Footnote 61, Part 3.
[75] Op. cit., see Footnote 62, Part 2.

by reneging on the Acadians' pledge to remain neutral in the midst of England's political dispute with France. Thus, in order for England to advance its devious plan against France, the former "… appointed Major Charles Lawrence as Lieutenant Governor of the Acadian Province in August of 1754 [because] England's position regarding the colony had changed drastically…Major Lawrence had had enough of [the Acadians'] French tongue…and with no legal justification whatsoever-he decided to get rid of this annoying problem once and for all and by any means necessary."[76] Major Lawrence coerced the Acadians into disarming themselves, and what happened subsequently was a Domino Effect.

First, on July 3, 1755, using the disguise of returning the Acadians' arms to them, Vincent Brault, and other leaders of the Acadian settlements were summoned to Halifax, Nova Scotia by Major Charles Lawrence "… where he demanded they abandon their neutrality and sign an unconditional oath of allegiance. When they refused, he summarily imprisoned the entire delegation; lured the Acadian men into the posts on some pretext, then arrested them all as enemies of the Crown. Separated from their men, the women and children would offer no resistance and could be loaded onto the English transport ships waiting offshore. Extended families would be broken up and distributed among British Atlantic seaboard colonies and sent to England."[77] The Grand Derangement and Expulsion of Acadians, from their homes in Nova Scotia, had begun. Second, two months later on September 5, 1755, in the community of Grand Pre,' 418 Acadian men were lured into a local Catholic Church using the pretext of discussing a decree regarding their land; instead, they were arrested, and five days later they were escorted by armed guards, including their families, to English Transport Ships and deported. Third, by mid-October 1755, most of the Acadian communities were reduced to ghost towns."[78] Fourth, the colonial government in Nova Scotia, acting on orders from the British Crown, "…abandoned its policy of deportation in exchange for one of outright and total extermination…Starvation and disease claimed "great numbers", but the British commitment to extermination was relentless. Between 1756 and 1758, the Nova Scotia government declared an official bounty on

---

[76] Ibid.
[77] Ibid.
[78] Ibid., Part 3.

Acadian prisoners. Unofficially, the bounty was on their scalps."78 Before the end of 1755, the Acadians, and the White Brault People from France were, for the most part, homeless and without a country.

Therefore, according to James H. Marsh, "between 1755 and 1763, approximately 10,000 Acadians were deported. They were shipped to many points around the Atlantic. Large numbers were landed in the English colonies, others in France or the Caribbean."[79] Many of the Acadian Refugees were deported to several of the English Thirteen Colonies-Massachusetts, South Carolina, Connecticut, New York, Maryland, Pennsylvania and so forth. During this time, or by the mid-18th Century, Spain had gained ownership of much of the land area called Louisiana today. Though none of the Acadian Exiles were recruited to Louisiana by Spain after their expulsion from Nova Scotia by the British Crown, the former was looking for anyone to give large Land Grants with only one obligation, which was to improve the land and make it productive.

E. White Brault Family Migration From Nova Scotia To St. Jacques de Cabannoce' Later Renamed St. James Parish

France ended its Seven Years War with England in 1763, roughly eight years after England expelled Vincent Brault and his family, and thousands of others, from Nova Scotia by any means necessary. When the spoils of this war were divided up, "...the Treaty of Paris ceded the area west of the Mississippi to Spain, (France's ally in the war), and east of the river to England."[80] By 1765, the expelled Acadians began arriving in the Louisiana Territory in search of land to rebuild their communities that were destroyed during the Grand Derangement in 1755. Duncan and Duncan stated "during the 1760's, at least one thousand Acadians migrated to Louisiana. In 1785 nearly sixteen hundred from France, alone, made their way back across the Atlantic, bound for the new land. Early immigrants settled in the plains areas and began raising cattle, while a group of members from the old Acadian Breauxs were settled along the west bank of the Mississippi River."[81] Vincent Brault's offsprings were likely among the

---

[79] Marsh, op. cit.
[80] Duncan and Duncan, op. cit., See Footnote 62, Part 4.
[81] Ibid., Part 4.

Acadians that settled on land bordering on the west bank of the Mississippi River "…at St. Jacques de Cabannoce'(present day St. James Parish)."[82] Interestingly, the St. James Parish's Name evolved out of the name of Jacques Cantrelle's (He was originally from Picardy, France) Plantation's name, which was Cabanocee', a name of a local bayou tributary connected to the Mississippi River. Cabanocee' eventually became known as the J.K. Cantrelle Plantation by 1858.

a. Vincent Brault: Source Of All Of The Brauds (Breaux, Breaus, Braud, etc) Who Migrated To Louisiana After The Grand Derangement In 1755

Duncan and Duncan stated "all of the Breauds (Breauxs, Breaus, etc.) of Louisiana are descended from one man who came to Acadia from La Chausseé near Loudun, France, not long after its founding. He was born ca 1631…he married MARIE BOURE there in 1661 and over the next 20 years, until his death in 1681, they produced five sons…"[83] Of the five children Vincent Brault produced with Marie Bourg Brault in Nova Scotia, Antoine Breaux was the link between his father-Vincent Brault-and the subsequent establishment of the White Brault Group on land located on the west bank of the Mississippi River after the Aadian Grand Derangement occurred in 1755. Antoine Breaux married Marguerite Basin Breaux, and they produced five children, namely, Antoine Breaux Jr, Charles Breaux, Alexandra Breaux, Jean Baptiste Breaux, and Pierre Breaux. Of the second generation of Braults born in Nova Scotia, Alexandra Breaux was the link between Antoine Breaux, his father, who eventually would produce four children, one of whom would end up in St. James Parish.

Particularly, Alexandra Breaux married Marie Dugas, and they produced four children, namely, Armand Breaux, Alexis Breaux, Joseph Breaux, and Cecile Breaux. Alexis Breaux is the only one of this Breaux Family Group who had children. He married Marie Breaux, and they produced seven children. They were: Honore Breaux, Joseph Breaux, Charles Breaux, Marie Breaux, Viveine Breaux, Anatasa Breaux, and Aleyisha Breaux. Alexis Breaux and His Family Group made it to New Orleans, LA in 1768. Initially, the Spanish Governor of the Louisiana

---

[82] Ibid., Part 4.
[83] Ibid., Part 1.

Territory, Antonio de Ulloa, wanted Alexis Breaux to settle in Natchez, MS 115 miles upriver from his other Breaux relatives, who had already settled in St. Jacques de Cabannoce.' Obviously, he was not happy about this order from the Antonio de Ulloa, and "...at the last minute ALEXIS and Honoré and their families jumped ship and went into hiding on the farm of one André Jung. Not long after, records indicate that ALEXIS purchased a farm at Cabannocé from Joseph Ducros."[84] When Spanish Governor Ulloa found out about Alexis, and his Breaux Family Group Plan, he ordered Alexis to be apprehended and tied up, or arrested. Before Alexis was scheduled to be sentenced, he escaped with the help of fellow Acadian he befriended in Nova Scotia, namely, Charles Gaudet. If sentenced, Alexis was certainly going to be deported. When the Acadian Militia was ordered to apprehend Alexis by the Spanish Governor Ulloa, they refused, and since the Acadian Militia was a loyal servant of the Spanish, Spanish Governor Ulloa rescinded his order, but he sternly warned Alexis, if he disobeyed future orders, he, and the whole lot of Acadians would be expelled from St. Jacques de Cabannoce', and all of their possessions would be confiscated. With his freedom assured, Alexis Breaux, along with his dear friend, Charles Gaudet, bought and farmed land side-by-side on the west bank of the Mississippi River in St. Jacques de Cabannoce'.

b. Origin Of The F. Braud Plantation In St. Jacques de Cabannoce' (Later Renamed St. James Parish)

The selfless intervention of Charles Gaudet, on behalf of his life-long friend-Alexis Breaux, which brought to an end his potential deportation, cemented their family's friendship that lasted for another 100 years. From the outset, Alexis Breaux and Charles Gaudet established ownership of farms adjacent to teach other in St. Jaques de Cabannoce'. Alexis Breaux's widowed sister, Cecile Breaux Cloatre', married Charles Gaudet. Thus, according to Duncan and Duncan, "...two years before the signing of the Declaration of Independence, the farms of Charles and CECILE Gaudet, of HONORE and MAGDELEINE Breaux, and of ALEXIS and MAGDELEINE Trahan Breaux were snuggled up one next [each]other on the west bank of the Mississippi in St. James. One hundred years later,

---

[84] Ibid., Part 4.

the Breaux and Gaudet descendants would still be next door neighbors, farming the same adjoining land (though both farms would have swelled into successful plantations with multiple families in residence."[85] Thus, by 1858, or 88 years after the Alexis Breaux and Charles Gaudet Family Groups began cultivating crops on farms located side-by-side, they evolved into two major plantations on the Louisiana River Road.

As I have already mentioned, these plantations were called the J.K. Gaudet Plantation and the F. Braud Plantation.

As these plantations began to grow and expand, the Acadians' feelings toward Blacks and Mulattos changed. A steady, dependable supply of labor was increasingly needed to insure increasingly higher profits from Rice and Sugarcane Production. The older generations of Acadians remembered the Grand Derangement and all the hardships and emotional traumas it caused them. As a result, at the outset "…the Acadians regarded blacks and mulattos as their social equals, working and traveling with them. In the 1770's, the St. James Acadians, usually young men with infant children - began purchasing young Negro women as nursemaids or simply as maids to assist their wives with the housework after childbirth or during the latter stages of pregnancy. Thus, our family's earliest slave acquisitions were prompted by familial, rather than economic considerations. Later, slaves were purchased to supplement the family labor pool in the fields…

The Creoles were scandalized."[86] Regardless whether Negro Women were purchased as nursemaids for Acadian Men's wives after they gave birth, the fact is from 1800 to 1860, the J.K. Gaudet and F. Braud Plantations, along with all of the others located along the Louisiana River Road, utilized African Slave Labor to operate them. As a reminder, I have thoroughly shown that by 1860, the ratio between the African Slave and Native White Populations was 3 to 1 respectively. I have also shown that two-thirds of the millionaires in the United States by 1860 lived on the Louisiana River Road. None of this prosperity would have been possible without African Slave Labor.

Therefore, African Slave Labor was a *premium*.

Armed with this knowledge related to how the F. Braud Plantation came into existence, it is time for me to answer two questions: How

---

[85] Ibid., Part 4.
[86] Ibid., Part 4.

did the Black Braud Group begin on the F. Braud Plantation? Were its members privilege to a portion of the profits received from African Slave Labor annually?

F. Crossover: Edouardo Breaux, Jr Marriage To The African Slave Woman Celestine And The Beginning Of The Black Braud Family Group On The Louisiana River Road

Honore Breaux[87] married Magdeleine Breaux, and they produced six children. They were: Edouardo Breaux, Sr, Madeline Breaux, Marie Breaux, Marguerite Breaux (Deceased), Elizabeth Breaux, and Joachim Breaux (He was a son Honore Breaux had with another woman). I have previously established that Alexis Breaux, Honore Breaux's father, was the founder of the F. Breaux Plantation; it follows that his son's identified children likely lived on this plantation during their childhoods. Duncan and Duncan stated "there…[is]…overwhelming [evidence] that this family homestead is a piece of the original Breaux plantation."[88] And, since I have explained African Slave Labor was used on the F. Braud Plantation also, it follows that there were a number of African Slave Women held captive on it as well. Edouardo Breaux, Sr married Rosalie Breaux. They produced two children, namely, Edouardo Breaux Jr. and Bienvenu Breaux.

It was during Edouardo Breaux, Jr's lifetime that the Black Braud Family Group came into existence via his marriage to an African Slave Woman name Celestine. She was the bridge that my Black Braud Family Group used to start this new branch on the White Brault/Breaux Family Tree, which dates all the way back to the early 17th Century in Western France with the birth of Vincent Brault in 1632. This *crossover* began the Black Braud Family Group Lineage in St. James Parish seven generations after the expulsion of the Acadians from Nova Scotia. Celestine's daughter, Leontine, was also called Ma'am George.

Throughout the 244 years of the American Slavery Institution, it was common practice for the slave master to engage in intimate relationships with African Slave Women. Usually, the slave master's encounters with African Slave Women were kept highly secretive. Normally, the public

---

[87] Honore Breaux had another female companion name Anne Trahan.
[88] Op. cit., See Footnote 62, Part 4, June 1995.

would find out about a particular encounter when a Mulatto Child would appear in its midst. However, it appeared Edouard Breaux Jr, and his Breaux Family Group, broke the template of traditional secrecy. Given the fact, a majority of the existing information contained in the *On The shoulders Of Giants: A History Of The Breaux Family,* Celestine would have been a slave on the F. Braud Plantation, or the J.K. Gaudet Plantation in as much as Edouard Beaux Jr's Great Uncle, Alexis Breaux, was a very close friend of Charles Gaudet. I believe Celestine was likely born on the F. Braud Plantation, or, if not, she was purchased from another one on the Louisiana River Road, or she was bought from a plantation owner located outside of the region. Duncan and Duncan stated "though the evidence is clear…our [White Beaux] ancestors…eventually…left the fields, moved into a Big house, and prospered in a slave economy. By 1810, 72% of the farms in St. James owned slaves."[89]

At any rate, Edouardo Breaux, Jr and Celestine did, in fact, meet each other; they apparently enjoyed each other's company very much; thus, their friendship blossomed through their early adulthoods into a marriage. Twenty-three years passed before they got married! Duncan and Duncan wrote "EDOUARD, JR. was only 20 when LEONTINE was born and the birth of a second child a few years later suggests a level of commitment beyond just a lustful, youthful folly. EDOUARD JR. appears to have genuinely loved CELESTINE and their children. We don't know CELESTINE's age, but she bore EDOUARD, Jr. a son 23 years later, so she cannot have been much older than 20 herself when their relationship began."[90] Edouardo Breaux, Jr. married Celestine after Emancipation,[91] which means if he waited 23 years to marry her, then, they had to have known each other during the 1840s. The table was now set for the Black Braud Family Group to take their place in St. James Parish History, beginning after the end of the American Civil War. The crossover was complete with the birth of Edouardo Breaux, Jr and Celestine Breaux's three Mulatto Children.

---

[89] Ibid., Part 5.
[90] Ibid., Part 5.
[91] Ibid., Part 6.

G. Manifestation Of The Crossover And The Beginning Of The Braud Family Group Lineage On The Gravel Road

Of all the places on the Gravel Road I could call the starting point of the beginning of the Black Braud Family Group, it was, based on available evidence, the original F. Braud Plantation. Duncan and Duncan stated "… the original Breaux plantation and the family homestead… fell very close to the town of Welcome, St. James Parish, where family members who visited the homestead said we would find it."[92] One of the landmarks that remains today, from the days of the past operation of the F. Braud Plantation, is "…Braud Road—and not far away, a mailbox marked "L. Braud".[93] The significance of the location of the F. Braud Plantation is, it is very likely the place where Edouardo Breaux, Jr and Celestine Breaux raised their three children. And, of particular importance here is the birth of their only son, namely Theophile Breaux (The White Breaux Family Group spelled their surname as shown, and once the Black Braud Family Group started during the mid-19th Century, it changed from Breaux to Braud). Because of the prevailing American Slavery Institution on the Gravel Road, the name change might be further explained as a way to make a distinction between the White Breaux Family Group and the Black Braud Family Group.

As it was in the beginning of the Crossover, it is here where I found the first fledgling of my Braud Family Group.

Edouardo Breaux, Jr and Celestine had three children. They were Leontine Breaux, Theophile Breaux, and Marie Leontine Breaux. In addition, Edouardo Breaux, Jr and Celestine Breaux's children's last name was the same as their father. According to the 1850 Census, Theophile Breaud was reported to be 8 years old, which means he was born in 1842. When the 1860 Census was recorded, he was reported to be an 18 years old Mulatto Male. As time passed, the way Theophile's last name was spelled changed again to Braud. As I mentioned earlier, Edouardo Breaux, Jr waited 23 years before he married Celestine; however, the census suggests their children were born during this interim period. By 1852, Leontine was 6 years old, which indicates she was born in 1846. And, when the 1860

---

[92] Ibid., Part 6.
[93] Ibid., Part 6.

Census was taken, she was 14 years old. Although our attention is focused on Theophile Braud (The 1850 and 1860 Censuses changed the spelling of Breaux to Braud), it is worthwhile noting for the record that Leontine Breaux, aka, "Ma'am" George" had a twin brother whose name was George Allen Breaux. And, "Ma'am George" gave birth to five children, namely, Mary Alice Allen Braud, who married Floriston Villavaso, Louis Braud Allen, Marie Isabella Braud Allen, Ann Braud Allen, and Betty Braud Allen. Mary Alice Allen Villavaso went on the distinguish herself as a pioneer in the field of Public School Education in St. James Parish. An opportunity will present itself later for me to elaborate more on education in this parish.

Thus far, I have traced the movement of the Brault Family Group from western France to Nova Scotia, Canada and, by the 19th Century, I documented its migration to St. Jacques de Cabannoce' later known as St. James Parish in the Louisiana Territory. I have now come to a fork in the road where the crossover between Edouardo, Jr and the African Slave Woman name Celestine has made it necessary for me to switch tracks, from the White Brault Family Tree to the Black Braud Family Tree; and henceforth I will, without any delay, begin to trace the footsteps of Theophile Braud, and thereafter, my own. Every flowing river has a source; the Mississippi River's is Lake Itasca in Minnesota and the Nile River in Egypt is Lake Victoria, which flows through parts of Uganda, Tanzania, and Kenya. The source of my Braud Family Group is my grandfather-Theophile Braud.

H. Braud Family Group And Selected Generations During The 19th And 20th Centuries

By 1860, Theophile Braud, aka Defeo, Dufino, etc. was 18 years old. That year the Census recorded his ethnic identity as being a Mulatto Male. As it was, Thoephile Braud's childhood years corresponded to the last 18 years of the American Slavery Institution's existence on the Louisiana River Road. Given what I know about his parents and the F. Braud Plantation, it is safe to say Theophile Braud was not a free man yet, but his family connections did not hurt his chances of survival. As the word spread among the Slaveholding Families along the Louisiana River Road that his father was Edouardo Breaux, Jr, Theophile Braud probably was viewed a bit more favorably by them relative to the generalized harsh treatment the majority of African Slaves endured throughout their entire lives, from birth to death. How long an African Slave survived most likely depended on his or her obedience to his or her slave master.

In short, Theophile Braud could have had access to a little more food, medicine, education, tools, land, and housing among others than most African Slaves due to his Braud name connection to Edouardo Breaux, Jr. The latter's great, great grandfather, namely, Alexis Breaux, started the F. Braud Plantation. So, his great, great grandson-Theophile Braud-could have benefited in some ways as a result. Nevertheless, he still had to work hard to provide for his family, which he started during the last three decades of the 19th Century.

Previously, I emphasized the southern Slaveholder Oligarchy Class made a deal with selected President Rutherford B. Hayes in 1876, which in essence, removed Federal Troops from the South; dismantled President Abraham Lincoln's Reparations Reconstruction Program after his assassination; and re-installed, without any impunity or punishment, this class to political, social, economic, and judicial power. The single goal was to re-establish slavery as close as possible to the way it was by 1860. Simultaneously, the southern Slaveholding Oligarchy Class passed legislation throughout the South, which made Jim Crow and legalized segregation the law of the land. And, worse, it created a domestic terrorism program with the KKK at his forefront, and this tactic unleashed a wave of violence against Freed Negroes, which the U.S. Census called them, which rippled across the South, and manifested itself in the forms of fear, physical beating, and lynchings. All of these repressive factors and others gained momentum during the last half of the 19th Century, and many of them lasted well into the 20th Century. The Civil Rights Movement came about as a direct result of this unbridled Tyranny.

Moreover, along the Louisiana River Road before I was born, it was documented earlier that at least 10 Freed Negroes were lynched. Therefore, this is the social climate in which Theophile Braud lived his adult life, and raised his family, which became the Braud Family Group I was born in a few decades after the turn of the 20th Century.

a. Braud Family Group: First Generation[94] On The Louisiana River Road In St. James Parish

Both Theophile Braud[95] and Louisa (Lise) Mulberry were born during slavery. The former was born in 1842 and the latter in 1851. Theophile Braud spent 18 years of his life during the slavery era, and Louisa (Lise) Mulberry 9 years. Thus, Theophile Braud spent two times longer in slavery than Louisa Mulberry. Regardless, both were Mulattoes, and they probably were born on the F. Braud Plantation. This possibility raises one important question in my mind, and that is, unlike a majority of Mulatto Children born on the F. Braud Plantation, and many others during slavery as a result of involuntary intercourse between a Free White Male and an African Slave Woman, normally the Mulatto Infant was not automatically given his or her freedom. The question here is because Edouardo Breaux, Jr married the African Slave Celestine after the Emancipation Proclamation became law on January 1, 1863, and because Theophile Braud was born in 1842 and Louisa Mulberry in 1851, were they classified as slaves when they were born? If so, together, both of them experienced the sting of slavery for at least three decades.

Either way, Theophile Braud married Louisa (Lise) Mulberry Braud after 1865 and before 1875.

Theophile Braud and Louisa Mulberry Braud produced the first generation of the Braud Family Group not long after the end of the American Civil War. Specifically, they produced 10 children. Louisa Mulberry Braud was 24 years old when she gave birth to Edna Braud-Blouin, who was born in 1875, ten years after the end of the war. Afterwards, she gave birth to Elouise Braud, Celestine Braud-Washington in 1887 when she was 36 years

---

[94] To avoid any confusion, the White Brault Family Group goes back in time at least seven generations, beginning in Loudun, France. Thus, the Black Braud Family Group only came into existence when Edouardo Breaux, Jr and Celestine (Former African Slave) got married. Although their only son, Theophile Braud was born in 1842, the generation count did not begin until he married Louisa (Lise) Mulberry, and they started producing children. Then, the Generation clock began to tick.

[95] Theophile Braud appears in the 1850 and 1860 Census with his name recorded as shown. However, there are several other ways Theophile Braud's name has been written through the generations. They are: Defeo, Dufino, and so forth.

old, August Braud, Helen Braud, Alta Braud, Wellman Braud,[96] Edna Braud, and Albert Israel Braud. These children formed the foundation of the Braud Family Group. Every subsequent generation appropriately stands on the shoulders of Theophile Braud and Louisa Mulberry Braud. They had to have strong shoulders to weather the head-winds of the times.

Interestingly, one of their daughters, namely, Helen Braud, had six children who were Irma W. Braud Punch, Mary M. Braud Hill, Roy Ferdinand, Delfeo Ferdinand, Winthrop Ferdinand, and Louis Ferdinand. It is worth emphasizing here that Helen Braud's son-Delfeo Ferdinand made a significant contribution to Jazz Music inasmuch as two of his grandchildren became nationally and internationally famous Jazz musicians. They are Winton Marsalis and Brandford Marsalis, who are masters of the Trumpet and Tenor Saxophone respectively.

The first generation of the Braud Family Group passed the survival of the fittest test because it was able to continue to sew the seeds of Theophile Braud and Louisa Mulberry Braud well into the 20th and 21th Centuries.

b. Braud Family Group: Second Generation On The Louisiana River Road In St. James Parish

I entered the Braud Family Group during its Second Generation. All of the new additions to the Braud Family Tree appeared during the early 20th Century, and I am one of them. Albert Israel Braud produced seven children. They are: Beverly Braud, myself-Joseph Pierce Braud, Elaine Cecile Braud, Geraldine Braud, Suky Chapman Braud, Edgar Braud, and Mary Ann Braud. Emma Braud produced Joseph Hall and Sidney Hall; Elouise Braud produced Wilfred Francis and Stella Francis; Celestine Braud Washington produced 12 children; August Braud produced 7 children; Helen Braud produced 6 children; and Edna Braud 3 children. A complete listing of all of the children born in the First and Second Generation are included in the Braud Family Tree in Appendix A.

Since the members of the Second Generation of the Braud Family Group, and particularly my own siblings, were born after the turn of the 20th Century, many of them probably re-settled in the village called Brookstown near Welcome, LA. Both of these communities originated on

---

[96] Wellman Braud was a famous musician, and during his professional career, he played with the Cab Calloway Band, Duke Ellington Orchestra, and Borne Brigard.

land that was once a part of the F. Braud Plantation. Other families also settled in Brookstown, or in nearby Welcome, LA. One of the families that eventually became a significant addition to the Braud Family Group was the Pierce's. Just how significant the latter was, in this regard, will be disclosed shortly. Meantime, I will identify the key members of the Pierce Family Group at this time.

I. Pierce Family Group And Selected Generations During The 19th and 20th Centuries

Standing at the top of the Pierce Family Tree, by the end of the American Civil War, was Phillip Pierce. Obviously, there were other Pierce Family Members who have occupied this position, and, like the movement of the hands on a generation clock, they passed on before Phillip Pierce's birth. His father was Pedro Pierce. Nothing is known about him beyond this fact. I can say with a reasonable degree of certainty that the Pierce Family Group were associated with the F. Braud Plantation, or another one in the nearby vicinity; every inch of arable land was a part of a plantation. However, after the American Civil War ended in 1865, some former African Slaves remained on the plantation, and others left and settled in small villages and towns such as Brookstown and Welcome, LA. Somewhere in the mix of this social change, Phillip L. Pierce was born in 1865. By the time he reached 20 years old, that year was 1885. It was probably around this time that Phillip Pierce married and started raising his family.

That being so, and according to the Pierce Family Tree, Phillip Pierce married Suky Chapman. Over the course of 20 years, they produced 12 children. They were: Phillip Pierce Jr, Arthur Pierce, Chapman Pierce, Leah Pierce, Mary Pierce, Roger Pierce, Louise Pierce, Ophelia Pierce, Evelyn Pierce, Franklin Pierce, Hugh Pierce, and Lillian Luellen Pierce. More details related to the other members on the Pierce Family Tree can be observed in Appendix B. Later, I will say something about the *special powers* Leah Pierce possessed when I was young boy.

Presently, I will focus my attention on the two people, who joined the Braud and Pierce Family Groups together by the early 20th Century; and, with a mother and father's anticipation, they welcomed me into their household as their second born child.

CHAPTER VII

JOE BRAUD AND LILLIAN LUELLEN PIERCE-BRAUD HOUSEHOLD

Of the 10 children produced by Theophile Braud and Louisa (Lise) Mulberry Braud, who were my grandfather and grandmother, Joe Braud was born in 1896. As I have already mentioned, the Sharecropping System was widely practiced after the American Civil War, and it lasted, to some degree as a form until the Civil Rights Era, which began during the late 1950s. I imagine the widespread trend of having a large family was a carryover from the American Slavery Institution inasmuch as the slaveholder wanted as many "heads" as possible to work in the field. As it was, I do not remember Joe Braud and Lillian Luellen Pierce Braud engaged in the Sharecropping System during my childhood. In order to survive, my parents possessed some character traits that enabled them to withstand the obstacles that were intentionally put in the way of Negro Progress at the time. I have already mentioned a few of them thus far.

A. Joe Braud's Character Traits

When my father was born in 1896, and shortly after his birth, his father, Theophile Braud passed away apparently by the beginning of the 20th Century. Louisa Mulberry Braud, no doubt, must have been traumatized with her loss. Because family values were a centerpiece of home life of the Brault Family Group in France for many generations, its members brought a strong love, for one another with them across the Atlantic Ocean, which flowed in their blood in the old country; they used this core value to build their families in Nova Scotia, Canada. Edouardo Breaux, Jr mixed this core value with Celestine's, and they passed it on to Leontine Braud, Theophile Braud, and Marie Braud.

When Theophile Braud passed away, his oldest daughter, Edna Braud Blouin graciously accepted the responsibility for raising Joe Braud. In her greatest time of family need, Edna Braud Blouin stepped in, and she raised Joe Braud, from a baby into adulthood. Without a core value of love for each family member that permeated the Theophile Braud and Louisa Mulberry Braud's household, there is no telling what might have happened to my father that would have significantly reduced his life expectancy. Joe Braud survived; he had a childhood; and he became a respected man in the Brookstown Village.

I have heard it said many times that *it takes a village to raise a child*. By the time my father arrived in the Brookstown Village during the early 1920s, he had developed into a well-rounded man.

Joe Braud was 5'11" tall. He had a light brown complexion and it accented his beautiful, wide smile. His hair was dark and somewhat kinky. In short, Joe Braud was an attractive man. More importantly, he was even tempered, and he listened to both sides of an issue before making a decision about what to do. While the Sharecropping System was in full swing during the decades following the American civil War, Joe Braud was not drawn into it with all of the odor of quasi-slavery. He was a self-reliant man who owned his tools and some land needed to produce a livelihood for his future family. Joe Braud was a disciplined person-someone who utilized the resources he had on hand wisely. Being a young, single, and eligible bachelor, Joe Braud would make a good partner for a lady in search of a fellow to spend her life around. Someone she could share a laugh with in the middle of the night when the children are fast asleep, and one she could communicate with with her beautiful eyes without speaking one single word. In addition, that lady would, no doubt, need a man she felt safe with and respected by White Jim Crow People. Joe Braud was a peaceful man but he would defend his family in self-defense to the end. In the Brookstown, and nearby Welcome, LA Communities, Joe Braud met that special woman, who became the apple of his eyes!

B. Lillian Luellen Pierce's Character Traits

Her name was Lillian Luellan Pierce, one of the 12 children of Phillip Pierce and Suky Chapman Pierce. She came from a good family lineage. In real life, I remember my mother quite vividly, who stood 5'6" tall. She was petite with a well-defined waist line, and she had a smooth, dark complexion. Her facial features reminded me of a Native American because her cheekbones were well defined also. Lillian Luellan Pierce had waist length, jet black hair that accented her oval, warm, charcoal eyes. Without a doubt, Lillian Luellen Pierce was a grossly attractive woman. With her outstanding beauty, she could be selective, regarding her choice of a male companion.

Besides offering some "lucky" fellow her charming, and loving attention, Lillian Luellen Pierce had other mental features to offer. She was not someone who was unable to engage in deductive thinking to solve a problem; to the contrary, Lillian was a deep thinker. And, after pondering a situation, by looking at both sides, and turning it inside out a few times, she made a decision, and though it might not have been popular to some, she had the fortitude and strong will to stand her ground without wavering, and "giving in" to someone's unsubstantiated, emotional claims. In short, Lillian Luellen Pierce had a *word* that could be depended on like the sunrise and sunset. In addition, she was organized, and her personal self and surroundings did not contradict the power of her organized mind.

Thus, these are a few of the gems Lillian Luellen Pierce had in store for the man who could appreciate them as part of her being; and, more importantly, he had to be secure within himself, and not be intimidated by her physical and mental powers. Sometime toward the middle of the second decade of the 20th Century, Joe Braud and Lillian Luellen Pierce met each other.

C. Joe Braud And Lillian Luellan Pierce Marry, September 11, 1921

During their late teens, Joe and Lillian found time for each other. Their relationship grew stronger. Apparently, Lillian Luellen Pierce felt Joe Braud was the man for her, and she was not shy about letting him know how she felt about him. Joe Braud, on the other hand, thought to himself that he could not miss out on being with the woman of his dreams, and he acted accordingly, and proposed to marry his sweetheart.

After many days of dating both of them realized that their relationship was right for each other, and on September 11, 1921, Joe Braud and Lillian Luellen Pierce got married in Ascension Parish. At the time they got married, Joe Braud lived in Brookstown, LA and Lillian Luellen Pierce Braud was a resident of Donaldsonville, LA. On their Marriage License, Theo is listed as Joe Braud's Father, and Phillip Pierce as Lillian Luellen Pierce Braud's. Image 1.0 below is a replicate of their Marriage License.

Image 1.0
Joe Braud And Lillian Luellen Pierce Braud's Marriage License Dated September 15, 1921 In Ascension Parish

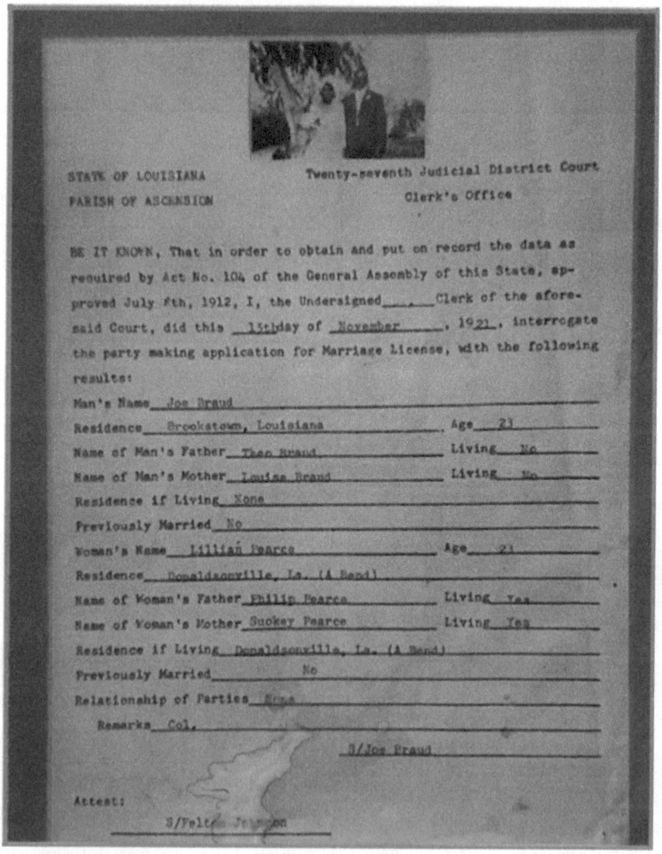

Source: Author

Briefly, the residence shown on the Marriage License is Brookstown, and the name of Joe Braud's father is Theo Braud. Recall, Edouardo Breaux, Jr and Celestine Breaux's second child was name Theophile Braud. Also, the name of Theo Braud's wife was Louise Braud, which is the same person, namely, Louise (Lise) Mulberry Braud.

Eventually, the newlyweds would set up their household in Brookstown, LA. Before I describe the Brookstown Village and the house they settled in to raise their family, it is appropriate for me to mention my birth.

a. Joseph Pierce Braud: Second Born Child Of Joe Braud And Lillian Luellen Pierce Braud On September 11, 1926

As I mentioned already, Joe Braud and Lillian Luellen Pierce Braud produced seven children. I was the second born; the oldest of my siblings was Beverly Braud. I was born on September 11, 1926, which was one year before the Great Mississippi River Flood in 1927. I was too young to remember anything about this event, which had a devastating and catastrophic impact on a combined 930,000 people in Mississippi, Arkansas, and Louisiana. Luckily, the Great Flood by-passed the Louisiana River Road, and flooded many parishes to the West, namely, St. Martin, St. Landry, and Iberia.

In addition, I have the unique distinction of having been born on the same day my parents got married-September 11, 1921.

I was born in a place called A-Bend near Donaldsonville, LA. Because there were no hospitals available for most Black Women to go to give birth to their children, the alternative was home delivery.

b. Home Delivery Assisted By Ms. Rose Williams-Midwife

During the late 19th Century and early 20th Century, most African-American Women in the rural South gave birth to their children at home. Segregation made Midwifery a common practice. Out of necessity, Black Midwives were up to the task of assisting Black Women with home delivery of their children because Midwifery was a tradition handed down to them through the generations, which go all the way back to Africa. Kelena Reid Maxwell stated "in 1921, the majority of women who gave birth under conditions that were indigenous…were the rural black women of the South. African American midwives and women of the South maintained the core qualities of the home birthing traditions, handed down through a matrilineal system of recruitment and training from the period of enslavement throughout the twentieth century."[97] Lillian Luellen Pierce Braud's home delivery of me was another one in a long line of such births, which was older than the American Slavery System itself. Ms. Rose Williams was not trained by White Doctors in a hospital to do Midwifery. She was trained by other Black Women, who had been trained by a stream of those, who were African Slaves before her. After the American Civil War, the Midwife Practice was handed down to Free Black Women, and Ms. Rose Williams was one of them who the torch was passed to, and with those *sacred skills*, which were older than America itself, my mother was assisted with them by the steady hands of Ms. Rose Williams, who helped her to safely deliver me into the River Road World that awaited me.

I was born in my grandparents' house in a place called A-Bend, which, at the time, was a rural suburban community of Donaldsonville, LA. My birthplace, namely, Jones Road, is located on the West Bank of the Mississippi River. A few days after my birth, Joe Braud and Lillian Luellen Pierce Braud returned to their home in Brookstown, which is about five miles from where I was born.

By the time I was about six years old, I remember we did not live too far from my grandparents' home where I was born. On occasion, my mother would bring me with her to visit her parents-Phillip Pierce and Suky Chapman Pierce. I remember my grandfather sitting in a black chair under two Pecan Trees during the day. There were one or two buildings in the yard behind the house. I do not remember what they were used for. In the front yard, there were several large Fig Trees, and a Water Well that was their water source. They also had a Cistern on the side of the house that was also used as a source of water. Of my grandparents twelve children, I only remember eight. One of them, and I cannot remember the name, I only saw once during my early childhood visits with my mother. By the time I was seven years old, my parents had already made a powerful impression on me related to the kind of characters they presented around me.

---

[97] Maxwell, Kelena Reid, "Birth Behind the Veil: African American Midwives and Mothers in the Rural South, 1921-1962," Dissertation, Rutgers, The State University of New Jersey, New Brunswick, New Jersey, 2009, p. ii.

D. Reflections Of Joe Braud's Character During My Early Childhood Years

My father was a very good fellow, and when he was going somewhere that he did not want me to come along, he would say that he was going to see "Turk take water." I never learned what he meant by that phrase. He smoked Bull Durham Tobacco. It was sold in small cloth bags with a draw string. He rolled his own cigarettes. The tobacco could also be chewed. On occasions the fellow would smoke a sweet tasting cigar called King Edward. There were times that he would let me light his cigarettes. Then, one day, rather than asking me to light his cigarette, he handed me a cigar to light; and, due to my youthful curiosity, I lit the cigar and took a couple of puffs from it. I got so sick from that cigar that I thought I was going to die! I learned a good lesson: That episode caused me not to smoke for many years. My father took me with him frequently, and he never missed an opportunity to tell anyone who would listen that he was going to send me to college.

For example, I casually remember when I was around four or five years old, he would take me different places with him. He was always telling his friends, and other people, that he was going to send me to Southern University to take up, or major in, Agriculture. As I got older, between seven and nine years old, my father did not stop saying he wanted me to major in Agriculture. As he expressed his educational desire for me to become an Ag-Man, privately, I would say to myself that I wanted to be a medical doctor. Something had planted this idea in my mind, but I would not figure out what did until I got a little older. He also felt that his children should go to school. Thus, none of us ever missed a day in school. In addition, my father was always helping others in the community to better their condition and life. My father taught me some valuable lessons related to how to work at an early age, which, at the time I did not know it, but they would play a significant role in my life as I got older.

Moreover, my father farmed for himself on a small scale, and sometimes he worked for other farmers for wages intermittently; he grew crops in partnership with other farmers. He was always looking ahead to see what he could do for his family. Joe Braud would take me into the Rice Field with him. I remember I was seven or eight years old. The Rice Field where my father grew rice was over a mile behind our stable. I remember the horses were muddy when we arrive near the house so we rode the horses into the pond behind the Mississippi River Levee. We were on several horses, and I would slip off of the back of the horse in the water. I did not know how to swim, but I learned very quickly! From that afternoon until today, I have been able to swim. I learned how to take care of the work animals on our farm, and I also learned how to grow and harvest rice. Earlier, I explained Rice Production in detail, and I learned how it works because my father taught me how the process works. I felt like a "man" when I was with my father; he taught me how to think through every challenged we faced working on the farm. I learned there was an objective logic in operation within every farm task we worked on together. In other words, there was a way things connected together, and if I made the wrong connection, the project I worked on either failed, or it did not perform like Joe Braud told me it was suppose to operate. I did not know it at the time but I was being prepared to search for the logic in my Medical School Course Projects, which, of course, were many years down the road in my future.

Overall, I remembered my father was a friendly man with a wide smile. I never remember him being angry for any reason. These reflections of my father made a life-long impression on me. On the other hand, I was also blessed to have Lillian Luellen Pierce Braud teach me the feminine perspective of life.

E. Reflections Of Lillian Luellen Pierce Braud's Character During My Early Childhood Years

Everyone knows there is no substitute for having a good, loving mother or mother surrogate. When times get tough, my mother, being the deep thinker that she was, seemed to always have a solution waiting to solve any problems I might have encountered, or any one another of my siblings might have experienced. She was a solution-oriented person. My mother had foresight, and she planned ahead to make sure we had enough of the basic necessities we needed to survive. For example, my mother stayed home and nurtured her children and managed her house. She also developed a first class vegetable garden in which she raised such items as snap beans, crowder peas, tomatoes, several kinds of peppers, melons, pumpkins, cucumbers, meletones, and so forth.

Moreover, I had grown accustomed to my mother's love and attention she gave me, and it made me feel wanted, safe, and secure. This is how I grew up feeling the first ten years of my life in Brookstown. I felt I had a place in the sun even before the Rhythm and Blues Singer-Stevie Wonder-popularized this thought in his song called *A Place In The Sun* in 1966. This is how my mother made me feel even when my way seemed hard and dark, she was always there providing the light.

When everything in the Braud Household seemed to be going so well, suddenly a life-changing event unexpectedly occurred, which, to my mother's surprise, caused her to dig deeper down inside of herself to bring forth a timely solution. It would determine the stability of the Braud Family Group. Because Lillian Luellen Pierce Braud rose to the challenge; stared it in the face; and offered a practical family plan, the Braud Family Group was able to quickly refocus itself, and proceed to excel in the education field in a way that actually exceeded anyone's grandest imagination then, or thereafter! Shortly, I will reveal what my mother did to produce something that never had been produced on the Louisiana River Road throughout its history.

Presently, I will describe the Brookstown Village where I spent my childhood years.

F. Brookstown: A Description Of My Home Village

This is the settlement where my parents lived, and the one I called my home when I was away going to elementary and middle school in New Orleans, LA during my childhood years. As it was, Brookstown could be hidden in New Orleans, LA, and the only person who would know where it is located is the person who hid my hometown village there. Brookstown was truly a tiny village. If a stranger passing through Brookstown was looking for it for some reason, and if he or she asked a local resident "how can I get to Brookstown?" the local resident would probably breakout into a loud belly laugh, and respond saying "You are in Brookstown now!" My hometown was not even on the Louisiana State Map, or any map for that matter. But, Brookstown was my home, and I still have many fond memories about the place I grew up. This was a time when life seemed so simple to me almost like a fantasyland. I knew what was going to happen because Brookstown was tiny enough to know nothing out of the ordinary was going to happen. It was my safe space, although Jim Crow was always around with its ears ease dropping on Black folks.

By 1926, the year I was born, Brookstown was a little settlement located on the Gravel Road, which paralleled the Mississippi River. In all of my years growing up in Brookstown, in my Braud Family Group and outside of it, I have never been able to get any information on how and why it was given that name. Maybe some wise person imagined since the settlement was located just across the Gravel Road from the Mississippi River, and because the latter is known to ALL as the "Mighty Mississippi River," its opposite is a lazily flowing small surface stream called a Brook. Could this be where the Brookstown name originated? I am interested to know what you think? At any rate, and true to its name, Brookstown had a total population of approximately three hundred people, including adults and children. I am sure everybody, who lived in Brookstown, knew their neighbors.

Regarding Brookstown's description, as I recall, there was a church, school (1-room), post office, two grocery stores owned by Oneal and Gerald-"Gerra"-Roberts, and houses. There were no streets-instead, there were lanes. Some of the lanes had names and others did not. There were three to four houses in the average lane. Some lanes were farther from the Gravel Road than other lanes, and this meant some of the houses, along the lanes, were farther from the Gravel Road than other houses. I wonder if this housing pattern was a carryover from the Pre-American Civil War Era? Slave houses were built in a uniform pattern, and they ALL looked just alike; this housing style was used to physically and psychologically control the thoughts and movement of the African Slaves.

Some of the families owned the properties where they stayed and some did not. Other families lived in houses on properties owned by non-family members. In addition, other families lived on plantations. And, some families lived on property owned by farmers, who also owned the local stores and post office. Recall my discussion of the Sharecropping System earlier, which was nothing more than quasi-slavery. I do not recall Brookstown having a Stop Sign, or traffic lights. There were no street lights so at night, the only light there was was Moonlight and StarLight. Free of artificial lights found in big cities, there was nothing more beautiful to me than to gaze into heavens on a Moonlit Night, or looking out on the expansive night sky at ALL of the twinkling stars in the Milky Way Galaxy. Those times were special to me growing up in Brookstown, and I never forgot them to this very day. The house I grew up in watching the night sky was nearly lost save for the foresight of my father-Joe Braud.

G. Description Of Joe Braud And Lillian Luellen Pierce Braud's House In Brookstown

Unlike many other Brookstown Families, they did not live on a plantation by the beginning of the 20th Century. However, as I have indicated earlier, the F. Braud Plantation was started by the White Breaux Family Group, which immigrated from France, and migrated to the Louisiana Territory at the beginning of the 19th Century. That being so, because the Black Braud Family Group was a spinoff from the marriage of Edouard Breaux Jr and Celestine Breaux, who was an African Slave, they produced a son, namely, Theophile Braud, who was Joe Braud's father and my grandfather. Although this family connection, between the White Breaux Family Group and the Black Braud Family Group, did not mean the latter inherited any money from the profits generated by the F. Braud Plantation, the Braud Surname may have benefited Joe Braud and his family to acquire land, farm tools, and animals during a time in which domestic terrorism was an everyday, prevailing fact of life, for thousands of African-Americans, who lived on the Gravel Road and elsewhere throughout the South and North.

Thus, as I recall during my childhood, Joe Braud and Lillian Luellen Pierce Braud Family did not live on a plantation; we lived in one of the houses on the family estate. Being a progressive man with foresight, and realizing the land where the house his family lived in on the family estate did not belong to him because no succession of the family estate property had previously been done, and, more importantly, my father realized, at any time, one of his sibling heirs to the family estate could claim the land where his house was located. To prevent such an occurrence, Joe Braud went to the courthouse and had the portion of land where he built our Braud Family house and barn removed from the Braud Estate Property.

One of Joe Braud's brothers gave him the idea to take this action to avoid any future trouble.

For example, many years later, my father's preemptive, legal maneuver paid off because the levee system of the west bank of the Mississippi River had to be moved in the area where we lived in Brookstown. One of my father's brothers lived in the house of my grandparents, and it was the first house on the Braud Property Estate, which was next to Highway 18 and the levee. Therefore, when it came time to move the levee, my father's brother had to move the house farther back on the Braud Property Estate. My father envisioned the day would come when this levee development would impact the latter. This was the reason years earlier that Joe Braud had our portion of the land removed from the Braud Property Estate in the courthouse. If he had neglected to take this action, my uncle would have made my mother and her children move our house. He tried to do just that, but legally he could not.

Ultimately, our house was the first house on the estate, and my distraught uncle had to have the house where he lived rolled behind our barn. He had a fit, but there was nothing he could do.

Joe Braud and Lillian Luellen Pierce Braud's house, as I recall, had two rooms with high ceilings, a kitchen that was separated from the house by a small porch. The front porch extended the width of the two rooms, and there were two posts on each side with center steps. The structure was old and there was a wooden cistern on one side with a draining trough from the roof, which syphoned the water from the roof when it rained. In order to get to the house from the Gravel Road, we had to go down the church lane. Ordinarily, we should have been able to pass through the family house yard in front of us, but I had a very funny acting uncle that lived in the family house. This is the one I mentioned earlier who tried to get my parents to move their house. Traveling from the Gravel Road to our house was a few blocks. When it rained, there was a lot of mud from the horses, wagons, and livestock. Our house was functional for several years, regarding its size; however, as my parents produced more children, a larger house was needed to accommodate more people.

After a few years, my father built a house that was located even farther down the lane. By that time, there were five children and we needed a larger house. I cannot remember who helped my father build his new house; I do know it was completed by the early 1930s. Our new house had five rooms and a kitchen. It was very modern for the time. Detached from our new house was a large barn in which my father stored food and his farm equipment.

H. Farm Equipment And Barn Behind Our House

Joe Braud and Lillian Luellan Pierce Braud had three or four horses that the former used for his farming. The animals were used to till the soil for raising rice, corn, sweet potatoes, snap beans, butter beans, cabbage, peanuts and so forth. We had had a large barn that had three sections. There was the section where sweet potatoes, white potatoes, and beans were stored for the winter months. The middle section is where corn, dried beans, and farm equipment were stored. And, the third section had stalls and shelter for the animals and livestock. There was a large yard, or lot, where the horses, cows, and hogs grazed.

Our hogs were raised for meat and lard (This oil is derived from pork by frying the outer layer of a slaughtered hog to make Hog Cracklins; the residual oil is allowed to cool and turn a white color. African-Americans used lard, for decades, to cook many of their foods. Over consumption of lard may cause unintended health issues). The hogs were kept in "pens," and every winter one or two of them were killed by a knife piercing their hearts. From the hog, we got cracklins, liver sausage, blood sausage (In southwest Louisiana, the Acadians and Black Peoples call it Boudin), pork chops, pork roast and so forth. There was a smokehouse where the meats were stored. In addition, we had cows for milk, and we made butter (The crème, or fat, that formed on the surface of the milk was skimmed off and saved; when enough was accumulated, it was placed in a churn and turned or shaken until butter formed), creme cheese, and so on. We also had steers, or young bulls, to take to the butcher shop in the winter, out of which was made ground meat, steaks, and other meat cuts. The butcher shop would package the meat for storage. There were also chickens, geese, guineas, and ducks. Thus, we were never without food, or any of the basic comforts of life. We thought we were good livers, and we even had a phonograph.

By the time I was ten years old, rice was the dominant crop grown by farmers in my Brookstown area. However, due to the "grassing problem," its prominence rapidly waned during my teen years, and it was eventually overtaken by sugarcane, which became the dominant cash crop. The only thing the farmers were unable to mechanize was grassing rice. They did have a trial on poisoning the grass and preserving the rice; however, that system was not economically feasible, and it was eventually cancelled. That is, the farmers stopped raising rice in my area and began the widespread cultivation of sugarcane.

I. Rise Of Wide-Scale Sugarcane Production During My Childhood Years

The Sugarcane Industry was mechanized by this time. Tractors and attachments were used to till the soil, harrow, construct rows, and so forth. Then, the farmers developed the sugarcane planter, sugarcane cutter, sugarcane stackers, derricks, etc. There was also an apparatus for loading the sugarcane on the tractor-wagons, tractor trailer trucks and so on. Thus, very few workers were needed. Workers needed for a farm to be productive were cut down fifty or sixtyfold. Unlike Rice Production, sugarcane does not require flooding the field to grow.

Briefly, I remember to produce sugarcane, the preparation of the soil would start in August and continue through February each year. That is, for new crops, the land was plowed, harrowed, and then built into rows using tractors. Later, pieces, or individual stalks, of sugarcane were placed in the trench opened in the top of each row. Afterwards, a tractor would pass a roller, which is shaped like a solid iron cylinder, and cover the stalks of individual sugarcane beneath the tilled soil. During earlier years before I was born, this method of sugarcane planting was done by humans; however, I have already mentioned, machines were used to plant the sugarcane after the soil was tilled, from beginning to the end of the process.

In early spring, the buried sugarcane began to germinate and sprout up through the soil. Sugarcane grows relatively fast depending on the variety. The rows, which consisted of thousands of acres of sugarcane, were cultivated with tractors with plows, or choppers attached, several times a year. During the early stage of the growth of the sugarcane, for example, when it reached a height of two or three feet, a fertilizer was applied. Once the sugarcane harvest was completed, its stubble remained in the ground, and the farmer did not have to plant new sugarcane stalks for several years.

The sugarcane harvest time is from the last of September to December. The intent is to have all sugarcane cut before the first freeze. Once sugarcane freezes, and thaws to a normal temperature, it spoils, or turn sour. As it was, during the early years of Sugarcane Production, the White Farmers had gangs, usually Black People, for cutting sugarcane. The latter consisted of topping, or cutting the narrow head off of the sugarcane stalk, removing dead leaves, and placing the sugarcane stalks in rows. Usually, the cut stalks were laid down in a horizontal manner across two rows. Sometimes the White Farmers would burn the dead leaves on the sugarcane stalks. At times, there was smoke pollution, in the air, all over the Brookstown area and others. Controlled fires would blaze, which burned the dried leaves off of the sugarcane stalks, from one end of long rows to the other. Pray that on the day of the burning, the wind did not blow in the direction of the village, or town, where I lived and other residents. The smoke pollution would cause many respiratory infections, especially it would inflame the sinus.

Once the sugarcane burning was done, and in order for the White Farmers to harvest their sugarcane, they used, literally speaking, Black Gangs and others, who would manually load the tractor wagons with the sugarcane stalks, and then they were taken to a designated area near the Gravel Road. In a short time, the White Farmers got machines that were able to raise the sugarcane stalks to the tractor wagons, and then it was taken to a designated area. The sugarcane stalks were then lifted by a derrick and transferred to a tractor trailer (Commonly known as an 18-Wheeler) Truck. After the tractor trailer truck was loaded, the driver would transport the sugarcane to the local sugar mill. The tractor trailer trucks would transport the the sugarcane stalks directly to the sugar mill.

Along the Gravel Road, there were several sugar mills where the tractor-wagons and tractor trailer trucks carried the loads of sugarcane stalks. When the loads arrived at the sugar mills, derricks unloaded the tractor-wagons and tractor trailer trucks; the sugarcane stalks were downloaded onto a conveyor belt that carried the stalks into the sugar mills. At this point, the sugarcane stalks were washed, and then they entered into massive grinders, where the juice inside of the sugarcane stalk was separated from the stalk itself. The liquid was then channeled into large boilers, and when subjected to various temperatures, molasses, brown sugar, and white sugar were produced for the American and International Marketplaces. The crushed sugarcane stalks were carried outside of the sugar mills, and placed in large, high piles. In southwest Louisiana, the crushed sugarcane stalks are called Bagas, which works good as a fertilizer in vegetable gardens and so forth. Over a period of time, the Bagas would turn into "Black Colored Dirt." This is an excellent fertilizer for vegetable gardens because it makes the plants more vigorous in size and color.

While Sugarcane Production supplanted Rice Production as the primary cash crop along the Gravel Road, although Rice was still grown to some degree during my childhood, and as this change was taking place, I started elementary school in 1931. I was five years old.

J. Brookstown And Education Opportunity For Black People By The Early 1930s

As I previously mentioned, it was a generalized education policy of the Slaveholding Families throughout the South, both before and after the American Civil War, that Black People, and other people of color, were forbidden to learn how to *read and write*. Legalized de facto segregation, underpinned by *Systematic Racism*, whose origin is in the American Constitution itself, created the *Separate But Equal Policy*, which established educational institutions, at all levels of education, which provided Black People, and other people of color, with an *inferior education* that characterized them as being inferior human beings, and simultaneously relegated many Black People in the South, and along the Louisiana River Road, to a second class citizenship status. The availability of education to me on the Gravel Road was no exception.

Because of the poor quality of public education in Brookstown by 1931, and thankfully, Joe Braud and Lillian Luellen Pierce Braud recognized its inferior quality, I began the First Grade in the New Orleans, LA Public School System. Nevertheless, for many of my peers, the public school available to them was a one-room building on the side of a ditch, which was located on the property of one of the White Farmers where most Black People on the Gravel Road attended public school. This was school for so-called Colored Children. The building was open and there were only two teachers, namely, Mary Alice Villavaso, who was Leontine Braud's daughter and Leola Washington. They taught the Colored Children to the sixth grade. Consistent with the Separate But Equal education Policy mentioned earlier, about two blocks away was a moderate size public school for White Children. It was built like a schoolhouse. It had six to eight classrooms and two offices. There was also adequate space for a playground. The one-room Colored School was not large enough to accommodate the number of Colored Children, who desperately needed an education to combat widespread illiteracy by the turn of the Twentieth Century.

If it was not for my Braud Family Group, I would have been lost somewhere in this Separate But Equal Educational Game. Fortunately, Beverly Braud and I attended public school in New Orleans, LA. We lived with my mother's three sisters, namely, Leah Pierce, Evelyn Pierce, and Mary Augustine Pierce (Aunt Leah moved into the house when I was in the Fifth Grade). They lived at 7820 Olive Street in the Gert Town Area near Xavier University. The former was an Adult Education Teacher and Evelyn Pierce was a Public School Teacher by 1931. For me, being in the household of my two loving Aunts as a First Grader was special; I had intimate contact with two educated relatives, which inspired confidence in me that I could also excel in education. For example, by the time I was four years old, I had started reading; I could read one children book I remember called Bob and Nancy. By five years old, I was reading the local New Orleans, LA newspapers, namely, Times Picayune and the State's Item. I remember reading newspaper stories about New Orleans, LA Mayor Chip Morrison and the New Orleans International Airport, at the time. Thus, living in New Orleans, LA with my two Aunts exposed me to a whole New World, which many of my peers on the Gravel Road could only imagine what it would feel like living and attending public school in New Orleans, LA.

Moreover, my Aunt Leah Pierce Argieard had a "special power" she shared with me, before I started the first grade and for years after I started public school. My Aunt Leah would regularly sit me down at her feet, and she would talk to me in a way I had never heard anyone speak before, including my own parents. Aunt Leah would not confine her information-sharing to what was happening in 1931 New Orleans, LA, but, interestingly, she talked about what life was going to be 70 years down the road from the present day. As I listened to her, I wondered to myself "How does Aunt Leah know these things she is talking about?" The central theme, or thread, that always tied everything together that she talked about was education. She constantly emphasized to me that education has a power, or key, that can unlock any door faced by people. Most of what Aunt Leah shared resonated with me in my "gut" I knew she was right; I was five years old listening to her message; and, I came to the conclusion that I would remember her teachings as I proceed down the road on my life journey. I had to live and have experiences to test the truth in the power of her educational messages she shared with me about the future, and where I fit in it. How my Aunt Leah's educational messages helped me to develop my life, beginning in elementary school in New Orleans, LA, is addressed in detail shortly.

Presently, I intend to give a flavor of what social life was like in Brookstown during the 1930s. In many regards, I must say, as a young boy growing up on the Gravel Road, it was a very interesting laboratory in which I observed how the legacy of the American Slavery Institution affected the behavior of some Brookstown residents. Surely, there were many observations omitted here because I did not witness them. I will share a few of the anomalies and others that I witnessed with my own eyes.

CHAPTER VIII

SOCIAL LIFE IN BROOKSTOWN AND SURROUNDING VILLAGES

Brookstown was home then, and it is still my home, although I have journeyed many miles away from it since I was born in 1926; but, quite frankly speaking, it still holds fond memories in my mind, although I have not lived there continuously since my childhood came to an end in 1943. Social life, for Black People in Brookstown during the early 1930s, was filled with a checkerboard of oddities. The legacy of the American Slavery Institution was still fresh in the minds of many Black People at the time, who were descendants of African Slaves.

A. Getting To The One-Room School On Side Of A Ditch

For most White People, who had anything to do with making it possible for Black People to get an education, did not consider the latter a priority. At best, those Black Children, who attended school had to walk to get to a one-room building. At best, those Black Children, who attended public school, had to walk to small halls and churches in various communities. In Brookstown, there was a small hall on the side of a ditch on Gerald Roberts Property near his store. I do not remember its name. However, in other communities like Jamestown, some Black Children attended public school at Help Hand Hall. Burton Lane had Good America Hall. A-Bend had a public school called A-Bend Benevolent Hall. And, in Pair Tree, there was a small schoolhouse that was located near the railroad track.

Sometimes the Black Children had to walk in the rain and cold. Oftentimes, they walked in mud to get to school in the communities I mentioned earlier. In Brookstown, there was an area where a small building stood next to the railroad tract that was used as an elementary school for Colored Children. I remember the principal of the school was a woman name Zenovia Love.

Moreover, in Brookstown, there was an area about one-and one-half miles from the Gravel Road where the railroad passed through. That small area was called a "Section," and there was a small house and maintenance building located in it. One of the families, who had children that attended the school by the ditch lived by the railroad tract. The father in the family worked for the railroad company. That is, he helped to maintain the railroad tracts and others in the "Section." It was like a small "Roundhouse." This father, and others, worked to keep the freight trains operating so the White Farmers Rice and Sugarcane, and other products, could be transported out of Brookstown to their intended markets. Obviously, the workingman did not share fairly in the revenue the White Owners of the railroad received for their transport services. They were always faced with more hard times to survive.

To get to school, the family(s) with children, who lived near the railroad tract, had to walk about two miles a day on a 'dirt road' to get to school. Once they reached this location, they had to walk another two miles, from the one-room schoolhouse, to get back home. This was not unique, but a very common practice for Black Children, who lived in the Brookstown area, and surrounding communities. What kind of education would one expect Black Children to receive under this social condition? Of course, everyone would stand and applaud any person who overcame this obstacle and received an education of some kind. But, the fact is, not many would be able to tolerate the hardship of walking this far to get to school every day. Many, as most White People hoped at the time, would give up, and dropout of school. Many did dropout, and others never attended school due to the walking distance. There were other oddities that caught my attention while growing up on the Gravel Road.

B. Two men Walking In Opposite Directions

Another situation that I thought was unusual caught my attention because of the frequency of its occurrence. There were two men, who met each other on the Gravel Road two or three times a week. Each man was traveling in opposite directions. For all intent and purposes, they chatted and were very cordial to each other. The irony of the situation is they were going to each other's house. The two men had six or seven children, but there seemingly was no crossover. That is, all of the children looked like the right man. While in many respects, this ordeal leaves much to consider in one's imagination; however, given the legacy of the American Slavery Institution on the Gravel Road, it can certainly be understood what such a sustained, generational impact it must have had on the psyche of thousands of Black People. This oddity was, no doubt, a physical manifestation of the unhealed biography tapes passed down through the generations, which was a part of the social life of the Brookstown I remember as a boy growing up there. Such an oddity will continue to be passed down through more generations until it is intentionally healed by the person's whose mind it resides inside of. There were other oddities that made up the fabric of the social life of Brookstown.

C. Christmas Gift Child And The Stepfather

I was always paying attention to my surroundings. Some things happen in people's lives, regardless of their age, and it flies right over their head, or go in one ear and exit the other as fast it came in. I was an inquisitive young boy filled with more than my share of curiosity. This trait would serve me well throughout my adult life. Before this time came, I continued to observe everything I could in front of me, both overtly and covertly.

For instance, there was a couple that had three grown children. Then suddenly, late in life the wife got pregnant. And, when the child was born, they named the child *Christmas Gift*. Imagine for yourself. Have you ever known in your lifetime parents who named their child Christmas Gift? I thought to myself I would not give any child of mine this odd identity. Would you? All I can figure is because the mother became pregnant later in her life, the parents were overjoyed all went well with the pregnancy and childbirth that the latter had to be a Christmas Gift. My explanation may seem as strange as the Christmas Gift name itself. But, this was part of the social life in Brookstown. Adding to its color was the stepfather.

The stepfather raised a male child to manhood. The stepfather would visit the stepson's house, and somewhere down the line, the stepdaughter-in-law had a child, who was the "spitting image" of the stepfather-in-law. That, to say the least, was very interesting! This made me wonder how these social relations came about in real time? What was the moral code? Or, lack-thereof-of one? My imagination kept a smile on my face even when times got hard working in the field. And, there were more oddities to go along with this one.

D. Powerful Women And Collection Day On The Gravel Road

There were also seemingly powerful women, who lived along the Gravel Road. One woman had a husband and there were three or four other men that she had living in the same house (They may have been her husbands also?). All of the husbands worked. The main husband worked in a city, and he would return home on the weekends. From all indications, there were no friction in the house. It may seem like there was a deterioration in the social fabric of the Black Family Household during this period; however, if the devastating affects the American Slavery Institution had on the Black family are taken into consideration, it follows what I observed in the household with the woman who had several men living in the same house, is relatively speaking, very mild, and on a scale of one to ten, family instability would be at a number 1, where one is low and ten is extremely high.

In addition, another lady had a husband, and she would travel up and down the *Gravel Road* to collect "goodies" from three or four other men. She made no bones, or excuses, about collecting from those men. I have not forgotten how much unpaid compensation the White Slaveholder collected from the unpaid labor of the African Slaves for 244 years. This collection far exceeded any that the Black Woman, who traveled up and down the Gravel Road, received. Apparently, the Black Woman's Collections were a drop in the bucket.

There was another family with strange occurrences. A husband and wife had five or six children, but none of the children looked like the father. Instead, they were the spitting image of another man. This situation was one that families had encountered during slavery. It was being repeated in Brookstown and surrounding villages several generations after the formal slave institution came to a close in 1865. Actually, one does not have to look too hard to find this situation among us in 2021. Its occurrence is like inertia; if nothing is done to throw an object off of its course in outer space, it will continue to move in the same direction endlessly. Such is the case with the husband, who was the father of five or six children, and none of them looked him; but, to the contrary, all of them look exactly like another man. If there is no intervention, this situation will continue to repeat itself, from one generation to the next.

These social oddities were widespread in Brookstown and surrounding villages during the 1930s. They are reflective of some of the challenges Black Families were confronted with four generations after the American Civil War. Much of the social life I grew up in the midst of in Brookstown and surrounding communities had an odor of the legacy of the American Slavery Institution. The inclusion of the foregoing information offers the reader a small glimpse into the social and economic inertia that many residents were faced with during my childhood. In my case, my Pierce-Braud Family Group guided me through this maze, which many of my peers were unable to escape. Although I witnessed this social life in Brookstown, my feet were set upon an educational path, which, fortunately, would play a significant part in breaking the stranglehold of illiteracy in my community in later years.

In addition, many of the local residents wanted to "go to town" and shop on Saturday to buy some goods they could not get at Gerra's local grocery store, or others, in the area where they lived. Some residents took a bus to Donaldsonville, LA on the weekend to shop for a wider selection of items.

E. Jitney Bus Ride Up And Down The Gravel Road To Donaldsonville, LA

For clarification, a Jitney Bus is one that transports passengers over a regular route on a flexible schedule. In Brookstown and surrounding villages, a truck would come to a specified location in the early morning, which would transport Black People to work in the Rice and Sugarcane Fields. On weekends, some local residents would walk to a certain location and wait for Mr. Joseph Robinson's Jitney Bus. He would transport his passengers, for a small fee, up and down the Gravel Road.

Mr. Robinson brought people to and from all the little settlements along the Gravel Road to the small township known as Donaldsonville, LA. The latter was a little town that had a few department stores, food stores, lumber companies, railroad station, banks, schools, fairgrounds, and one or two honky tonks and so forth. The bus driver was married, but another woman made the trips up and down the Gravel Road with the bus driver. The bus schedule was in late morning and in the evening during the week. On Saturdays, there were four or five trips a day. On Saturday nights, there was always a late trip. One could talk to the bus driver and, if you were going to be late, he would always wait for you. If someone was going to the honky tonk, or hole in the wall, he or she would let Mr. Joseph Robinson know ahead of time. A designated place for late pick up would be agreed on, and everyone would go to the "hole in the wall" and have a good time. The farthest some Brookstown Residents ever traveled was the few miles to Donaldsonville, LA. This was the extent of how large their world was at the time. As I will explain to you, I have traveled all over the world, and, given the fact I grew up in Brookstown, I was not ever suppose to spread my wings that wide. The secret, sure enough, of what made my life experience so different from what might have been expected by others, was quietly formulated inside the Braud Family Group.

Before I made ten years old, I did not know exactly what was happening that made my life's outlook different from my peers. I would learn what the cause was soon. But, in the meantime, I continued to enjoy my childhood. One of the big events in Brookstown was what was known to ALL as Baptism.

F. "Big Sunday" Baptism Process Day And The March To The Mississippi River

Big Sunday Baptism was the main event that brought most of the Brookstown Residents, and those from other surrounding communities, together to celebrate, worship, and praise God. This major community affair occurred once per year; and, as I understand it, those persons selected to participate in the Big Sunday Baptism Celebration had to go through a ritual process. That is, those potential persons, who would be baptized,[98] had to pray over a period time, and they, at some point during this prayer period, would testify in church that God had spoken to them in some recognizable way. By testifying that God had spoken to them, during which the person would reveal to the church congregation how they were spoken to by God, the Pastor, Deacons, and Stewards would certify this or that person qualified to be baptized. This was a big event! Given ALL the hardship Black People faced on the Gravel Road presently, and during previous generations, and if someone selected that might qualify to be baptized was spoken to by God, this was a huge revelation that there was hope for a better life, for Black People on the Gravel Road, because God was watching over them.

The Baptism Process was not for everyone, but everyone thought it was for them. Some local residents went through it and they were baptized; others were not able, for some reason, to complete the Baptism Process. I tried to go through it, but I was not successful. One of my siblings-Geraldine Braud Bernard-completed the Baptism Process.

In effect, it was the baptism for the local Baptist church. The name of the church was Mt. Calvary Baptist Church located in Brookstown; it had a membership of roughly 200 people. The pastor was Rev. Daniel Jones. Generally, for each Baptism Process, an average of between three and eight candidates were pre-selected for baptism. The candidates would go into a semi-closed place where they would pray for several weeks. They would have varying 'travels' or visions they would have encountered while praying. There were always interpretations of the travels, or visions, throughout the period. Sometimes the candidates had a deacon or sister of the church that would be their counsel during the period. All candidates presented their travels and visions to the church congregation. Then, they would attend church on Sundays until the baptism. They had a scarf or other to denote that they were candidates for baptism. The word related to an upcoming Big Sunday Baptism spread throughout the Gravel Road like a raging wildfire.

---

[98] When a person is baptized with water, it is an act in which the one baptized commit oneself to be an obedient believer in God's Teachings in the Bible. During the Pre-Baptism Ritual Process, the seeker aims to repent his or her sins, and make a change to live a spiritual life. Selfishness, pride, and ego are placed before the Lord.

People came from near and far to witness the baptism. And, on the day of the Big Sunday Baptism, there was a very long procession, beginning at the church. The church's banner, or flag, was flown that day. Usually, the same two men always led the procession as they marched across the Gravel Road, and up one side of the Mississippi River Levee. The procession followed a pre-determined path. The marchers were led along a path slightly above horizontal; otherwise, if the path was a vertical march up the levee, some parishioners would not be able to ascend the steep climb directly up the levee. As the procession marched along the above horizontal-friendly path, the people would be singing such hymns as "Poor Mourner Got A Home," "At Last," and "Down By The Riverside." Their echoes could be heard for miles around! The fields were alive with the sounds of human voices.

Once the procession descended the other side of the levee, the baptism was performed in the Mississippi River. That is, the deacons of the church would have already found a suitable place on the bank of the Mississippi to conduct the baptism. Water depth, and other safety factors, had to be considered before a spot was chosen. They always tried to find an area on the bank of the river that was suitable to be roped off, and secured to posts that were placed soundly into the Earth. The area was usually twelve x twelve feet. The Ole Mississippi River usually had a tarnish, brown color (This was sediments being transported to the Gulf of Mexico to build the Louisiana Coast). The water was about five feet deep.

Within that secluded area, the minister was on one side, and the deacon was on the other side. Then, there were two more deacons between three and five feet from the minister. Two more men were stationed another two to three feet from the last set. In addition, there were two or three sets of deacons, and stewards that further lined the walkway.

The procession was sometimes a fourth to a half mile long. They marched from the lane beside the church, across the Gravel Road, and up the levee on a slant, carrying the flag and banners to the top. The minister and the deacon wore black trousers and a white shirts; the deaconess (A deaconess is the same as a steward) wore long white dresses; the baptismal candidates wore white; males wore white shirts and pants; females wore long white gowns and white head wraps. As they marched in single file, they sung the mentioned hymns. The procession marched on the top of the levee until they were near the baptismal area. Upon arrival, the leaders of the procession, who carried the church flags and banners, descended behind the levee along the battery (This was surplus dirt leftover by workers who did various jobs aimed at strengthening the Mississippi River Levee) to the roped off area. When they arrived at the roped off area, the pastor stood at the break of the water, and the deacons and deaconesses lined up. The church members, family, friends, guests and so forth formed an amphitheatre like arena. All of the baptismal candidates stood in line.

At this time, the pastor of the church would give the pre-baptismal sermon. Some of the deaconesses got happy, or filled with the Spirit, and began to shout. Some of the baptismal candidates also got happy and they were hard to contain. The pastor, deacon, and deaconesses treaded the water of the roped off area and made an aisle for the baptismal candidates to walk down to the minister. When they reached the place where he stood, they turned and their neck and back was placed on the arms of the minister and the head deacon. It was then that the minister placed his hand over the nose and face of the baptismal candidate. He then called their names and said "I baptize thee in the Name of the Father, Son, and the Holy Ghost." The candidate's head was then dipped in the water with "Amen." Some of the baptismal candidates reacted in varying ways; some got stiff; others shouted; and others had no special response.

After all of the baptismal candidates were baptized, they would be wrapped with blankets and so on, and taken to their homes, or some designated place to remove the wet, baptismal clothing they wore. At once, they would put on their post-baptismal garments. After which, the baptismal candidates would return to the church for the baptismal sermon and Lord's Supper commonly known as communion (This ritual consisted of a piece of cracker that symbolized Jesus' physical body, and the wine represented his blood). This ritual is as old as the Baptist church itself. Sometimes the pastor of the church gave the sermon, and, on some occasions, it was delivered by a guest minister.

Once the Big Sunday Baptismal Process' main activities were completed, they were followed with a baptismal dinner or reception in the church hall. There were times when the reception took place at one of the member's home. Beneath the surface of the Baptismal Process is where the true meaning of it resides. That is, on Big Sunday Baptismal Process

Day, the threads that bound Brookstown, and surrounding communities' families together were reaffirmed. Black People got a chance to talk to their neighbors about how they were doing, and what one neighbor could do to help another. Differences, open wounds, and festering feuds were variously discussed, and some active ones brought to the Big Sunday Baptismal Process Day were released by the time the closing receptions took place. Old friendships were reinforced, and new ones were formed.

The Big Sunday Baptismal Process Day was an annual routine affair. It had been going-on before I was born in 1926. And, it continued uninterrupted throughout my childhood in Brookstown.

Another event occurred in my life when I was five years old, namely, I received an educational revelation that would change Brookstown, the Gravel Road, and myself forever. Although I was too young to realize it at the time, an educational seed was planted in me that gave me a vision that I was destined to become a medical doctor, and through my efforts, more physicians would stream out of Brookstown like the Mississippi River had been flowing pass it for millenniums. In short, unlike any other village, settlement, town, or city in Louisiana, Brookstown, the home of the Pierce-Braud Family Group, would produce more medical doctors, and other highly trained professionals such as lawyers, doctors of philosophy, and nurses than anywhere else statewide during the last half of the 20th Century. Unless I tell you how this development got started, no one would believe it. Moreover, who would believe a young five year old boy received a message that would later change Brookstown, St. James Parish, the River Road, Charity Hospital in New Orleans, LA, and African-American Educational Achievement in medicine, academia, and, law in Louisiana forever?

G. Joseph Pierce Braud's Unlikely Early Inspiration To Become A Medical Doctor ?

When I was seven or eight years old, there was a medical doctor in the area that I would pass occasionally from a distance. I would get close enough to him to observe his unusual dress. It was very different at the time. Imagine the Gravel Road when it was hot and dry, the wind would stir up the dust. When it was rainy, or during the winter when it would rain quite frequently, the Gravel Road would oftentimes be muddy. With this as a backdrop, the medical doctor I am referring to always dressed in white clothing, i.e., hat, shirt, necktie, pants, coat, socks, and shoes, from head to feet-Always. Every time I saw him, whether it was raining, muddy, or a sunny day, the medical doctor would be dressed this way. No change!

I never said more than hello to him during those years-early 1930s. Nonetheless, I always said to myself that is what I would like to be when I grow up-a medical doctor. No doubt, the man dressed in all white clothes made a lasting impression on me. I thought "that must be a cool way to make a living wearing an all-white uniform." When I worked on the farm, I would get dirty; but, I thought, "if I have a white uniform on when I go to work, I would have to work on a job where my white uniform would not get dirty like the medical doctor's I first saw in my life who wore all-white clothes on the Gravel Road, and his never got dirty. The name of the medical doctor was Stephen Campbell, MD. Some of my peers saw Dr. Campbell dressed up in white clothes, but I wonder if any of them gave it a second thought how his white clothes were connected to his medical doctor profession? I gave it a second thought, and I turned the image of Dr. Campbell's white clothes into a vision, which I held onto and nurtured inside of myself even though my father was always proud to tell all of his friends that he was going to send me to Southern University to get a college degree in Agriculture.

As it was, my father continued to tell the family and friends that he was going to send me to college to study Agriculture. I would still say to myself that I was going to be a Medical Doctor again and again. Aristotle once remarked "What we repeatedly do, we become." I never voiced my feelings, but I would say to myself that I was going to be a Medical Doctor. There was one Black Medical Doctor, namely, Dr. John Harvey Lowery. His medical practice was located in Ascension Parish so I did not get a chance to see him in Brookstown. Dr. Lowery was the first Black Medical Doctor from this mentioned parish. I enjoyed thinking I would be the first one to come out of Brookstown in St. James Parish, and many others would follow in my footstep. I was going to be a trailblazer! Although my father was certain I was going to study Agriculture at Southern University because it is what he lived and breathed on the Gravel Road.

However, in the Pierce-Braud Family Group, I was fortunate be around relatives who were unafraid to think outside of the box. Thus, in this family group, especially on my mother's side, there was always talk and conversation going-on about education. As I mentioned earlier, there were several educators among my mother's siblings. One of my aunts taught Adult Education and another taught in one of the local school systems. There was the aunt that told us that she envisioned that it would take a good education to live well in years to come. She talked about people moving around in space; she envisioned the NASA Program nearly a half century before it came into existence. In addition, my aunt stressed that one should do his or her best in school because you can never tell what types of opportunities one will encounter in life. I learned these valuable lessons before I enrolled in the First Grade. By the time I was ready to go to elementary school, my mother sent me to live with her two sisters in New Orleans, LA so I could get a better education than the one I was suppose to receive in an overcrowded one-room school located on the side of a ditch near the railroad tract in Brookstown.

H. Danneel Elementary School Years In New Orleans, LA School District, 1931 To 1936

I moved in with my mother's three sisters. Leah Pierce Argieard lived at 3511 Audubon Street; Evelyn Pierce and Mary Augustine Pierce lived at 7820 Olive Street in the Gertown Section of New Orleans, LA near Xavier University. Aunt Leah moved into the house in Gertown when I was in the Fifth Grade. I was a long way from the Gravel Road; and, fortunately, I was being exposed to a whole new world. This was the perfect place for me to begin my elementary education. I enrolled at the nearby Danneel Elementary School.

It was 1931, and the Great depression was two years old by the time I was in the First Grade. Many people were thrown out of work. Some of them loss every possession they had, and many loss their minds too; and, others committed suicide in large numbers. While these and other social developments were taking place around the nation, I was blessed to be living in my aunts' household. And, they had jobs during the Great Depression. Table 1.19 shows the years I attended Danneel Elementary

School (DES) and the teachers who taught me, from First Grade to Sixth Grade.

Table 1.19 Danneel Elementary School Years From 1931 To 1936

Name	Teacher	Grade	Years
Danneel Elem. Sch.	Ms. Dumonee	1st	1931
DES	Ms. Landix	2nd	1932
DES	Ms. Ferris	3rd	1933
DES	Ms. Steel	4th	1934
DES	Ms. Reed	5th	1935
DES	Mr. Hart	6th	1936

Source: Author

I had a mixture of male and female teachers. The Danneel Elementary School had several rooms; a cafeteria; and a playground. It was designed the way you would imagine and elementary school should look. The Danneel Elementary School was more advanced and sophisticated than the one-room school I would have to attend, if I did not have the former as a valuable option. I entered the Danneel Elementary School knowing how to read for my age. Of course, I had a whole lot more to learn about each subject, I felt I was making good educational progress. As I recall, I was reading when I entered first grade. Seemingly, I did well in reading, spelling, and penmanship. I won all of the spelling matches in the school. I was excited to be doing well academically, and I had my Aunt Leah, Evelyn, and Mary to guide me when I had any homework that I needed help with understanding and completing for the next school day. I was in good health and absorbing as much information as I could from my teachers. I was a sponge soaking in everything put before me to learn. And, I was in excellent physical health all the time. When summer came, and school was out, I went back home to Brookstown in the country.

During the years I was enrolled at the Danneel Elementary School in New Orleans, LA, a new public school was built for the White Children to attend in Brookstown and Welcome, LA. They were bussed to their new school, which was much larger with more classrooms and other facilities such as a playground. When the White Children's new school opened, the public school they formerly attended was handed-down to the Black Children. There was nothing equal about the St. Louis School the Black Children inherited; however, it was separate. Interestingly, this school was painted white, and, for the first time, it resembled what an elementary school should look like. The St. Louis School had a principal and five or six teachers. Originally, the principal was a lady; a short time later, a male principal took her place. There were more Colored Children that had to go to that school, but there was no transportation. The Colored children had to walk long distances.

As I mentioned earlier, the White children were bussed to a new, modern school facility. Interestingly, as long as White Parents' Children were being bussed to keep them from attending public school with Colored Children, bussing was acceptable to them. However, when White Children were forced, by legal mandate, to attend school with Black Children toward the end of the 20th Century, White Parents rebelled vehemently against bussing. It was a bad thing! On the Gravel Road, during the early 1930s, Colored Children still had to walk long distances to attend the St. Louis School. The United States Supreme Court's Separate But Equal Ruling in the Plessey v. Ferguson Case, which was handed down in 1896, was very much *alive and well* on the Gravel Road. My first six years of elementary school went by pretty smoothly and productive.

I. St. Louis School Given To Black People Due To White Flight, 1935

By the time I was in the fifth grade at the Danneel Elementary School, the St. Louis School came into existence in Brookstown, which is the same location as Welcome, LA. My mother-Lillian Luellen Pierce Braud decided to enroll me in the school. Her decision to do so must have been influenced in part by the untimely loss of her husband-Joe Braud-who was my father. I will spend some time explaining some of the impacts the death of my father had on me and my Pierce-Braud Family Group shortly.

Meantime, Mary Alice Villavaso was the principal of the St. Louis School. I completed my seventh grade year there with some anxiety. As much trouble as most Black People have had with White People, who used "skin color" as a determinant of who is the superior and inferior race, I encountered some of the same color issues within the St. Louis School, regarding the fact that Principal Villavaso seemed to make decisions related to the student body based on the old White Supremacist Paradigm I mentioned earlier-skin color. Nevertheless, Principal Villavaso thought the world of me as a student, and she was very pleased with my academic performance.

As it was during my seventh grade year at the St. Louis School, for some reason the teachers in the school began to treat some students different from other students. There seemed to be cliques, favorites, and other unlawful acts. One situation stood out very vividly near the time of my graduation from the seventh grade. The students were in preparation for graduation when there were two or three students that the teachers and principal did not allow to graduate. They could not walk across the stage. In the group they let graduate, only one went on to attain further education. Eventually, the administration of the school was changed. Mrs. Mary Alice Villavaso was removed as principal of the St. Louis School, and this was a big change; the latter began to turn out better students. Given this internal strife going-on inside of the St. Louis School, my parents decided I should return to New Orleans, LA to continue my education. Table 1.20 below shows the teachers and the courses they taught me at J. W. Hoffman Junior High during my 8th and 9th grade years at this school.

J. J. W. Hoffman Junior High School Affectionately Known As The "Chicken Coup", 1938 To 1939

My fellow students and I called J.W. Hoffman the Chicken Coup because ALL of the buildings of the school were painted white. I imagine since there was no central air conditioning in the school, the white-colored paint on the buildings helped deflect the ultraviolet sunrays. Maybe all white colored building helped the air temperature in the classrooms to remain relatively cooler. On the other hand, could the all-white buildings be a message to me that "anything worth having, or good, is white; those with another color, like myself, is not good. At any rate, I feel I got a good education at J.W. Hoffman, one better than I would have obtained, if I did not have the Hoffman option, relatively speaking. My teachers are shown in Table 1.20 below.

Table 1.20 J.W. Hoffman Junior High In New Orleans, LA From 1938 To 1939

Name	Teacher	Subject	Grade	Year
J.W. Hoffman	Mr. Richards	Homeroom	8/9	1938/39
JWH	Ms. Perkins	English	8/9	1938/39
JWH	Mr. Wheeler	Carpentry	8/9	1938/39
JWH	Mr. Speaker	Auto Mechanic	8/9	1938/39
JWH	Mr. McGivens	Mathematics	8/9	1938/39
JWH	Mr. Lear	Algebra	8/9	1938/39
JWH	Mr. Meade Grant	Civics	8/9	1938/39
JWH	Ms. Lee	Literature	8/9	1938/39
JWH	Ms. Brazile	History	8/9	1938/39
JWH	Ms. McGregor	History	8/9	1938/39
JWH	Mr. Segue	Science	8/9	1938/39
JWH	Mr. English	Science	8/9	1938/39
JWH	Ms. Durnford	Mathematic	8/9	1938/39

Source: Author

My two years at J.W. Hoffman were productive. My grades were average. And, I was growing older, wiser, and being a good teenager, who suddenly knew more than anybody, including most adults. I made some growth spurts during my Middle School Years; I grew taller and my voice started to change noticeably. I guess my hormones became more activated around this time. But, I was cool, and I did not get into any trouble with my teachers or the girls. One embarrassing incident occurred in my science class; Mr. Segue ask me to explain how the Mercury in the barometer work to my science class. He was teaching his science class about Gallileo and Torricelli and the Barometer. I have not forgotten to this day what my response was when Mr. Segue called on me to explain the Mercury' behavior in it. I said "the mercury in the barometer had done gone down." I even had to laugh at myself later. Mercury does not go down in a barometer; it changes according to the prevailing, surrounding temperature; but, I said "it had done gone down." My Science Class got a kick out of my answer and so did I. This was not a Charlie Brown Class Clown Moment; I had to buckle down and study harder. Oh well, the lesson was learned. I had expected to finished high school in New Orleans, LA, but a strange incident occurred that set my aunts off like a Five

Alarm Fire! You know the sound-sirens blaring and lights blinking in all directions. Well, I already mentioned it is during the middle school years that one's hormones necessarily increase in boys and girls, which signals a time of change from pre-teens to teenage.

In a nutshell, my aunts made a mountain out of a grain of salt. This is how the imaginary mountain was constructed.

I attended school in New Orleans, LA until the tenth grade. As it was, I was performing very well academically. But, like Murphy Law warns, *if something can go wrong, it will.* During that summer going into my tenth grade year, or it might have been sometime during the beginning of that year, one of my "nosey" aunts went into my wallet and saw a prophylaxis. Rather than us having our usual sit-down discussion when an issue needed our attention, my mother was notified immediately to get me out of New Orleans, LA by any means necessary! Just the sight of the prophylaxis in my wallet was enough to Rush To Judgment that I was on the verge of becoming a player, or a ladies man. Actually, I didn't know what any of that lifestyle was all about. I was just trying to be "hip" like my male peers and nothing more. But, the prophylaxis was enough to cause my mother to "serve me papers" requesting that I come back home immediately, and finish my high school education in Brookstown on the Gravel Road. I did not resist; I followed my mother's order.

Reflecting on this incident over the years, I finally realized why my Aunt Leah responded so emotional about it. It was a test my aunts felt I needed to pass, if I was going to succeed in achieving my educational goals. If I imploded and became so angry that I would stop studying my lesson, and maybe dropout of school, then, I would have failed the test my aunts presented to me. I passed their test because I enrolled at the high school in Donaldsonville, LA, and I became one of its leading academic lights.

Therefore, by the start of my tenth grade year, I had changed schools, and I was on my way. What I learned from my Aunt Leah Pierce Argieard was solidly imprinted in my mind forever.

K. Lowery Training School In Donaldsonville, LA Located In Ascension Parish, 1940 To 1943

I enrolled in the Lowery Training School located in Donalsonville, LA in Ascension Parish. Table 1.21 shows the teachers and the subjects they taught me.

Table 1.21 Lowery Training School In Donaldsonville, LA

Name	Teacher	Subject	Grade	Year
Lowery Training School	E.C. Land, Prin.	N/A	N/A	1940/43
LTS	Ms. Oceola Chatters	Music	10-12	1940/43
LTS	Mr. Jackson	Science	10	1940/43
LTS	Mr. Hiram Martin	Carpentry	11	1940-43
LTS	Ms. Hazel Smith	Home Econ.	10-12	1940/43
LTS	Ms. Mattie Foster	English	10-12	1940/43
LTS	Ms. Vivian Franklin	Science	10-12	1940/43
LTS	Mr. Murray	Music	10-12	1940/43

Source: Author

When I got to the Lowery Training School, I took my first course in Biology. By the time I had finished that subject, I had been exposed to all of the major systems of the human body as well as those of some rodents, fish, and insects. When I entered college, after my graduation, I had no difficulty understanding the sciences. This was also true in graduate school and medical school. Mr. Jackson had prepared me very well! Moreover, in high school, I played football, and I had one of the leading parts in the high school play called "Leave It To Leander."

In order to get to the high school from where we lived on the Gravel Road, I had to walk four or five miles, which was going and coming from school daily, in order to get a ride to Donaldsonville, LA. There were many days that I ran the four or five miles. That is, from my Brookstown residence, I had to walk five miles one way to a designated location, which was near the cemetery, where a few days Henry Tribit and Rosemary Tribit came along in their automobile and gave me a ride to my destination. The next year, Earnest Pedescleaux would give me a ride to the Lowery Training

School. Remember, earlier I mentioned that my White Peers rode the bus to school. They did not have to run like I did to get to school; they did not have to worry about the weather that was a constant challenge; and, they did not have to get their shoes and clothes wet or dirty before they got to school. I should point-out here the Louisiana Department of Education did not award a "Diploma" to Black High School Graduates by 1943, the year I graduated from high school, Isn't that amazing?! In addition, this fact indicates how ingrained Systemic Racism still was in this Louisiana Institution as well as others.

What I went through to get my education was nothing short of miraculous! Many of my peers did not even try to get to school; they were already exhausted caused by the Separate But Equal System. My vision, to become a medical doctor later in my life, served to help me "keep on pushin" like my Pierce-Braud Family Group told me to do; I was determined to "movin on up." Curtis Mayfield, several decades later, wrote these lyrics in one of his hit songs. I was living his words nearly forty years earlier before he wrote them! With this steel determination to nurture my dream of becoming a medical doctor, and having to navigate through all of the obstacles thrown in my way by those White People, who cared less if I graduated from high school or not, I finished high school at the Lowery Training School in May 1943. That year, I received a certificate, which was neatly rolled in a cylindrical style, and it had a ribbon tied around it to prevent it from unrolling.

One of the biggest obstacles that unexpectedly stood in my way, or should I say, it was the "Grand Shock" of my childhood, which was the untimely passing of my father-Joe Braud-when I was at the tender age of ten years old. As a growing young boy, I thought I would have my father around to teach me the "ropes" about teenage and adult life. As fate would have it, this was not going to happen. How I managed to weather this storm came in the form of my mother's-Lillian Luelle n Pierce Braud-timely family leadership. Without her sustained intervention, my ship, and those of my siblings, could have drifted out on an angry ocean on a dangerous and uncharted course. How Lillian Luellan Pierce Braud made a course correction, after the passing of my father, laid the foundation for me to eventually become a medical doctor, and it gave Brookstown the *unique distinction* of producing more medical doctors, and other highly trained professionals such as lawyers, Doctors of Philosophy, Teachers, Nurses, and so forth, relative to any other families in Brookstown, White or Black etc., along the Louisiana River Road, or anywhere else in Louisiana. The one thing is for a village as small as Brookstown, a large number of medical doctors got their start there. It is worthwhile to reiterate here, from my previous discussions of the demographics on the River Road, that Louisiana led the nation in illiteracy after the American Civil War. How the Pierce-Braud Family Group turned this formidable obstacle, in addition to the loss of my father, into an Education Gold Standard is, by all accounts, nothing short of a miracle!

CHAPTER IX

JOSEPH PIERCE BRAUD'S CHILDHOOD WORLD TURNED UPSIDE DOWN IN 1936

A. Untimely And Sudden Death Of Joe Braud In 1936

From all indications, my father-Joe Braud-was a healthy man. He never complained about any mental or physical health problems[99]. Every day he customarily went about his farm work as planned. My mother was happy to see my father with his wide smile only he possessed. My mother loved it; she loved Joe Braud's work ethic; she loved the attention he gave to their seven children; and, at the end of the day, and after all of the work and questions were answered for that day, she knew Joe Braud was saving some of his attention for her. For fifteen years, and for at least ten of them, I recall this loving relationship in my household.

Although I have discussed my school years thus far, I have to rewind my tape, and go back to 1936 so I can capture the impact my father's death had on my mother, my siblings, and myself. By the time I was in the sixth grade at the Danneel Elementary School in 1936, something quite unexpectedly happened to my mother, myself, and my siblings. The Pierce-Braud Household, with me inside of it, was turned upside down in the matter of a blink of an eye. No one expected when we woke up, from our

---

[99] Sometime between 1915 and 1918, which was three years before my parents got married, Joe Braud was accidentally struck in the head by a falling can of grease on a dredge boat. He was employed at the time engaged in Mississippi River Levee work. After this accident, I was told my father was unconscious for several months. Joe Braud recovered from this accident, and by 1921, he married Lillian Luellan Pierce, and they raised seven children together in Brookstown before his death.

night sleep; put our clothes on; brushed out teeth; and ate our usual family breakfast, none of us could have imagined that before we went to bed that night, our father would pass away, which, no doubt, forever changed our household unlike any changes it had undergone before.

As I recall the day my father died in August 1936, I was 10 years old; I was a pre-teenage young boy, who was on the threshold of becoming a teenager, which was a time I would need my father's male energy to guide my footsteps through the second half of my childhood. Having no reason to think my solid relationship with my father would change when I became a teenager, I, no doubt, would have a lot of male questions that Joe Braud would have been best suited to answer for me. Since he took me almost everywhere he went during my pre-teen years, I am certain we would have many opportunities to talk with each other during the time we would continue to spend alone together.

On the August Day my father passed away, he was home alone with his seven children. My mother had gone to some type of meeting in one of the neighboring communities. All of us children were sitting around talking (Being school age children, most of our talking was about school-related things like who was the teacher we liked best, or who was a handsome boy and beautiful girl etc.), laughing, and playing. Suddenly, in the midst of our cheer, and sometimes temporary displeasure with a comment made by one of us about another, my father seemed to have passed-out. I immediately went to the backyard and put a bridle on one of the horses named Fannie, and I rode her as fast I could on the side of the Gravel Road to the doctor's office. In an excited voice of trouble, the doctor, after quickly learning from me what was transpiring, Dr. Stephen Campbell wasted no time; he quickly gathered his medical bag; and, then he got in his Model T Ford Car and rushed to my house, which was about two miles from his office. As before, I re-mounted my horse, and galloped full speed back to my house! My horse must have known something unusual was happening because she seemed to run faster than I ever remember riding her before. I am sure I rode the two miles back to my house in record-setting time; if I had a stop watch to time myself, no doubt, it would have affirmed my claim.

When Dr. Stephen Campbell arrived at the house, he said that my father had already died. My seven siblings were between one and thirteen years old. When Joe Braud passed way in August 1936, I went into a state of feeling melancholy; I felt sad; I felt Like I lost something that was irreplaceable like my right arm or eyesight; I felt down; some of my peers tried to cheer me up, and some of them helped me to break a smile about one thing or another. It would take me a little time to bounce back from the unchangeable thought Joe Braud was now, for the Pierce-Braud Family Group, only a warm and loving memory.

B. The 1929 Great Depression

The loss of my father coincided with the 1929 Great Depression. By 1936, the latter was only half way over. I was born in 1926, which was three years before the 1929 Great Depression started, and this meant my first ten tears of life paralleled one of the worst social and economic catastrophes hitherto known in America save the American Slavery Institution. This catastrophic event was caused by unwise investment transactions on Wall Street in New York City.

The American Civil War ended in 1865; and, slavery by another name continued well into the last half of the Twentieth Century. By the end of the American Slavery Institution, African Slaves loss a cumulative $4.3 Trillion in uncompensated labor. This money continued to pile-up, during the 64 years following the American Civil War, in the form of interest earned off of it by the American Elite Class, or the half-of-one percent of the American Population. With so much readily available money to invest, many Wall Street Investors, in their desire to earn higher profits off of uncompensated labor, made many unwise investments, which resulted in the 1929 Great Depression.

There was hardship and pain everywhere you looked, from New York City, New Orleans, LA, Los Angeles, CA to Washington, D C. Rural communities, both towns and villages, did not escape the wrath of the 1929 Great Depression. Working people everywhere, especially poor Whites and African-Americans, and other people of color, loss nearly everything they possessed; millions loss everything, and some committed suicide. Fortunately, living on the Gravel Road in Brookstown, I was connected to the land, and, with the knowledge I had gathered about "Seed To Table" from my father and mother, I felt I could produce food to survive. When my father died in August 1936, he left the Pierce-Braud Family Group in relatively good shape, regarding having a food source.

C. Pierce-Braud Family Safety Net Before And After Joe Braud's Death In August 1936

A few years before my father passed away, and as I mentioned earlier, he took the important step of transferring the Pierce-Braud Property into his name. When the Mississippi River Levee work got underway during the early or mid-1940s, some of the houses near the river had to be moved in order for the work on the levee to be completed. My father's brother-August Braud-made an attempt to get the house where we lived moved farther away from the Mississippi River Levee. August Braud was unsuccessful because Joe Braud had already gone to the courthouse and placed his part of the Braud Estate in his name. Thus, when he passed away in August 1936, my Uncle August Braud, could not make us move off of our land, or move our house, before or after my father passed away. This was one issue my Pierce-Braud Family did not have to be concerned about moving forward. In addition, because my father was a hard-working man, he left his family in good shape for the time being; that is, we had enough food saved in our barn, along with other tools to produce more when we needed it. But, I felt, and my siblings did to, that we needed a plan to guide the Pierce-Braud Family during, what was sure to become with the passing of my father, some difficult days ahead.

D. Lillian Luellen Pierce Braud's Strategic Family Development Plan

I was still too young to come up with this timely and important plan. Even if I had written one down on paper, I did not have the experience to get my other siblings to carry-out their part in it. What was needed was someone with very strong leadership qualities. And, we were blessed to have that someone with us all the time-my mother.

We had reached what I call a "crossroads." That is, it was usually Joe Braud's role to plan what was going to happen when it came to farming. As a result, and being initially caught off guard, my mother did not know what we were going to do. This is not unusual when some significant emotional shock occurs in one's life, which requires him or her to make a 100% change such as taking on totally new and different responsibilities, for the very first time. For example, my mother did not work and she did not have any special skills. She, of course, would prove me wrong. My mother was also thrusted unexpectedly into a new role during the waning years of The 1929 Great Depression. There was not a lot of money available to anyone on the Gravel Road, or elsewhere especially if you were an African-American, during that period. Therefore, we had to put together the things we had at our disposal. Without a loud drumroll, Lillian Luellan Pierce Braud introduced her Strategic Family Development Plan in 1936, and it would remain in effect for the next 22 years. As new family life inputs demanded that her plan change, she remained flexible and recommended a new action step whenever a different time required an adjustment be made to it.

a. Sustainability

My mother said it was best that we get rid of the excess livestock because that required extra feed to maintain. Before this modern idea called sustainability came along in the early 2000s, Lillian Luellen Pierce Braud was already practicing it in our Pierce-Braud Family. My mother was teaching my siblings and I the *importance of sustainability* 86 years before it became a household word in government, education, business, and environmental settings. No doubt, this was one of Lillian Luellen Pierce-Braud special skills. Along this line of thinking, we also disposed of some of the farm equipment. In all, we downsized our operation in the areas of livestock and farm equipment. There was no need to carry a large inventory with Joe Braud no longer around to use them. My mother built into our Strategic Family Development Plan a Food Acquisition Component.

b. Food Acquisition And Evariste "Fray" Washington Commitment

After downsizing, we still had to plan farther ahead. We had the barn, two horses, wagon, two cows, hogs, chickens, Guineas, ducks, and Geese. My mother stated that she would grow a garden to supply us with vegetables. There was also an uncle that talked with us and promised that he would see that we got a load of corn and a load of sweet potatoes every year to help take us through the winter months. That uncle was my father's sister-Celestine Braud-Washington's-husband, namely, Evariste "Fray" Washington. That was a big sacrifice on his family because he had twelve children. No doubt, this philanthropy was driven by the family values brought from France by Vincent Breault several generations earlier. Obviously, there was a strong bond between Lillian Luellen Pierce Braud and Celestine Braud-Washington manifested by the latter coming to the aid of her sister during her critical time of need.

Evariste "Fray" Washington lived on one of the plantations, namely, Salsburg, where he worked and, in addition, he farmed on the side. He lived next door to the "Big House-Livermouth." The family in the big house had a son who was very friendly. His name was "Geeto," who was the son of the owner of the Salsburg Plantation. Whenever I visited my Uncle Fray's home, that little fellow would always come over to play with me. We were 10 years old. There were times, I remember, when we had our disagreements, but it was never anything serious. My Aunt Celestine Braud-Washington use to get upset because she did not want me to leave her house. I imagine she did not want me to leave her eyesight because, after all, social relations between White and Black People, in 1936, were still saturated with racial inequality(s). However, there I was playing with the slave master's son like slavery never existed on the River Road. Nevertheless, the little fellow would always find me. We were about the same age as I mentioned earlier. My friendship with "Geeto" did not translate into any particular favors offered to my Pierce-Braud Family Group. It was a daily struggle to survive, although we had slightly more of the basic necessities than most of our Brookstown Peers. In fact, my family group went on welfare in 1936.

c. Aid To Families With Dependent Children (AFDC) Recipient In 1936

We had a steady food supply chain thanks to "Fray," and our Food Acquisition Component was stable. During this time, the Pierce-Braud Family Group, including all of my siblings, would get together regularly to decide what and how we were going to do things. It was during this period we got on welfare, or Aid To Families With Dependent Children. The welfare organization gave the eight of us $18 per month(!) in addition to commodities such as cheese, grits, and dried milk. The $18 per month meant each one of us had $2.25 to live on for this time period. Yet, by 1860, as I previously indicated, two-thirds of the millionaires in the United States lived on the River Road at that time and thereafter. In light of the challenges my mother faced while raising her family, she was able to develop her Strategic Family Development Plan, and using leadership skills I did not know she had, ALL-of her children became willing stakeholders in it. I do not know if any other Brookstown Families setup a plan like ours', which laid the foundation that eventually produced more medical doctors whose DNA is forever linked to a place with such a small number of people. By 1936, the total population of Brookstown, on a good day, was 300 or less. Lillian Luellen Pierce-Braud's Strategic Family Development Plan consisted of five interrelated components.

E. Five Components Of The Strategic Family Development Plan In 1936

The success of any plan is directly dependent on its practical application toward solving the immediate problems faced by the people whom the plan was setup to assist. Ultimately, the best laid out plan usually fails, if the people who have to implement it are not *disciplined*. Instant gratification has been the downfall of countless good plans, which fail because its workers fall prey to *impatience*. The Pierce-Braud Strategic Family Development Plan consisted of the following:

- Everyone would go to school come hell or high water,
- Monies from the welfare (AFDC) would go toward buying shoes and clothing,
- Every summer we would (a) scrap rice from the rice fields and (b) scrap white potatoes (Spuds) from the White Farmers Fields after they had harvest their crops (c) pick berries, etc.,
- I would grass rice or work for the truck gardener (This was a farming entity that raised Turnips, peas, butterbeans, okra, and peanuts for market), and
- I would work at the Rice Thrasher

Every component identified above served the primary one, which was ALL of my siblings would go to public school and college. This was the "super glue" that held the plan together. My mother knew if she could get one sibling through public school and college, this would generate funds to help the next older sister or brother to do the same and so forth. The end goal was to produce an educational legacy, which, surprisingly, would be unmatched by any White or Black Family on the River Road, or elsewhere in Louisiana or the nation. That being so, we wasted no time implementing my mother's plan. It looked good on paper, and the words were easier said than done. We had to implement our plan.

F. Scrapping Rice And Irish Potatoes During 1936 And Thereafter

We had the two horses and the wagon to use whenever we went out to scrap rice, potatoes, peanuts, and so forth. The horses and the wagon would remain on the headland, or if we were near the house, they would stay at home until we would get a load. It was always amazing that other people in the community would tell their folk to get to the fields before Ms. Lillian's children because we could scrap ten times more and faster than anyone of the others. We were so proficient with scrapping rice that we would have our half day at the main White Farmer's Rice Thrasher to thrash our rice. Our scrapping for the summer would always be between ten and twenty sacks of rice. Scrapped rice is usually without any foreign seeds and so forth, and it is excellent for planting. However, we would have rice for our family and we gave to others in the community during the winter months. We never had to buy rice for several years at a time. Sometimes the White Rice Farmers would buy a few sacks of our rice to conduct experiments at the beginning of the rice growing season. There was also a nearby "rice mill" where we could have the rice processed; that is, it would remove the husk. The cover of the rice seed is removed and it is called "bran." Bran is fed to hogs to improve the meat, especially the ones in the pen for slaughter in the winter time. We used the same approach when we scrapped Irish Potato Spuds, peanuts, and so forth. We always had enough rice and potatoes for the entire years, or until the next season. All of those foodstuffs were stored in our barn.

In addition, throughout the year, my mother would grow snapbeans, butterbeans, peas, okra, tomatoes, cucumbers, cantaloupes, melons, and so forth in the vegetable garden. Thus, we could have fresh, as well as, canned vegetables all year. My mother also raised the chickens, collected their eggs, geese, ducks, and guineas. Again, we were able to supply the neighbors, friends, and less fortunate people with all types of food throughout the year. Interestingly, because of my Pierce-Braud Family Group Plan, many people in the community, and nearby surrounding area, would always say that we were "well-off." Imagine that? I was ten years old, and I had just loss my father. I was far from being well-off, materially speaking. But, no one should forget the human toll the American Slavery Institution had on the physical and mental well-being of many descendants of African Slaves, who were still feeling the social limitations of this system during the 1930s.

All-in-all, our source of monies came from the welfare program called Aid To Families With Dependent Children, and from what I could earn working, or from what members of the family were able to donate. Though monies were limited, not one of my sisters, brother, or me, ever missed a day of school, unless there was an illness, which was rare. No one was ever without clothes or shoes. Whatever activity either of my siblings wanted to participate in, we could without difficulty. More importantly, my Pierce-Braud Family Group realized it was sustainable as long as each one of my siblings followed the disciplined path my mother's Strategic Family Development Plan demanded of me and my siblings. As long as we followed the plan, we were, in fact, well-off!

G. Shoe Shine Boy On Carrollton Street And Tulane Avenue In New Orleans, LA In 1938

I was enrolled at J.W. Hoffman Junior High in 1938, and on weekends, several of my good friends and I would walk down to Carrollton Street and Tulane Avenue to shine shoes. Charles Nero and Clarence Nero, both brothers, and I got together and found us a spot to shine White Males' shoes, who were either coming to attend a New Orleans Pelicans Minor League Baseball Game, or leaving the game after it was over. It is necessary to point-out here that segregation was on full display, from the first pitch to the last out in the 9th Inning. The baseball players were ALL WHITE. The baseball stadium was located in Haneman Park. Segregation did not bother me; I was in the midst of a stream of paying customers, and my Pierce-Braud Family Group could use the money I earned toward the upkeep of my family household. It should be kept in mind that every since I was around five years old, Dr. Stephen Campbell, the White Medical Doctor, who dressed every day in all white clothes, had already planted the seed in my mind that I wanted to be a medical doctor when I grow up. So, shining the "Man's" shoes did not bother me at the time. My dream was alive and well to attend medical school. I trusted the process, and shining shoes was only a small part of it. After my father passed away unexpectedly, I was thrusted into the role of being the "man" in the house by the time I reached the tender age of ten years old.

During a typical baseball game day, I earned between $.10 and $.25 to shine a pair of shoes. On average, I earned $2 to $3 dollars for my days' work. The Nero Brothers and I had to be careful because there were some older boys, who checked us out, from a distance, when we were shining shoes. Their intention was to rob us of our money on our way back home. But, we knew their game so we told our parents to come to the New Orleans Pelicans Stadium, at a certain pre-determined time, to get the money we made so the "bad boys" would not take it away from us. I shined shoes regularly during the two years I was enrolled at J.W. Hoffman Junior High. As I already mentioned earlier, I left the latter and enrolled at the Lowery Training School during my high school years. I graduated in May 1943.

I remained true to our family sustainability plan throughout my junior high and high school years.

H. Stevedore Work Removing Mud From The Hole Of Cargo Ships In New Orleans, LA During The Summer 1943

After I graduated from high school, and during the summer 1943, I got a job with a stevedoring company in New Orleans, LA working in the hole of cargo ships. Briefly, the "hole" is an opening in the cargo ship's bow, which is beneath the surface of the water. The purpose of the "hole" is to allow water to pass through the ship so it will not tilt over when traveling through rough seas. The water in the bow of the cargo ship has sediments in it, and, over time, some of it accumulates on the base of the ship. The sediments eventually turn into mud, and it must be removed from the bottom of the cargo ship. If it is not removed, eventually the wet mud will cause the metal of the hull of the cargo ship to rust, and, if the mud is not timely removed, this could end in the catastrophic sinking of the ship. That is, if too much water gets inside of the cargo ship, there is a high probability that it will sink. Moreover, removing mud out of the hole of a cargo ship is not the safest occupation because gaseous fumes accumulate in it, and, though it rarely occurs, an explosion could happen due to spontaneous combustion. I was blessed nothing like this happened to me. In addition, my Stevedore job also involved moving cargo from the ship. For example, I helped load cargo onto Pallet Boards; once this was done, a derrick, either attached to the cargo ship or the dock, removed the cargo from the ship to the wharf where it was then loaded onto trucks for distribution.

With all of the pros and cons taken into consideration, the pay was relatively good. After all of my obligations were taken care of, I saved about $75, which was enough for my room and board, including food, for one semester at Southern University in Baton Rouge, LA. Without Lillian Luellen Pierce Braud's Strategic Family Development Plan, which required me to get as much education as I could, regardless of any prevailing difficult circumstances, I may not have taken the summer job working in a Stevedore Occupation. So many of my peers were not fortunate as I was to have parental guidance that strongly emphasized the value of education and family.

Although World War II was raging by 1943, and the Soviet Union's Red Army, by that year, had defeated Hitler's Barbarossa War Plan, which was designed to crush the former, and eliminate, from the Earth as many Jewish People as possible, I was on schedule to enroll at Southern University in the Fall 1943.

CHAPTER X

SOUTHERN UNIVERSITY EDUCATION TEMPORARILY PUT ON HOLD TO JOIN THE MILITARY TO ADVANCE THE PIERCE- BRAUD STRATEGIC FAMILY DEVELOPMENT PLAN

My father told me when I was five years old, and everybody else he came in contact with, that he was going to send his son to Southern University in Baton Rouge, LA to study Agriculture. This was my father's dream, and I made it a reality when I enrolled at the university in the Fall 1943. I enrolled in Agriculture like my father wanted me to do. I was given several scholarships by the Agriculture Department at Southern University. However, they wanted me to work on the farm on Saturdays and Sunday. At that time, I did not want to do that, so at the end of the Fall 1943 Semester, I changed my major, from Agriculture to Liberal Arts because I wanted to go medical school. Because I did not seek any department advisement, and if I had done so, I could have finished college in Agriculture and still gone to medical school too. One of my roommates went through and graduated in Agriculture, and he subsequently went on to medical school. Thus, the old cliché that says "What you don't know won't hurt you" is not true. I made my own road difficult because there was some information I did not know, and it did adversely affect my college curriculum. After attending Southern University for one year, I had to make, or we-my siblings-some strategic changes in the Lillian Luellan Strategic Family Development Plan.

A. Joined The Navy To Help Lillian Luellen Pierce Braud To Financially Support My Six Siblings

By 1945, I had attended Southern University Baton Rouge Campus for one year, the situation in my Pierce-Braud Family Group was as follows: One of my siblings, including myself, were in college (Beverly Braud and Joseph Pierce Braud); two of my siblings were in high school (Suky Chapman Braud and Geraldine Braud); and two of us were in elementary school (Edgar Braud and Mary Anne Braud); one sister-Elaine Cecile Braud-had died a few years after my father. The best I recall she passed away between 1938 and 1940. Notwithstanding the pain the passing of my sister caused my siblings and I, there was not enough cash money coming into the family so I decided that I should temporarily withdraw from Southern University, and enlist in the military service. By doing so, then I would be able to receive an allotment[100] for my mother and the rest of my family. It is rare to find anyone, both then and now, who would selflessly put aside their own personal goals and work toward the improvement of the family, group, or organization.

I should add here that during my Freshman Year at Southern University, which was 1943 to 1944, I pledged and became a member of the Alpha Phi Alpha Fraternity. This was, traditionally speaking, the most academic-oriented fraternity on campus relative to the others. In addition, when I pledged Alpha Phi Alpha, there were only two students "on the line," namely, Henry Bardell and myself. The Alpha Phi Alpha Fraternity was not for everybody.

When I enlisted in the Navy, this made it possible for my oldest sister-Beverly Braud-to remain in college, and my other siblings could continue to attend elementary and high school. Having established an allotment for my Pierce-Braud Family Group, from then on, there was smooth sailing for a few years. While I was in the service, I had one or two part-time jobs. As is the case for all of the branches of military service, there is an initial indoctrination period, generally speaking, called Boot Camp.

---

[100] The allotment I received from the Navy was between $200 and $300 per month. No doubt, this sum was far more than the $18 per month we received from the Louisiana Welfare Department's Aid To Dependent children Program.

B. Years Of Service In The Navy, 1945 To 1948

When I initially enlisted in the Navy, I went to Great Lakes, Illinois for Boot Camp Training. On the day I left New Orleans, LA, I wore a two-piece suit, sport shirt, regular underwear, shoes and socks; I thought that I looked like a million. We left New Orleans, LA in February 1945, and it was warm. However, I was in for a rude awakening when we reached our Great Lakes, Illinois destination. It was freezing cold; snow was on the ground; and for five or six days, I almost froze because of the lack of adequate clothing for that type of weather. No one back in warm New Orleans, LA ever told me to bring heavier clothes because I would need some to change into immediately upon my arrival at Boot Camp in Great Lakes, Illinois. It was cold, and unlike others I had experienced in the South, the Illinois Cold was one that felt like it penetrated all the way down into my bones. It could make anyone shiver and when their warm exhalation mixed with the cold, frosty air, a white fog would instantly appear.

a. Boot Camp And Company #311

I was placed in Company #311 in Camp Robert Smalls for Boot Camp Training. There were several other recruits from New Orleans, LA in this Boot Camp. However, most of us did not know each other save a fellow by the name of Charlie Hamilton. He and I had gone to the Danneel Elementary School together, and we lived in the same section of town known as Gert Town located near Xavier University. All of us from New Orleans, LA became friends, and we met with each other after we finished our military service. Some of the fellows stationed with me at the Great Lakes, Illinois Boot Camp were Warren Bowman, Willie Graves, Alfred Andrus, and Salvador Margin. Another fellow name Ambrose Pratt was from Louisiana, and he-too-met with us when we returned to civilian life. Robert Brewington was from Los Angeles, CA, and he became friendly with the gang from Louisiana. Brewington informed us that he had been an "extra" in the "Our Gang" Series, which was a Hollywood Movie. After we completed our military service, Robert Brewington met with us when we held reunions during subsequent years. Our Boot Camp Training lasted roughly six weeks; at the end, we were allowed to go home on what the military called a furlough.

My furlough lasted a week or two. It was a time to exhale and relax a little, and catch up on the happenings on the Gravel Road since I was gone, and I spent some quality time with some of my siblings. Of course, I visited with my mother as well. She was happy to see me as usual. The friends I mentioned earlier and I were all on the same train when we left Great Lakes, Illinois for New Orleans, LA, and we were all on the same train when we returned to Great Lakes, IL from New Orleans, LA. When I got home, I had an opportunity to wear my new Navy Uniform. I looked very sharp and handsome in my uniform. Everybody was proud of me. Furloughs are always too short; when I got back to Great Lakes, IL, my military orders sent me to Camp Perry in Virginia. Soon after I arrived, I received new Military Orders that sent me to Port Chicago, San Francisco, California.

b. Port Chicago, San Francisco, California Preparations For Overseas Station In Japan, 1945

Soon after my return to Great Lakes, IL, I was sent to Port Chicago, California. After Boot Camp Training, most of us were transferred there. Several months before, there had been a severe explosion in the ammunition depot, which caused the loss of many soldiers' lives. Interestingly, one of the casualties involved in that explosion was from Brookstown. We stayed in Port Chicago, CA for several weeks in preparation for overseas duty. That is, we were stationed there for embarkation so there was no liberty; I could not go into town. However, there was a sailor who had found a small metal door at one side of an old ball stadium. When darkness came, we put on our dress sailor uniforms and used the metal door to escape Port Chicago. We went out in such cities as San Francisco, CA, Oakland, CA, and Berkeley, CA a number of times. We went AWOL (Absent Without Leave) for a number of nights; backtracking the way we left, we returned late at night by way of the metal door.

So, the situation was not so sterile for us brave hearts. We just turned our lemon barracks into sweet plum nightlife. Of course, we did not overdue the situation; we worked within the rules. From Port Chicago, CA (San Francisco Bay), we were sent to Okinawa, Japan.

c. From Port Chicago, San Francisco, CA To Okinawa, Japan In 1944

After being stationed at Port Chicago, CA for several weeks, we were sent to Okinawa, Japan on the USS Randal, a cargo ship. While on our way to Okinawa, we encountered a "Tidal Wave" off the coast of Hawaii, which forced us to change course. A Tidal Wave, which is usually generated by an earthquake in the ocean crust, and, this event oftentimes triggers a tsunami due to the sudden release of energy into the ocean waters. When this happens, a Tidal Wave between 10 and 100 feet can result. Anything in its path is at risk for serious damage or destruction. This is why the USS Randal I was sailing on was forced to change its original course on our way to Okinawa, Japan.

Upon arrival at Okinawa, Japan, we were removed from the ship and taken to a Seabee Camp on small landing craft boats with landing gear and ramps. The living quarters were nice; we were housed in Quonset Huts. I was very glad to get off of the vast ocean; at times, as far as my eyes could see, in any direction, all I could see was water out to the horizon, and beyond the horizon, there was more ocean water. Interestingly, we had arrived on Okinawa on D-Day (The Normandy Landing in Europe was the largest landing operations, and associated airborne operations on June 6, 1944; the Allied Forces landing was the largest seaborne operation in history); however, we were later informed that the USS Randal had been bombed by enemy airplanes sometime after we had been removed from the ship. I guess during a war, one might say "those soldiers who survived had to have a little luck on their side."

Several weeks later, there was a typhoon (This is what a hurricane is called in Asia) that hit Okinawa, and the Quonset Huts where the troops stayed were blown away by the strong winds, from the typhoon. We were without food for several days. After the storm, I promised not to ever throw food away. Here I was in Okinawa, Japan without any food for several days; when I was growing up on the Gravel Road back home, I never went one day without food. There is a lot of truth in the saying "everything is relative." Robert Brewington came to the rescue of those of us from New Orleans, LA because the Officers' Club had food; he sang with a trio for the Officers' Club, and when he finished singing, he brought us some food. Whenever Brewington sang at the Officers' Club, he would bring the Louisiana Crew steaks, cake, and so forth. Before I continue my story related to my stay in Okinawa, it is necessary to point-out here that many years after we were all discharged from the service, we would visit with each other intermittently. Brewington would visit New Orleans, LA, and I would visit Los Angeles, CA. A few times we had a reunion at my house in New Orleans, LA. Warren Bowman, Alfred Andrus, Willie Graves, Ambrose Pratt, Salvador Margin, Robert Brewington all attended. We would have food, music, and talk and laugh about our experiences in the Navy, from boot camp to discharge. I am the only one still living in that group today. Amen.

We stayed on Okinawa for several months. After the storm, we had to take showers in water by an Okinawa Cemetery on the side of a hill. This experience was gruesome. Eventually, we were shipped from Okinawa with a stopover in Guam on our way to Siapan. I was transported on the USS Benner to the Tinian Island, which was a small Aircraft Carrier.

d. Saipan And Tinian Island In 1946

When I arrived in Siapan, I became ill and was taken off of the USS Benner to a hospital. The ship attendants placed me on a gurney in the direct sun for several hours. During that time, I perspired profusely, and when I got to the hospital, I was no longer ill. I believe I released the toxins in my body that caused my illness via my profuse sweating in the direct sunlight. After a week or two stay in the hospital for observations, the Navy Commanders subsequently gave me orders to join my outfit on Tinian Island. I was stationed there for several months. Since World War II had come to a close in 1945, there was no direct threat from the Axis Powers; however, because the war had recently ended, we still had to operate with maximum precautions.

While stationed on Tinian Island in the Pacific, my military rank was a Third Class Pharmacist Mate. I was assigned to work in the Navy dispensary; specifically, my responsibilities were similar to a nurse inasmuch as I did patient intake to determine what ailment(s) the latter came to see the doctor seeking medical help. I took a host of vital signs, ranging from body temperature to blood pressure. Generally, most patients sought the doctor's advice related to colds and allergies. I performed these duties for several months, and after this time, the Navy Commander gave me orders to return to the United States.

Return To Camp Elliot In San Diego, CA From Tinian Island: Then To The Naval Supply Depot In New Orleans, LA: Then To Camp Moffet In Great Lakes, IL: Then To The Jacksonville Naval Station, 1946

I sailed on the USS Benner, from the Tinian Island, to Camp Elliott located in San Diego, CA. I was at this Naval Station for only a short while before I received new orders to go to the Naval Supply Depot in New Orleans, LA (Algiers is where the Naval Supply Depot was located). I was happy about this assignment because I was close to the Gravel Road where I grew up. While stationed there for several months, I got a chance to enjoy the nightlife in New Orleans, LA and surrounding area. I was right at home, and this felt good to me. I could see my mother and some of my siblings periodically. After a couple of months, the Navy Commander gave me a new order to return to Great Lakes, Illinois. It was during 1946 that I re-enlisted in the Navy while I was at the Naval Supply Depot.

When I arrived in Great Lakes, IL, I was stationed at Camp Moffett. I worked in the dispensary (A room where medicines are prepared and provided similar today's Walgreen, CVS, etc.) for the two months I was stationed there. It was like a vacation again. I was able to visit Chicago, IL, and I got a chance to visit relatives. I also met several other people in the area. From Camp Moffett in Great Lakes, IL, I was stationed in the Infirmary of the Jacksonville Naval Station. I was stationed at a number of Naval Bases in and outside the South. However, taking all of them together, the social relations at the Jacksonville Naval Station were, by far, the absolute worse I had experienced in my Navy Career thus far.

As it was, the Jacksonville Naval Station, which was located in a suburban community called Yukon, FL, was the worst base for Negro Service Personnel. That is, the transportation from the city to the base had a lot to be desired. There were buses leaving a certain point in the city in order to get to the base. Black Sailors had difficulty getting seats on the buses because of the large number of White Sailors. The buses filled up rapidly with White Sailors above and behind the screens, and the Black Sailors had no place to sit or stand. And, to add insult to injury, the White Sailors did not want the Black Sailors to stand over them. Therefore, there were always fights, name calling, cursing, and other racial slurs going-on.

The Sailor MPs (Military Police) were as bad as the other White Sailors. The commander of the base did not do anything about the problem. Duty in the infirmary was not so bad because the White Sailors were subtle with their "hatred" during the workday.

For those who may not be aware, the year was 1946, and the United States had just concluded its involvement in World War II, or the fight against Adolph Hitler's Third Reich. Many of the Black Sailors, who were treated less than human beings at the Jacksonville Naval Station, had fought against Hitler during WWII; many died fighting for the Freedom of the White and Jewish Peoples of Europe; but, unfortunately, those who survived this life-threatening ordeal tragically returned from Europe *only* to discover that they were still being treated less than human beings like they were before they went to war; and, their freedom here in America meant nothing to their fellow White Sailors. I nearly loss my life when I got to Okinawa because the USS Randal was bombed by enemy aircraft only a few hours after the Black Sailors, myself included, disembarked the ship. I was not on vacation; I was fighting in World War II so other peoples could enjoy their Freedom; yet, many Black Sailors and I were denied ours' here at home.

What I experienced at the Jacksonville Naval Station I attributed to Systemic Racism. I had witnessed it when I was growing up in Brookstown on the Gravel Road; and, it was still alive and well by the end of WWII in America. The racism my fellow Black Sailors experienced at the Jacksonville Naval Station was not limited to it, but it had become an ingrained part of the social fabric of American Society. When something is systemic, like a decayed tooth, where the pain from the exposed nerve causes a toothache so bad that one cannot sleep, and like the decayed tooth, Systemic Racism has to be uprooted so the social relations between races can be healed by the people of different races themselves. No amount of legislation can do the job alone. Novocaine can only deaden one's pain for a period of time before it returns worse than before. For example, the Civil Rights Bill of 1964 was passed 18 years after my experience at the Jacksonville Naval Station, and 57 years after it was passed by 2021, more than 45 State Legislatures have drafted laws potentially aimed at rolling back the voting rights guaranteed to African-Americans by the Fifteenth Amendment to the U.S. Constitution.

That being so, while I was stationed in Jacksonville, I had a number of occasions to visit Edward Waters College. Now, I think its name has been changed to Edward Waters University. I met some very nice people during my visits to the college. Because my visits were brief in nature, there was nothing discussed that turned out to last any length of time. Most of the time, my group spent our liberty, or off duty time, on and around Davis Street and the Blodgett Apartments and homes.

C. Davis Street Incident In 1946

Davis Street can best be described as one you might run across in the French Quarters in New Orleans, LA. Because the Black Sailors, including myself, were functioning in difficult racial circumstances in the Deep South, and we had just come through the dangerous World War II, where one's life could be ended in the blink of an eye, we would spend some of our off-duty time hanging-out with Black People-oftentimes-just laughing, talking about the war, shooting pool, drinking a beer, listening to music, and talking about social life in America. These were times when we could relax for a moment. On Davis Street, we would sometimes get our tension off with a "Pepper Head." There were good Black People down on Davis Street.

On one occasion when my group went to Davis Street, something very interesting happened one night while I was there. Seemingly, out of nowhere, a young girl, who was adult age, appeared in an alley between a trash bin and a building. She was about eighteen years of age. The girl was very attractive and she had a beautiful ebony color. We became friends and eventually she showed me the way to her house. That young girl would be at her house alone every night. However, her grandfather, or uncle, lived next door. When we would make out, she would always cover my mouth with hers to absorb any sound or noise. Each time I would leave to go back to the Jacksonville Naval Base, she would say that she was afraid that I would not return. For months, we totally enjoyed each other's company.

As anybody who has been in the military for any length of time, it is not uncommon to receive new orders to relocate to another base. Eventually, I received orders to go to The National Naval Medical Center located in Bethesda, Maryland to take a course in Physical and Occupational Therapy.

I had an open train ticket. I could leave Jacksonville in a reasonable time. My luggage was placed in a storage locker, and I returned to my ever-awaiting friend. As always, when I was ready to leave, she said I was not going to return. That time, she was right. The sad part is I only remember her first name, and I knew where she lived; but I did not know her address. Thus, I was never able to communicate with her again.

D. Transferred To The National Naval Medical Center In Washington, DC, 1946

I arrived in Washington, DC and was able to get to Bethesda, Maryland by way of local transportation. The National Naval Medical Center was a long way out in suburban DC. The living quarters for the Naval Personnel was very nice. There were several specialty schools for Naval Personnel.

One day, I went to the cafeteria in the National Naval Medical Center trying to get some food when I ran into another sailor like me. That was Bill Hicks. He stated that he had been in the area about one week. He was in Dental Corps School and I was in Physical and Occupational Medicine School. We were the only Black Sailors in the school. Bill had found his way to downtown Washington, DC, and we also met a few people who worked at the National Naval Medical Center. During our travels around DC, we went over to the USO and made some life-long contacts. We met people like Fannie, Rosie, Mary Vernice, Ira, etc. On several occasions, Fannie and her brother made trips to Louisiana, and I would come down with them. So, I was pleased with making some new friends because it made my work and stay at the National Naval Medical Center easier.

The program that I was in was very rewarding. It was of value for me in later years. That is, it was valuable for my medical practice that became a reality many years later. By now, it should be no surprise, and forgive me if I sound redundant, that my dream of becoming a medical doctor was still very much alive since the day Dr. Stephen Campbell inspired me, back on the Gravel Road, to become a medical doctor when I was five years old. I had traveled extensively since that time, and with each passing year, I felt I was getting closer to brining my dream to reality.

At the end of the course, the class members were certified and all of us were assigned to varying areas around the United States. I was transferred to Treasure Island, California.

E. Transferred To Treasure Island, California And Unexpected Reunion With Edward Turner In 1947

There were remnants of the structures used for the San Francisco World's Fair still standing. At the time I arrived on Treasure Island, there were civilian crew demolishing the structures. I had been walking around the area for some two weeks when I ran into one of my friends from New Orleans, LA. We had not seen each other for a number of years. We had gone to the same elementary school (Danneel); we would shine shoes together in the Carrollton Section of New Orleans, LA; and we lived around the corner from each other. What a pleasant coincidence to meet such an old friend so far away from home.

Being a stranger in the Bay Area, it was quite rewarding to see someone that dated back back to my childhood. In addition to going to the downtown area of San Francisco, I was able to visit my friends and his family in South San Francisco. There were parties in the area near my friend's home. Also, there were a number of other people from the New Orleans, LA area where I grew up; I shared some of my late teen years with them. I was having a good time in the San Francisco, CA and Bay Area. Everything was going well. However, by 1948, I had come to the end of my second two-year re-enlistment in the Navy. I had to make a decision. To either re-enlist or retire from military service.

F. Discharged From The Navy After Four Years Of Service Was Over In 1948

My time was up in the Navy. I knew it somewhere inside of me. But, since I was having so much fun in the Bay Area, I put the thought in the back of my mind. I was not in denial like so many people manufacture an illusionary defense when they do not want to face the truth about something they did. I knew I was a "short timer" as the old cliché goes. Anyway, I had signed up for two years, but I did not get out because the Navy people could not find me. I thought that was strange. I was walking around in plain sight! I reported to my duty station in the infirmary every day and was paid at my regular pay periods.

However, one day some Navy personnel came looking for me and I was given an ultimatum to either sign up again, or get out of the service. It was a hard decision and I thought about it for two or three weeks. Finally, I was discharged from the Navy on Treasure Island. Life was full of adjustments I had to make at the time, and some say they are the "Spice of Life." I was a young man, and I was ready to take on everything I had to adjust to head on. One of the first adjustments I had to make was getting back into the swing of every day civilian life. I thought I was a handsome guy, smart, and maybe-maybe-I might be able to turn my mental and physical attributes into becoming an actor in a Hollywood Movie. Hmm? For a moment, I thought to myself "it would be really cool to see myself featured in an acting role on the "Big Hollywood Silver Screen." This notion was not unique to me because more people, who come to Sunset Blvd, end up in Hollywood never making it to the "Big Screen" relative to those few who actually do so! Like those people before me, I was willing to give it a shot!

G. Hollywood And Dreams Of Being Discovered By Metro Goldwyn Meyers (MGM) In 1948

From Treasure Island by the dock of the San Francisco Bay, a few years before Otis Redding left his home in Georgia, I went to Los Angeles, California before I returned to mine. I had been in contact with one of my cousins, and she gave me a place to stay. Check that box. I had been walking around the city looking for work. During that time, I had the feeling that someone from Hollywood would discover me. LA is a big city, and nearly everybody had a hidden aspiration of being discovered by Hollywood. So, I kept looking and waiting for the day circumstances would come together, and I would land on the lot of a Hollywood Movie Set. I would be offered an audition for a role in a movie, and then I would sign a big contract. This is how the fantasy plays out in people's mind every day out here. Similar to thousands of others, after a few months I was not discovered, and I, fortunately for me, woke up from this "Hollywood Acting Dream," and decided to return to Louisiana and pursue my college education. This was reality 1.0. I thought it was better to leave the acting to others like Sidney Poitier, who later became a big movie star.

Having come to my timely awakening about most people's Hollywood Fantasy, I did like Gladys Knight and Pips sung a few later: I took the midnight train back to the Gravel Road by way of New Orleans, LA. The only dream and hopes I pawned were my Hollywood Fantasy of becoming a movie star. I always held on to my *real dream* of becoming a medical doctor one day. And, to re-start my academic work toward realizing my dream of becoming a medical doctor, the next step in the process was for me to re-enroll at Southern University Baton Rouge Campus in the Fall 1948. I did.

CHAPTER XI

RETURNED TO SOUTHERN UNIVERSITY TO COMPLETE MY UNDERGRADUATE DEGREE IN THE FALL 1948

A. Southern University Football Powerhouse And My Attempted Tryout

When I enrolled at Southern University Baton Rouge Campus in the Fall 1948, its football team was a powerhouse. In 1948, Southern University was the Black College National Co-Champion and SWAC (Southwestern Athletic Conference) Champion. The team's 1948 season record was 12-0 (7-0 SWAC). The Head Coach was Arnett William "Ace" Mumford. He coached at Southern University for 13 seasons, and during this time, Southern University won 11 Southwestern Conference Athletic Championships. Having played a little football myself during my high school days, I thought there might be a position on Southern University's winning team for me. Thus, again, I attempted to try out for the football team, but, as I mentioned earlier, in 1948, Southern had a powerhouse, and I did not show Coach Mumford enough to be considered.

At any rate, I did not return to Southern University to become a professional football player but a professional in the medical profession. My dream of becoming a medical doctor began to take shape because I excelled in the sciences seemingly with little difficulty and with ease. I was on my way. I could taste my dream. It was like a developing photograph taken with a Poloroid Camera. My academic life at Southern University was coming into focus and taking shape.

B. Academic Curriculum Change From Agriculture To Biology And Sciences

Henceforth, I decided to become strictly academic. The fellow was proud of himself even though he was not discovered by anyone in Hollywood, nor was he accepted on the football team. On the academic side, I excelled in the sciences, and because I did so well, one of my professors, namely, Dr. J. Warren Lee, who was so dear to my heart as a mentor, wanted me to go to graduate school and return to Southern as an instructor. In addition, I joined, or was given an invitation to join, several of the honor societies. My grade point average (GPA) was only one or two points from becoming a member of the highest honor society on the Southern University Campus. Agriculture was no longer in my academic crosshairs. I was "all in" with the sciences.

During this time, I had the G.I. Bill to supply my family and I with a flow of money. My younger sister-Geraldine Braud-was in college also, and I was able to contribute money toward her room and board. In addition, I worked in the "The Café" that was in the middle of the campus (My first job was during my Freshmen Years in the Fall 1943). The Café was operated by Mrs. Sarah Netterville Phillips, who was Dr. G. Leon Netterville's sister. During the early 1970s, the latter served as President of Southern University. Mrs. Sarah Netterville Phillips treated me like I was her son, and she covered all of my meals and some of my school supplies as compensation for the work I did at The Café. I worked as an orderly and waiter. It is worthwhile noting that the Nettervilles and I shared a common experience on the Gravel Road. They were from a village called Dutchtown near Gonzales, LA located in Ascension Parish.

There was also a small job in the Biology Department I was given by Dr. Lee. Specifically, I was assigned to work with students in the Biology Laboratory. I helped them to work out some of the problems they encountered while completing various homework assignments given to them by their professors. In addition, I started my own carwash business on campus. I mainly washed professors' cars such as Dr. J. Warren Lee, Dr. Posey, and so forth. I washed their cars behind The Café. I also, to a lesser extent, washed the cars of some of the students. I earned between $3 and $5 for washing a car. This is what I did to nurture my dream of becoming a medical doctor, and to help my mother provide financial resources for my siblings. Shining shoes, scrapping rice and potatoes, washing students and University Professors Cars, and working as a waiter were all jobs I proudly did to help me to financially reach my goal of one day becoming a Medical Doctor. Unfortunately, many youth today are misled by social media to forego their real life goals for the instant gratification an object they seek provides, regardless of how fleeting their feelings are that they receive from this or that item of consumption.

When I was not heads down in my science books, I was earning extra money to help my Braud Family Group advance their education goals. In short, I allocated my time studying, working, dating, and praying.

C. College Dating In 1948

No doubt, Southern University had some of the prettiest young women on campus that I had ever seen in one place. I was one of the beneficiaries of a few of their attention. For instance, one Saturday afternoon there was a party in one of the buildings. It might have been in the "Union" where students usually congregate before or after their classes. There was an attractive young lady, namely, Mary Antoine, who I had seen a number of times on the campus, and we struck up a conversation. From all indications, she had everything working for her. She was very beautiful and smart. We had a sizzling time in the torrid zone. All of our moments together after that were ecstatic! She graduated from college before I did and we lost tract of each other.

Moreover, I encountered another peculiar situation while in college. There was this ultra beautiful young lady, whose name was Janice Roy, and I discovered she had a boyfriend who was a womanizer and a physical abuser. She and I ran around in the same group of friends. She was my secret passion, and how I wished she was mine. As years passed, this young lady had several marriages. Because I was on another trajectory in my life, I lost contact with her after I graduated.

There was one acquaintance I made with a very good-looking young woman when I first enrolled at Southern University in the Fall 1943. Her name was Swedie Weary. Nothing happened in the dating department then but Swedie Weary made an impression on me that I encoded in my mind.

Strangely, a few years after I graduated from Southern University, Swedie Weary resurfaced in my life. Since she and I did not spend much time together in 1943, and because she graduated from Southern University in 1947, I focused on my academic studies in the Biology Department. I still had a few years to go before I graduated.

D. Biology Project Lesson And Personal Growth

When I was in high school at the Lowery Training School, Mr. Jackson really taught me the ABCs of Biology and Anatomy. By the time I enrolled at Southern University in the Fall 1943 and re-enrolled in the Fall 1948, I had learned from Mr. Charles Jackson's instructions nearly everything about these subjects, which made me a standout. I was so prepared that Dr. J. Warren Lee, Chair of the Biology Department, sketched out his academic plan for me. He wanted me, upon my graduation from Southern University, to go to graduate school; obtain and advance degree in Biology; and return to Southern as a faculty member. This was definitely a possibility; but, I had to factor into the equation my mother's Strategic Family Development Plan for my Braud Family Group. That is, a cash flow was necessary to insure that all of my siblings received their first college degree. This was the primary priority.

In the meantime, I did not shut any doors to my immediate future; I left all of my options open. So, I continued to study hard, and Dr. Lee rewarded me with a job in the Biology Laboratory. I thought I was doing really fine. However, nothing can substitute for experience; this is not a cliché or a wives tale. For example, one of the most hurting situations I encountered in college occurred during the summer 1950.

I enrolled in a Biology Course called Embryology, and at the end of the summer school session, I had an almost perfect average in both lecture and laboratory. All of my assignments were turned in before the due date. I had all of my grades. Being one who gave my fellow peers the benefit of the doubt to conduct themselves in a moral way as I tried to live my own life day-to-day, low and behold-one of the students in the class asked me to see my laboratory drawings and laboratory book because he was not up-to-date. That student attempted to turned in my drawings and so forth, by trying to erase my name off of the pages of my Biology Project.

Because I write hard, he was not able to cleanly remove the imprint of my name. The student tried to put his name in the place of mine. One could see on each drawing the imprint of my name. Committed to his deceptive scheme, the student turned my work into the instructor.

Interestingly, my instructor, who was Paul Brown, blamed me for that student's deceptive scheme, and gave me a failing grade. I had to take the course again. Mr. Brown, in my opinion, did not handle this matter with justice as his guiding light. I imagine you are wondering what did I learn from my unfortunate experience? I learned there is a sharp difference between giving my Biology Project to my classmate rather than sitting down with him and explaining how he should go about understanding the assignment, which would empower him to do his own work. I also learned there are no short-cuts in life; everyone must go through an experience so they can learn a skill that will serve one for the rest of his or her life. I did not give anymore students my completed homework; I advised them to meet me in the Biology Laboratory so I could demonstrate how they can conduct an experiment and complete their own Biology Projects. Thus, the lesson I learned from this experience was more valuable to me in the long run than the "A" I received in the Biology Course when I took it over. This experience also taught me to look for the "silver lining" in every difficult situation because, although I might not see it immediately, I just have to *knead it out* like the gradual picture unfolds when it is taken by a Polaroid Camera. I was a shining star in the Biology Department, and I received help with my college education in President Felton Clark's Office.

E. Mrs. Patrick, President J.S. Clark's Administrative Secretary And The Reading Lessons

Before I went into the Navy in February 1945, during my Freshman Year, I worked in The Café on Southern University Campus, and when I re-enrolled in the Fall 1948, I got my old job back. As a Freshman, and through my job in The Café, I had an opportunity to meet many of the administrators and professors who worked for the university. One of the persons, who I struck up a conversation with one day, was Mrs. Patrick, who was President J. S. Clark's Administrative Secretary (J.S. Clark was the President of Southern University at the time). While talking to Mrs.

Patrick on several occasions, she told me emphatically that "I am going to teach you how to read." Personally, I thought I was a pretty good reader already. Instead of becoming offended in any way, I kept my mind open. My goal was to become a Medical Doctor, and Mrs. Patrick might teach me a technique that could help me reach my goal easier.

Nevertheless, she invited we to come to her office in the administration building, and that I should bring one of my books I use for class with me. I followed her directions. When I got to her office, Mrs. Patrick ask me to open my book and begin reading from chapter I was studying in my Biology Course. As read for a while, she stopped me, and Mrs. Patrick told me I could read better. So, as any good teacher does, she took my book and she began to read what I had already read to her aloud, and almost instantly, I could hear a different cadence and intonation. Then, I tried to duplicate what I heard. It took me a while to master Mrs. Patrick's suggested reading style. Over several months, I was able to read the new way she instructed me to do so. From that time forward, I became a much faster reader, and, more importantly, my ability to comprehend information greatly improved. In short, I became a "speed reader" years before this reading style became a household practice for many. During all of my future studies, I applied the speed reading style, and I felt I was able to get my assigned coursework projects done faster and with a higher degree of accuracy. My first big test using my new reading style came during my last semester before I graduated from Southern University.

F. Medical Aptitude Test Taken At Louisiana State University In 1950

During the last semester in college, I took the Medical Aptitude Test (MAT). Generally, this type test was a timed one so my speeding reading style was put to the test. The test was scheduled to be taken at LSU, and there were two Black Students in the assembled group to take it. The test was held in a large auditorium. The two mentioned students were Elijah Richardson from Jonesboro, LA and myself. Given the existing practice of racial segregation in the South, to our surprise, there was no special seating. This was not because LSU had purged itself of racial segregation practices by 1950, it was, more than unlikely, due to the fact not too many Black People show up to take the MAT during any given cycle when it was scheduled. In addition, in case one or two Black People did show up as we did, there was a Colored Sign, which was placed over the bathroom door in full view, for any Black Student to use, in case someone(s) showed up to take the MAT. All-in-all, Elijah Richardson and I must have done very well on the Medical Aptitude Test because we both were subsequently admitted into Medical and Dental School respectively. These milestones would be achieved a few years after our graduation from Southern University in the Spring 1951.

Elijah Richardson was accepted into Meharry Medical College's Dental School, and he went onto have a long and distinguished career in the Medical Field. He retired from his Dental Practice in 2008.

That being so, and after I graduated from Southern University, my Pierce-Braud Family Group reached a new crossroad.

G. Lillian Luellen Pierce Braud Strategic Family Development Plan Reached a New Crossroad Between 1945 And 1950

As I have already mentioned, my mother's Strategic Family Development Plan was successful because periodically an adjustment in it was made due to some changing social and financial conditions. The plan was fluid.

a. Education Status Of The Pierce-Braud Family Group

This family group had been taken off of Aid To Families With Dependent Children ($18 per month for seven people) when I entered the Naval Services. After my discharge from the Navy, I had some four years on the G.I. Bill. We were able to continue our education journey. My oldest sister-Beverly Braud-had finished college in 1946 and working now. There were two of us that were about to finish college-Geraldine Braud and myself. There was the next sister-Suky Chatman- that had graduated from high school. She entered college and eventually thought it was too challenging, and decided to enroll in a trade. The last two in the group-Edgar Braud and Mary Anne Braud-were graduating from high school at the same time that Geraldine Braud and myself were graduating from Southern University.

We had entered, therefore, into another crossroad. We still needed my financial input to continue our educational journeys. Soon after I graduated from Southern University, I was offered an interview by Crieghton University in the Midwest, to attend Medical School. Though this was exciting, there was so much at stake, and being a young man on the rise, I was plain afraid. Really, my fear centered around my internal feelings related to my siblings; I knew what Medical School would demand of my attention, and that could mean less I would have to put toward making sure my siblings achieved their educational goals. Thus, for the time being, I did not respond for the interview; this did not mean I aborted my childhood dream of becoming a Medical Doctor; it simply meant I adjusted my strategy to *get it done*. The Lillian Luellen Pierce Braud Strategic Family Plan required me to make this adjustment to the new demands of my family group.

b.   Part-Time Employment As A Laboratory Assistant In The Biology Department

Therefore, after I graduated from Southern University in the Spring 1951, I accepted a part-time job in its Biology Department as a Laboratory Assistant. This job provided me with some funds I could use to keep my mother's Education Plan for the Pierce-Braud Family Group viable.

CHAPTER XII

POST-SOUTHERN UNIVERSITY AND THE BEGINNING OF MY PROFESSIONAL CAREER IN 1951...

A. Charles H. Brown High School Science Teaching Position In 1951

After working as a Biology Laboratory Assistant for about two months, a teaching job at Charles H. Brown High School in Springhill, LA in Webster Parish became available. That is, there was an opening for a science teacher there. I would earn more money than I was earning as a Laboratory Assistant so I accepted the job. Low and behold, there were several teachers employed at Charles H. Brown High School, who were my classmates at Southern University during my Freshmen Year, and when I re-enrolled at the university after I was discharged from the Navy. Thus, my reception at the high school was cordial and uneventful. I had a built-in social network that caught me up on those things I could benefit from at the high school as well as those that I needed to stay away from.

a. Science Classroom Facility

Charles H. Brown High School was a practically new school but, from an architectural standpoint, it had a lot to be desired. Its floor plan consisted of a gymnasium; a large room for Industrial Arts; a large room for Home Economics; and the rest of the classrooms were open space with a blackboard. The classroom for Industrial Arts was equipped with carpenter tables for constructing joints and so forth. It was the same for the Home Economics Classroom. There were tables, stoves, ovens, dishes, linen ware, and other kitchen related items such as utensils. The rest of the classrooms had no equipment, teacher aids, and so forth. The Biology Classroom had no tables or equipment I could use to provide my students with some elementary level Biology Instructions and Experiments. No doubt, the underlying message, then, was educate Black Students to become Blue Collar Workers, and do not prepare them to become highly skilled professionals such as medical doctors, lawyers, doctors of philosophy, and nurses among many other White Collar Occupations.

When I arrived at Charles H. Brown High School, the White School Board Members, and other city fathers from the private business and judiciary sectors, had already given their blessings to the United States Supreme Court Ruling related to Separate But Equal Facilities for White and Black Students at the high school level. As I have already mentioned, the White City Fathers in Webster Parish considered the Black Students' *place* was either working in construction related occupations (Blue Collar), or in those that pertained to household maintenance (Cooks, waiters, domestic laborers, and service occupations generally, etc). Knowing what I had learned about the plantation culture on the Gravel Road where I grew up in St. James Parish, this over-emphasis on Blue Collar Educational Training I found at Charles H. Brown High School, when I arrived there to teach science, was far from being a surprise to me. I picked up on what was going-on at Charles H. Brown High School right away. That is, the Black Man and Woman was going to continue to be relegated to doing manual labor like our ancestors had done during the 244 years existence of the American Slavery Institution. Its legacy was being acted-out right here in Charles H. Brown High School in plain sight. I wanted to try to change that in some small way, for my students, while I was teaching science at the school. My parents were proud people, and I was raised to believe in myself, and I was taught, by my Pierce-Braud Family Group, and my Aunt Leah Pierce Argieard in particular, that education was the key that unlocked the future.

b.   Industrial Arts Teacher Ask To Build Biology Style Tables

I reached-out to Mr. Claude Newton, who was the Industrial Arts Teacher at Charles H. Brown High School when I got there. Specifically, I ask him to build two Biology Style Tables for my classroom. I turned my lemon classroom into a setting where Black Students could learn Biology Theory as well as conduct some science experiments. Some of the Black Students, who took Mr. Claude Newton's Industrial Arts Course, probably played a part in building the Biology Style Tables, which they used to do their science experiments when they came to my science class. I recognize the academic talents of many of the Black Student who I taught, and, it was so unfortunate that the City Fathers in Springhill, LA and Webster Parish did not see in them what I saw. I think self-hatred had blinded their ability to see the "great potential" in the Black Students I taught, and in Black People in general. This was tragic inasmuch as the community, in the long run, suffered because many talented Black Students I taught eventually went to college but they did not return to share their talents with the people in the communities where they grew up.

Once I got the Biology Style Tables built and installed in my classroom, I used them to improvise my science instructions. With those tables and textbooks, the students were able to do basic experiments, including those related to frogs, fish, insects, and so forth. Most of the specimens we used in these science experiments were collected by my students in the community where they lived. This means the School Board did not provide any science equipment for the science experiments we did. What kept me from crying on my way to school each day was the determination and energy my students brought to class. They knew the deck of cards was missing some of its cards, and the hand they were being dealt was faulty. Nevertheless, they put their cards on the table, and we improvised science learning like the great Jazz Musician-John Coltrane-did so well when he was playing a jazz tune at the Apollo Theatre in Harlem, New York. My student and I's greatest resource were each other; we leaned on each other to get through the Separate But Equal Maze. The racial segregation problem was widespread in nearly every corner of the land.

c. Southern University Thirteen In 1956

I worked in that Webster Parish School System for four years. During that period, a number of the students I taught went to college and even received advanced degrees. One of my best Black Students became one of the so-called Southern University Thirteen, following the 1956 Sit-ins in Baton Rouge, LA. That student was John Johnson; he was one of the "Southern University Thirteen," who sat-in at the segregated Kress Gallery Lunch

Counter. The sit-in was called the Kress Gallery Sit-In. "...the Kress lunch counter in downtown Baton Rouge was segregated. On March 28, 1960, a group of seven [The total number of Southern University Students was 13; I was closely connected to Southern University by 1951, and though my contacts thereafter this year, 13 is the number of students I was told, who were involved in the sit-in]... Southern University students challenged the norm and held a sit-in...The seven students were expelled from Southern for participating in the sit-in."[101]

All thirteen students were EXPELLED from Southern University, by Felton G. Clark, President, for peacefully protesting against the system for their human rights. Some of the students were readmitted to the university but the "tell-tale signs" and power of White Supremacy still ruled over the Black Community throughout Louisiana, and at all levels of human discourse by 1960 (Twelve years later, two Southern University Students were murdered on the campus during a student protest that continued over the years since the Kress Gallery Lunch Counter Sit-Ins). I should point-out here that John Johnson was a first year Law Student at Southern University when the Kress Gallery Lunch Counter Sit-Ins occurred. John Will Johnson continued his pursuit of a law degree at another university, and he eventually became an AT & T Lawyer.

During the summer months of the four years I taught at Charles H. Brown High School, I enrolled in graduate school at the University of Illinois Urbana Champaign in its summer program in Entomology. I went every summer beginning in 1951. This was done in case I had to return to Southern University to work in its Biology Department.

B. Reunited With Swedie Weary Brown At Charles H. Brown High School In 1951

As I have already mentioned, during my Freshmen Year at Southern University in 1943-44, I met a number of female student friends. However, there was one I met named Swedie Weary, from Columbia, MS. Swedie Weary was a very good-looking, and fine woman. From all indications I got from her during our very brief acquaintance, is she was also very smart

---

[101] "Dozens gather to remember historic sit-in," www.wafb.com Mar. 29, 2013.

too. As it was, she went about her college life and so did I. I probably did not get to know Swedie Weary more intimately at the time because I withdrew from the university in 1945 to join the Navy. Thus, by the time I returned to Southern in September 1948, Swedie Weary had already graduated. So, I thought, "Oh well, that's how things go; there is no way one man can know the whereabouts of every pretty girl on campus." I didn't have a magic wand one would need to do so. This made sense to me, and I went on with my life and pursuit of my "Medical Doctor Dream."

So, I walked into Charles H. Brown High School feeling like I was on my way up to bigger and better things. And, as fate would have it, unexpectedly, up walked Swedie Weary Brown, and my first thought was "What is she doing here?!" When I reported for my first day of class, I did not know Swedie Weary Brown was a teacher at the school. However, to my surprise, I quickly found out Swedie Weary Brown was one of the teachers employed at the high school. We had been in the freshmen Class at Southern University in 1943. Our paths crossed in a couple of classes and about the campus. Eventually, I enlisted in the Navy Armed Services. This is worth repeating because of all the places in the world I could have been employed, I chose the same employer Swedie Weary Brown did. It seemed we made a Divine Plan to meet each other at Charles H. Brown High School when we met briefly at Southern University eight years earlier.

In short, we were co-workers at the high school. And, during the school year, we began seeing each other on a friendly basis. Swedie Weary Brown had been married, and she had one child. Her name is Brenda Brown; The latter was born in Minden, LA on October 11, 1948. I also had a child, namely, Brownsyn Braud, who was the same age. Brownsyn was born on January 30, 1948 in Washington, DC when I was stationed at the National Naval Medical Center located in Bethesda, MD. I got custody of Brownsyn Braud in 1948-49, and I brought her to stay with my mother on the River Road in our family house in Brookstown. Brownsyn and another son-Glenn Braud-will not live with Swedie and I until I completed Medical School, which was still a few years away in the future.

Louisa (Lise) Mulberry
Delpheo wife ca. 1850

Joe Braud and Lillian Luellen Pierce Braud
Married on September 15, 1921

Joe Braud and Lillian Luellen Pierce Braud
September 1921

Aunt Leah Pierce Argieard
African Griot and Adult Educator, ca. 1935

St. Louis Elementary School Former segregated White School turned over to Negro community ca. 1933-1934

Lillian Luellen Pierce Braud
Ca. 1989

O'neal Roberts Grocery Store Purchased food supplies, i. e., milk, bread, eggs, etc., circa. 1930-1950. Structure stands today-2022.

Leonard "Big Boy" Melancon Post Office, Grocery Store, and Residence. Purchased food supplies and picked up mail.

"Big Boy" Street Sign and Welcome, LA Water Tower.
Erected in 1980s.

Welcome, LA Water Tower
Erected during1980s. Indoor running water replaced the cistern.

Lillian Luellen Pierce Braud Family House
My childhood home, circa. 1934-1960

Braud family Group who lived in family house at 8883 Hwy 18, St. James Parish, LA as children-Dr. Joseph Pierce Braud, Geraldine Braud, Edgar Braud, and Mary Anne Braud Edwards. Braud Family Group, 2017

Lillian Luellen Pierce Braud Family House with Hurricane Fence in front. House remodeling began in the 1970s.

Lebeouf/Braud Street Sign
This street sign separated Braud and Lebeouf Property in Brookstown.

Three generations of Braud Medical Doctors from Brookstown-Dr. Joseph Pierce Braud, Sr, Dr. Brownsyn JoAnn Braud on Right, (Second Generation), and Anya R. Hancock (Third Generation) Dr. Joseph P. Braud Home, ca. 2005-2006

CHAPTER XIII

MARRIAGE TO SWEDIE WEARY BROWN IN 1952

Swedie Weary was born in Columbia, MS on January 24, 1925, which was one year before I was born in 1926. She was the second daughter born to Ollie and Lora Weary. Interestingly, I was also the second child of Joe Braud and Lillian Luellen Pierce Braud. Swedie Weary completed four years of high school at the Marion County Training School in Columbia, MS. Likewise, I graduated from the Lowery Training School in Donaldsonville, LA. After high school, she enrolled at Southern University and earned a B.S. Degree in Vocational Home Economics. I earned a B.S. Degree in Liberal Arts (Sciences) from Southern University in the Spring 1951. As I mentioned earlier, Swedie Weary's and my path briefly intersected during our Freshmen Year at Southern University in the Fall 1943. Then, after eight years, we made a second intersection on our paths when we met again as teachers at Charles H. Brown High School in Springhill, LA.

A. Home Economics Teacher

When we met at this high school, Swedie Weary Brown was a Home Economics Teachers in the Webster Parish School System. This was her academic turf. She was the one who took those "diamonds in the rough" students who enrolled in her class, and polished them with proper etiquette and protocol, of which a majority were unaware of. Swedie Weary Brown taught Black Students how to walk between their culture and mainstream White Culture without sacrificing their own personal identities in the process. She taught her students skill sets, and knowledge of when and how to use them to accomplish their goals such as making a favorable impression during a job interview, participating in a dinner setting, or, more importantly, knowing how to solve social problems when they arise on any level. Swedie Weary Brown, in my view, was the total package.

B. Description Of Swedie Weary Brown's Character

Swedie Weary Brown was quite attractive, and was very talented. She could take any kind of fabric and make, or design, whatever she wanted. The young lady could cook and prepare most foods. We had marvelous times together. Swedie was a thinker; she could take a problem and analyze it, and then arrive at a good decision. I found her to be a balanced person where her emotions were kept in check when a sober perspective was needed. Swedie was able to listen before rushing to a conclusion that may come back to haunt her later. She was a good conversationalist, both when she was wearing her professional hat, and when we were out among our friends.

So, from the outset of us rekindling our friendship, I did not detect any major "Red Flag" that would alert me to be aware she may have a contrary tendency in this or that area of our emerging relationship. Thus, it "seemed to me" so goes the old cliché that I had found my love. I guess this is the feeling that stimulated the songwriters Wilson Pickett, Willie Schofield, and Robert West to write their Rhythm and Blues song called "I Found A Love." Later, although this song was covered by many individual and group artists, Percy Sledge's rendition seemed to have struck a deeper chord with the masses when he sung it. However, as the old saying goes "All that glitters ain't Gold;" I have heard it uttered many times during my young life; it is a fact *one will never find out who a person truly is until they live together every day.*

Honestly, in my mind, I was "Head Over Heels" for Swedie Weary Brown, for all of the good reasons I have already mentioned above. Therefore, eventually, we decided to get married.

C. Double Ring Wedding Of Joseph Pierce Braud To Swedie Weary Brown And Alphonse Jackson To Ruby Helen McClure In Shreveport, LA In 1952

My best friend from my Southern University Days and the two ladies got together, and we had a small Double Ring Wedding. For the reception, we had a wedding cake that was made in the shape of the #8. Shortly after our wedding, we bought a new house in Springhill, LA in the community where we both taught high school. It was not far from the Charles H. Brown High School where we worked. It was a modern, three-bedroom green colored house with a wood and siding exterior and carport driveway. There was a living room, dining room and kitchen. There were two bathrooms. The house sat on a corner lot with a lawn in the front and backyard; we paid $10,000 for our house, and back in 1952, that was a lot of money. My marriage to Swedie Weary Brown Braud was everything I thought it would be.

a. Family Life In Springhill, LA In 1952 To 1955

Everything moved along smoothly. We had no difficulties, and given the fact we had our summer months off from teaching, we were able to travel and spend time in the summer in Chicago. If we decided to teach summer school, we still had enough time left to vacation there and other places. In addition to taking vacations, we continued to pursue more education. Swedie enrolled in Graduate School at the University of Iowa, which was located in Iowa City, IA, to work on her Masters Degree; her focus of study was Home Economics with an emphasis on Family and Textiles. I enrolled in Graduate School at the University of Illinois Urbana-Champaign where I pursued a Masters Degree in Entomology. I continued work toward this degree during the summers, from 1951 to 1954. For several years, this was the routine after working in the high school during the school session. We were teaching and advancing toward achieving our education goals; everything was going smoothly at this time. We were happy being together. And, we had made some good friends in our local area.

b. Social Network Of Friends In Springhill, LA And Surrounding Area

During the school year. We had a group of friends that we socialized with. Some of them were Ruthie White, Joann Hughes, Myrtle Veals, James Veals, Claude Newton, and eventually Harry Jackson joined our friendship circle. A few times we shared some activities with Harry Jackson and his wife-Ruby Helen. Our usual pattern was we would go from house to house and on occasions, we went to Shreveport, LA, Grambling, LA, or Monroe,

LA. During football season, we attended the Grambling-Southern Games. The old saying "Time is Flying By" has some truth in it. Before I knew it, I had worked two years going-on three in my capacity as a teacher at Charles H. Brown High School. Our children were also growing older too.

D. Adoption Of Children Problem Emerged In 1953

Remember earlier I said one does not know what is truly inside the heart of another person until the two people involved in a relationship live together over a sustained period of time. I do not mean six months but at least three to five years. Swedie and I had been married going-on two years; we hadn't reached this threshold yet but the issue of adoption surfaced, which I felt would be a routine matter. Brownsyn Braud and Brenda Brown were the same age, and they were getting larger by the day it seemed. So, one day the subject of adoption came to the forefront; it had been dormant in Swedie's mind for a while too. She told me she wanted me to adopt her child-Brenda Brown-but she did not want to adopt mine-Bronsyn Braud. Interestingly, Swedie said we could adopt Bronsyn at a later date. I went along with her desires. I adopted Brenda Brown willingly and voluntarily. Brenda Brown Braud was a cute, lovable, and smart child. So was my child-Bronsyn. I was happy to adopt Brenda Brown; she was my daughter, namely, Brenda Brown Braud now.

Time continued to pass and we had an opportunity to get a baby boy name Glenn Braud. That was alright but no adoption. God seemed to bless us, and in all other aspects of family life, we progressed. We were able to pursue further education, and our children were getting larger; they were growing up too. Being a sensitive person, I noticed something strange in our relationship that also surfaced around the question of Swedie's adoption of my children.

The peculiar situation that became ever present since the adoption issue was first raised by Swedie was her sibling's interference in our marriage. It has been said many times before that the mother-in-law has a tendency to interfere in their children's marriage, regarding decision-making. In my case, it was Swedie's siblings-in-laws that became a growing problem overtime. Specifically, Swedie's family members did not have any respect for me. I had not once ever given them any reason or cause to have the attitude they had against me. Her siblings just acted like she was the husband. I called this feeling I had about Swedie's siblings to her attention on a number of occasions. They were not around most of the time; thus, it did not seem so acute to the well-being of our relationship at the time.

E. Swedie Weary Braud's Siblings In-Laws Interference In Our Marriage

There were a few times when all five of us (Brenda Braud, Brownsyn Braud, and Glenn Braud) went to Chicago, IL, and one could sense the subtle negative treatment of the girl and boy-my two children. I believe the negative vibe originated from the White Supremacy idea imprinted in Black People's minds, regarding "skin color." It is so subtle in its implications and manifestations. No one told my children their skin color was darker outright, but the self-same message came across all the same as if someone verbally voiced this painful commentary. Usually, the subtle message was conveyed in such a simple way as which child was served first, or spoken to first and so forth. The manner and ways this message can be delivered is endless. Skin Color is still being used today across America to remind Black People, and others of color, that they are inferior human beings.

Brownsyn Braud and Glenn Braud were beautiful children; Brownsyn had a movie star appearance at an early age. The children could obviously feel the ripples of negative vibes aimed at them. Again, a number of times the situation was discussed. However, Swedie never did anything to resolve the situation, which was an emerging contradiction in our marriage. Interestingly, everything else was going along great except her resistance to adoption of my children. I mentioned earlier that Swedie's siblings in-laws played a role in keeping her resistance to adoption of my two children alive.

Specifically, her brothers were the main actors in the gathering drama. They were against my wife adopting my children, although their resistance remained subtle and unspoken. The primary one I remember, who played a leading part in this play, was Swedie's older brother. For many years, I often wondered why a person as nice, and loving, as Swedie Weary Braud was, would not readily agree to the adoption of my two children? This was a mystery to me until very recently. One day as I sat down reflecting on my life, and talking privately with a few people, I came to the realization that money was the main driver underlying Swedie's resistance to adoption. For example, she enthusiastically encouraged me to adopt her child-Brenda Brown. I told Swedie I did not need a reason to justify my adoption of Brenda. I love her from day one as my own child, and my adoption of her was the most natural thing for me to do when we got married.

To the contrary, Swedie's resistance was more than likely privately instigated by her siblings, who I referred to `earlier. Like a ton of bricks, the answer to her resistance to adoption hit me right between my two eyes. It was hidden in plain sight for years. That is, when I adopted Brenda Brown, she automatically became an heir to our estate, and if anything happened between Swedie and I such as a divorce, other permanent separation, Brenda Brown would be an heir to my individual estate like my two children, and any others I would have in my life later. When this fact was brought to her attention by her siblings in-laws, and in my opinion, I believe they privately counseled Swedie to disagree to the adoption of my two children because they would become automatic heirs to her estate in the event we divorced each other later. Moreover, if the situation ever involved writing a Last Will And Testament, the true feelings of the author would be revealed, if one of us would exclude one or more of our children from the document.

There is nothing sinister (Swedie was a good person as I mentioned earlier) about this fact at all. It is one of the historical legacies of the American Slavery Institution. During the 244 years of tenure of American Slavery, African Slaves were dirt poor; their descendants were not much better off financially for many years after slavery purportedly came to a quasi-end in 1865; in fact, poverty was widespread in Black Communities across America well beyond the first half of the 20th Century. Thus, Swedie Weary, and her siblings, were born in Columbia, MS during this time; and, since money was not easy for Black People to come by, which is not to say it once was, the former may have been conditioned by the *generalized scarcity feeling* that ran deep inside of the DNA of a majority of Black People.

In Psychology, there is a concept called behavioral default.[102] That is, even when financial circumstances change for a person, who once grew up poor, and now there is more money available due to educational achievement and so on, the affected person has a tendency to relate to money by default, or respond to it when more money is available, the same way they were conditioned to respond to money while growing up poor during their childhood.

In spite of the resistance I faced regarding Swedie's adoption of my two children, and as painful as this was for me, I had resolved within myself, several years earlier on the Gravel Road, that I was not going to allow anything to disrupt my dream of becoming a Medical Doctor. I knew something would have to be done to reconcile the adoption issue, but I felt the labor pains within my soul that the time for me to *step out on faith*, and give birth to my dream of going to medical school, had arrived. I knew this rung was on the ladder, namely, teaching science at Charles H. Brown High School, and I was ready to reach upwards for my dream, by letting go of the rung that was known to me and *venture into the unknown*. I was ready for the adventure.

F. Dream Of Attending Medical School And The Lillian Luellen Pierce Braud Strategic Family Development Plan In 1953

In the meantime, it had been three or more years since I had been teaching science at Charles H. Brown High School. My mother and my siblings came together for a family meeting in January or February 1954 to have a discussion about my making a *last try* to get into medical school. *This was it!* As you may recall, I have mentioned throughout that my mother's plan was relevant as long as it was flexible and could adapt itself to the Braud Family Group's changing social and economic challenges it faced. During

---

[102] According to Stephen Altrogge, "People prefer to carry on behaving as they have always done even when the circumstances that might influence their decisions change…Default behaviors are the actions you take without thinking. They're your *habits, routines,* and compulsions. With more than 40% of our daily actions controlled by our defaults, they're powerful tools for helping (or hurting)…," "What to change your life? Start with changing your default behavior," www. rescuetime. com, September 26, 2019.

our family discussion, we agreed that it was worth the try. How beautiful those words sounded to my ears to hear my family group offering its unconditional support of my dream to attend Medical School! Therefore, we had to make some adjustments for finances and family business.

My brother-Edgar Braud-had decided to quit his pursuit of his college degree, at Southern University, after two years. That is, he enlisted in the Armed Services. We tried to advise him that was not the most prudent move. In addition, there were two siblings still in college at Southern University, namely, Mary Anne Braud and Edgar Braud. Once I met with my Braud Family Group, including my wife Swedie, together, we made the necessary adjustments to my mother's plan, which consisted of tentative plans for my going to medical school. We all agreed to the following:

- Swedie would take care of our responsibilities in Springhill, LA
- My oldest sister-Beverly Braud-would take care of the responsibilities of my youngest sister and brother-Mary Anne Braud and Edgar Braud-so they could graduate from Southern University
- My oldest sister-Beverly Braud-who finished from Leland College would would also help me in Medical School
- Geraldine Braud would assist me while I was in Medical School
- My youngest brother-Edgar Braud-would help to take care of our mother and
- Suky Chatman Braud would assist my mother with her daily routine because she lived in the family home with her

This was our updated Braud Family Plan, which was geared toward helping everyone, who wanted a college degree to earn one, and it included unanimous support for me to go to Medical School. I was happy my family Group could easily reach a consensus without any dissension or personality discard. This was a rare power we exercised within the privacy of the Braud Family Group. I had a very interesting encounter with the principal of Charles H. Brown High School on the last day I worked at the school. This meeting with the principal occurred after I was assured I would be accepted in the Howard University Medical School.

G. No Respect For "Authority" Revelation In 1954

I was on my way out of the door of Charles H. Brown High School by the summer 1954. My departure was imminent. And, I was ready to go because, as I will explain shortly, I was granted an interview by the Howard University Medical School in August 1954 to determine if I would be accepted into its Medical School. I had stepped out on faith like a commercial jetliner roaring down the runway with wheels-up in a matter of seconds. There was no turning back! My Medical School Dream could not be aborted. Following the school's protocol, I had to meet with Mrs. Landry, who was the Black Supervisor for the Black Public Schools, to inform her that I would not be available to teach science in the Fall 1954 or thereafter. I also spoke with Mr. Starr, the White Supervisor for segregated White Public Schools about my plans.

There was an incident that occurred during the first or second year of my science teaching career at Charles H. Brown High School. Specifically, I helped the junior and senior students prepare decorations for their Prom. One day, while I was in the gymnasium supervising the students toward completing this task, and in the midst of working with students preparing decorations laid-out on the gym floor, and there, of course, was talking, laughing, and a lot of excitement going-on among the students, Mr. Starr and Mr. J.T. Coleman, Black Principal, walked into the gym. I did not see them come into the gym but, at some point, their presence was made known to me by a student, and I stopped what I was doing and walked over to where Mr. Starr and Mr. Coleman were standing. I greeted them with a handshake and I let them know I was unaware of their presence when they walked into the gym. I explained to them the students were preparing for their Prom, and I was their supervising teacher. Our conversation seemed routine, and after a short period of time, Mr. Starr and Mr. Coleman left the gym, and I resumed my supervision of the students' decoration preparations for their upcoming Prom. Mr. Starr's disapproval of my actions that day would be revealed to me, during my Exit Interview, that took place on my last workday at Charles H. Brown High School.

It is necessary to point-out here one fact. That is, during my second and third year of teaching at Charles H. Brown High School, I received very good evaluations from its administration. That being so, I was being considered to become the principal of Charles H. Brown High School. However, when I learned I was accepted to attend the Howard University Medical School, as I mentioned earlier, I notified my Black and White Supervisors about my future plan (For clarification, due to Jim Crow's presence in the Public Education System at the time, Black Teachers had a Black Supervisor, and my White Teacher Colleagues had a White One). My Howard Medical School Interview was forthcoming. Since it was favorable, I will provide a few more details related to my ultimate departure from Charles H. Brown High School.

a. Post-Howard University Medical School Interview And Exit From Charles H. Brown High School In The Summer 1954

When this interview was over, I was told that I should get a favorable letter from the Registrar, and that I could either call the Webster Parish School Board and let them know that I would not be returning to work in the school system for the Fall Semester 1954 because I was accepted in medical school, or I could go back to Louisiana and get all of my personal business and affairs in order. I chose the latter course of action.

I returned to Webster Parish and explained to my supervisors, both Mrs. Landry and Mr. Starr, that I would not be able to continue my employment at Charles H. Brown High School because I was going to Medical School, beginning Fall Semester 1954. Mrs. Landry seemed to be happy to see that I had made plans to advance myself by going to Medical School. On the other hand, Mr. Starr was less than enthusiastic; his attitude was indifferent and aloof. Of course, he was aware how to be politically correct. He may have said he was happy for me but on the inside, Mr. Starr was the same guy who did not champion the educational cause of Black Students in Webster Parish before, or after, I arrived to teach them science.

As the old saying goes "Actions Speak Louder Than Words." As a matter of fact, during my Exit Interview from the school, I was informed that someone else was going to be put in my place, and that I was being transferred to a smaller school. This is the news I was given even as I told my supervisors I was going to Medical School in the Fall 1954. Habits are very difficult to break, and racism, for many, has been a daily thought in their minds for decades. The affected people no longer can distinguish between their racist habits and reality. Most White People, for example, will quickly tell any person of color that they are not racist. In fact, they will get very angry, if a person of color calls out their racist behavior in this or that situation.

Being a bit naïve, I did not understand this sudden deflation of my value as a science teacher at the school. Had I not gone to Medical School, I was destined to be transferred to a smaller school somewhere in the outback of Webster Parish, where I would likely face even more overt and covert racism, both in and outside of the smaller school I would be reassigned to teach. Worse, and overnight, I went from being considered to become the new principal of Charles H. Brown High School to being just another Black Male Teacher in Webster Parish, who hardly anyone would remember after working 30 years or more. I would be just another brick in the wall is a fair description of how I felt about the situation.

b.   Stay In My Place And Don't Rock The Boat Syndrome

Earlier, I mentioned my encounter in the Charles H. Brown High School Gymnasium with Mr. Starr and Mr. J.T. Coleman, Principal. If you are still wondering who Mr. Coleman is, he is a Black Man. Apparently, Mr. Starr spoke with Mr. Colemen and related to him his dissatisfaction with me since I did not somehow miraculously realize he was in the gym, and I did not come running over to shake his hand and acknowledge his presence with my head halfway bowed. I eventually discovered what I felt about Mr. Starr, at the time the incident occurred, was accurate.

As it was, I remember on the last day of school, the principal-Mr. J. T. Coleman-informed me that "I would not work at the high school during the coming Fall Semester 1954" (I had been considered for the principalship of the school and that person-myself-would be transferred). I said "Oh! Thank you (I had been informed of my planned transfer by my other friends and co-workers a few weeks earlier)." I heard the news through the Grapevine so I was not shocked by Mr. J.T. Coleman's *revelations*. Therefore, as Clarence Carter later sung in his song Turn Back The Hands Of Time, as I was about to walk out of the office door, Mr. J.T. Coleman ask me if I wanted to know why I was being transferred? I stopped in my tracks; I turned around, and said "To think of it, Why?" He stated that "I did not have respect for authority." To myself, I said "What authority?" I knew exactly what he meant, and with all of the educational challenges the students in Webster Parish have, both Black and White, I laughed to myself feeling we still have such a long way to go because our priorities are upside down.

I had bigger fish to fry so I put a pin in this "No Respect For Authority" thing, and I continued to prepare myself to leave Louisiana for Medical School in Washington, DC.

To avoid any confusion, and similar to the layers that makeup and onion, my Howard University Medical School Interview occurred in August 1954, and my Exit Interview from Charles H. Brown High School occurred a few days later during the same month and year. Thus, my intent was to explain the latter first and my Medical School Interview last because I included it in the next Chapter, which focus primarily on my Howard University Medical School Experience.

CHAPTER XIV

HOWARD UNIVERSITY MEDICAL SCHOOL IN WASHINGTON, DC FROM 1954 TO 1958

A. Howard University Medical School Mystery Letter

For some strange reason, the above sent me a letter that informed me I was on its schedule to be interviewed in Atlanta, GA during the summer 1954 to determine whether I would be accepted into its Medical School. As I have pointed-out repeatedly thus far, going to Medical School was as important to me as every inhalation and exhalation I took 24 hours a day! Either I received the letter, and in the process of dealing with the demands of my recent marriage to Swedie Weary Brown Braud, I may have inadvertently misplaced my invitation letter to follow through with scheduling an interview with the Howard University Medical School, or it may be possible Swedie got the invitation letter and forgot to tell me about it? So, to this day, I still am unclear what happened to my invitation letter. My chance of going to Medical School was in jeopardy.

In fact, since I did not timely respond to the Howard University Medical School Invitation Letter to schedule an interview, its administration assumed I was not interested. In the early summer of nineteen hundred fifty-four, I got a letter from the Howard University Medical School stating that I had not reported for an interview it scheduled for me in Atlanta, GA. Consequently, I read in their follow up letter that they were going to close my application. Had I missed my once in a lifetime chance to go to Medical School is all I could think about? But, I quickly gathered my wits about me and I immediately contacted the Howard University Medical School and ask If I could still have the interview? I informed this Medical

School that I was going to the University of Illinois for the summer 1954 session. I was greatly relieved to learn the Howard University Medical School re-assured me that it would get someone to interview me on the University of Illinois Urbana Champaign Campus, or in Chicago.

B. Howard University Medical School Interview Day In August 1954

Toward the end of my summer session of graduate studies at the University of Illinois Urbana Champaign Campus, I had not heard from the Howard University Medical School about when someone here would interview me. I called this Medical School and I was told if I would come to Washington, DC, I could have the interview whenever I arrived. When I ended this telephone conversation, I was happy as a Lark, and singing like a Mockingbird at the beginning of springtime on a warm and breezy day! I was overjoyed, and I did all I could not to break out running and hollowing at the top of my voice. I knew with an interview I could talk my way through it successfully, and simultaneously demonstrate to the interviewer that I possessed the *Right Stuff* to be an asset to the Howard University Medical School Culture. I prayed I had not misled anyone because I was not overconfident or cocky. I had my apprehensions so I intended to take all the precautions I could to have the best interview I could. The first thing I planned to do was carefully listen to every question I would be ask so I could reply as clearly and specifically as possible.

When I received word via my telephone conversation with someone from the administrative staff of the Howard University Medical School that informed me, if I travel to Washington, DC, an interview would be set up. Since I was at the University of Illinois Urbana Champaign when I confirmed I could have an interview upon my arrival in Washington, DC, I had to figure out a way to travel to the latter. A fellow graduate student lived in Washington, DC, and when I told him I needed to go to the city for an interview, he agreed to let me ride in his car with him. Our journey to Washington, DC went very smoothly. It took us a day to drive there.

When we arrived, I was dropped-off at the Dunbar Hotel located on U Street. As you can imagine, I was really excited and happy because I had taken a "big leap of faith," from the security of working at Charles H. Brown High School, toward realizing my childhood dream of becoming a Medical Doctor. For the first time in my life, while I sat on the bed in my hotel room, with the moisture of tears in my eyes, I imagined what it might feel like being a Medical Doctor? What I felt was more than just my imagination running away with me; my thought of being a Medical Doctor felt good to me, and I was young, gifted, and ready for the challenges ahead.

It was Friday afternoon; I was in DC; and I was ready to enjoy a few minutes with some of the people I made friends with while I was on active duty in the Navy. Once I got some rest, I contacted a few friends, who I knew beforehand during my travels. One of them was Bill Hicks, who I formerly met in the US Navy at the National Navy Medical Center in Bethesda, MD in 1947. We spent some time together, along with a few other good friends that weekend. I had a glorious weekend getting to see many of my old friends from the National Naval Medical Center days. It was good to see all of them, and they all looked so well. We reminisced about our past experiences together; I told them why I was in Washington, DC, and what my plan of action was. Everyone was so happy for me, and wished me their best. When my weekend festivities came to an end, it was time for me to take care of my business.

The first thing I did was to make sure I dressed appropriately. I also made sure I was very clear on why I wanted to become a Medical Doctor.

C. Joseph L. Johnson, MD And Dean Of The Howard University Medical School Conduct Interview

The day of my interview was on a Monday. When I got out of bed, I did my usual bathroom routine, and I ate my breakfast. Afterwards, I made a telephone call to the Howard University Medical School during the mid-morning. I informed the staff administrator that I was in Washington, DC, and I wanted to schedule an appointment for an interview. The lady told me that I could have the interview whenever I arrived at the Medical School. I was given all of the necessary directions. I realized I needed to dress as business-like as I could because first impressions are usually lasting ones. That is, non-verbal is 90.0 percent of communication. Toward this end, I put on my favorite two-piece suit; it was an olive green color with a conservative tone; I wore a white shirt and matching necktie. I looked very dapper and ready to have my interview. I felt good and there were a few butterflies, or a little nervousness, which I planned to use to my advantage during my interview. Once I was fully dressed, I called a taxi cab to bring me to the Howard University Medical School. It was a short drive from the Dunbar Hotel on U Street and 16th Street.

When the taxi cab pulled up in front of the Medical School, I was very impressed with the building and its architecture. It looked like it was a Four-Story Building. It had an aura of purpose, and it gave off a feeling that whoever enter the Howard University Medical School, that person would be transformed into a Medical Doctor. As I sat momentarily in the taxi cab, my mind reflected back to the first day I saw Dr. Stephen Campbell dressed in all white, which is the same day I decided I wanted to become a Medical Doctor also when I grow up. So, there I was sitting in the taxi cab all grown up, and about to take the *first step toward becoming my dream in real time*. This feeling seemed like it lasted for an hour; it surfaced in my mind; and, disappeared again in my subconscious in a matter of a few seconds. I paid the taxi cab driver; picked up my small briefcase, and I walked up the steps of the Medical School Building and walked through the door, and made my way to the administrative office on the First Floor. I was greeted warmly, and I was escorted to the Howard University Medical School Dean's Office Conference Room.

It was a large room with a big, polished, wooden, table in it. I was told to have a seat. I placed my notepad on the table in front of me, and I thought to myself "This is the moment I have been dreaming about for a long time, and now it has arrived." I reminded myself to listen carefully and use my nervousness as a positive energy to demonstrate my desire to study medicine and become a Medical Doctor. Everything was going as I had envisioned they would.

Moments later, I was greeted by a distinguished looking gentleman, who told me he was the Dean of the Medical School, and he would be the interviewer. This was Dr. Joseph L. Johnson. He was short with large penetrating eyes and he wore eyeglasses. Dr. Joseph L. Johnson was a champion in the struggle to breakdown the doors of racial segregation that had barred many Black People from pursuing their dreams of becoming a Medical Doctor. According to Herbert M. Morais, "he urged that the medical schools of the South and the border states, including those of the

District of Columbia, abandon their racial restrictions in the admission of students...the main burden for training Negro doctors still rested on Howard and Meharry. Of the 588 Negro medical students in 1947-48, 49, or 84.2 per cent, were enrolled in these schools. In 1955-56, Howard and Meharry had 525 students, or 69.0 percent of the 761 Negroes enrolled in the country's medical colleges."[103] I was about to be interviewed by one of the pioneers, who led the struggle to get Black People like myself into Medical School. I dearly wanted to receive the medical School Training Howard University Medical School had to offer so I could take up the sword in the fight to breakdown the racial barriers that were inhibiting our people from obtaining a Medical School Education, especially in the South. I was a willing and potential Medical School soldier! During my later Professional Medical Practice Years, I also became a pioneer like Dr. Joseph L. Johnson when I broke down the door that had barred Black Physicians from doing their Residency Training in Anesthesia at Charity Hospital in New Orleans, LA.

After Dr. Joseph L. Johnson greeted me, we sat in a conference room and the interview began. Dr. Joseph L. Johnson was very polite and relaxed. On the other hand, I was somewhat nervous but tried my best not to make it so noticeable. We discussed all of the usual things about education, college, graduate school, military and so forth. Dr. Joseph L. Johnson was measuring my ability to recall various experiences I had in the past, and relate them systematically to contemporary topics. In other words, has anything changed in graduate education since I entered the University of Illinois Urbana Champaign?, for example. There was also discussion on family and family relations.

a. Medical School Tuition Payment Question

Midway through the interview, Dr. Joseph L. Johnson ask me this question: "Young man, you say that you are married; you have two or three children; you have no father; your mother is a widow; how are you going to finance a medical education? I had anticipated this question might come up, and

---

[103] Morais, Herbert M., THE HISTORY OF THE AFRO-AMERICAN IN MEDICINE, The Publishers Agency, Inc., Cornwells Heights, Pennsylvania, 1978, p. 138.

I was ready with an answer for it. I was eager to inform him that I had the following means: (1) one-and a-half years left on my GI Bill, out of state aid, (3) wife support, (4) Teacher Retirement that I could cash-in, and (5) there was a potential oil well discovery on the Braud Family Estate in Louisiana. Regarding the oil well situation, I informed Dr. Joseph L. Johnson an oil company was actively surveying our property in Louisiana for oil. The former gave us a meager thirty-five dollars a month for each family group. It wasn't much money to talk about but it could help my situation in some small way. The second item listed as a part of my financial means to pay my way through Medical School is very interesting, and it is directly linked to the southern climate of segregation in the South.

b. Louisiana "Out Of State" Tuition Program

During the 1950s, the Louisiana Department of Education, and given the fact it enforced a razor sharp division between White and Black Higher Education (Jim Crow and Separate But Equal), barred any Black Person, who desired to obtain a Masters Degree, Doctoral Degree, or Medical Doctor Degree, from acquiring one from an accredited four-year higher education institution in Louisiana. This department, instead, developed a Jim Crow Out Of State Tuition Program, which provided any approved Black Person with a $5,000 Scholarship to attend any Graduate School, or Medical School of his or her choice to obtain one or more of the mentioned degrees. The tuition payment was available as long as one pursued their degree(s) at any school of higher learning outside of Louisiana. Normally at the time, a Black Student could not apply for admission at any university with a Graduate School in the South. Jim Crow placed a lock and chain on the entrance door. This was the case, everywhere in the South as late as the mid-1960s, and everyone who is still alive today remembers, James Meridith and Vivian Malone were initially barred from admission to the University of Alabama. President John F. Kennedy's Assassination can be partly attributed to the fact he tried to help Black People, and others of Color, to obtain their human rights.

It is very interesting that the Louisiana Department of Education would develop such a racist program, given the fact all of the data indicates that African Slaves provided all of the labor required to build and sustain the southern economy for several centuries. Yet, the descendants of African

Slaves were forced to leave the South to obtain their advanced degrees. The most egregious and cold-hearted thing about this "Out Of State" Tuition Program is the descendants of African Slaves were barred from attending the four year accredited Louisiana universities that their ancestors built with their labor. The purpose of education is to demonstrate that such behavior is short-sighted, ungrounded in reality, and is an affront to human dignity and integrity; and worse, it shows that prohibition of Black Students from obtaining advanced degrees at Louisiana Institutions of Higher Education is a violation of their human rights.

In addition, there was another source of Out of State Tuition offered in Louisiana, namely, the Emily Bundick Tuition Program. It was supported by money provided by Emily Bundick, who was a White Female Philanthropist. The $5,000 Scholarship was available to Black Students, from Louisiana, to go to Medical School. In either case, Black Students were usually successful in getting a higher education degree from a university located in the West, East, or Midwest. As I remember, I took advantage of this program by the beginning of my second semester in the Howard University Medical School.

c. Grass Cutting Business During Medical School Study From Fall1954 To 1958

As I have often mentioned before, I was not going to allow a lack of money to be a determinant whether I completed Medical School. To insure I had money in my pocket, I started my grass cutting business during the first year I was in Medical School. I had the tools to get the job done quickly and effectively. I would cut the neighbor's lawns on the weekend, holidays, and sometimes on days when I had a light course load. I had a lawnmower and some other tools to edge around shrubs and the sidewalk. I advertised my grass cutting business with a sign that read-Lawn cutting, $3 to $5.

I operated my grass cutting business for four years. I wanted my Medical Doctors Degree bad enough that cutting grass was very easy to do. Some people's pride kept them from achieving their life goals because many today feel cutting grass is beneath them. If one has an earned college degree, and the only job they can get is cutting grass, then that is a "serious problem." The work involved did not scare me because I grew up in Brookstown working on the farm. I was use to working hard, and I transferred my willingness to work hard to my Medical School Courses. I did not mention my plan to start my grass cutting business to Dr. Joseph L. Johnson because I had to wait until he informed me whether I would be accepted into the Howard University Medical School. By the time my interview with the Dean was over, I knew I had been accepted by this school.

At the conclusion of my interview with Dr. Joseph L. Johnson, he told me I would receive a favorable letter of acceptance to attend the Howard University Medical School. And, as I have already mentioned, he told me to go ahead and terminate my employment at Charles H. Brown High School. I did. "At last, my love had come along." I felt the way Etta James did when she bellowed-out these famous words in her song with the same title. At Last, I was accepted into Howard University Medical School; it had been 23 years since I first decided I wanted to be a Medical Doctor while I was growing up on the Gravel Road in Brookstown. When My interview was over, I returned to my home in Springhill, LA briefly in August 1954.

D. Howard University Medical School First Year From Fall 1954 To Spring 1954

Swedie Weary Braud continued to teach Home Economics at Charles H. Brown High School during the 1954-1955 School Year. For a few weeks in August 1954, we spent this time getting everything together, including but not limited to, all of my finances and business. We had to workout where the children were going to school; where were monies coming from in order for the situation to work smoothly. We had recently purchased a new house that had a substantial mortgage. With the Lillian Luellen Pierce Braud Strategic Family Development Plan in place, part of which called for Geraldine Braud to provide me with some financial assistance while enrolled in Medical School, and my other siblings, who had completed college, would see that our youngest sibling finish college. In addition, Swedie and I made arrangements for me to go to Medical School also. Overall, everything seemed to have fallen in place.

Swedie Braud would stay in our Springhill, LA home, and continue to teach Home Economics at Charles H. Brown High School. Regarding our children, Brenda Brown Braud began the First Grade at Charles H.

Brown Elementary School, which was a part of the high school complex (Charles H. Brown High School went from Kindergarten to the Eleventh Grade), in Springhill, LA; Brownsyn Braud began the First Grade at the St. Louis Elementary School in Welcome, LA (Brookstown). By the time I started my first year of Medical School, both of my children entered the First Grade respectively. I left my home in Springhill, LA a few days early so I could get myself registered in my medical school courses as well as give myself some time to meet some of my medical school classmates. I also had to locate a place to live.

a. 11th Street Apartment

I returned to Washington, DC on the Greyhound Bus. When I arrived, I took a taxi to a home owned by a woman who I became good friends with while I was in the Navy. Her name was Fannie Harang. Thomas Harang, Fannie's brother, also lived in the home with her. Fannie and Thomas Harang were from Hammond, LA. I met Fannie Harang and Brownsyn Braud's mother at the USO Club in Washington, DC a few years earlier. My travel back to the area was uneventful but all of my senses were filled-up with great hope of succeeding in my new adventure. By the time the medical school opened for the Fall 1954 Semester, I had secured a place to live, and I had located a place where I could get regular meals. Specifically, on the first morning of the first day of the beginning of the semester, there were a group of my classmates standing on the concrete steps of the Howard University Medical School. I said a warm hello to my classmates, and one of them, in particular, I was drawn to talk to. His name was Zebedee Nevels. He caught my attention because he was more jovial than the rest of my classmates, and I guess I wanted to be around his energy because going to Medical School was, of course, new to me. While talking to Zebedee, he told me he was looking for a roommate to share his apartment, and, coincidentally, I was looking for a place to stay. There is something to the idea of synchronicity. I moved in Zebedee Nevel's apartment after my first day of medical school courses ended Monday afternoon. The apartment was located on 11th Street NW not far from the medical school. The other thing Zebedee Nevels and I had in common is we were both married, and our wives did not come with us to live until the end of our second year in Medical School.

The 11th Street NW Apartment was located in the Black neighborhood. And, there is one thing you can count on and that is, there are some Black-Owned Restaurants where one can get some "finger-lickin'" good, tasty, down home food. Zebedee and I located just such a restaurant on Georgia Avenue. It is what many know today as a "greasy spoon" restaurant. Many days while we were on our way to this restaurant, we could smell the scent of soul food cooking in the air. The menu usually consisted of different types of beans, rice, cornbread, chicken, both fried and stewed, greens of various kinds, pork chops, steaks, various deserts and more. In short, this food was very nurturing to me because it always reminded me of the Gravel Road where I grew up in Brookstown. At the time, I could buy a full course dinner for no more than $2.

b. Fall Semester 1954 Medical School Coursework

When I enrolled in the Howard University Medical School, my class consisted of 70 students. There were 4 student carryovers from a prior enrolled class in our group. Of the 70 original students I started Medical School with in my class, there were 40 Black Males (57.1%); 18 White Males (25.7%); 7 Black Females (10.0%); 1 Asian-American (1.4%); 1 Indian-American (1.4%); and, 1 White Female (1.4%). Interestingly, there was one Black Male student in my class from Donaldsonville, LA. His name was George Wilkins. As I remember, his family operated a shoemaker and repair business in Donaldsonville, LA. George Wilkins had a sister name Olga Lou Wilkins, who was one class ahead of me when I attended the Lowery Training School during my childhood.

Finally, I was in Medical School, and I was ready to dive into my coursework; I was ready to learn all I could and more. It did not take very long for me to become adjusted to Medical School. A good portion of my Freshman Year was geared toward Anatomy. As such, my Anatomy Courses and Anatomy Lab were like a refresher course for me since I got a good foundation in the subject matter from the Lowery Training School and Graduate School at the University of Illinois Urbana Champaign. I was in good academic shape!

As far as my finances were concerned, everything fell in place. I had multiple sources of funds that I mentioned earlier. And, I operated my grass cutting business between classes and on weekends and holidays. I was also given textbooks from several organizations through the years. As it turned out, I had more money while in Medical School than I had my whole life. Everybody flourished; Swedie and our children were in good shape, and they did not want for anything. I was able to meet all of my obligations with a few dollars to spare. When I got down to the "nitty gritty" of my Medical School Coursework, I did run into a slight hiccup.

c. Professor Moses Young And Neuro-Anatomy Coursework

As I mentioned already, I arrived at the Howard University Medical School with a strong foundation in Anatomy. Mr. Jackson, my 10th Grade Science Teacher at the Lowery Training School, taught me everything I needed to know about Anatomy. Remember, from the time I was five years old, I decided I wanted to be Medical Doctor so, by the time I got to Mr. Jackson's Science Class, I was a total sponge because Anatomy made me feel like one. The more difficult Anatomy became, the easier it was for me to learn how all of the parts of the human anatomy work together.

So when I took Professor Moses Young's Neuro-Anatomy Course during my Freshman Year in Medical School, I was "on top of my game" as the old saying goes. Professor Young was a Black Man. Occasionally during class, Professor Young would make the comment "You fellas think you know." I thought my purpose was to know and learn more so I could know more and so forth. Because I knew Neuro-Anatomy well, and I also knew I had some room to learn more about the subject matter, every time Professor Young class met, and no matter what the Neuro-Anatomy question of the day was, he would "always" call on me to answer it. And, I did. I did not understand why Professor Young Always called on me because there were students in the class who were Phi Beta Kappa, and they were very smart. But, he would not call on them but mostly me.

After one of the class sessions, some of the other students came up to me and said some nice things to me like "Wow, you are really well versed in the Neuro-Anatomy." Or, some said "How does the subject come to you so easily." Or, one said "You have a very good way of articulating some very difficult Anatomy Relationships, by reducing them down to a very clear and understandable level of comprehension." By the end of my conversation with some of my classmates about the situation, one of them said "Professor Moses Young is either going to give you and "A" grade in

Neuro-Anatomy or and "F" grade." I was just being myself in the Neuro-Anatomy Class. But, I understood what the remark meant. Somewhere on the inside of Professor Moses Young was his heart, and I knew in his heart, he wanted his students to excel academically. So, I went on about my coursework, and I continued to be called upon by Professor Young to answer more questions.

What is more, Professor Young would often drop-in on my Anatomy Lab Class to see how I was doing. I guess he wanted to see if I was able to apply the theory he taught me in his classroom to actual experimental conditions in the Laboratory. In the end, I did earn an "D" grade in Neuro-Anatomy. Actually, I performed well in most of my courses and associated labs such as Bacteriology, Neurology, Bio-Chemistry, and Physiology among others. While everything was going along just fine during my Freshman Year of Medical School, everything was not all "Peaches and Cream."

Medical School, under the best of circumstances, is quite demanding academically, and I had to *stay in the books to stay on the top shelf.* Being a human being with feelings, I was, at times, afraid and anxious; I had occasional thoughts of self-doubt; and, I went through periods when I did not trust myself as much as I did during other less stressful times. I worked through my feelings, and one of the things that kept me afloat is the fact becoming a Medical Doctor was *my dream, and there was a price to pay.* I was willing to pay it! The other thing that steadied my hands was my mother's belief in me that I could become a Medical Doctor one day, and my siblings' shared love, which they gave me unconditionally.

While I was going through my first year of Medical School, and in October to be exact, a riot broke-out at Anacostia High School in 1954.

d. Anacostia High School And The 11th Street Riot And The 13th-16th Street Riots In 1954

Washington, DC Public Schools were segregated by the early 1950s. A Consolidated Parents Group, which consisted of Parents and Students who lived in Northeast Washington, DC, had been struggling to desegregate public schools since 1947. According to Washington Area Spark, "the District's Integration took place following the Supreme Court's Bolling v. Sharpe decision in May 1954 that was brought about by the consolidated

Parent Group. Consolidated represented parents and students living in Northeast and led a seven year fight that began with a boycott of deplorable conditions at the all black Browne Junior High on Benning Road."[104] "White students chase newly admitted African American students October 4, 1954 at Anacostia High School...The most intense resistance took place at Anacostia where rallies of up to 1,000 students took place including an attempt to march across the 11th Street Bridge to rally support at other schools."[105] This was a very intense riot, and it went on within a stone's throw of the Nation Capitol. I was enrolled at the Howard University Medical School because no other Medical Schools would open their doors to train Black Medical Doctors. I received money from the Louisiana Out Of State Tuition Program, which is evidence that no Black Student could earn a Medical Degree from a university that offered them in the state. Little Black Girls and Boys were barred from the best educational facilities based on the Supreme Court Separate but Equal Ruling. This was the state of play across the country and in Washington, DC.

Being enrolled in the Howard University Medical School, and having grown up on the Gravel Road where plantations dominated the landscape as I have shown earlier, it is a miracle that I was in Medical School at one of the most prestigious centers of Black Learning in America, at the time the 11th Street Riot broke-out. I did not get involved in it, but I vowed to never forget the pain my people felt with so many doors locked that barred them from achieving their dreams of getting a good education. In addition, there was also a riot that broke-out in the area of 13th and 14th Streets. This riot was likely an extension of the injustices Black People were faced with in their lives. Rather than high school students in the vanguard of the 13th to 14th Streets Riot, it was led by adults of varying ages. There was a lot of window breaking; some looting; and a few fires were also set. While these riots were going-on near Howard University Medical School, I never got involved in them, or lost sight of what my Aunt Leah shared with me during my childhood.

---

[104] Washington Area Spark, "White students terrorize Anacostia black students: 1954," www.flickr.com. For more information, go to www.flickr.com/gp/washington area spark/564wW3

[105] Ibid.

My Aunt Leah told me during my childhood that education is the *Key* that unlocks the future. She told me, years before there was NASA, that people would be moving around in space. An education she injected "would make that possible." Segregation was designed to keep Black People from realizing education is the key they need to unlock the educational door. Without one, Black People, and others of color, would move around only within the confined space of the ten blocks in the neighborhood where they live.

E. Completion Of First Year Of Medical School And Navy Reserve, Fall 1954 To Spring 1955 And Summers 1955 To 1958

All-in-all, my first year was highly productive in the classroom. My grades were outstanding, and my efforts paid-off because I finished the year within the Top 10% of my Freshman Class. This was great because I was in a class with some heavy hitters; I was around some very talented students, and I was right at home in their company. I had come a very long way from the days when I would go in "Gerra" Roberts Grocery Store, and purchase a few items my mother sent me their to pick up. I always laugh when I think about how "Gerra" would put his hands over his wrinkled ledger notebook to keep me from seeing what he had written down in it. Now, I was studying Medicine, and one day I might have an occasion to administer medical assistance to him or a relative. I was rolling along like a well-oiled wheel; there were no squeaky sounds or chinks in my self-determination armor. I wasted no time.

After my beautiful Freshman Year, I spent a month and a half in the Navy Ensign 1995 Program. I was stationed at the Portsmouth Naval Yard located in Portsmouth, VA. It was a Naval Reserve Program for Medical Students, which provided them drill requirements at the end of the school year.

The program was rewarding and it was an honor to wear the Naval Officers Uniform. I was in all probability one of the first Black Officers, who was accepted in this program. During the late forties and early fifties, there were very few Black People wearing the Naval Officers Uniform. Moreover, the Navy Ensign 1995 Program was also a source of income to help me with Medical School and personal expenses. With a portion of the allotment I received, I was able to send my mother some funds also. I participated in the Navy 1995 Program for three years, or during each summer I was enrolled in Medical School.

In short, during the mid-1950s, there were very few Black People wearing the Naval Officers Uniform. As one might expect, Systemic Racism, similar to termites in wood, had permeated every branch of the military and civilian institutions, and the Navy was no exception. No doubt, this was one of the major factors that accounted for the low number of Black Navy Officers in the Navy Ensign1995 Program.

At any rate, I am proud of the fact I was one of the early pioneers that broke down the door that barred Black People from becoming an officer in the Navy Ensign 1995 Program.

After my summer duty in the Norfolk, VA area, I returned to Washington, DC a week or so later. I started back with my weekends and holidays grass cutting business. This fellow had all of the tools needed for the business. I was a forerunner of today's landscape business in which there are hundreds of such businesses operating in villages, towns, and cities, from coast to coast. Swedie came to Washington, DC for the summer 1955. We stayed in my original apartment I shared with Zebedee Nevels; he moved out because his wife came to live with him. They got another apartment in the same building. We were able to go a few places such as New York City. We visited with my friend Bill Hicks and his wife and some of their friends. We went to a Broadway Play.

The children did not come, which was somewhat of a setback. Brenda Braud was taken to visit with her relatives in Chicago, IL. Moreover, while Swedie was visiting with me, and given the fact we had both agreed 100% that we felt it was a good plan for me to enroll in the Howard University Medical School, seemingly out of the blue, she made a very strange comment to me that I did not expect to ever hear.

Summer vacation from school had come and gone. It was time to get back to business. For some unknown reason, Swedie got in her head that she was sorry that I had gone to Medical School. That comment caused me to get upset and worry more than I should. Seemingly, I was unable to get it together. I became very depressed, and could not get that funny feeling off my back.

F. Swedie Braud Came to Washington, DC To Stay In May 1956 To 1958

Before Swedie Braud left Washington, DC at the end of the summer 1955 to return to Springhill, LA to resume teaching Home Economics at Charles H. Brown High School, she planted a seed of doubt in my mind about Medical School. I had never had any doubt about what I was doing; I was certain I would finish Medical School but when my intimate partner uttered some disbelief in my achieving my Medical Doctor Dream, that was a "Big Deal." Swedie's doubt in my dream affected my academic performance. I was afraid to talk to anyone about my dilemma, and my grades went down. My second year in Medical School, from the Fall 1956 to Spring 1957, was consumed with some doubt in my mind. It took almost my entire second year for me to get back on target. I did get a few scholarships for books, which was encouraging. I was struggling because I was pregnant with the idea of giving birth to becoming a Medical Doctor, and some doubt could cause me to abort my dream. I had scrapped rice and potatoes back on the Gravel Road so I had to call upon ALL of my determination I learned from my Braud Family group to weather the storm raging on the inside of my mind. When I remembered where I came from, and where I was going, and similar to a pinhole in a balloon, the doubt planted in my mind slowly began to dissipate, deflate, shrink, and disappear. And, I felt a turnaround and stronger too.

At the end of my second year in Medical School, Swedie came to Washington, DC to stay. By the time she arrived, I had self-examined and done some consistent self-reflection. I was in a good balanced place. I was determined as usual to complete Medical School come "Hell or High Water." No mountain was high enough to keep me from getting my Medical Degree and becoming a Medical Doctor. And, no matter how hard anyone tried they could not stop me now from achieving my goal. I said it loud within myself every day, both when I was awake and sleep. I breathed Medical School; it was oxygen to me! Therefore, things progressed very well, and I was again in pursuit of finishing Medical School. Swedie was able to get employment as a Dietician with DC General Hospital, and she also worked in the same capacity for St. Elizabeth Hospital. There were no financial hardships, we were able to attend a few shows, movies, plays and so forth. In the Greek Language, this *anthropas estin kalos*. Translated in English, the sentence means "this man is in a good place and happy. When the summer 1956 arrived at the end of my second year in Medical School, I returned to Portsmouth Naval Hospital to participate in the Ensign 1995 Program.

a. Third And Senior Years In Medical School From 1956 To 1958

I adjusted to Swedie Braud being with me during this time. I was now in the heart of my Medical School Coursework. I could begin to see a glimmer of light at the end of the tunnel. Swedie was working as a Dietician for the hospitals mentioned earlier; thus, she was busy working and I was busy working my Medical School Program. We were dancing together and seldom did we step on each other's feet. As it is written in the literature, *as the horseman rode toward the windmill, it continuously receded into the distance.* For me, I was steadily moving toward reaching the end of my Medical School Work. My third year in Medical School was uneventful. It seemed I had squashed the doubt thought that plagued me after Swedie Braud mentioned to me that my going to Medical School may not have been a good idea. Time has a way of healing anything so I persevered on, and my third year in Medical School was a good one. I may have earned even higher grades than I did in my courses, if I did not have to deal with an emotional setback. There was no time for second guessing! In a little while, I would be a senior in Medical School.

During my third year, Swedie and I enjoyed some of our weekends with my friends. For example, we spent a weekend in New York visiting my friend Bill Hicks (He was my old buddy from the days at The National Naval Medical Center). We had a very enjoyable time attending several social events. We attended a dinner dance where Swedie wore a dress that she designed; it was beautiful and she wore it most ravishingly. If any of the males in attendance noticed me, they would clearly see my shoulders were erect and my chest was stuck-out because I was proud of my lady. Before the dinner dance was over, we were able to meet several members of Bill Hicks Family. During the summer 1957, I returned to the Portsmouth Naval Hospital for the Ensign 1995 Program. Everything went smoothly. As usual, at the end of the summer, I returned to my 11th Street Apartment, and prepared myself for my final year of study at the Howard University

Medical School. Swedie continued to work as a Dietician at the DC General and St. Elizabeth Hospitals.

b. Areas Of Specialization In Medical School From 1954 To 1958

During my Medical School Career, all of my classmates studied the same curriculum. Taking our common curriculum, each one of us was free to choose our particular area of specialization. For example, in the universe of possibilities, one could choose to specialize in Surgery, Gynecology, Neuro-Anatomy, Anesthesia, and Pediatrics among many others. Initially, I chose General Practice. I had acquired expertise to diagnose and prescribe a treatment method for most of the ailments an individual would experience, including children and adults. I did not specialize as a surgeon but I could do surgery related to stitching up an open wound; removing minor external growths; and opening up a wound and stitching it closed. Moreover, if a patient presented a health issue that I considered would require surgery of some kind, I was trained to refer the affected person to an appropriate surgeon, who could perform the necessary surgery. In addition, my Medical School Training prepared me to prescribe medicine to a patient whenever it was necessary.

However, by the time I graduated in the Spring 1958, I was also nurturing an interest in Anesthesiology. This specialty would turn out to be a centerpiece of my Medical Practice a few years later.

Thus, I had reached the end of my Medical School Training at the Howard University Medical School by the end of the Spring Semester 1958. More than you can imagine, I was overjoyed! My graduation from Medical School was imminent. To say the least, and according to the Greek Language, *Anthropas Estin Kalos*, which means this man was happy and in a good place at the time. This summed up perfectly my state of mind! I had turned the sour taste of Systemic Racism's Roadblocks, which cut short so many Black People's Dreams along the Louisiana River Road, into *honey*.

My journey from the Gravel Road was a long, bumpy, and-oftentimes-academically tedious one; however, all of my early teachers, including Aunt Leah Pierce Argieard, Mr. Jackson, my science instructor at the Lowery Training School, and Professor J. Warren Lee, Chair of the Biology Department at Southern University-ALL-prepared me to achieve my goal of becoming a Medical Doctor. The Lillian Luellen Pierce Braud Strategic Family Development Plan provided me with crucial emotional and financial support to endure the rigors of Medical School. And, my siblings were my biggest supporters and cheerleaders! They still are today too. Their collective energy gave me the constant boost I needed when I felt somewhat overwhelmed, and there were times when I did. I am a human being.

G. Graduation From Howard University Medical School And Passage Of The Maryland Medical Board Examination In The Spring 1958

On the day of my graduation in May 1958, my Braud Family in Louisiana and Washington, DC were very happy for me. Most of my Braud Family Group came to celebrate my graduation with me. I was proud to have them at my graduation. In attendance were Lillian Luellen Pierce Braud, my mother, Edgar Braud, my brother, Geraldine Braud, my sister, Suky Chapmann, my sister, Mary Anne, my sister, and Bill Hicks, my good friend from my Navy Days. Swedie and Brenda Braud were excited; Brenda Braud was ten years old. She was old enough by the time of my graduation to grasp some of the significance of my accomplishment. Everyone of my siblings did; they were all happy for me, and especially my mother-Lillian Luellen Pierce Braud. She had walked the Gravel Road with me for many years, and if my statistics are correct, I was the first African-American, who began a trend of a procession of Medical Doctors, whose origins can be traced back to my Braud Family Group on the River Road. Lillian Luellen Pierce Braud, and Joe Braud, who was deceased 22 years by the time I graduated from the Howard University Medical School, were the source of this unprecedented trend. I am in complete gratitude for the love and efforts they gave to my development through the years.

The weather was perfect. I could not have ordered any finer day in which to graduate; I could see more blue skies than clouds. I was elated, happy, and overjoyed all at the same time. My Graduation Table was prepared before me, and my cup truly overflowed. There were 69 Medical Students seated at our Graduation Table. This was my class forever. Our graduation ceremony took place outdoors near Crampton Hall.

My Graduation Program consisted of two parts, namely, a Baccalaureate Ceremony and a Commencement Ceremony. Dr. Mordecai W. Johnson, who was the President of Howard University delivered the Baccalaureate Address, and the Honorable John Sherman Cooper, US Senator, delivered the Commencement Address. Both speakers urged my Graduation Class to not forget the work that went on by others that paved the way, or opened doors, so my/our Graduation Class could obtain a Medical Degree. We were also told to avoid becoming selfish; rather, do everything we could to help those prospective Medical Students, who were aspiring to achieve a Medical Degree. All-in-all, my entire Graduation Celebration was something to behold!

Moreover, as an appreciation of our academic achievement, the Howard University Medical School Senior Class went on a one-week vacation before my graduation day. There were a lot of activities going-on such as golf, various card games, and sporting games among others. It goes without saying, there was also a lot of good food available to choose from, including soft and hard drinks. We were celebrating surviving four rigorous years in Medical School. My Senior Class took a one-week vacation held at Bear Mountain Resort near New York City. It was sponsored by one of the pharmaceutical companies.

From the first day of my Medical School Training, where I met Zebedee Nevels and my other classmates standing on the steps of the Howard University Medical School, and after mowing the lawns of numerous local residents, on the weekends and holidays, to make extra money to support myself while I was in Medical School, to the last day when I marched across the graduation stage, ALL of my efforts, both in the classroom and outside of it, had paid me a handsome dividend. By the time my gradation came to an end, I was now Joseph Pierce Braud, MD. My Medical Doctor Dream, which was born in my mind on the Gravel Road 27 years earlier, when I was five years old, had finally come true!!

That being so, and in order to legally open-up my medical practice in the near future, I had to pass the Maryland Medical Board Examination to do so. By 1958, Maryland had one of the most challenging board examinations because, if a graduate of a medical school passed it, he or she would be eligible to practice medicine in every state. This is called reciprocity. For example, Louisiana is my home, and I would be able to practice medicine there, if I successfully passed the Maryland Medical Board Examination. Howard University Medical School was one of the best in the nation, and I had no doubt the medical training I received was sufficient for me to pass this board.

As it was, I took the exam soon after I graduated; I believe I took it during the same month I received my Medical Degree-May 1958. My exam score was in the upper percentile. Of all those who took this test, I was happy to be among the group whose test score fell in this category. Those test scores in this group were considered among the highest earned on the board exam. I was extremely satisfied with my academic performance. The next move, or decision I had to make, is where would I do my Post-Medical School Internship? With my graduation, my four years of Medical School came to an end. But, it was not the end because Swedie and I had to make plans for the upcoming 1958-1959 School Year.

CHAPTER XV

POST-HOWARD UNIVERSITY MEDICAL SCHOOL INTERNSHIP DECISION AND FAMILY MATTERS

When I started my Medical School Training, it looked like it would not ever come to an end. Every day there was work and more work to do. There was one course lecture and lab after the next. Remembering what my Aunt Leah Braud Argieard told me years earlier that Education is the Key," I "stayed the course" with all kinds of days following each other, both happy, sad, and sometimes indifferent. Yet, through it all, I graduated with my Medical Doctors Degree, and it was time for my family and I to decide what is the "best" next move to make?

A. Howard University Medical School Hospital Internship Program, Fall 1958 To Spring 1959

My decision was not a complicated one to make. It was a matter of staying in Washington, DC, or relocating to another part of the United States to do my Internship. Very few, if any, hospitals paid a stipend to interns. My family would make out better if there was an Internship Program that gave a reasonable stipend, and provided a place to stay, including food. I had come to enjoy the Washington, DC lifestyle and cultural atmosphere, and it would be somewhat difficult to uproot my family and travel somewhere new to do my internship work. My daughter, Brenda Braud, would have to change her school; leave her friends; start over at a new school; and make some new friends. I wasn't too concerned that Brenda Braud could not make the adjustment; children are, generally speaking, easy-going and resilient.

My family's decision was to leave the Washington, DC area, and do my internship work elsewhere. So, we packed-up out things, and placed them in a U-Haul Truck. We decided to go to Youngstown, Ohio.

B. Youngstown, Ohio Hospital Association Fall 1958 To Spring 1959

After a lengthy deliberation, we decided to go to Youngstown, Ohio because the Youngstown Hospital Association paid a reasonable stipend, lodging, and food. That gave the family a chance, for the very first time, where we could all be together. Therefore, Swedie, myself, and three children eventually went to Youngstown, Ohio. We did not travel directly to the latter.

Rather, having made my decision to do my internship work at the Youngstown, Ohio Hospital, and because I had roughly two weeks before my report date, Swedie, myself, and Brenda traveled to Springhill, LA. We still maintained our house in this city while Swedie and I lived in our 11th Street Apartment in Washington, DC. Our red, cream-colored Studebaker Car was towed behind our U-Haul Truck. Upon our arrival in Springhill, LA, and after resting for a day or so, we drove our car to Brookstown to my mother's house. While I was in Medical School, my mother kept my two children, namely, Brownsyn Braud and Glenn Braud. We visited with my family and friends in Brookstown for a few days. After our visit, it was time for us to leave so I could stay on schedule to arrive in Youngstown, Ohio to begin my internship. There were enough hugs, kisses, handshakes, and tears of joy to last me for quite a while.

As I mentioned earlier, this was the first time in my life that I had all of my children in the same household. When we left my mother's house, I had Brownsyn Braud, Brenda Braud, and Glenn Braud in the car with us. I really felt good about the prospect of the joy that I would experience being around my children on a daily basis. All I could see was blue skies ahead of me now. When we arrived back in Springhill, LA, Swedie and I transferred the children's belongings into the U-Haul Truck, along with other essential items we would need when we got settled in Youngstown, Ohio. Once all of our preparations had been made, we embarked for the latter.

After arriving in Youngstown, we got a three-bedroom apartment that was supplied by the Youngstown Hospital Association. Swedie was also able to get a job as a Dietician at one of the hospitals in the area; the children entered school, and I was one of the interns in the hospital system. How did my internship program work?

a. Rotating Internship Program Fall 1958 To Spring 1959

By 1958, it was still a standard practice that a recently graduated Medical Doctor would spend at least a year in an internship program. The value of participating in an internship program would allow a Medical Doctor to do two things. One, he or she would get an opportunity to rotate through a hospital to observe how the various departments in it operate. For example, most hospitals, especially the larger ones in metropolitan areas consisted of-but not limited to-the following departments: Neurology, Oncology, Pediatrics, Anesthesiology, Surgery, Obgyn (Obstetrics and Gynecology), Pathology, and Internal Medicine among others. Second, the Medical Doctor would, while rotating through the various departments, get a feel for a particular area in which he or she would like to specialize such as Anesthesiology.

As I rotated through the various departments, I was attracted to Anesthesiology. The latter is closely tied to Surgery inasmuch as the patient had to be scientifically given the exact amount of Anesthesia to maintain one in a sleep state. The Anesthesia Dose had to be the exact amount to insure the area of surgery would remain numb, and the patient would not regain consciousness until the entire surgical process was completed. Otherwise, it could end up in what the Greeks call a *Katappobi*, or catastrophe. In short, my internship offered me an opportunity to get some hands-on experience, by observing experienced Medical Doctors at work. This is an invaluable experience because in a year or less, I would be in the drivers seat attending to my own patients. As the old saying goes "one can never receive enough training."

b. Internship Experience Today

Over the past 25 years, the Internship has become less a standard practice. In todays Post-Medical School Training, generally speaking, a Medical Doctor moves from graduation, and go directly into his or her chosen specialty. This could be due to a number of factors such as (1) the Medical

Doctor feels stressed about the prospect of another one or two years of Post-Medical School Training (2) he or she is anxious to begin their Medical Practice, and (3) one feels it is time to earn some money to pay off some of the debt accrued during Medical School. Either way, the rotating experience one would receive, by participating in an internship program, is bypassed. Time will tell what impact, if any, this modern trend will have on the patient. In the meantime, as an intern, I was a sponge because the experience gave me an opportunity to observe the Laws of Nature at work. For example, I saw quantity and quality, interpenetration of opposites, and negation play out daily as Medical Doctors worked to relieve the pain of their patients and, ultimately, save their lives. Though I was learning so much about the implementation of theory into practice, there was something still unsettled in my personal household.

C. Adoption Problem Resurfaced As An Elephant In The Room By 1959

Youngstown, OH was a steel town. It was different with its big molten furnaces, towering smokestacks, which were a constant reminder of the Co_2 released into the atmosphere, and the humming sound of the factory itself. With this backdrop which gave Youngstown, OH its economic identity, there were several crossroads that came to the forefront in my household.

Swedie Braud had been married before, and she had one daughter-Brenda during her first marriage. I knew Swedie Weary dating back to our Freshman Year at Southern University in 1943. I had not been married but I had a daughter name Brownsyn; I also had a male child, who I was raising. Everyone, that is, Swedie and I, was aware of the situation, and it had been discussed for a number of years. However, a peculiar thing happened. I adopted Swedie's daughter-Brenda-in 1959 but she could not, or would not, adopt my two children.[106] There was a difference in their ages; and they were all the same size.

---

[106] Swedie Braud was under the influence of her biological family regarding her aversion to adoption of the children. She was likely coached by her brother. He may have planted the thought in her mind related to inheritance. My children would become heirs to Swedie Braud's Estate if something happened to her. By not adopting my children, this fact would never come to pass, or become a reality.

Moreover, Swedie was not very cordial to my two children. Her behavior was noticed by individuals that were not in the family. Besides the inheritance factor, skin color was probably another subliminal thought in Swedie's Mind because, although Brownsyn Braud was beautiful with a chocolate skin tone, pre-conditioning did not allow her to adopt and accept Bronsyn Braud as her own daughter. I did not have any resistance to the children. However, Swedie seemed to have had a great burden on her hand. She had an older brother who tried to tell her how to live with her husband and family. The tension grew and Swedie finally moved out and left me and my two children in the apartment. Th children were large enough to take care of themselves in preparation for attending school. At best, there were no financial troubles, and general living was comfortable. After two months had passed, I managed to get my two children, who were with me, to a safe haven, by bringing in a caretaker to help me while I was doing my Internship Work at the hospital.

D. Bank Meeting Coincidence In Early 1960

Swedie Braud moved out of our apartment into another one toward the end of my Residency Program. This was symbolic of her deep-rooted resistance to adopting my two children. As much as we talked about her doing so, her position, which was shrouded in resistance, had become hardened like soft mortar mix does a few hours after it is poured to form a foundation of a house or other. To break up the concrete, a jackhammer would be needed, or a heavy-duty Caterpillar Tractor. Swedie was not going to change her mind about adoption of my two children, and that was final.

I was in Youngstown, Ohio for approximately two years, and had finished one year of internship and midway through the years of my General Practice Residency. One day I went about my usual routine of getting ready to go to my General Practice Residency at the Youngstown Association Hospital. I helped to get our three children ready for another day of school. I made sure they had everything they need for that day. I did not do anything that day out of the ordinary. However, one of the most non-ordinary things happened.

a. Swedie Braud Moved Out Of Apartment

That is, once the children left for school, I followed behind them shortly. Swedie worked at one of the hospitals, and she also prepared herself for her usual days work. When I returned home on the day the most non-ordinary thing happened in my life thus far, I discovered Swedie Braud had secretly planned to move out of our apartment without giving me any prior indication that she intended to do so. When I unlocked the door and entered our apartment, I found everything in their normal places except Swedie Braud. She had moved out of our apartment! I was shocked! And, afraid is an understatement of how I felt.

I was home when Brownsyn Braud and Glenn Braud arrived but Brenda Braud did not come home from school with them. She was with her mother, and I did not know where she was either. When I sat down in a chair to think about what was happening, what kept coming up in mind was two things: One, Swedie Braud was dead-set on not adopting Brownsyn Braud and Glenn Braud. And Two, Swedie's brother had visited with us two weeks before she left me and my two children. After one month or so, I manage to stabilize, to some degree, the impact of Swedie Braud's absence on my two children, by getting a middle-aged Black Woman, who was recommended to me by a friend, to come to my apartment a few days a week to help out with cooking, washing clothes, keeping the floors and dishes clean, and sometimes going to the grocery store to purchase groceries when I had to work on weekends. At this time, I was half way through my one year of General Practice Residency. Soon, I would be faced with a decision about what would be my next move after I completed my General Practice Residency.

Now, it was time for me to decide where to go, and what to do with the family that I had scattered in Youngstown, Ohio. Neither one of us knew anyone in that city. We had managed to make a few acquaintances. I had difficulty trying to make the right decision. For example, if I left Swedie and Brenda in Youngstown, OH, and no matter where I decided to go, we would be very far apart, regarding physical distance. We were very far apart when it came to emotional distance. But, survival is an interesting idea Charles Darwin used to prove how species originate, develop, and adapt to their environment. I found myself in a place of having to adapt to some major changes that had recently occurred in my personal family life.

b. Decision To Reunite Amidst Unspoken Internal Dialogue

Specifically, I felt somewhat guilty because I brought Swedie and my children, from their Louisiana Homes, to several distant cities, namely, Washington, DC and Youngstown, Ohio. As I mentioned earlier, we were mostly strangers in these cities. So, in some ways, I felt it was my responsibility to not leave Swedie and Brenda so far away from Springhill, LA. I had difficulty trying to make the right decision.

Therefore, as fate had it, one day I went to a local bank and accidentally ran into Swedie Braud most unexpectedly. Though she left me, I was happy to see her again. We talked for a while in the bank and on the outside. And we decided to make amends. It should be pointed-out here that I knew clearly, from past experience, that Swedie was not going to rescind her resistance to adopting my two children; I also knew this was likely going to eventually be the "Straw That Broke The Camel's Back," or that is, what would eventually cause us to get a divorce. This is not what I desired but I could not see anyway around this inevitability. These thoughts played out in my subconscious mind as I talked with Swedie in the bank. On the other hand, Swedie was eager to make amends and get back together with me, although she knew in her heart she was not going to adopt my two children, and she also knew she was not going to treat them warmly as a mother, if she did not freely and voluntarily adopt them. Nevertheless, she wanted to get back together because she knew I was nearing the completion of my General Practice Residency, and she also knew my Braud Family Group lived in Louisiana and that I would likely return there once I completed my residency. So, we both had our subconscious agendas in play.

c. Decision Made To Return To Louisiana After Internship And General Practice Residency Successfully Completed In Early 1960

After our Bank Meeting, Swedie moved back in with me the next day! I got everybody together, and we prepared to return to Louisiana. I was the one who took them to Youngstown, Ohio, so I felt good that I was taking them all back to Louisiana. My internship and residency work was successfully completed. I was a Medical Doctor and my next move was to open up a Medical Practice in Louisiana somewhere. I had not decided on a city location but I am sure that decision would not nearly be as hard as the one I made to get my family back together under one roof.

Toward this end, Swedie and I packed up the things we had and placed them in the U-Haul Truck I rented for our journey back to Springhill, LA. When I packed the truck, I put everything in it that was going to Springhill, LA first. I packed Brownsyn and Glenn items last because I intended to drive to my mother's house in Brookstown and leave them there. Getting their things off of the U-Haul Truck would be easy, rather than looking through everybody's items to try to locate theirs.' The reason I packed the truck this way is because Swedie Braud was not going to adopt my two children so I faced this fact, and I was ready to let the chips fall wherever they did. Once the U-Haul Truck was packed, we headed South with our Studebaker Car in tow.

CHAPTER XVI

LOUISIANA HOMECOMING AND RETURNED AS A MEDICAL DOCTOR

A. Triumphant Return To Louisiana As A Medical Doctor

When I left Louisiana and the Gravel Road in September 1954, I only had my dream of becoming a Medical Doctor to hold onto, which I had been nurturing since I was five years old. By early 1960, my dream became a reality; my name was now Joseph Pierce Braud, MD. I was from Brookstown, and I was the first Black Medical Doctor with this distinction, from this village, since the beginning of the American Republic; and, inclusive of every stage of its development but not limited to, the 1776 American (Bourgeois) Revolution, the enactment of the US Constitution, American Slavery Institution, Civil War, Abraham Lincoln's Reconstruction Reparations Program, World War I, The Great Spanish Influenza Virus in 1918, 1929 Depression, World War II, and the Korean War to name a few. I was not the first Black Medical Doctor from St. James Parish, or from the Louisiana River Road. There were a handful of others before me.

Dr. John H. Lowery was the first Black Medical Doctor to hold this distinction. According to Michael L. Wilson, "...he...studied medicine at the Flint Goodridge Hospital in New Orleans and graduated with a Doctor of Medicine Degree from New Orleans University in 1894...Dr. Lowery established his medical practice in the town of Donaldsonville along the Mississippi River...He also owned and operated...one of the first pharmacies in Donaldsonville."[107] Being an outspoken proponent for education for Black People, Dr. John H. Lowery organized a movement to construct a modern public school for Black Students in Ascension Parish. Wilson added **"in 1937, Dr. Lowery sponsored a movement to build a new modern school for Black youths in Ascension Parish, Louisiana. His generous contributions led to the school being named the Lowery Training School in his honor. When the school fell on hard times, he personally paid the teachers' salaries for a year. The elementary and intermediate schools in Donaldsonville still bear his name."**[108] John H. Lowery, MD "... died at the Flint-Goodridge Hospital in New Orleans, Louisiana, on September 25, 1941...he is interred in the Ascension Catholic Cemetery in Donaldsonville, Louisiana."[109]

Regarding the Louisiana River Road, there were several other Black Medical Doctors in the area. They were: Dr. F. N. Ezidore, St. James Parish; Dr. Speight, Ascension Parish; Dr. C.C. Haydel, Sr., St. John Parish, and Dr. C.C. Haydel, Jr., St. John Parish. It is necessary to mention here that Dr. C. C. Haydel, Jr became a Medical Doctor several years after I completed my Medical Doctor Degree at Howard University Medical School in 1958. Former Mayor of New Orleans, LA, Dutch Morial married Dr. C.C. Haydel, Sr's daughter, who was a Medical Doctor. I believe in the Haydel Family Group there were three Medical Doctors; none of the others had this many in theirs.' By the time I graduated from Howard University Medical School, and finished my internship and residency at the Youngstown Association Hospital, there was a disproportionate number of Black Medical Doctors nationwide, relative to their White Counterpart. For example, in an AMA (American Medical Association) Report, which includes information on Black Medical Doctor's participation in it during the Civil Rights Movement, from 1955 to 1968. By "1956 Louisiana is the only Southern state without at least one black physician member of a local

---

[107] Wilson, Michael L., Secretary, "Dr. John Lowery, Louisiana Activist born," John Harvey Foundation, 509 Lessard Street, Donaldsonville, Louisiana, www.aaregistry.org

[108] Ibid.

[109] Ibid.

medical society."[110] This was the state of play two years before I completed my Medical Degree at Howard University Medical School in 1958.

That being so, the only Medical Doctor in the Brookstown area I had ever heard of, or frequently seen, was Dr. Stephen Campbell, the White Medical Doctor who gave me my very first inspiration that a Black Person could become a Medical Doctor. Since there were so few Black Medical Doctors around during my childhood, I seldom, if ever, saw one. Therefore, as I have hitherto discussed, I set my sights on becoming one at a time when the only thing a *Negro* was expected to do was either be a domestic worker or a manual Laborer. My Aunt Leah Pierce Argieard, the one I have already mentioned who had an unusual ability as a *Seer*, who could foretell what would be happening 70 years into the future, helped me to see, when I was seven years old, that the distance between Brookstown and Southern University, University of Illinois Urbana Champaign, Howard University Medical School, and the Youngstown Hospital Association's Internship and Residency Programs could be shortened and eliminated, if I would apply myself and obtain a good education. I believed my Aunt Leah's words when I first heard her speak them to me in New Orleans, LA, and by early 1960, I had mastered them with the fires of education, and they transformed me. I no longer dreamed of becoming a Medical Doctor.

I returned to Louisiana the first Black Medical Doctor to ever come out of Brookstown, a village with no more than 300 residents. No one outside of the Braud Family Group could have suspected this outcome because the fact is, by the early 1960s, White Medical Doctors still dominated the Medical Profession, and the total number of African-American Doctors continued to lag far behind the former in Louisiana and nationwide. As I mentioned earlier, Dr. Stephen Campbell was the only Medical Doctor who served the Brookstown Residents' healthcare needs during my childhood and after I left home for college. By the early 1970s, and following in my footsteps, the number of Black Medical Doctors with a connection to Brookstown steadily increased. In fact, from a per capita perspective, my Pierce-Braud Family Group started a trend in which six of its members earned Medical Doctor Degrees. This

---

[110] "African American Physicians and Organized Medicine, 1846-1968, Medico-Historical Events, https://www.ama-assn.org/media/14066/download, p. 7.

educational achievement was unmatched by others on the Louisiana River Road, including Louisiana as a whole.

Having taken my two children to live with mother on the Gravel Road, I was ready to take the first step toward opening up my first Medical Practice in Louisiana.

B. Return To Springhill, LA In Early 1960

The elephant was obviously still in the room in Swedie and I's household. Glenn Braud and Brownsyn Braud did not return to Springhill, LA with us. Only Brenda Braud did. Because I grew up in a very functional Household, where Lillian Luellen Pierce Braud and Joe Braud taught my siblings and I the value of building and maintaining a strong bond with each other, it is clear that I was not happy with the separation of my children from each other. I guess Smokey Robinson's words had some meaning in my life here when he sang this lyric in one of his songs: "Fantasy, we're all prone to fantasize." I was still vaguely clinging to the hope that Swedie would soften her position about adopting my children. When I thought she might do so, I always ended up with a sinking feeling inside of me that she would not do so.

With the U-Haul Truck packed with Brownsyn Braud and Glenn Braud's belongings in the rear of it, I could drive straight from Youngstown, Ohio to my mother's house. When I got there, I left my two children, as I mentioned earlier, and a day or two later, Swedie, Brenda, and I drove to north Louisiana. Our trip from Youngstown, Ohio was uneventful. The biggest downside of the entire trip was our children were now separated from each other; two in Brookstown and one in Springhill, LA.

Nevertheless, at last we were back in the house and turned on the utilities. For a few weeks, I scouted around for some type of employment. There was a clinic where the physician had recently expired. I negotiated with the medical owner of the A. Phillips Medical Clinic in Minden, LA; I wanted to see if it would be possible for me to take over operation of the Medical Practice. The amount of money ask for was more than I could afford at the time. The possibility of taking control of the Springhill, LA Clinic did not work out. Being new to the city, I was undecided if I wanted to remain in that area. When that venture fell through, I took a trip to visit my mother and two children in Brookstown. Another reason I was uncertain if I wanted to stay in Springhill, LA was due to some hidden differences in my domestic situation.

Deep down inside, I really wanted to go to the west coast. Swedie had a job offer at Grambling College and she was going over there to work in the Home Economics Department. That was a secure move. I was still searching for somewhere to begin my Medical Practice. Being the largest city in Louisiana, I decided to go to New Orleans, LA and check out what it had to offer.

C. New Orleans, LA: A Virgin Territory To Set Up A Medical Practice In 1960

I caught a Greyhound Bus to New Orleans, LA. Riding the bus down South gave me some time to reflect and rest because the Greyhound Bus seemed to stop in every little town along the way. I was alright with that because I knew by the time I reached my destination, I would be in New Orleans, LA. It was a long way from my five years old days on the Gravel Road where I first hatched my idea of wanting to become a Medical Doctor. I was now going to set up my Medical Practice in the city, which was bustling with people, history, culture, and life. I was a young man and that was a very exciting prospect. The New Orleans, LA environment was far different from the lazy pace of Springhill, LA. When I arrived in the city, I stayed with my two Aunts, who were Evelyn W. Pierce and Mary Augustine Pierce; at the time, they lived at 7820 Olive Street in Gerttown near Xavier University. As a reminder, I lived with my Aunts when I attended Daneel Elementary School, beginning in 1931. Aunt Evelyn W. Pierce allowed me to use her new car to get around in New Orleans, LA. This made my life so much easier. I began exploring the Medical Practice Landscape; there seemed to be some opportunities for a new physician. However, as I looked around, I still had it in the back of my mind I wanted to go to the Los Angeles, CA area because there were a number of my classmates that were in residencies or practicing. This thought was quickly laid to rest because I had run out of money, and I was becoming a burden to my Braud Family Group. I was closer to getting myself together, with my own Medical Practice, than I realized. The axiom that says "life is a process" is true. That is, the cake will bake according to the necessary amount of time it takes for all of the ingredients to metamorphosize, from its batter form to a baked cake ready to eat. I was in the process of setting up my Medical Practice in New Orleans, LA.

a. Dr. Anthony Hackett Breakthrough In 1960

Of all the people[111] in New Orleans, LA at this time, I was very fortunate to come across a Medical Doctor, namely, Dr. Anthony Hackett, who owned and operated his medical practice in the city for several years. As it happened, I visited one of the local hospitals, which was Flint Goodridge, in New Orleans, LA, and met several of the Black Physicians who were on its staff. After looking around New Orleans, LA, I thought it was *Virgin Territory*. Timing is a key factor in any endeavor; if any situation is acted upon at the precise point, or intersection between the person involved and available opportunity, the latter will occur seamlessly and almost mysteriously. This is exactly what happened to me when I met Dr. Anthony Hackett. If I had visited Flint Goodridge Hospital two days before or after the time I did, Dr. Hackett may have already gone on vacation.

Because my *Timing* was synchronistically correct, I met Dr. Anthony Hackett when he had a need for someone to operate his medical practice while he was away on vacation; and, simultaneously, when I also had a need to make some money and, ultimately, set up my own Medical Practice in New Orleans, LA. After many years of working in the Medical Field with my own established Medical Practice, I still do not know, presently speaking, exactly what made it so easy and effortlessly for me to initially setup my Medical Practice in New Orleans, LA. It seemed like everyone had been waiting for me to come to New Orleans, LA since the time I first put it in my mind I wanted to become a Medical Doctor, when I was five years old growing up on the Gravel Road. It seemed they were all relieved to see me as if I was an old friend, or family member, they had not seen in a long time.

---

[111] Besides Dr. Anthony Hackett, a few of the other Black Medical Doctors I had the privilege to meet were Dr. Joseph Epps, Sr, Dr. Thelma Boute, Dr. George Thomas, Dr. William Adams, Dr. Alvin Smith, Dr. Henry Braden, and Dr. Norbert Davidson among others.

Specifically, one of the local Black Physicians, namely, Dr. Anthony Hackett, was going on a month-long vacation and he asked me if I wanted to work in his office until he returned from his vacation? Divine synchronicity must have been at work because Dr. Anthony Hackett did not know me and I did not know him; yet, he was perfectly willing to allow me to operate his Medical Practice in his absence. I still wonder today why Dr. Hackett placed his confidence in me, who, for all practical purposes, I was a stranger to him, nevertheless, he trusted me to operate one of his most valuable assets? Trying as hard as I could to contain my excitement and my yes answer, I thought it was a relatively good offer because I was "out of money" and in dire need of work. The job offer, which I accepted unhesitatingly, enabled me to give staying in New Orleans, LA a higher priority than going out to California. When Dr. Hackett returned from his vacation, he took another two or three more weeks for rest recuperation. So, I was in good shape.

I was learning hands-on how to operate a real Medical Practice, where the patient and medical skills intersect on a daily basis; and, I was also learning the "nuts and bolts" of what it takes specifically to setup and operate my own Medical Practice.

b. Medical Practice Setup At St. Bernard Avenue And North Claiborne Avenue In 1960

I setup my first Medical Practice at this address. All of my life, this is what I aspired to do. And, now I was ready to walk through the doors of my very own Medical Practice. Therefore, staying in New Orleans, LA was one of the *best decisions* that I could have ever made. The *Gods* were looking out for me. It is true "Good Things Come To Those Who Wait." And, now I was reaping all of the benefits of the *good* I had done for people in my life thus far.

All kinds of opportunities were coming from all directions. There were a number of office spaces around the city that were geared for doctors that had no office, or those who wanted to expand their practices. I chose to start working in an office on St. Bernard Avenue at North Claiborne Avenue. Similar to my Aunt Evelyn Pierce allowing me to use her new car to get around in New Orleans, LA to explore what medical opportunities were available, and Dr. Anthony Hackett putting in my hands the responsibility to operate his Medical Practice for more than a month when I needed some money the most even though he did not know me and vis-à-vis, another offer was made to me at the precise moment I needed to setup my own Medical Practice. I could not believe what happened next because I did not believe my fortunes could get any better than they already had been, given the fact I had just gotten off of the Greyhound Bus less than two months before the newest development occurred. All I could think is everything that was happening was incredible!

Here is what happened.

c. Circle Food Store And Available Office Space Use For Free In 1960

There was some very nice office space, which I felt would be perfect to setup my own Medical Practice located at the identified address. Of course, I did not have much money to invest in securing the site. But, I did not allow money to deter me from asking who owned the available office space? I found out it was owned by the Circle Food Store. The available office space was located across the street from this store. When I sat down with the owners of it, I knew my meeting would be brief because, as I stated before, I did not have any money in an amount that I would need to secure the property. Contrary to my belief, the owners told me I could use the office space for free. I tried hard to contain my excitement again like I did when Dr. Hackett allowed me to manage his Medical Practice while he was away on vacation. I kept a Poker Face and maintained my businesslike composure. Inside of me, my mind was racing a thousand miles per hour(!) because my Medical Doctor Dream had two parts: One, I had to first graduate with my Medical Doctor Degree, and, Two, I needed office space to open up my Medical Practice. The latter came true when the owners of the Circle Food Store, who also owned the available office space, agreed to allow me to use the property free without any conditions. Although the Circle Food Store had a Pharmacy on the inside, I was not under any obligation to write a prescription, for one of my patients, who would have to get it filled at the Circle Food Store Pharmacy. If someone had told me this is the way I would get my Medical Practice setup before I left Springhill, LA, I would have laugh at them, and ask them "Have you been drinking?"

When I got the keys to the office space at St. Bernard Avenue and North Claiborne Avenue, I discovered all of the basic facilities and equipment for a practicing physician were available. I did not have to purchase examining tables, medicine cabinets, prescription pads, chairs, and so forth. It was up to me to get supplies such as gauze, dressing pads, minor surgical equipment sterilizers, and band aids among others. Gee! I was on my way! Moreover, each day the situation got better and better. This was true Virgin Territory(!) as I had envisioned. It was not too long before I was able to get a better automobile and apartment. I was able to gradually become self-sufficient.

That is, after setting up my Medical Practice, and shortly thereafter, I began accumulating more money than I had accumulated in my whole life up to this time. As my financial situation grew stronger, then, I began to ask for the opinion of several of the medical practitioners, who had been in the area where I setup my Medical Practice for a number of years, this question: How and what did they do with monies that their practices generated? They seemed stunned because it was not their experience to have large sums of money coming from their practices. They told me I must have been crazy. Therefore, I began asking individuals in the financial area, and they provided me with a wealth of information to consider.

D. Flint-Goodridge Hospital Of Dillard University: A Light Post For Black Physicians In New Orleans, LA By 1960

By the time I arrived in New Orleans, LA in early 1960, I was a newly minted Black Medical Doctor, who was young, gifted, eager, and hungry to get started with my Medical Practice in the "Big Easy," which turned out to be on one hand, the best decision I made to stay in New Orleans, LA, and on the other, I had made a quantum leap forward, regarding how quickly and seamlessly I was able to meet the right people, who were, for unknown reasons to me, very willing to help me get a foothold in its medical landscape. I felt empowered and on the move in the right direction. In addition, what made everything even better is New Orleans, LA was my home away from my real one on the Gravel Road where I grew up. I could get in my car, and within less than two hours time, I could visit my mother, my two children, and some of my siblings.

And, when it appeared to me that my fortunes could not get any better, suddenly they did. Like a majority of the Black Physicians, who came to New Orleans, LA before me, I was drawn, similar to the way gravity pulls on living and non-livings things, to Flint-Goodridge Hospital of Dillard University. It is not an exaggeration when I say this hospital was a *Mecca* for Black Doctors since its dedication in 1932, which was six years after I was born in 1926. As I will explain later, Systemic Racism was a primary contributing factor because Flint-Goodridge Hospital of Dillard University was the *only* one in New Orleans, LA where a Black Doctor could obtain employment to practice his or her medical craft. Therefore, I got on the staff of Flint-Goodridge Hospital of Dillard University for this reason. Before I delve deeper into my medical practice at Flint-Goodridge Hospital, a brief history of the beginning of the hospital will demonstrate how it evolved over time in an-oftentimes-unfriendly racist environment.

CHAPTER XVII

FLINT-GOODRIDGE HOSPITAL OF DILLARD UNIVERSITY GLORY YEARS FROM 1959 TO 1982

Flint-Goodridge Hospital of Dillard University did not come into existence in a vacuum immune from the many prevailing influences of Systemic Racism that permeated if not all, nearly all-modern American Institutions, including Medicine. As recent as June 13, 2021, Lindsey Tanner reported the American Medical Association is making a move to overthrow Systemic Racism in its ranks. Specifically, he stated "the nation's largest, most influential doctors group is holding its annual policymaking meeting amid backlash over its most ambitious plan ever-to help dismantle centuries-old racism and bias in all realms of the medical establishment."[112] Dr. Gerald Harmon, incoming president, admitted "…racism and white privilege exist in the medical establishment and have contributed to health disparities… racism is a public health threat."[113] Before 1932, Flint-Goodridge Hospital of Dillard University did not exist. It would later emerge and operate in this atmosphere. Several White Institutions joined to form a nurse training school at New Orleans University. This is where I will begin my discussion of the soil out of which Flint- Goodridge Hospital of Dillard University would later germinate and develop.

---

[112] Tanner, Lindsey, "AMA meets amid backlash over racial equity plan," Associated Press, June 13, 2021.
[113] Ibid.

A. Phyllis Wheatley Sanitarium And Training School For Nurses

In October 1896, The Journal Of The National Medical Association (JNMA) stated "a small group of Negro women known as the Phyllis Wheatley Club...formally opened an institution, which they named the Phyllis Wheatley Sanitarium and Training School for Negro Nurses."[114] The institution began very small with seven beds and five students. Usually unable to meet its operating expenses, the Phyllis Wheatley Sanitarium seemed like it was doomed to fail. However, realizing an opportunity to expand its curriculum offerings, the JNMA added "New Orleans University came to the rescue by assuming the indebtedness and taking all of the of the Club and making the Phyllis Wheatley Sanitarium an adjunct to its medical school."[115] New Orleans University (NOU) official, Bishop Mallalieu contacted Mrs. Caoline Medge of Boston, MA., who gave a $25,000 gift to NOU to purchase a lot adjoining the latter. This financial contribution was so timely that by 1901, the NOU's Board of Trustees decided to change the name of the hospital to Sarah Goodridge Hospital as a memorial to Mrs. Caroline Medge's mother, namely, Sarah Tannett Goodridge. Thus, this is where the Goodridge name originated; not long thereafter, Bishop Mallalieu was able to secure more funds for the New Orleans University Medical School. He secured a $10,000 gift from Mr. John D. Flint, who lived in Fall River, MA, to purchase a property at the corner of Canal and South Robertson Streets. The Board of Trustees of New Orleans University renamed its medical school Flint Medical College.

The Flint Medical College life was short-lived. In those early days, medical requirements were increasingly influx caused by new and elevated standards of practice, whereby it became very difficult to raise more external funds for the Flint Medical College. Such fundraising efforts were limited due to the changing medical standards fixed by the American Medical Association. Consequently, the Flint Medical College of New Orleans University, which was established in 1889, was forced to close its doors in 1911. All of its students were "...transferred to Meharry Medical

---

[114] "THE HISTORY OF FLINT-GOODRIDGE HOSPITAL OF DILLARD UJNIVERSITY, Journal OF The National Medical Association, Vol. 61, No. 6, November 1969, p. 533.
[115] Ibid., p. 533.

College at Nashville, Tennessee"[116] During its 22 years tenure, the Flint Medical College of New Orleans University was very productive. As a matter of fact, with support from the Methodist Episcopal Church, the Flint Medical College developed into a three story structure, 22 by 114 feet; it had graduated 75 students by 1905; and, if those graduates who took the state boards between 1906 and 1911 are added in, the total number of graduates during the 22 years of its existence came to a total of 116 medical graduates.[117] With the Flint Medical College closed, a new hospital was formed using the former Flint Medical College infrastructure.

B. Flint-Goodridge Hospital Of Dillard University And Dillard University Established, 1911 To 1932

The pathway was created to eventually merge two medical facilities together to produce the Flint-Goodridge Hospital. As it happened, the buildings previously occupied for medical practice work, "…since 1901 had been used jointly by the Flint Medical College and the Sarah Goodridge Hospital and Nurses Training School were converted into a 50 bed hospital and the name changed to Flint-Goodridge Hospital,"[118] according to the JNMA. After its first fifty years of operation, another major change occurred that would have a major impact on the future development of the Flint-Goodridge Hospital. Its mission would change also.

By 1930, the groundwork was laid for the birth of Dillard University in New Orleans, LA. A movement was initiated to merge New Orleans University, which was affiliated with the Methodist Church, and Straight college, which was affiliated with the Congregational Christian Church, into one institution. The JNMA stated "a fund of $2,000,000 was raised for the purpose of establishing the new institution. The trustees of the new institution, composed of representatives of the Board of Education of the Methodist Episcopal Church, the American Missionary Association of the Congregational Church, and other citizens, named the institution after Dr. James Hardy Dillard, formerly president and director of the Jeanes

---

[116] Ibid., p. 533.
[117] Ibid., p. 533. This data is taken from Cobb, W. M., Progress and Portents for the Negro in Medicine, NAACP, N.Y., 1948, p. 12.
[118] Ibid., p. 534.

and Slather Funds."¹¹⁹ At a cost of $500,000, the initial unit constructed at Dillard University was its hospital addition. By February 1, 1932, the hospital moved into its newly constructed physical plant. According to JNMA, this building, housing 88 beds and 12 bassinets, was modernly equipped throughout, and fully approved by the American College of Surgeons. It was also approved for the training of interns by the American Medical Association. The old Phyllis Wheatley Sanitarium, later known as the Sarah Goodridge Hospital, and still later as Flint-Goodridge Hospital, is now known as Flint-Goodridge Hospital of Dillard University."[120] Image 1.1 below shows how the Flint-Goodridge Hospital looked in 1916.

Image 1.1 Flint-Goodridge Hospital In 1916

"The Flint-Goodridge Hospital in 1916. The buildings were used jointly by the Flint Medical College and the Sarah Goodridge Hospital and Nurses Training School from 1901 to 1911, when the medical school was closed and the hospital continued as the Flint-Goodridge Hospital."[121]

---

[119] Ibid., p. 534.
[120] Ibid., p. 534.
[121] Ibid., p. 534. Prior to 1958, Flint-Goodridge Hospital was a four-story building with a separate building that had a small living quarters for nurses, and a house

Through the years, Flint-Goodridge Hospital of Dillard University had been able to serve the indigents in the New Orleans, LA community. This was made possible by small grants received from charitable organizations, private organizations, governmental agencies and others. With these funds, it was possible to serve non-paying patients. In addition, during its early years, Flint-Goodridge Hospital was guided by a strong educational mission. Being a predominantly minority serving institution, the JNMA stated "it offered residences for young physicians who had graduated from medical schools and were seeking to better prepare themselves to enter practice. Many of the physicians practicing in New Orleans have done intern or resident training at Flint-Goodridge Hospital. Its annual Postgraduate Courses were of vital importance to physicians of Louisiana, Texas, and other adjoining states. Flint-Goodridge continues as one of the few Negro institutions offering training for nurse anesthetists."[122] This was the only medical institution in which young Black Doctors and Nurses could receive Postgraduate Intern and Residency Training in Louisiana. Most of them, like myself, were forced to seek intern and residency training outside of the South as I did in Youngstown, Ohio.

C. Dedication Of Flint-Goodridge Hospital Of Dillard University In 1932

The formative years of the Flint-Goodridge Hospital of Dillard University were moving along relatively smoothly. It acquired a new name, and an expanded mission during the A.W. Dent Administration. Joe Richardson stated "in January, 1932, a twenty-seven year old, physically imposing, fair-skinned African American, Albert W, Dent, arrived in New Orleans to superintend Dillard University's new Flint-Goodridge Hospital."[123] That same year and month, Flint-Goodridge Hospital of Dillard University was

---

that was for the administrator. It was a hospital where the nursing students from Dillard University did some of their clinical training. There was also a Nurse Anesthesia Program that trained Black Nurse Anesthetists from all around the United States.

[122] Ibid., pp. 534 and 535.
[123] 123 Richardson, Joe M., "Albert W. Dent: A Black New Orleans Hospital and University Administrator," The Journal of the Louisiana Historical Association, vol. 37, No.3, (Summer, 1996), p. 309.

dedicated, which marked the beginning of its tenure under the direction of Dillard University. A large gathering of people gathered in front of the hospital to see and listen to how the hospital intended to serve the New Orleans, LA Community. Image 1.2 below shows the dedication ceremony that took place in January 1932.

Image 1.2 Flint-Goodridge Hospital Of Dillard University Dedication Ceremony In January 1932

Source: Bedou, Arthur P., Photographer in the archivesD@xula.edu

D. Mr. A. W. Dent Superintendent Of Flint-Goodridge Hospital Of Dillard University And President Of Dillard University

From 1932 to 1942, Mr. A.W. Dent served as the first superintendent of Flint Goodridge Hospital of Dillard University. One of his notable achievements that received nationwide acclaim was his "Penny-a-day Plan" Insurance Plan. Also, during Mr. A.W. Dent's Administration, he instituted the Postgraduate Course Curriculum Program for young Black Physicians in the South, which enabled them to do their intern and residency at Flint-Goodridge Hospital of Dillard University. Image 1.3 below shows the Postgraduate Class of 1944.

Image 1.3 Black Physicians And Postgraduate Course In 1944

L.to r. First row.Dr.J.Covington, Houston, Tex.;Dr.Peter M.Murroy, New York; Dr.X.A.Hill, Prairie View, Tex.; Dr. E. 1.Jones, Talladego, Ala. Dr. Rivers Frederick, New Orleans, La. Dr. Walter A. Younge, St. Louis, Mo.; Dr. M. A. Clark, Wynnewood, Ore. Dr. P. S. Moten, Birmingham, Ala. Second row. Dr. C. W. Smith, Hattiesburg, Miss. Dr. J. A. Philips, Minden, La. Dr. J. L. Welch, Port Arthur, Tex. Dr. P.R.Stewart, Port Arthur, Tex. Dr.S.D.Hil, Monroe, La. Dr.W.A.Anderson, Alexandria, La. Dr.Harrison Joseph, Baton Rouge, La. Third row. Dr. E. F. Aarons, Pensacola, Fla. Dr. A. W. Dumas, Natchez, Miss. Dr. N. L. Lacy, Franklin, La.; Dr. H. H. Huggins, Baton Rouge, La. Dr. Ino T. Stocking, Daytona Beach, Fla. Dr. J. H. Murray, New Orleans, La. Dr. 0. H. Smith, Ardmore, Ore. Fourth row. Albert W. Dent, president of Dillard; John L. Procope, superintendent of Flint-Goodridge; Dr. August C. Terrence, Opelousas, La. Dr. H. C. Scoggins, Algiers, La.
Source: Journal Of the National Medical Association, Vol. 61. No.6, November 1969, p. 535.

By 1942, the Board of Trustees elected Mr. A.W. Dent President of Dillard University. President Dent is shown in the Fourth Row in Picture Number 2, and standing beside him is John L. Procope, who was appointed superintendent of Flint-Goodridge Hospital of Dillard University to replace him. Interestingly, both Mr. Dent and Mr. Procope did not carry the Medical Doctor title, yet they were in charge of hospital matters that affected physicians and patient care. This could have been a useful strategy designed to foster an objective perspective in decision-making and policy matters. World War II had some adverse effects on the operation of Flint-Goodridge Hospital of Dillard University.

From the day Mr. John L. Procope took over the day-to-day management of the hospital, various problems surfaced. According to the JNMA, "...Mr. John L. Procope...was faced with many problems which were magnified by the war situation. The patient load reached its peak and the nursing shortage became very acute. When Mr. S. Tanner Stafford became superintendent of the hospital in 1946, the hospital was faced with its most difficult financial problems. The indebtedness became so great that it was feared the hospital would be closed. In fact, because of the shortage of personnel and patient demand, the fourth floor area was closed."[124] After World War II ended, the financial health of Flint-Goodridge Hospital of Dillard University improved significantly.

Accordingly, the JNMA stated "it was not until October, 1949, when Mr. C. C. Weil became superintendent of the hospital, that the financial cloud began to lift. An indebtedness of some $37,000 was soon paid of, making most of the hospital's accounts current."[125] Flint-Goodridge Hospital of Dillard University was back on a solid economic footing. In 1949 dollars, $37,000 worth of debt may not seem overwhelming; however, if the sum is computed in today's dollars, it would likely amount to several hundred thousand dollars? At any rate, the development of Flint-Goodridge Hospital of Dillard University was about to undergo a major expansion around the time I was teaching at the Charles H. Brown High School in Springhill, LA. Although I did not know it at that time, my future employment, as a Medical Doctor, was inevitably linked to this hospital.

E. Flint-Goodridge Hospital Of Dillard University Expansion During Mr. Albert Walter (A.W.) Dent's Presidency Of Dillard University From 1941 To 1969

President A.W. Dent moved the Flint-Goodridge Hospital of Dillard University into the modern era. In order to attract a high quality and skilled medical staff, President A. W. Dent was well aware of the importance of paying the hospital doctors, nurses, and administrative staff a competitive salary. In fact, during the early months of his administration, the JNMA

---

[124] op. cit., Journal of the National Medical Association, p. 535.
[125] Ibid., p. 535.

added "a salary scale was effected comparable to that of the other hospitals in the city."[126] In addition, several other additions were made to the Flint-Goodridge Hospital of Dillard University during his tenure as president.

They were as follows:

- "Roughly 65 per cent of all equipment was replaced during this period [Early 1950s].
- A grant to set up the School of Anesthesia and other educational activities was procured from the Edward G. Schleider Foundation. Under the directorship of Dr. John Adriani, the School of Anesthesia trained nurses not only from our institution, but others from hospitals throughout the South.
- Toward the latter part of 1950, a very much needed blood bank was established."[127]

There were more key improvements added to the Flint-Goodridge Hospital of Dillard University during the mid-1950s. Before I mention them, one administrative change in particular would inevitably have an irreversible impact on the overall operational health of the hospital three decades later.

That is, according to the JNMA, "in 1953, the Trustees of Dillard University established a Board of Management and delegated to them the full responsibility of the operation of the hospital. Thus the hospital which had been run by an institution of higher learning for over 50 years, began operating as a community enterprise."[128] At the outset, the Board of Management of Flint-Goodridge Hospital of Dillard University was instrumental in obtaining $1,360,000 in philanthropic contributions to launch a major expansion and modernization program in 1958. It was completed in 1960. Between 1958 and 1960, some key additions were added to the infrastructure of the hospital. According to the JNMA, a brand new four-story wing was added to the existing Flint-Goodridge Hospital of Dillard University. It reported "the new four-story addition,

---

[126] Ibid., p. 535.
[127] Ibid., p. 535.
[128] Ibid., p. 535.

completely modern, houses 96 beds. All rooms are private or semi-private, equipped with bath facilities, telephones, piped oxygen, and audio-visual patient nurse intercom system. A new physical therapy department, dietary service, medical records, central supply, and conference room are also in this new wing."[129] The Board of Management had transformed the Flint Goodridge Hospital of Dillard University into a competitive force in the New Orleans, LA Community, and it represented hope in the Black Community that it could receive the types of medical care it needed within a reasonable expectation of delivery of health services. Major medical surgeries such as heart, lung, and colon among others were referred elsewhere. Image 1.4 below shows the new wing addition to the Flint-Goodridge Hospital of Dillard University when I started working there full-time in 1960.

Image 1.4 New Wing Addition To The Flint-Goodridge Hospital Of Dillard University In 1960

Source: Journal Of The National Medical Association, vol. 6, No.16, November 1969, p. 533.

This was where I obtained employment shortly after I arrived in New Orleans, LA from Springhill, LA. Earlier, I mentioned coming to New Orleans, LA to seek a place to begin my medical practice was one of the *best decisions I ever made*. When I arrived in New Orleans, LA, I started

---

[129] Ibid., p. 535. There was only one set back, New Orleans, LA only had roughly 30 Black Physicians to utilize. The 96 bed hospital, therefore, had to depend other ethnic physicians, particularly White Ones.

out managing Dr. Anthony Hackett's Medical Practice while he was away on vacation for several months; I also established my own medical practice when the Circle Food Store allowed me to use the office space across the street from it on St. Bernard Avenue at North Claiborne Avenue. Then, my Guardian Angels led me to Flint-Goodridge Hospital of Dillard University where I was employed for more than two decades, from 1960 to 1982. During this time, more innovations were added to the hospital.

F. Flint-Goodridge Hospital Of Dillard University Glory Years, Including Black Physicians And Nurse Anesthetists-1960 To 1982

How everything came together, like the perfect pieces of a puzzle that fell into place out of an infinite possibility of others, regarding the establishment of my medical practice in New Orleans, LA, is still a big *mystery* to me today. As I reflect back on each of my footsteps, when I first walked into New Orleans, LA in 1960, only the higher power could have guided the steps I made during the Flint-Goodridge Hospital of Dillard University Glory Years. Without a doubt, I realize now, with the right medical preparation, situations that seem impossible beforehand become possible. When preparation intersects with opportunity, educational dreams are transformed into reality. I went through the Fires of Purification at the Howard University Medical School in Washington, DC, and the Spirit anointed me with a cup that *runneth* over with opportunities opened to me at Flint-Goodridge Hospital of Dillard University in New Orleans, LA a few years later.

a. Began Employment at Flint-Goodridge Hospital Of Dillard University In 1960

By the beginning of the early 1960s, the Flint-Goodridge Hospital of Dillard University was the only hospital in New Orleans, LA where physicians of color were welcome. That being so, I was hired to work for Flint-Goodridge Hospital of Dillard University in New Orleans, LA in 1960. This hospital had recently undergone new construction and expansion. Before the expansion, Flint-Goodridge Hospital of Dillard University was a thirty beds hospital, but since the expansion, it had become a one hundred bed hospital, which nearly tripled its bed capacity.

On the day I walked into Flint-Goodridge Hospital of Dillard University, I inherited a modern hospital facility. It was, in many ways, equipped with the latest technology required to effectively serve the healthcare needs of the Black Community in New Orleans, LA. My initial job duties consisted of providing medical care for my people on an "on call" basis. At the outset, I did some work in the Emergency Room of Flint-Goodridge Hospital of Dillard University.

Being on the staff of the hospital, there were times when I was "on call." The latter's schedule was not random but it was worked-out in advance with some of the other hospital physicians so that, on any given weekend for example, if a medical issue came up with a patient of mine, or one of the other doctors on the hospital staff, the physician "on call" would be contacted by the hospital to come in immediately to deal with the medical situation at hand. Being "on call," I was contacted by the hospital to come in during daytime hours and at night. The time was determined by the person who needed medical attention. Being a young, gifted, and Black Physician in 1960, I was ready to practice medicine. For me and my fellow Black Physicians, it was the beginning of the best of times at Flint-Goodridge Hospital of Dillard University. It is what I think of as being the Glory Years at Flint-Goodridge Hospital of Dillard University.

b. The Glory Years Of Flint-Goodridge Hospital Of Dillard University And Black Physicians-1960 To 1982

Those were the beginning of the Glorious Years for Flint-Goodridge Hospital of Dillard University. It was also, in my view, the glorious years for Black Physicians. All of us practiced with dignity, and the hospital had, as I mentioned before, all of the modern equipment. Although everything was moving along like a well-oiled engine without any "knocks" or "smoking," and as the old saying goes, if something is going so well, "it may be too good to be true." The expansion and modernization program I discussed thus far did not come without a *big price*. The latter was like a newborn baby; it would take some years for the baby to grow up and mature; similarly, it would take some years for the "big price" to manifest itself in the day-to-day operation of Flint-Goodridge Hospital of Dillard University. I will get back to this point much later on.

Meantime, and in the lyrics of the Famous Trumpeter, Louis Armstrong, "I see blue skies, people smiling and shaking hands saying 'how do you do' (Paraphrase Mine). This is the way I saw life inside of Flint-Goodridge Hospital of Dillard University during the Glory Years, which for me, really got started around 1963. From 1960 to this time, I developed my medical practice on St. Bernard Venue and North Claiborne, and, by 1964, I opened up a medical practice on La Salle Street at Louisiana Avenue. So, for roughly three years, I worked on building my medical practice in this location. However, another mystery occurred when I decided to venture into an Anesthesia Practice at Flint-Goodridge Hospital of Dillard University. As before, of the infinite pieces of the puzzle, one fell into place, which would inevitably change my medical practice fortunes at Flint-Goodridge Hospital of Dillard University, for the entire duration of time I practiced medicine there, which lasted more than two decades.

c. Nurse Anesthetist Training Program And The Dr. John Adriani Policy In 1960

When the Phyllis Wheatley Club started its Sanitarium and Training School for Negro Nurses in October 1896, and since that time, the nurse training program at Flint-Goodridge Hospital of Dillard University evolved into the above program. While the hospital had stopped taking interns and residents for training, it continued, by 1960, to train Nurse Anesthetists, including other nurses. That is, Flint-Goodridge Hospital of Dillard University was the one that served as the Dillard University Nursing School.

Before I proceed any further with my life work in the New Orleans, LA Community, of which the Flint-Goodridge Hospital of Dillard University was a medical player, I take time here to remind everyone that Segregation and Systemic Racism, whether in its De jure or De facto forms, were presently, still more the norm than the exception. I have already mentioned earlier that the only hospital that Black Physicians and Nurse Anesthetists were welcome was Flint-Goodridge Hospital of Dillard University. No White Hospital in Louisiana welcomed us during the early 1960s. In short, there was a Color Line waiting to be broken. By 1960, it was unbroken and *Alive and Well!* As I proceed with my telling my story about the time I worked for Flint-Goodridge Hospital of Dillard

University, I will interject instances of racism, as I remember them, which existed at the time. Nevertheless, in spite of racial barriers, my colleagues and I persevered and moved forward with our medical practices in face of some seemingly overwhelming resistance to change.

As it was, Flint-Goodridge Hospital of Dillard University was one of the few institutions in the South for training Black Nurse Anesthetists or Black Nurses.[130] The Black Nurse Anesthetist Students got their academic training with the Nurse Anesthetist Students of Charity Hospital, of whom many were White, in New Orleans, LA; they also engaged in hands-on training at the Flint-Goodridge Hospital of Dillard University. This Charity Hospital Training Program had been in existence for a number of years. One of the Black Nurse Anesthetists, whom I would work with for a few years while I was employed at Flint-Goodridge Hospital of Dillard University, was Mrs. Mrytle Garrison.

Mrs. Mrytle Garrison told me due to racial segregation, "Black RNs were not admitted to the Anesthesia Schools located in Texas. The Texas RNs had to seek admissions in out-of-state Schools of Anesthesia. After doing some research, and not being deterred, Mrs. Garrison applied to four hospitals in other states, and the Charity Hospital was among the group. Interestingly, with Louisiana being located in the Deep South, the Charity Hospital School of Anesthesia accepted her application. Unknown to her, the Charity Hospital School of Anesthesia sent her application to Flint-Goodridge Hospital of Dillard University because, by 1960, this hospital was segregated and "admitted White RN Students only." Thus, the Charity Hospital School of Anesthesia did not accept Mrs. Myrtle Garrison's application but, rather, it sent it to Flint-Goodridge Hospital of Dillard University (FGHDU) where Black Physicians and Nurses were welcome. Initially disillusioned, when Mrs. Myrtle Garrison arrived at FGHDU, she was introduced to Mrs. Eloise Lyons Baker, BSN, CRNA, who was the Director of the Anesthesia School at FGHDU and Miss

---

[130] A Nurse Anesthetist is a person who is a registered nurse, who has completed two or more years of additional specialized training and education and is certified to administer anesthetics. This person is a Certified Registered Nurse Anesthetist (CRNA). He or she is qualified to administer Anesthesia required to put a patient

Shirley Patterson, BSN, CRNA, who was the Clinical Supervisor[131] for the same. Mrs. Myrtle Garrison was shown to her apartment at the rear of the hospital, and she moved in. This is factual evidence of the state of play at the Charity Hospital School of Anesthesia at the time.

Between 1960 and 1964, the FGHDU continued to modernize. It was an island amid many surrounding racial barriers as Mrs. Myrtle Garrison put the patients to sleep; while monitoring their vitals during a surgical operation; and assisting the patients return to an awake state after a given surgery is completed. The CRNA is a highly skilled medical professional. Garrison's experience testifies. For example, there was an expansion in the hospital's Medical Obstetrics, Surgical, Orthopedics, Anesthesia, and Pediatrics Departments. Everyone was proud of the progress this small hospital had made in the community. There were more Black Physicians in the specialties coming to New Orleans, LA such as Anesthesiologists, Internists, Obstetricians, Gynecologists, Orthopedists, Urologists, Surgeons, Neurosurgeons, and so forth. These glorious years of FGHDU lasted from 1960 through 1981. As it was, the latter was a fairly well-equipped, small hospital that attracted many specialists.

Although the Charity Hospital School of Anesthesia publicly barred Black Nurses from its Anesthetists Training Program publicly, privately, based on an agreement between Dr. John Adriani, who was the Director of the Charity Hospital School of Anesthesia and Mrs. Elosie Lyons Baker, Director of the Anesthesia School at Flint-Goodridge Hospital of Dillard University, only two Black Nurses would be allowed admission into the Anesthetists Training Program per year with one non-negotiable condition. As I mentioned earlier, this agreement had been in use for several years before Mrs. Myrtle Garrison arrived at FGHDU as a prospective Nurse Trainee. Based on Dr. John Adriani's Terms and Conditions, the Black Nurse Anesthetist Students, without any exception, entered Charity Hospital on one side, and the White Nurse Anesthetist Students entered on the other

---

[131] According to Mrs. Myrtle Garrison, "Mrs. Baker was a graduate of Flint-Goodridge [of Dillard University] School of Nursing, which was no longer in existence in 1960. Miss Shirley Patterson Theodore was a graduate of Dillard University School of Nursing and Flint-Goodridge Hospital of Dillard University School of Anesthesia. There was no Physician Anesthesiology Resident Program at Flint."

side. They were prohibited from entering the Charity Hospital through the same door, or together. Moreover, the Black and White Anesthetist Students had their classes together in the same auditorium or classroom. Dr. John Adriani demanded that "nothing be said; no comments; and no advertisement." This was the unbreakable Adriani Policy during his tenure as the Director of the Charity Hospital School of Anesthesia Program. Specifically, those Black Nurses accepted in the program followed this process to the letter.

d. Nurse Anesthetist Training In The Charity Hospital Anesthesia Training Program By 1958

By 1958, as it is recalled by Mrs. Myrtle Garrison, who successfully received her Anesthesia Training in this program, "Flint accepted two (2) Anesthesia RN Students per class per year [The Charity Hospital School of Anesthesia did not accept any Black Nurses in its program directly but referred those who applied to Flint-Goodridge Hospital of Dillard University, which, in turn, recommended two per class per year to be trained as [Anesthestists]. The course of instruction, combined with the Clinical Practice, was one year. The tuition was free with free room and board, laundry, and a $20/month stipend. The stipend was increased to $60/month after 1958. The students paid for daily bus transportation to Charity Hospital Anesthesia Lectures each afternoon [given by Dr. John Adriani, Chief Anesthesiologist, Monday thru Friday]. The latter's Lectures took place each day at 1 PM sharp. The students had to purchase their textbooks, which Dr. Adriani was the author."

Moreover, Mrs. Mrytle Garrison stated "Dr. Adriani lectured to the vast majority of Anesthesia Physician Residents and Nurses in training in New Orleans, LA, who came from Tulane University, Louisiana State University (LSU), Oschner Foundation Hospital, Charity Hospital, Hotel Dieu Hospital, Charity Hospital School of Nurse Anesthesia, and Flint-Goodridge Hospital of Dillard University. Mrs. Adriani, Dr. Adriani's spouse, was the Director of Charity Hospital Nurse Anesthesia School." Racial Segregation was the norm rather than the exception because Mrs. Mrytle Garrison witnessed firsthand "the Flint Hospital [of Dillard University] Black Students were not allowed to see nor rotate in the Charity Hospital Operating Rooms; nor were they allowed to observe those various

Surgical Anesthesia Cases, which were not performed at Flint Goodridge Hospital of Dillard University." If the professionally trained Black Nurse Students' Anesthesia Training was forcefully limited in this manner, so much is left to the imagination how Black Patients and others of color's health was treated, behind the closed doors that barred the Black Nurse Anesthetists Trainees from observing the Charity Hospital Operating Rooms? (!)

In addition, and more disturbing, is Mrs. Mrytle Garrison's recollection "Flint[-Goodridge] Hospital [of Dillard University] provided Anesthesia to only Black Patients. The Blood Transfusions were labeled "Black" and "White" Blood. According to the Louisiana Law, White Patients were not under any conditions to receive blood from Black Donors, and Black Patients were not to receive blood from White Donors." For example, a young college age student, who I will call Johnny F., went to Charity Hospital in New Orleans, LA with a blood disorder; after a short stay at the hospital, he died. There is no way to obtain data on how many Black Patients met this same fate, but the imagination is left to wonder under the prevailing conditions mentioned thus far. Moreover, Mrs. Myrtle Garrison added "the Anesthesia Students provided ALL General Anesthesia for the scheduled Surgical and Obstetrical Patients during the day before 12 Noon. At lunchtime, we traveled by city bus across town to Charity Hospital on Tulane Avenue for [Dr. John Adriani's] daily lectures-Monday thru Fridays. We returned to Flint Hospital and took emergency surgery and OB Calls during the evening and night shifts-(Without Supervision)." This deficit would be corrected toward the end of the 1960s. One other point Mrs. Myrtle Garrison made, and that is, "due to segregation in 1960 in Louisiana, Black Nurse Anesthetists, nor Black Physicians, were not accepted as Staff Positions in any hospital that accepted White Patients, who required Anesthesia Services." Moreover, Mrs. Myrtle Garrison noted before I became Chief of the Anesthesia Department at Flint-Goodridge Hospital of Dillard University, Nurse Anesthetists were grossly underpaid for their services relative to the White Physicians who came to the hospital to administer Anesthesia to those patients scheduled for a particular surgery.

In the meantime, the Adriani Policy was similar to today's saying "What happens in Vegas stays in Vegas." Regarding our Anesthesia

Training at Charity Hospital, it was "business as usual." No coverage was permitted in the newspapers, or on the radio. While this Adriani Policy was in effect at the Charity Hospital, across town at FGHDU, Black Physicians were going about the day-to-day care of their patients.

During the early 1960s, Black Patients, who had insurance, or could pay, could only go to Flint-Goodridge Hospital of Dillard University. This fact would later come back to haunt the latter. Nevertheless, the only other hospital for Black Patients was Charity Hospital of Louisiana. White Physicians, who treated Black Patients, were only able to take them to Flint-Goodridge Hospital of Dillard University. This is added testimony of the existence of Segregation and Systemic Racism, which permeated every facet of American Life, and Medicine was no exception to the *rule*. For that reason, and that reason only, enabled the census of patients, for Flint-Goodridge Hospital of Dillard University, to be maintained, or it stayed in the larger percentile.

Around this time, if a FGHDU's patient required surgery, and he or she needed to be put to sleep and so forth, Mrs. Myrtle Garrison observed "when an emergency situation arose, a Resident Physician in Anesthesia was called from Charity to Flint to provide assistance. To my knowledge, there was no staff Anesthesiologist hired at Flint until 1960. Dr. Robert Wood Jr., MD became the Director of the Department of Anesthesia at FGHDU. Dr. Roberts replaced Dr. Woods; and, Dr. Roy E. Boggs replaced Dr. Roberts. There was a growing need for another trained Anesthesiologist, and, fortunately for me, I was at the right place at the right time. Before I share how I got involved in the Anesthesia Training Program at Charity Hospital, I will update what was happening in my life after work at my private medical practice and FGHDU.

G. Private Medical Practice And Family Life Between 1960 and 1963

During this time, I relocated my medical practice from its St. Bernard Avenue and North Claiborne Avenue location. My decision to move my medical practice was due to my interest in getting it closer to the Flint Goodridge Hospital of Dillard University. Obviously, this would be a win-win situation for my patients and myself. Toward this end, I relocated my medical practice to Louisiana Avenue at LaSalle Street. The office space I rented had an Exam Room, a Waiting Room, and a Secretary Area where Patients Records were kept secure. I was now located across the street from FGHDU. Although I gave up the free use of office space at my former medical practice address mentioned earlier, I was now contracted at my new medical practice address to pay monthly rent and utilities. My contract lease for my new office space was with FGHDU. By 1963, my medical practice fate was aligned with FGHDU, and I was an *Anthropas Estin Kalos*, or a happy man in a good place.

When I completed my day's work at my medical practice or FGHDU, I would go to my Aunts Mary Augustine Pierce and Evelyn Pierce's house on Olive Street in Gert town near Xavier University. I stayed with them for about four months, and, afterwards, I moved into my own apartment located on Treasure Street near Dillard University. I stayed in my Treasure Street Apartment for about one year. I also went to my mother's house on the Gravel Road to get my two children, who I introduced earlier as Brownsyn Braud and Glenn Braud. While all of these changes were taking place, I was still married to Swedie Braud, who was living in our house in Springhill, LA. I would spend some of my weekends with her, and usually returned to my medical practice by Monday morning. Sometimes I would bring Brownsyn and Glenn with me to visit with Brenda Braud, but most times I left them at my mother's house on my way to Springhill, LA. Moreover, at this time, I ceased bringing up the matter of adoption with Swedie. I resolved in my mind and heart to let it go. And, I did so.

Eventually Swedie earned her Masters of Arts Degree in Home Economics from the State University of Iowa, Iowa City, and her Doctoral Degree in Higher Education from Southern Illinois University at Carbondale, Illinois. Swedie would soon obtain employment at Grambling State University where she would spend her entire professional career working as a Professor in Home Economics, and later as a Special Assistant to the Vice President for Academic Affairs. Meantime, right before I made a major leap forward in my medical career at the Flint-Goodridge Hospital of Dillard University, I moved out of my Treasure Street Apartment into a house I rented located on DeBore Drive in Ponchatrain Park. Toward the end of 1962, I moved out of the house I was renting, and moved into another one at Providence Place, which I purchased. My new house was adjacent to Southern University New Orleans commonly known as SUNO. Interestingly, many New Orleanians today think Hurricane Katrina was the first big flood event in New Orleans, LA. Of course, that is far from being true. Hurricane Betsy, which struck New Orleans, LA in 1965, caused widespread flooding at the time, and my Providence Place House was flooded with water. As it is often said, Katrina was not my "first rodeo." The truth is I have been dipping water out of my homes for more than 40 years! Hurricane Betsy pounded New Orleans, LA before I began my Anesthesia Training at the Charity Hospital Residency Anesthesia Training Program. Louisiana, geographically speaking, is in a bowl six feet below sea level. California is prone to having earthquakes so we ALL play the analytics commonly known as the odds that neither one of these catastrophes will occur. Only time will tell…

H. First Black Physician Admitted To The Charity Hospital Residency Program In Anesthesia In 1965

Without a doubt, this was a time of several momentous, or Earth-shattering Events. On November 22, 1963, President John F. Kennedy was assassinated on live Television! Though the average American Working Class Man and Woman did not know it at the time, and given the firestorm of emotions that followed the Kennedy Assassination, the latter was another effort to prevent People of Color from advancing up the economic ladder, from the lowly rung their lives clung to since the beginning of the American Republic. The South was still in near total resistance to Black People, and others of Color, from making any real significant gains across the social, economic, political, and judicial spectrum of American Life.

As evidence of this fact, on the very day of the Kennedy Assassination, Mrs. Mrytle Garrison reported a firsthand conversation she had with Dr. Roy Boggs, who was then the Chief of Anesthesia at Flint-Goodridge Hospital of Dillard University. She reported "Dr. Boggs went to Charity and was given a tour of the hospital by Dr. John Adriani, Chief of Anesthesia on the very day that John Kennedy was assassinated in Dallas, TX. Dr. Boggs stated to me that members of the hospital staff were rejoicing, singing, and dancing in the Charity Hospital [L]obby with the happy news of President Kennedy's Death. Racism was at an all-time high then! This was the state of play at Charity Hospital in 1963, which was one year before a plan was being made for me to begin my Anesthesia Training.

Since the beginning of the first day Charity Hospital opened its doors, no Black Person, male or female, had never been accepted into its Residency or Internship Programs. However, as fate decreed, I dreamed of becoming a Medical Doctor when I was five years old, and as the old saying goes. *"To whom much is given, much is expected in retu*rn." Like Malcolm X once remarked to Minister Louis Farrakhan, and I paraphrase, "Brother, I wish I could pass this cup to you because the responsibility and burden is so great." Malcolm X made this remark when he had to make a decision related to taking the moral high ground, or settling for the low place of mediocrity. By 1964, I was about to voluntarily be thrusted into the position of being the *First Black Physician to be accepted in the Charity Hospital School of Anesthesia by 1965*. There was no precedent for me to fall back on to learn from; I was the precedent in the making for another generation of Black Medical Doctors and others of Color, regardless of gender and religion and so forth. I was breaking down a racial barrier for People of Color everywhere in the South in particular. I was about to do what Rosa Parks did when she refused to give up her seat on a bus during the Montgomery, AL Bus Boycott. For me, I was about to take a seat in the Charity Hospital Anesthesia Residency Program, which had been denied to Black People since the Charity Hospital was established.

Before I go into more details related to my Charity Hospital Residency Training Experience, Image 1.5 below shows the physical plant of Charity Hospital in 1931. It operated sharply along racial lines. There were no gray areas where Black and White Physicians interacted except under the strictest racially-motivated operating guidelines.

Image 1.5 Charity Hospital Physical Plant And Its Racially Divided Healthcare Practice In New Orleans, LA By 1931

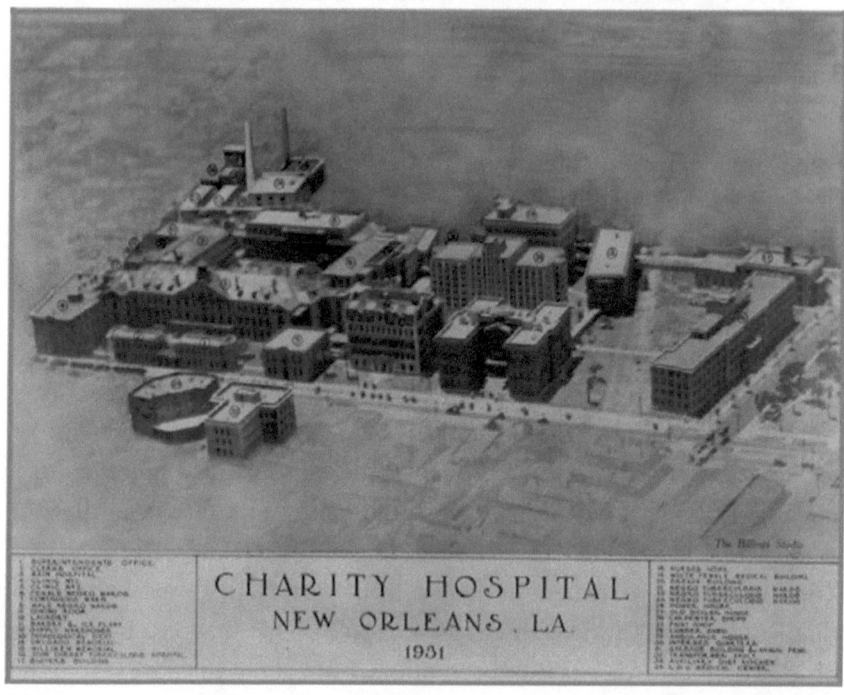

Source: Louisiana. New Orleans. Charity Hospital Complex, ca. 1931. Newman Louisiana Aviation Collection (MSS6) Folder 91. University of New Orleans, Earl K. Long Library, https://collections.uno.edu/repositories/2/archival object accessed February 24, 2022

According to the legend in Image 1.5, the Main Building is the one in which I did my Residency Anesthesia Training. My training took place on the top floor in this building in the auditorium. Moreover, a close inspection of the legend shows there were separate Male and Female Wards and several separate Negro Tuberculosis Wards. In addition, the building labeled Number 19 was the segregated White Female Medical Building. The LSU Medical Center was also segregated inasmuch as "no" Black Physicians held a staff position there, nor were Negro Patients allowed to receive "any" healthcare services there either. Moreover, according to Mrs. Myrtle Garrison, who was trained as a Nurse Anesthetist at Charity Hospital during the time I was there, told me there were two entrances to the Charity Hospital Main Building facing Tulane Avenue. During the

Christmas Holidays, there was a White Santa Claus, who took pictures, at one entrance with White Parents' Children, and at the other entrance, there was a Black Santa Claus, who took pictures with Black Parents' Children. As it was, racial segregation was not limited to healthcare but it permeated the general cultural life throughout New Orleans, LA. The same racial segregation, regarding healthcare practices, was in effect when I was accepted into the Charity Hospital Residency Anesthesia Training Program 33 years later.

Therefore, on June 1, 1965, I ventured off into Anesthesia Training at Charity Hospital. Dr. John Adriani, Dr. Roy E. Boggs, and I got together and discussed my getting trained in Anesthesia. It was understood that I would be trained with the Residents in Anesthesia at Charity Hospital. As I stated earlier, I had, by this time, already completed my Internship Program at the Youngstown Hospital Association in Youngstown, Ohio. If I had not already completed it, I would have to complete my Internship Program before I could receive my Anesthesia Training. Because I had already completed it, I was the first Black Physician to be trained at Charity Hospital of Louisiana in its Residency Anesthesia Program. This was orchestrated by Dr. John Adriani, and the program was labeled Charity Hospital-Flint-Goodridge Hospital of Dillard University.

When all of the pre-planning discussions were done, I began my Anesthesia Training on June 1, 1965. One year earlier, another milestone was reached; the first Black Intern was accepted at Charity Hospital in its Surgery Internship Program. A Silent Revolution took place but not a word was ever heard about it anywhere in Louisiana, or the nation.

I. Silent Revolution At Charity Hospital In New Orleans, LA In 1965 To 1967

Little Black Children, who took my place on the Gravel Road in St. James Parish where I grew up a generation earlier, never heard about the precedents Dr. Earnest Kinchen, Surgeon and Dr. Joseph Pierce Braud, Anesthesiologist set for them. I can only reflect back to that time-now-what a positive impact this news would have had on my Gravel Road Friends, regarding motivation and inspiration to get an education, if it had been timely made known to them that a young boy, who lived next door, actually scrapped rice and potatoes, and shined shoes; and, in spite of these perceived hardships, he went on to graduate with his Medical Degree. Then, not stopping there, he eventually broke down the racial barrier door of the Charity Hospital Residency Anesthesia Program, and became the first Black Medical Doctor to be accepted in its Residency Anesthesia Program in 1965. In addition, Dr. Earnest Kinchen, a colleague of mine and surgeon, was the first Black Doctor accepted into the Charity Hospital Surgery Internship Program, where he went on to receive his Certificate of Completion of that Program as a Heart Surgeon. Both of us made more than waves; we made history.

As you may recall, the day I resigned my teaching position at Charles H. Brown High School, I was told during my Exit Interview that I did not have "No Respect For Authority." And, upset as I was about this remark, I chose to remain peaceful, and live to fight another day. That day was June 1, 1965 when I broke down the barred door that had kept Black Physicians from doing their Residency Training at Charity Hospital since it was first established. Timing is everything, and the moment I was needed *by change to make a significant change*, which would later impact American Society forever, I was prepared to make this change with my educational pedagogy in Medicine. Since this landmark breakthrough was made by me, there have been an influx of young, gifted, Black Physicians, and others of color, both male and female, who, today, are able to do their chosen Internship and Residency Programs at most major American Hospitals in Louisiana and elsewhere. I am proud of my accomplishment as well as the one made by Dr. Earnest Kinchen and others, who I do not know but benefited from the change. Image 1.6 below shows the certificate I received for completing my program as a trained Anesthesiologist.

Image 1.6 Certificate Of Completion Of The Charity Hospital Residency Anesthesia Program, From June 1, 1965 To June 30, 1967

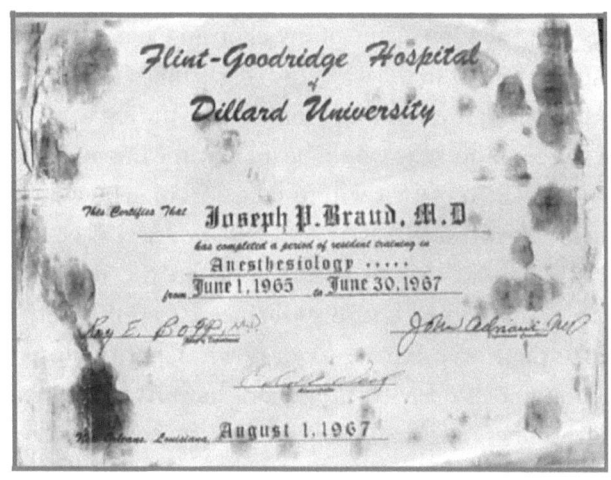

Eventually Dr. Earnest Kinchen and I were the first Black Intern and Resident in the Charity Hospital Anesthesia and Surgeon Programs. There was no publicity. My Anesthesia Achievement, nor his Surgeon work, were never mentioned in the local newspapers-Times Picayune, States Times, etc.-nor was it ever mentioned in circulating papers around the hospital. There was nothing said, no comments, and no advertisements of any kind. Ralph Ellison's book titled *Invisible Man* hit the nail squarely on the head: We were two real people but publicly we were not seen or spoken about. Ralph Ellison said we were only "figments of a White Person's imagination." This is the way the situation was but we were absorbing all of the wonderful scientific information necessary to lead our individual medical practices in the near and long-term. As I noted already, this was the Terms and Conditions of the Adriani Policy. As it was practiced in real time, *It was a Silent Revolution. We ate lunch in the regular cafeteria for interns and residents. The Adriani Policy was subtle at best-we were ignored.* I did not despair because I knew the difference between where I came from and the seat I sat in in the Charity Hospital Residency Anesthesia Program. I was a long way from scrapping rice; I was being prepared to manage the Anesthesia that would mean the life or death of a patient, regardless of race, if the setting on the fluid infusion machine was mis-calibrated by as much as a *single strand of hair*. I knew what the stakes were, for my patients, so I ignored the Adriani Policy, and gave my full attention to his valuable lectures. There is a season for everything, and I knew I would weigh in on the matter later, at a later time of my choosing and in manner I would choose to respond similar to the way I did, regarding the Charles H. Brown Situation mentioned earlier. At that moment, the timing was not right, and I knew what the consequences would be if I became impatient like so many of our people do, which cause them to fall short of achieving their goals.

In the end, the Residency Anesthesia Program was Dr. Adriani's "Baby." Because he was able to keep the lid on the Racial Segregation Bottle, the program worked out so well since I completed it; Thereafter, or once I broke the Racial Barrier Door down, Charity Hospital, Tulane Medical School, and LSU Medical School have had continuous as well as increasing numbers of Afro-American Interns and Residents in their respective programs. I think my being the first Black Medical Doctor accepted in the Charity Hospital School of Anesthesia Program had a lot to do with this change for the better. Wouldn't you agree with me?

Besides the improvements made in getting more Black Doctors accepted as interns and residents, there was also a number of Black Nurses accepted in the Charity Hospital Anesthesia Training Program. We received our Anesthesia Training in the same auditorium. One year before I completed my Anesthesia Residency Program at the Charity Hospital, I made some changes in my personal life.

J. Marriage To Swedie Weary Braud Comes To An End In 1966

Leading up to my completion of the Charity Hospital Residency Anesthesia Program on June 30, 1967, my marriage to Swedie, which began while I worked for Charles H. Brown High School in Springhill, LA, came to an end. We got divorced in 1966. By that time, Swedie had reinvented her life in the Grambling State University Culture as a Professor of Home Economic. Much has been said about the problems that come along with "long distance" relationships. After I set up my Medical Practice on St. Bernard Avenue and North Claiborne Avenue, and later at LaSalle Street and Louisiana Avenue near the Flint-Goodridge Hospital of Dillard University, more and more of my time was devoted to nurturing my

Medical Practice, and, after I broke the "Glass Ceiling" as the first Black Medical Doctor accepted into the Charity Hospital Anesthesia Training Program, the scientific rigors of completing my Residency Program in Anesthesia consumed nearly all of my time. At the end of a typical workday, during which I conducted the business of my Medical Practice; and, after which, I attended my class in the Residency Anesthesia Program and, oftentimes, I was exhausted.

Thus, traveling to Springhill, LA became more challenging, especially since Swedie had made it clear to me years earlier, in spite of my timely protestations to save our marriage, she would not change her mind about adoption of my two children. As I said earlier, I stopped asking her about doing so, but that did not make it any easier for me as a positive stimulant to make the long drive to Springhill, LA. Therefore, before the end of 1966, we got a divorced. Our breakup was amiable, and, interestingly so, we remained friends many years after we got divorced. A few months after Swedie and I divorced, I met and dated a woman whose name is Susan Ducre.

Susan Ducre and I were married when I completed my Residency Anesthesia Program at Charity Hospital. We enjoyed each other's company, and the natural next thing to do was get married. We did and Susan Ducre moved in with me in my house located in the Ponchatrain Park Section of New Orleans, LA at Providence Place. We were all happy, including my two children-Bronsyn and Glenn. Susan Ducre Braud adored them before and after we were married. I had a new wife, and I was about to obtain employment in one of the most prestigious jobs I have had the good fortune to work in during my Professional Medical Career.

K. Named Chief Of Flint-Goodridge Hospital Of Dillard University's Department Of Anesthesia And Phase-out Of The Nurse Anesthetist Program By 1968

Before 1960, Nurse Anesthetists were the only skilled Medical Professionals, at Flint-Goodridge Hospital of Dillard University, who could administer Anesthesia during a Surgical Operation. Unfortunately, the Nurse Anesthetists rarely received the notoriety and equal compensation other White Medical Doctors received, who administered Anesthesia during surgery. The Nurse Anesthetists were told they not Medical Doctors, which is the reason they received less pay and recognition for doing the same job as White Medical Doctors. By 1968, Flint-Goodridge Hospital of Dillard Hospital Staff underwent some key changes. At the end of my Residency Anesthesia Program, I began working in the Anesthesia Department of Flint-Goodridge Hospital of Dillard University with Dr. Roy Boggs. Everything was going fine, and for some reason Dr. Boggs resigned and relocated to another area in the United States. He must have had all he could take of the subtle racism that permeated every aspect of institutional life in the Deep South? Whatever his reason was for leaving, his resignation created a vacuum in the Department of Anesthesia at FGHDU by 1968. If asked to assume this highly important and technical position, I felt ready to step in and accept the torch and the demands that came with it. When Dr. Roy Boggs resigned, surprisingly but not unexpected, the Medical Staff of Flint-Goodridge Hospital of Dillard University voted to have me become the head of the Anesthesia Department. Without a doubt, I was elated, blessed, and accepted the responsibility for all decisions, both good and bad, that could arise during my tenure. I knew there was no room for a lack of Surgical Preparation, and this meant the margin of error was so slim one could not see it save looking through a microscope. I realized this fact and conducted the day-to-day business of the Department of Anesthesia accordingly. There were other Department Heads who assumed such duties at Flint-Goodridge Hospital of Dillard University.

a. Black Physicians Became Department Heads At Flint-Goodridge Hospital Of Dillard University In 1968

For example, from the early sixties, following the renovation and enlargement of the FGHDU, the different departments of the hospital that were headed by other ethnic groups were gradually replaced by Black Physicians (Specialists). At the time, FGHDU had approximately 30 Black Medical Doctors or less, *give or take one or two*. Oftentimes, the latter called upon some White Physicians for help, and with Systemic Racism notwithstanding, they kept their private sentiments about the matter mostly to themselves, and assisted the FGHDU Medical Doctors in the interest of the patients, who needed their timely help. Things went well for a while. The first group to change department heads at FGHDU was the following:

- Richard Timpton, MD, Radiology
- Roy Boggs, MD, Anesthesia
- Odell Dean, MD, Obstetrics &Gynecology

At the same time, there were several more Black Physicians, who came to New Orleans, LA to practice, namely, Joseph Labat, MD, Emile Riley, MD, Reginald Woods, MD, Roy Marerro, MD, Warren McKenna, MD, Jerome Medley, MD, and Errol Quintal, MD. This list does not exhaust the Black Physicians, who continued to arrive in New Orleans, LA, who were searching for a place to practice. Although New Orleans, LA was still a very good place to practice as I had found it to be true when I arrived there in 1960, it was still a place where racism's foothold was quite strong by 1968. Appendix C includes a list of the Black Physicians who held Staff Positions at Flint-Goodridge Hospital of Dillard University by 1968.

b. American Medical Association Denial Of Membership And Phase-out OF Flint-Goodridge Hospital Of Dillard University's Nurse Anesthetist Program By 1968

Only three years earlier, by 1965, Mrs. Myrtle Garrison wrote, "Dr. William R. Adams, a Staff Physician at Flint [Goodridge] Hospital [of Dillard University] sought membership in the American Medical Association and staff privileges at Charity Hospital, and he was denied due to segregation." Herbert M. Morais added "in one Southern state, Louisiana, no local affiliate of the American Medical Association would admit a colored physician, regardless of his professional qualifications. When Negro doctors in New Orleans applied for staff privileges to Charity Hospital, a tax-supported city institution, they were told to seek membership in the Orleans Parish Medical Society."[132] Given this Carte Blanc denial of Black Physicians entry into the American Medical Association, along with its prohibition of staff privileges, Dr. William R. Adams was quoted in a press dispatch saying the following: "…when we made application there,

---

[132] Morais, op. cit., p. 177.

we were turned down flatly, with no effort at subterfuge. We were told Negro physicians were not accepted."[133] Many changes were made within the internal organization of FGHDU; however, externally, many, if not all Black Physicians, still had a difficult *row to hoe*. Although this was the sign of the times then, I felt empowered to do my best medical practice at FGHDU.

When I became Department Head of Anesthesia at Flint-Goodridge Hospital of Dillard University in 1968, its Nurse Anesthetist Program was gradually phased-out. There was a loosening of employment restrictions by other hospitals in America, which had hitherto barred African-Americans from practice. Slowly, various hospitals in New Orleans, LA opened their doors, and began hiring Afro-American Certified Registered Nurse Anesthetists (CRNA). That being the case, some of the Nurse Anesthetists moved to greener pastures where they could earn more income and work with state-of-the art Anesthesia Technology. Mrs. Myrtle Garrison is an excellent example of this emerging trend by the late 1960s. Mrs. Garrison is retired and lives in Houston, TX today.

At least four years after the 1964 Civil Rights Bill was passed by the United States Congress, and like an iceberg that has been frozen for a century or more, gradually there was some slow "drip" employment of Nurse Anesthetists at some of the White Hospitals in New Orleans, LA, which had, for more than a century, barred them from working there.

In Mrs. Mrytle Garrison Case, she belonged to the First Unitarian Church in New Orleans, LA. As a member, she met Dr. John Wait, who was also a member of the congregation. "Dr. John Wait, a cordial White [Medical Doctor]… was also the Chief of Surgery at U.S. Public Health Hospital. He stated to [Mrs. Mrytle Garrison] 'Myrtle, now that the integration laws have been passed, we need Black People to fill those positions. Will you consider applying for a position on the Anesthesia Staff at U.S. Public Health Services Hospital in New Orleans, LA?' Mrs. Myrtle Garrison took Dr. John Wait's advice and applied for a staff position in the Anesthesia Department and she was hired. Mrs. Garrison "…was the second Black Nurse Anesthetist to be employed at the [U.S. Public Health Hospital] in 1965." Though she was employed in this Staff Position, Mrs. Mrytle Garrison said "…she encountered great resistance and racial

---

[133] Ibid., p. 177.

discard from the White Male Coast Guard Patients, who would voice their reluctance to have me, a Black Person, administer Anesthesia to them when their physical status was critical and life-threatening...For some who had received the "Last Rites," Racism was relentless!" For example, a Coast Guard Patient, who was dying, refused to allow Mrs. Myrtle Garrison to put him to sleep for surgery! It was true then, and it is still true today that one can "legislate change" but a law enacted "cannot change" an affected person's racist behavior. However, overtime, may be a generation or more, the Civil Right Laws had some affect on producing an integrated Nurse Anesthetist Group.

At any rate, by 1968, FGHDU was still going through its "Glorious Years," and as Head of its Anesthesia Department, I had a front row seat because surgeries of various types were being done, which required my department's constant services.

L. Flint-Goodridge Hospital OF Dillard University And Its Surgery And Anesthesia Groups From 1968 To 1982

Without being naïve and redundant, I must mention the obvious, which is, no surgery could take place without Anesthesiologists, Nurse Anesthetists, and Surgeons working closely together on a daily basis. As it was, the Anesthesia Department did predominantly "bread and butter" surgery. That is, Gall Bladders, hernias, fractures, hysterectomies, pregnancies, and nerve blocks among a host of others. *As long as the hospital was able to perform less imposing types of surgery, it stayed in the black, regarding cash-flow.* Make a note of this fact because I will circle back to it later to make a significant point that was threatening to the Flint-Goodridge Hospital of Dillard University financial health. For now, everything was going very well.

For many years, I was the only Anesthesiologists at FGHDU, and I had a staff of two or three Nurse Anesthetists. The Surgical Scheduling was rather efficient. That is, the Surgical Crew and the Anesthesia Crew worked very well together. Many days the schedules were heavy and I had to get anesthesiologists from other hospitals to give us a hand. There was more demand for surgery than there was an available supply of Anesthesiologists. The philosophy that says "when there is a need, the Spirit will send a solution to address it." Because of the prevailing Systemic Racism I have mentioned throughout my life journey thus far, it did not discriminate between people of color but affected them equally in an adverse way.

That being so, then, a Korean Doctor, whose specialty was Anesthesiology, came to FGHDU, and he was hired by the hospital. Prior to that time, my coverage in Anesthesia came from Anesthesiologists from other hospitals outside of FGHDU. I occasionally called upon Dr. Zepernick, who held a staff position at Mercy Hospital in New Orleans, LA and Dr. Elmore Ogeron, who held a staff position at East Jefferson Hospital. Their assistance was needed only when our surgery caseload at Flint-Goodridge Hospital of Dillard University was higher than normal. Usually, FGHDU performed an average of 20 to 30 surgeries per week. If this average significantly increased, then, I would call in the Medical Doctors mentioned earlier. In addition, when I had to attend local, regional, or national symposiums, I would schedule the Medical Doctors to come in and provide pre-and post-surgery assistance. They would "Make The Rounds" the following day to make sure that any patients, who had surgery the day before, were recovering according to what was expected.

In addition, I also had a group of Certified Registered Nurse Anesthetists, who came in to assist with surgery, in my absence. They were namely, Mrs. Mattie Hansberry, Ms. Loudella Fleming, Ms. Ardella Fleming, twin sister of Loudella, Mrs. Shirley Theodore, and Mrs. Mrytle Garrison. Thus, I had a compliment of available Medical Professionals, who helped FGHDU's Department of Anesthesia, to provide the highest quality of continuum of care possible. Although the work provided by these healthcare professionals was timely and necessary, I was blessed to have Dr. T. Luke Yang join my Department of Anesthesia at FGHDU.

At last, we now had coverage in-house. This was a milestone development in so many ways, regarding making the Surgery Schedule easier to manage. Dr. T. Luke Yang And I formed and Anesthesia Group; we covered the Surgery Schedule for each other, which reduced my need to bring in external Medical Doctors and Nurse Anesthetists to assist with surgery. Flint-Goodridge Hospital of Dillard University continued to have glorious years, from 1968 to 1982. Those were great years for all concerned. This was a time when Black Physicians were empowered to engage in their Medical Practices at Flint-Goodridge Hospital of Dillard University. As I have established, it was a time when none of the White Hospitals would allow Black Physicians to work in their specialties due to Systemic Racism. FGHDU filled the void, and the Afro-American Community in New Orleans, LA was the direct beneficiary.

During the Glory Years of Flint-Goodridge Hospital of Dillard University, and as I made known earlier, less sophisticated, or complex surgery, was its Bread And Butter staple. While serving as the Department Head of Anesthesia, I was right in the middle of the action, from 1968 to 1982. In the words of Charles Dickens, "It was the best of times." Unfortunately, Black Physicians were not allowed to perform surgery at the local White Hospitals in New Orleans, LA. Such Jim Crow restrictions, no doubt, adversely impacted the quality of patient care. What happened to those Black Patients, like "JF" who needed a medical treatment only a White Hospital could provide?

At any rate, while I was having the greatest time of my life doing what I loved to do working as the Chief of Anesthesiology at Flint-Goodridge Hospital of Dillard University, my family life was changing.

M. Family Life-Work Life Balance From 1960 To 1982

When I set up my Medical practice and also held a staff position at Flint-Goodridge Hospital of Dillard University by 1968, my family life underwent several changes during this time. Initially, when I decided to do the former, I lived in New Orleans, LA with my two Aunts-Mary Augustine Pierce and Evelyn W. Pierce, my mother's sisters, on Olive Street. Swedie lived in Springhill, LA in our house there while she continued to work at Charles H. Brown High School, and later at Grambling State University. Swedie and I agreed, since we were living apart from each other, it was a good idea to put our children in a Boarding School. That is, my two children, namely, Brownsyn Braud and Glenn Braud. Brenda, on the other hand, would continue to go to school in Springhill, LA at the high school where Swedie worked in 1961.

Boarding School seemed like the best option to choose under the circumstances, given the fact I was a "Newly Trained Black Medical Doctor" in New Orleans, LA by 1961, and I did not have anyone at home, who could help me with the day-to-day demands of raising my two children. In this Spirit, I searched the available universe of Boarding Schools in my area, and settled on enrolling my daughter-Bronsyn Braud-at the St. Mary Academy Boarding School on Bourbon Street. There are other academic activities going-on on Bourbon Street besides the world-famous party life most New Orleanians and Tourist have come to love about it through the years. Bronsyn Braud was 11 years old when I enrolled her in this Boarding School in 1961. Later that year, I moved into my Treasure Street Apartment. I would have Bronsyn Braud home with me during the holidays, and I would visit with her periodically at the Boarding School. She never expressed to me any uneasiness about being enrolled at St. Mary. If she had done so, I would have disenrolled her and looked for a better alternative. Everybody was happy, and my sometimes unpredictable work hours at FGHDU did not directly impact my daughter.

Glenn Braud, my younger son, lived with my mother, Lillian Luellen Pierce Braud in Brookstown on the Gravel Road. In fact, Glenn attended the St. Louis School where many of my peers attended school during my childhood. He attended the St. Louis School, from 1960 to 1963. That year, I enrolled all of my children in another Boarding School located in Lafayette, LA, namely, Holy Rosary Institute, which was located on the Old Breaux Bridge Highway (Holy Rosary Institute is closed today but some efforts have been made to reopen part of the school and preserve it as a historical landmark). Brownsyn Braud, Brenda Braud, and Glenn Braud were enrolled there. For those who do not know anything about Holy Rosary Institute, it was a Catholic School, which adhered to the Roman Catholic Church Philosophy. So, from 1963 to 1967, they were enrolled at this Boarding School. The female teachers, or Nuns, wore the typical dress characterized by an ankle-length, loose-fitting, black dress, white shirt, and a dark headdress. Their education was a combination of the secular and religious teaching.

Brownsyn Braud and Brenda Brown Braud both graduated from Holy Rosary Institute in 1966 and 1967 respectively. As evidence of just how deep the Catholic Education she received had impacted her, when Brownsyn Braud graduated from Holy Rosary Institute in 1966, she enrolled in Immaculata College located in Bryan Mawr, Pennsylvania. She sincerely thought the day she graduated she wanted to become a Nun like the Sisters at Holy Rosary Institute, who taught her the Catholic Doctrine and way of life; Brownsyn Braud also wanted to become a Medical Doctor. Brownsyn Braud was not alone in her thinking; there were many young women before her and after, who, likewise thought they wanted to become a Nun too. The religious curriculum was widespread throughout the academic course offerings. Brenda Brown Braud took a different path when she graduated in 1967; that is, she enrolled in college at the University of Denver, Denver, Colorado. Denver, Colorado is known as the Mile High City because it is, in fact, 5,280 feet above sea level.

Denver, Colorado in 1967 was, by any estimation, a growing liberal place where secular thinking, that is, viewing the world around oneself differently, and cultivating a willingness to be open to new ideas that challenge the status quo, was encouraged by her Professors. This was also a time when the Civil Rights Movement, and Feminine Questions, which for decades had been *Taboo*, were being openly discussed. There was so much inequality that existed between Blacks and Whites that more young minds were needed to get into the struggle for justice at the grassroot level, or any level for that matter. Brenda Brown Braud was immersed in the Denver Community, and she, no doubt, had many opportunities to question some of the Catholic Teachings, which she learned while enrolled at Holy Rosary Institute. She received her undergraduate degree in the Sciences in 1970. Interestingly, Brownsyn Braud had a personal epiphany, during the summer 1967, which changed her direction in life 1800, from the direction in which she was headed after she graduated from Holy Rosary Institute.

Brownsyn Braud came home, for the summer 1968, after she completed her Freshmen Year at Immaculata College. Like young college age women were then and still are today, she was gregarious and open to have new experiences. As it was, she started visiting Xavier University where some of her friends were enrolled she knew in the community. One, in particular, was Winifred Johnson. Brownsyn and Winifred became very good friends, and Winifred would bring Brownsyn to some of the Civil Rights Meetings, and other social functions, that were held on Xavier University Campus. Brownsyn Braud met some of the male and female activists and even some who claimed to be revolutionaries. Brownsyn Braud's Epiphany was her eyes were opened-up to many of the inequalities Black People and others of Color faced, which she hitherto had not given much time and attention to before now.

The activists made a deep impression on Brownsyn Braud's mind because they suggested grassroot people had the "Power" to change their personal lives and the racial disparities in their communities, both singularly and collectively. This realization resonated so deeply inside of Brownsyn Braud's Mind that she felt she could *be and do more for the people and self through collective action, rather than giving her burdens to a deity, of whom she reasoned she did not know much about other than what was routinely taught to her by the institution.* By becoming active in grassroot work, Brownsyn Braud reasoned she could change herself; and, she could engage in social education and learn a philosophy consistent with her need to work-out her day-to-day contradictions on both a personal, group, and community level. I am sure Brownsyn Braud likely overheard me talking about some of my own challenges I faced in the area of *Race Matters*.

By the summer 1967, I had already broken down the closed door, which barred Black Physicians from being trained in their chosen specialties at the Charity Hospital Anesthesia Residency Program. As I have already stated, I was the first Black Physician in Louisiana to be accepted in this program in June 1965. My daughters and son knew generally what this meant but they still had to live a few more years to gain some more experiences of their own to understand the breakthrough I made for Black Physicians in Louisiana, and for those who chose to come to New Orleans, LA to do their Internship and Residency work from another state. Dr. Ernest Kinchen and I were already fighting in the Civil and Human Rights Struggle before my daughters and son completed high school.

My achievement was not widely advertised when it occurred, but here I have an opportunity, which I am taking now, to inform my Braud Family Group, all of my Gravel Road-Brookstown-Family Groups, and the World Family, how my efforts made getting into a Residency Program in Louisiana a whole lot easier for the children of color of mothers, fathers, and friends everywhere on the Planet. I was proud of Brownsyn Braud for her change of mind then, and I will always be now, and for the rest of my life. I am equally proud of all of the members of my Braud Family Group, and of their educational achievements. And, they know it too!

Brownsyn Braud did not return to Immaculata College but, instead, she enrolled at Xavier University in Fall 1968. My personal life underwent a change at that time. I entered into a marital relationship with Susan Ducre Braud. Moreover, Brownsyn Braud completed her undergraduate degree at Xavier University in 1971. She, then, got accepted into Meharry Medical School in Nashville, TN where she went on to complete her Medical Doctors Degree in 1976. When Brownsyn Braud graduated from Xavier University, my marriage to Susan Ducre Braud came to end. We departed amiably, and we remain friends today.

Glenn Braud left Holy Rosary Institute in 1967 when Brownsyn Braud graduated. He went to live with my mother in Brookstown where he enrolled in Magnolia High School; he graduated in 1971. He attended undergraduate school at Southern University New Orleans, LA (SUNO) and Southern University Baton Rouge, LA (SUBR).

All-in-all, my children grew into young adults during my "Glory Years" at Flint-Goodridge Hospital of Dillard University, which coincided with the first five years of my staff position at the hospital where I served as the Director of the Department of Anesthesia. With the exception of my divorce from Susan Ducre Braud, everything went along quite well for me at Flint-Goodridge Hospital of Dillard University. I worked with a strong team of Black Physicians and Nurse Anesthetists. There were no internal problems I could discern on the hospital's horizon yet. I was happy being the Director of the Department of Anesthesia at FGHDU, and by 1972, Medical Doctors were permitted to incorporate their practices for the first time.

N. Medical Practice Incorporation In 1972

That year, I incorporated my Medical Practice, which was inspired by Mr. John Becker, Financial Planner with Fringe Benefits Inc. I met with Mr. Becker and listened to his instructions related to how I could benefit, if I incorporated my practice. It made sense for me to incorporate; there were more advantages, if I did so than otherwise. I decided to move forward with incorporation.

Unlike beforehand, when I incorporated my Medical Practice, I became an employee with a salary. As an employee, I received medical insurance, unemployment compensation, pension plan, Defined Benefits Plan, and a Defined Contribution Plan, which included funds for my eventual retirement whenever that day arrived? All of these benefits of incorporation had to be approved by the Federal Government through its ERISA Program. The latter was necessary to make my incorporation of my Medical Practice valid. Also, I filed an application with the Louisiana Secretary of State Office. This was done because I needed to obtain the necessary documents so for my newly incorporated Medical Practice would meet all of the Louisiana State Government requirements. As I mentioned earlier, everything was going smoothly with my work as the Director of the Department of Anesthesia at Flint-Goodridge Hospital of Dillard University, including my incorporation of my Medical Practice. Two of my children were away in college and my son was going to high school in Brookstown. As it was, everything was lovely during the early 1970s.

The 1970s is when Flint-Goodridge Hospital of Dillard University became full grown, and reached the top shelf as a healthcare Power. But, there is a nemesis called "Success Anxiety," which is a mental state where an organization's success causes it to lose sight of its mission; and, rather than continue to build on the formula that it used to get it to the top, it takes on a new mission without fully vetting whether it will harm the organization in way it cannot recover. Managers must be clever, subtle, listen, and make tough decisions to stay on course, although the sustained success of an organization might make it appear the timing is right to add a new program to its operation, which actually does not help it grow but cut short its life expectancy. The great Motown lyricist and Singer, whom many know today as Smokey Robinson, wrote a song about the Temptations Rhythm and Blues Group, that captures what laid ahead for the Flint-Goodridge Hospital of Dillard University. Its name is: "Be Careful What You Wish For." In essence, the message embodied in this song is timeless, and it is be careful what you wish for because some dreams should never come true. Success can destroy you (Paraphrase Mine).

No one at FGHDU could imagine this was possible. All things were going so well; revenues were in the "black;" and smiles were in abundance. The 1970s were good years. This is how I went into them very optimistic that FGHDU would keep using the formula that works. I was all in.

CHAPTER XVIII

FLINT-GOODRIDGE HOSPITAL OF DILLARD UNIVERSITY RISE AND UNTIMELY FALL FROM 1960 TO 1982

When the 1970s began, Flint-Goodridge Hospital of Dillard University was operating at a high level but because of the relatively small number of Black Medical Doctors in Staff Positions, and not discounting the fact that Systemic Racism was still very much alive in the New Orleans, LA Medical Practice Theatre, any unusual external variable could send the Doctor-Patient Ratio into a downward spiral, regarding cash-flow going into the hospital treasury. At this time, there were approximately 30 Black Physicians were on staff at Flint-Goodridge Hospital of Dillard University. And, the hospital's bed capacity was 100. To the casual observer, this number of Black Physicians were far less than the number the FGHDU needed to serve a potentially growing patient demand. That is, with a much larger and diverse Black Medical Doctor Pool at the hospital, the latter could care for more patients, and I might add, it would be able to weather any unforeseeable change that might arise. One such occurrence was the Hill-Burton Act passed by the United States Congress in 1946.

Before I go into details about the events that collectively contributed to the downfall of Flint-Goodridge Hospital of Dillard University, which did not occur until the early 1980s, it is timely to mention here that my fellow Black Physicians and I continued to create the "Glory Years" of the hospital, from 1968 through 1980. Every one of the Black Physicians I worked with successfully practiced their specialties. Segregation made Coaches Mumford of Southern University and Eddie Robinson of Grambling

State University College Football Legends in Louisiana. When integration arrived, sadly, these football powerhouses never were able to achieve their former greatness.

A. Surgery And Anesthesia Department At Flint-Goodridge Hospital Of Dillard University During The 1970s

I had a very good working relationship with Dr. William R. Adams, Gynecology Surgeon, Dr. W. Barial, Surgery, Dr. H. E. Braden, Surgery, Dr. William Jones, Surgery, Dr. A. Pratt, Surgery, Dr. M. Epps, Sr, Surgery, and Dr. Riordan, Hand Surgeon (White Physician). There were others not named here who performed surgery at Flint-Goodridge Hospital of Dillard University during the 1970s, whom I also enjoyed a good working relationship. The one thing that every surgeon had in common was the surgeries they performed fell within the supporting capabilities available to them to perform this or that surgery at the highest quality level. Reflecting back, I do not recall any Black Surgeon scheduled a surgery that was highly risky due to the fact FGHDU did not have the equipment, or technology necessary to perform the surgery safely and successfully. The surgeons, patients, and the Anesthesia Department were on the same page the vast majority of the time. I would go so far as to say 100.0 percent of the time. That being so, the financial health of Flint-Goodridge Hospital of Dillard University remained in the "black." In short, the hospital was able to pay its "bills," and it made a profit. The Black Physicians did very well financially also. The 1970s were a continuation of the "Glory Years." For myself, everything was going well in the Anesthesia Department. Under my leadership, there were no mistakes made. Dr. Yang and I constantly cross-checked each other, for the purpose of weeding out any potential complications before we "prepped" a patient for surgery. That is, we made sure our patients stayed asleep during their surgery, and they woke-up at the planned time after their surgery was over. We adhered to the formula that worked; that is, surgeons performed surgeries within the boundaries of the available technology. While everything was sunny for me at FGHDU, I got married in this sunshine and started a family during the 1970s.

B. Angela Dixon And Our Children During The Flint-Goodridge Hospital Of Dillard University Glory Years Of The 1970s

While my work at Flint-Goodridge Hospital of Dillard University was oftentimes quite demanding characterized by long hours and overwork, I still found time to enjoy the New Orleans, La social scene. I often heard it said through the years that "All work and no play, makes Johnny or Susan a dull boy or girl." To avoid this trap, and in order to keep my Medical Intellect and emotional self balanced, I made friends with people in New Orleans, LA, and I spent time with them at parties, balls, and Mardi Grau among others.

During the early 1970s, I made friends with Dutch Morial, who owned his law practice in New Orleans, LA. Specifically, I befriended Mr. Overton Thierry, who worked at his law practice. One day Mr. Thierry introduced me to a woman who worked for the Dutch Morial Law Practice. Her name is Ms. Angela Dixon. At the time, when I first laid my eyes on her, I thought to myself, Angela Dixon is the most beautiful woman in New Orleans, LA! I see why Roberta Flack sung this lyric: "First time I ever saw your face I thought the sun and the moon rose in your eyes" (Paraphrase Mine). This is what I felt when I was introduced to Ms. Angela Dixon for the first time. I thought the sun and moon rose in her eyes! She was so beautiful, and I had to find a way to make her my lady. We agreed to see each other again, and I felt like a young boy in a candy store. We went to dinners, restaurants, balls, movies, and just hung-out at the park, or visited a museum. I knew I had found a love, which was the kind the great Rhythm and Blues Singer Johnny Taylor sung about. I felt like he wrote that song and sung it just for me.

After dating for about two years, we decided to get married. Angela Dixon became Mrs. Angela Dixon Braud on March 10, 1973. After a year or so, our first child was born, namely, Shannon Braud. She was our lovely baby girl; I tried not to spoil her but I do not know if I was successful not doing so. Before Shannon was old enough to attend school, we placed her in Mrs. Marva Doughty Day Care; the latter was owned by Mrs. Marva Doughty, a Black Woman. Afterwards, Shannon spent a year in kindergarten. Then, she was enrolled in St. Raphael Elementary School, from first thru fourth grade. Shannon Braud attended Jean Gordon during her fifth and sixth grade years. During her high school years, she attended St. Mary Academy, from seventh to twelfth grade. Shannon Braud graduated from high school in 1991.

The next step on her educational journey was Xavier University; she did her undergraduate work, from 1991 to 1995. Shannon Braud earned a Bachelor of Science Degree with a major in Biology and a minor in Chemistry and Spanish. After undergraduate school at Xavier University, Shannon Braud enrolled in the Tulane School of Public Health in 1996 where she earned a Masters Degree in Public Health (MSPH). During this time, Shannon Braud wrote a Violence Prevention Grant for the Tulane School of Public Health. The Housing Authority of New Orleans, LA funded her grant for $250, 000. Because Shannon had a desire to go to Medical School, she enrolled in Meharry Medical School in Nashville, TN in 1997. By 2001, she graduated with a Medical Degree. Shannon Braud was my second daughter to earn a Medical Degree. She did her Residency at Methodist Charlton Hospital in Dallas, TX, which Shannon Braud completed in 2004. She established her Medical Practice in Dallas, TX in 2005.

Today, Shannon Braud resides in Dallas, TX, where she practices Hyperbaric Medicine and Family Medicine. She is also the Director for Wounded Hyperbaric Medicine at the Methodist Hospital for Surgery in Addison, TX. I am very proud of Shannon Braud's educational achievements. In addition, she is still my lovable daughter after all of the years of ups and downs. We had many more upsides to talk about when we get together for Thanksgiving and other occasions.

One year after Shannon was born, the Board of Trustees of Dillard University selected a new president in 1974. Dr. Samuel Dubois Cook took over the responsibility for the leadership of the Flint-Goodridge Hospital of Dillard University. He relied on the Board of Management to keep him informed about its day-to-day operation via quarterly reports or others. Dr. Cook remained president of Dillard University, from 1974 to 1997. He would later make a critical decision related to the hospital. A year later, our second child was born.

In 1975, Angela and I's second child was born on July 7, 1975. His name is Joseph Pierce Braud Jr. Of all my children, Joseph P. Braud Jr was my first-born son so I named him after me. He was also the apple of Angela and I's eye. Joseph P. Braud Jr began his education at Crescent Academy in New Orleans, LA. He graduated from high school at Marion Abrabrison High School in 1994. Joseph P. Braud Jr graduated from Southern University Baton Rouge in 1999. Then he enrolled in Meharry Medical School, and in 2005, he received his Masters of Science in Public Health (MSPH) Degree. Joseph P. Braud Jr stayed at Meharry Medical School and entered its Dental School where he earned his Doctors Degree in Dentistry Science in 2009. After returning home to New Orleans, LA, Joseph P. Braud Jr enrolled in the LSU Dental School in New Orleans, LA where he earned a Periodontics Degree. Always interested in expanding his practice, Joseph P. Braud Jr enrolled in the Jacksonville School of Orthodontics. He graduated with his Orthodontic Degree in 2014. Joseph P. Braud Jr was our third child to graduate with a Medical Degree. Similar to the way Joe Braud, my father, took me nearly everywhere he went, I cherished the times I took my son, Joseph P. Braud, Jr with me to different places also. I am proud of him and his many educational achievements too.

Every three years, Angela and I were adding another child to our Braud Family Group. Particularly, in 1978, our third child was born, namely, Kyle Braud. He did his K-12 Education at Saints Academy Boarding School. Kyle Braud graduated from high school in 1998. Then, enrolled at Southern University Baton Rouge. He graduated in 2002. Kyle Braud passed away untimely in 2015.

The last of our children was born on December 30, 1981. Her name is Falon Braud. Shannon Braud and Falon Braud formed the book ends of our household with two boys in the middle. Falon Braud favors her grandmother-Lillian Luellen Pierce Braud. She was an adorable baby, cute as a blue sky on a sunny day and smart too. Falon Braud did her K-6 Education at Jean Gordon Elementary School, which she finished in 1985. She enrolled in Lusher Middle School the next year in the 7th Grade; Falon Braud went to McDonald 15 in the 8th Grade; and she graduated from McDonald 35 High School in 1999. Thereafter, Falon Braud enrolled in Southern University in 2000 but she decided to switch colleges in favor of Fisk University where she graduated in 2005. Today, Falon Braud is employed as a LPN Nurse, and she has a near-term plan to become a RN Nurse. Falon is the youngest in the family, and how I feel about her is no different from the way I feel about my other children. She holds a warm, loving place in my heart like my other children. Likewise, I am proud of Falon Braud and her educational achievements as well.

As it was, the 1970s were good to me. I had a beautiful wife-Angela Dixon Braud-and four beautiful, lovable, and fabulous children; we also had Brownsyn Braud and Brenda Brown Braud, who were away in college. I could not ask for anything more. I enjoyed my work at Flint-Goodridge Hospital of Dillard University, and I had a wonderful family to come home and snuggle-up with on those rainy nights when it was thundering and lightening, and on those many others when the mosquitoes would allow us to sit outside and view the gorgeous moonlight, and just engage in small talk and laugh about nothing, or sometimes about serious matters.

C. Brownsyn Braud Graduation From Meharry Medical School And Outpouring Of Brookstown Appreciation

It is timely to point-out here that the year after Joseph Pierce Braud Jr was born in 1975, Brownsyn Braud graduated from Meharry Medical School in 1976. I was overjoyed thinking about her achievement, and to celebrate it, the entire Brookstown Village was invited to travel to Nashville, TN to witness one of their own graduate with a Medical Degree. Brownsyn Braud was my first child to do so. She raised the bar, lit a candle for her siblings, and paved a path for some of my other children to follow in the not too far off distant future. To get those in Brookstown to Nashville, TN, who wanted to attend Brownsyn Braud's graduation, I chartered a Greyhound Bus to transport everyone there. We had a glorious time, and Brownsyn Braud was happy to see the outpouring of support and appreciation, from the community, for the years of hard work she had done at Meharry Medical School. Many Brookstowns Residents, between 40 and 50 people, who knew, or heard of, Brownsyn Braud as a little girl growing up on the Gravel Road, made the trip, in spite of the years of grinding work they had done beforehand in the Rice and Cane Fields on the River Road, which left its signs of arthritis and other health challenges on their faces. Not to be discouraged by health concerns, they, nevertheless, adorned their hats and put on their "best" Sunday Church Clothing to honor one of their own with their presence. Those Brookstown Residents, who were unable to get a seat on the Greyhound Bus, drove their own vehicles to Brownsyn

Braud's Graduation Ceremony. Some residents, who did not have a car, rode in others with someone they knew who had one.

Regardless of their physical conditions, they pushed through them, by calling upon a part of their last determination to witness one of their own daughters, who had exceled at the highest academic level in the Medical Field. To the Brookstown People, this was a "big deal!" It was like the Edwin Hawkins Choir shouted "Oh Happy Day!" The Brookstown People, learned indirectly through Brownsyn Braud, that it was possible for Black People to get an education, and their "little girl" affirmed their feelings, by giving them a moment to celebrate, and enjoy a little peace of mind and hope between their tears of joy, and no doubt, a few were shed on that glorious day. This was an opportunity for the Brookstown People to feel proud, exhale, and stick out their chests after somebody had told them for decades that they were inferior. This myth had been shattered into many pieces by Brownsyn Braud's achievement. Amen.

After 1976, and especially toward the end of the 1970s, some forces outside of Flint-Goodridge Hospital of Dillard University had some lasting impacts on the well-being of the hospital. One of the most important among them was the Hill-Burton Act of 1946, which was enacted into law by the United States Congress during the Truman Administration. World War II had just come to an end, and there was a need to expand the availability of healthcare to the American People.

D. Hill-Burton Act Of 1946

Unforeseen Federal Restrictions is how I explain the Hill-Burton Act's impact on the Flint-Goodridge Hospital of Dillard University by 1970 and thereafter. As it was, this act was passed by the U.S. Congress thirty-four years before this time. However, with the passage of the Civil Rights Bill in 1964, suddenly there was some interest, both quasi and real, to assist African-Americans' minority serving community hospitals with available Federal Funds. The latter often came with conditions, or a *quid pro quo*. That is, I will give this money to the hospital but the recipient of the Federal Funds would be required to adjust their internal operations to accommodate changes that the Federal Government insisted upon before releasing any funds to it. For example, if the Federal Funds were provided to Flint-Goodridge Hospital of Dillard University by 1960 without any conditions, the money could have been used to increase the total number of Black Doctors, and rather than the 100 beds being too many, some of the Federal Funds could have been used to build more wings on the hospital to expand the total number of beds, let us say, from 100 to 200 and so forth. Instead, there was no Hill-Burton Act money flowing into FGHDU at the time. It would take another 10 years before any did.

As background, John Henning Schumann stated "the Hill-Burton Act was signed into law by President Harry S. Truman on August 13, 1946 — and its effect on health care in the U.S. was nothing short of monumental... Hill-Burton provided construction grants and loans to communities that could demonstrate viability — based on their population and per capita income — in the building of health care facilities. The idea was to build hospitals where they were needed and where they would be sustainable once their doors were open."[134] The law was named for Senator Harold Burton of Ohio and a southern Democrat name Senator Lester Hill of Alabama. Schumann added "...the law codified the idea of "separate but equal" in hospitals and health care facilities."[135] Interestingly, if the Hill-Burton Act was left this way, Flint-Goodridge Hospital of Dillard University would likely remain intact as it was by 1960. However, the federal court presented a legal challenge to the Separate but Equal Code, and it was overturned in 1963, and "...Hill-Burton went on to become a major driver of hospital desegregation."[136] To accomplish this goal, the Federal Government placed various stipulations on a hospital to receive federal monies.

a. Federal Government Restrictions On Hospitals That Received Federal Funds By 1963

One of the chief Federal Restrictions placed on hospitals that received Federal Funds was "...hospitals receiving federal monies are obligated to

---

[134] Schumann, John Henning, "A Bygone ERA: When Bipartisanship Led To Health Care Transformation," Shots, https://www.npr.org/sections/health-shots/2016/10/02/495775518/a-bygone-era-when-bipartisanship-led-to-health-care-transformation, October 2, 2016.

[135] Ibid.

[136] Ibid.

provide free or subsidized care to a portion of their indigent patients... Another idea rooted in Hill-Burton is federal-state matching, meaning that federal appropriations must be matched by dollars from states, which is how Medicaid is financed."[137] In Louisiana, with its long history of Systemic Racism, it is safe to say its Department of Treasury was not hurrying to match Federal Funds so Flint-Goodridge Hospital of Dillard University could receive much need injections of money to support and expand its healthcare services. This was a game changer inasmuch as the Hill-Burton Act mandated that Flint-Goodridge Hospital of Dillard University provide "free" subsidized care to indigent patients in the local New Orleans, LA Community. No doubt, this was a *gathering storm* that would significantly affect the cash-flow and financial health of the hospital.

b.   Low Income And Underinsured Population

Accordingly, the Hill-Burton Act "...requires various health care facilities, including hospitals and other locations that have been granted federal funds for facility construction, modernization, or reconstruction to provide patients with free or low cost health care services...This in effect means that if a medical provider receives any type of federal aid, they are required to help patients that have a low income or are underinsured."[138] Moreover, the Hill-Burton Act only paid for facility costs; the Black Physicians' Doctor Bills for their services provided were not. "Not all medical bills are paid for. Only the facility costs are paid for and not your private doctors' bills... [When a person] apply for Hill-Burton medical care, the obligated facility or hospital needs to provide you with a written statement or documents that tells you what free or reduced-cost care services are available."[139] On one hand, medical care for the indigent population that was previously unavailable to it, was now available the through the Hill-Burton Act. This was good for the low-income patient, but not so good for FGHDU and its Black Physicians. Larger White Hospitals, like Tulane, Ochsner, and so forth could survive, if they took advantage of the Hill-Burton Act

---

[137] Ibid.
[138] "Free healthcare from the Hill-Burton federal program," https://www.needhelppayingbills.com/html/hill-burton act free healthcar.html
[139] Ibid.

because their number of White Patients, who had medical insurance, was higher than African-American Patients with medical insurance, who went to FGHDU for their medical care. Once more indigent patients started seeking medical care at Flint-Goodridge Hospital of Dillard University, many of the African-Americans with medical insurance went elsewhere.

Before the Hill-Burton Act came along during the 1970s, prior to this time, all of the Black Physicians in staff positions at Flint-Goodridge Hospital of Dillard University experienced the "Glory Years" of the hospital, including myself. Dr. Emily A. Largent, PhD, JD, RN stated "...black physicians had been "so successful within the confines of the segregated [Louisiana Medical] system..."[140] What Black Physicians needed at FGHDU was access to membership in the American Medical Association, and state funds to operate without restrictions. The hospital was a Black Institution like Ochsner and so forth, and with sustained, equal state financial support, it would grow and remain a valuable one to which the New Orleans, LA African-American Community could continue to view with great pride. Nevertheless, Hill-Burton Act was real and it would, in time, produce some real unintended impacts on the Flint-Goodridge Hospital of Dillard University's financial well-being. As Chief of the Flint-Goodridge Hospital of Dillard University's Department of Anesthesia, I had a front row seat in which I was privilege to observe firsthand exactly how the Hill-Burton Act impacted the hospital.

E. Hill-Burton Act Impacts On The Flint-Goodridge Hospital Of Dillard University From 1970 to 1982

In the early, or middle seventies, came the Hill-Burton Act. This Act was predicated on hospitals accepting all creeds, color, and ethnic groups to the hospital for services and so forth in order to receive Federal Government Funding. This was the crossroads for hospitals that were predominantly for Afro-Americans, including small hospitals and some private hospitals. There had been a number of hospitals around the United States such as Kate Billings, Flint-Goodridge Hospital of Dillard University and so

---

[140] Largent, Emily A. PhD, JD, RN, "Public Health, Racism, and the Lasting Impact of Hospital Segregation," <u>Public Health Report</u>, 133(6): September 17, 2018, PP. 715-720.

forth in which the number of physicians in the community had a direct effect on the percentage of beds that were to be filled. The Afro-American Hospitals were the hardest hit because of the small number of Afro-American Physicians. They could not depend on their White Physician counterparts because they were taking all of their patients to one or more White Hospitals. The Black Physicians, who were small in number, were not able to refer enough patients to the Black Hospitals around America. Thus, the Afro-American Hospitals gradually withered away and perished.

That being so, the "Pre-Madonna Days" of the Black Physicians gradually began to decrease. Patients able to pay for their healthcare progressively declined. Those with no health insurance increased. This is what happened at Flint-Goodridge Hospital of Dillard University during the 1970s. The latter was not unique because wherever there was only one Black Hospital in a community or city nationwide, the Hill-Burton act, generally speaking, sealed their fate. Usually, the Black Hospital had an average of 30 Black Physicians on staff. Therefore, most of the Black Hospitals in America gradually closed their doors. Flint-Goodridge Hospital of Dillard University was among the very first to close. Today, there are only three or four left in the United States. As I mentioned earlier, while the Hill-Burton Act Footprint was spreading, and Black Hospitals across the country were falling like dominoes, my colleagues in the Anesthesia Department thought FGHDU might "dodge the bullet." So, we kept on delivering Anesthesia Services, and in the meantime, I continued to take care of the healthcare needs of my patients in medical practice throughout the 1970s.

a. Anesthesia Associates Of Flint-Goodridge Hospital Of Dillard University Established In 1981

My aim, as it had always been since I took over the Department of Anesthesia, was to continue to strengthen it with as many qualified Medical Doctors as possible. The Hill-Burton Act (Axe) had not fallen yet, nor did any of the Black Physicians I worked with, on a daily basis, knew exactly what was coming down a few years ahead of us. We were not like the three-person orchestra, which continued to play music, while the Titanic was an hour or less away from sinking completely beneath the cold waters of the North Sea. Honestly, I thought FGHDU had many years left to grow and serve the community.

That being so, another Black Anesthesiologist came along and wanted to work alongside Dr. Yang and me. I was in favor of letting him in our group because it was a possibility that the Korean, Dr. Yang may want to move, and I would find myself alone again. Dr. Yang was not totally in favor, but after lengthy discussions of pros and cons, we decided to consider taking him into our group only if we incorporate. So, we proceeded to form Anesthesia Associates of Flint-Goodridge Hospital of Dillard University. It took several months to get the necessary papers, attorney, bank account, contracts and so forth.

The corporation had not been negotiating for much more than a month when this new anesthesiologist went to another hospital in New Orleans, LA, and the hospital hired him to head its Anesthesia Department. However, he did not want to share the compensation from the hospital. He wanted it for himself, even though he wanted to share the compensation from Flint-Goodridge Hospital of Dillard University. In addition, he wanted us to be his backup and on call responsibilities.

Under those circumstances, Dr. Yang and I decided not to finalize incorporating with this individual.

In the ensuing months, the Flint-Goodridge Hospital of Dillard University was moving along fairly well when this new anesthesiologist that had trained in the Charity Hospital Anesthesia Residency Program got with the "Staff Medical Politicians" of Flint-Goodridge Hospital of Dillard University, and sold them a "bill of good," stating that Flint-Goodridge Hospital of Dillard University could go on record for doing all kinds of surgical procedures. The staff members forgot about the "Glory Years" of Flint-Goodridge Hospital of Dillard University.

I was very disappointed with the doctor's behavior, and his actions violated what I had been taught a long time ago on the Gravel Road, and that is, "if a man or woman does not have a word, one has nothing no matter how brilliant and educated he or she is." The thing that hurt my feeling the most about the change of mind is every day I had to watch each step I made in the Systemic Racism Mind-field in New Orleans, LA. While I was carefully navigating one obstacle after the next, I discovered an enemy is not defined by "skin color," but more accurately by motivation and intent. The doctor was a Black Man, and he was being accepted into our Anesthesia Associates Group. Yet, his skin color did not inhibit him from violating my trust but his "hidden" intent did the damage. This was a painful experience for me but I had to, as before, deal with my emotions, and move forward with my life and work.

To resolve this matter, Dr. Yang and I had to get legal assistance to remove the doctor from the corporation. Just when we put out this fire, another one even more serious sprung up. The "Glory Years" the Black Physicians were experiencing during the 1970s were progressively blinding FGHDU's Board of Management and Medical Staff. The hospital was about to move away from its "Bread and Butter" Surgeries and move into "uncharted territory," when it changed course or operating policies, which allowed the hospital, for the first time, to do much more complex and sophisticated surgeries, which Flint-Goodridge Hospital of Dillard University was not equipped to perform. As the head of the Anesthesia Department of Flint-Goodridge Hospital of Dillard University, I did not believe, based on my experience at the hospital, that this was not a viable and sustainable move to make.

b. Black Medical Politicians And Flint-Goodridge Hospital Of Dillard University Board Of Management

A few months after my Anesthesia Associates issue I mentioned earlier was resolved, another huge problem surfaced.

During the coming months, the Flint-Goodridge Hospital of Dillard University was moving along fairly well. The new anesthesiologist wasted no time selling his Surgery Plan to FGHDU's Administration, or Board of Management. The Flint-Goodridge Hospital of Dillard University's Board of Management and Medical Staff embraced the "Bill of Goods," namely, that the hospital could increase its revenues, if it changed its surgery policy(s). The former was thinking of the "Glory Days" of Flint-Goodridge Hospital of Dillard University.

The Black Medical Staff Politicians, which is a name I coined for them, went to work to implement it. Everyone put on their "blinder;" they were necessary so nothing contrary could enter the discussion to challenge the decision to abruptly start performing more complicated and complex surgeries. The first big move the Medical Staff Politicians had to make was remove me as being head of the Department of Anesthesia at Flint-Goodridge Hospital of Dillard University. The Medical Staff Politicians on one hand, truly believed Flint-Goodridge Hospital of Dillard University could effectively perform more complicated and complex surgeries; and, on the other, they did not see what their decision to go this route would do to the hospital's sustainability in the short-term and longevity in the long-term.

I have already said by the early 1970s, Flint-Goodridge Hospital of Dillard University was going through its "Glory Years!" Black Physicians were doing great! We were all standing in the sunshine on a cloudy day!

However, as things unfolded, I was terminated from my staff position as being head of the Anesthesia at Flint-Goodridge Hospital of Dillard University in early 1981.

F. Out As Flint-Goodridge Hospital of Dillard University's Chief Of Its Anesthesia Department In Early 1981

As the Medical Staff Politicians, or Board of Management, likely reasoned in private discussions among themselves, in order for Flint-Goodridge Hospital of Dillard University to make the transition to performing more complicated and sophisticated surgeries, they decided to get rid of me being the head of the Anesthesia Department of Flint-Goodridge Hospital of Dillard University. The Black Medical Staff Politicians of Flint-Goodridge Hospital of Dillard University had to go to work.

Toward this end, they set up a Medical Staff Meeting. When it came time for a vote on the matter, the Medical Staff Politicians kept their true intentions a secret, regarding when and how they were going to make their move. Everyone was lounging around and talking while waiting for the meetings to begin. Seemingly, the meeting was held up for some reason.

a. Terminated As Chief Of The Department Of Anesthesia At Flint-Goodridge Hospital Of Dillard University In Early1981

Dr. Yang was off-duty that fateful day, and I decided to go up to the Anesthesia Department Office to get the Surgical Schedule so I could make "pre-op" rounds, and so forth. When I returned to the meeting, the

Medical Staff Politicians had already voted me "out" as being the head of the Anesthesia Department of Flint-Goodridge Hospital of Dillard University by June 1981. This was a very strategic maneuver.

I was not exactly alone in my place of pain and disappointment. There were those of us who knew the Medical Staff Politicians were taking a "giant" step. Flint-Goodridge Hospital of Dillard University was, by June 1981, standing "At The Precipice." Its sustainability, viability, and overall health was now in jeopardy.

b. Absence Of Data To Support Medical Staff Politicians' Decision

We all knew that before any organization make any radical changes, they should do studies, evaluations, projections, and so forth. None of these things were done. The Medical Staff Politicians did not bother to ask if there had been any previous studies, evaluations, or projections. Typically, Top Level Management relies on baseline and historical data to help it arrive at the best possible decision under the prevailing circumstances.

However, as it was, the Medical Staff Politicians felt they did not need any projections data to guide their decision-making to determine whether a shift in surgery priorities was the right and best decision to make for Flint-Goodridge Hospital of Dillard University. Instead, a decision was made to make a change in favor of the hospital performing more complicated and sophisticated surgeries. I knew I would be alright, though it was painful for me to stepdown as being head of the Anesthesia Department of Flint-Goodridge Hospital of Dillard University. I resolved to continue to focus my attention on my Medical Practice in the New Orleans, LA Community.

G. Picking Up The Pieces And Moving Forward With Medical Practice In 1982 And Thereafter

Dr. Yang and I had to do some readjusting. He decided that he would practice Acupuncture in his office at his home. I had no idea as to what I would do. My workday had to be rearranged, or changed from rising early in the morning to get to the operating room in the hospital in order to see that scheduling was followed, and the Anesthesia Group was prepared.

Having been recently terminated from my post as being the head of the Anesthesia Department of Flint-Goodridge Hospital of Dillard University, I no longer had to perform these tasks so I had to deprogram myself, and restructure my time management. I had no idea what the work routine did to workers' mind and body until I was put in the position where the schedule I followed for years no longer existed, and although my conscious mind knew my normal schedule no longer existed anymore, my subconscious mind still made me feel disoriented similar to the way someone feels when they lose a cherished relationship, or some valuable item that had a lot of sentimental value.

Thus, to re-balance myself, like someone whose car is out of alignment and the wheels pull heavily to one side, I settled down and got some much-needed rest. After a few weeks of rest, I continued to wake up about five o'clock in the morning. Once I got out of bed, and after helping Angela Dixon Braud with satisfying our children's needs, whether they were home or away, I began working in my yard at home. This was my chosen form of therapy, during which time, I could do some calm reflections and begin to let go of some of the things I once thought were important but had become irrelevant. I discovered how some of them had a self-imposed control on me at work. To loosen up my mind and release things that no longer served me, I planted flowers of different colors, which in a short time, my backyard was very colorful and pleasing to the eye. The more time I spent gardening, the better I started to feel every day that passed. Some of the contacts I made at Flint-Goodridge Hospital of Dillard Hospital while I was there, I was informed the Medical Staff Politicians continued to use the staff Nurse Anesthetists to administer Anesthesia during Pre-and-Post Surgery. They also gave me the privilege of doing Anesthesia on a consultant basis at two or three hospitals. There were those physicians who were desirous of my services still such as Dr. Williams Adams, Dr. Joseph Epps Sr, and Dr. Lemeul Clanton.

a. Landscape Therapy And Refocus

For the most part, I worked in my yard at home; I grew up on a farm; my father was a farmer; and my mother had the best green thumb for growing vegetables of all kinds and flowers. I spent many days on our farm in Brookstown doing agricultural work. So, being outdoors after leaving

Flint-Goodridge Hospital of Dillard University, was the prescription I ordered for myself. I knew, like it did before on the Gravel Road, that working in the dirt would go a long way to heal anything that ailed me.

Therefore, in my yard, I grew all types of shrubbery; on one side of the driveway, there were Willow Oaks that were groomed in the shape of umbrellas of varying heights down the driveway; on one side of the front of the house was a Weeping Hackberry Tree; directly in the front of my house, there was a Hackberry Tree that I groomed into a "Bonsai Shape" (That became the descriptive name of my house). On the wall of the house behind the Bonsai Hackberry Tree were ground cover that spelled-out (The Wiz); on each corner of the front of the house, there were Holly Trees in the shape of cones; in the center of the front lawn, there was a ground cover in the shape of a deer, and on one side of the front lawn was a Conifer Tree. The flower beds in the front of the house had ground cover and Azealeas that were kept manicured.

As someone entered the backyard, one noticed there were four Palm Trees alone the fence with Shrubbery lining the fences on both sides of the house with beds covered with ground cover. Directly in the back of the house was a bed in the shape of a mound with four Palm Trees that were so spaced that one could span Lake Willow, moving their eyes from east to west and vis-à-vis.

While landscaping my yard at home, I continued to work my Family Practice. Also, I was preparing to expand my practice with the potential addition of Disability Evaluation Physician work. This was a new need that was rising in the New Orleans, LA Community. That is, when someone gets injured on their job, and one is unable to function in it like they did before their injury, I recognized this as a new opportunity for Medical Doctors to evaluate a patient to determine if he or she could return to work after an injury occurred. I went to conferences and symposiums, where Disability Evaluation Training was held in such cities as Chicago, Los Angeles, and other cities around the country. I participated in trainings at these sites, from 1975 to 1982. However, with all of the commotion taking place at Flint-Goodridge Hospital of Dillard University, regarding a change in trajectory for surgery, along with my dismissal as the Chief of the Anesthesia Department, I was unable to fully prepare myself to take the qualifying examination to become a Certified Disability Evaluation

Physician. That being so, I continued to do my landscaping activities at home, and work in my medical practice.

For example, during the spring and summer months of each year, I would have "pots" around the borders of the yard in front and back with Portulascus, or Mossy Rose of varying colors, per season, such as red, white, and yellow. They were breathtaking! In the fall and winter months, I would rotate different colors of Petunias-yellow, red, wine, and white. Some years there were varying colors of Periwinkles and Pansies. The yard was colorful the year round. One year, maybe 1982 or 1983, I had cabbage plants in pots around the whole yard. That was the year that the Neighbor Banner stayed in my yard for several months. Moreover, the "Bonsai" Tree had a mushroom shaped top, and just below it, there was a one or two feet space before the next cluster of mushroom shaped branches were located. Below this cluster, there was another cluster of branches with mushroom shaped ends. I am sure I imprinted in my mind how my mother had her yard landscaped around her house in Brookstown. She had so many colorful flowers neatly arranged, which made most passersbys, walking up and down the Gravel Road, take a second or third look at its beauty. I relived the memory of my mother when I landscaped my yard around my house in New Orleans, LA.

b. Mind, Body, And Soul Gradually Deprogrammed

With each passing moment I spent landscaping my home environment, I felt stronger and better. My mind and soul were gradually deprogrammed. There were no residuals from my days working at Flint-Goodridge Hospital of Dillard University. I allowed the "drama" to surface in my mind without attaching any judgment to it. This non-attachment allowed me to "let it go!," rather than continue to internalize it. Otherwise, the drama would consume me like a California Wildfire. I would, no doubt, would end up a broken man, who was filled with guilt and regret. To avoid this Dante Inferno, I called upon my memories of the Gravel Road, and they served me well. The Gravel Road built me up where I was weak, and my Braud Family Group, along with the Higher Power, made my hands strong. One would have never known how rewarding it is to have something else that one enjoys doing. The one referred to here is me. I stepped in the joy I learned from my mother, and called upon the power she used to overcome the devastating loss of her man, Joe Braud, when he passed away in 1936. I felt empowered! Thus, all of the other family matters and so forth, which I needed to give my attention, were addressed head-on and carried-out. As I regained my health and strength, Flint-Goodridge Hospital of Dillard University became weaker, and its life, by early 1982, hung in the balance. Its vital signs were trending toward the negative. Similar to someone in the Intensive Care Unit, who has COVID-19, and is struggling to breathe.

H. Flint-Goodridge Hospital Of Dillard University And Its "Last Rites" In 1982

The hospital was on its death bed; that is, it was on the verge of the unthinkable for many who loved Flint like I did, which was now "the lights were about to be turned off, and the door closed-forever! The latter six months of 1982, Flint-Goodridge Hospital of Dillard University gradually went downhill. For the first time, the hospital was operating in the "red," which it had not done so for more than twenty years. Personnel in the Finance Office of the Hospital had to ask the Anesthesia Department and the Surgical Department to stop whatever they were doing because their surgical schedules were costing the hospital increasing funds, and the surgical cases were not bringing in enough revenue to justify the procedures. Remember earlier, I mentioned the Medical Staff Politicians removed me from my post as head of Anesthesia, and they took a "knee-Jerk" Leap into performing more complicated surgeries. Thus, the "Chickens were coming out to Roost." FGHDU was bleeding-out and there was nothing that could be done to stop its operating in the "red." The Louisiana State Government certainly was not in favor of saving the hospital in view of the prevailing Systemic Racism everywhere at the time.

As expected, when things get tough, Attorney General John Mitchell once remarked during the President Richard Nixon's Watergate Hearings, that "When things get tough, the tough get going." As it was, the Medical Staff Politicians never admitted to themselves that what they started was destroying the hospital, except for one of the general surgeons, namely, Dr. Joseph M. Epps Sr, who probably had the largest practice in the hospital. He decided that after his vacation, he was going to have me administer Anesthesia to his patients. Dr. Epps Sr was going on vacation to England and other parts of Europe during his travels. Unfortunately, as Dr. Epps Sr was about to board the plane at New York John F. Kennedy International Airport, he collapsed and died. This tragedy, in an instant, left a gaping whole in Flint-Goodridge Hospital of Dillard University's Patient Population. I have already mentioned how the Hill-Burton Act of 1946 played an adverse role on the survival of Black Hospitals. It is worth mentioning how it affected Flint-Goodridge Hospital of Dillard University in real time.

a. Hill-Burton Act Of 1946 Impact On Flint-Goodridge Hospital Of Dillard University By 1982

Remember, the action of the Medical Staff Politicians at Flint Goodridge Hospital of Dillard University was not the only reason for its destruction or demise. One must include the philosophy of the Hill-Burton Act of 1946. On the other hand, it was bound to come because of the disproportionate number of Black Physicians in the general population. Because of the small number of Black Physicians at FGHDU, which was between 30 and 40, the latter was not large enough to attract the patient population that would have been needed to keep the hospital afloat. The Titanic was listing at a 450 angle; the hospital was, metaphorically speaking, sinking similarly and rapidly. Following the implementation of the Hill-Burton Act, the general Medical Community began to undergo rapid change all over America. There was a move to put special emphasis on specialization. Even the Intern and Residency Programs began to undergo change. Most of the physicians in training were in specialty programs. There were less physicians going into general or family practice. Internship Programs became less and less. A young Medical Doctor started the first year of training to become the first year of a specialty instead of an Internship. The young Medical Doctor was able to shave at least one year off of his or her medical training by by-passing doing an Internship and going straight into one's chosen specialty. Another change that threatened Flint-Goodridge Hospital of Dillard University was the introduction of subsidized Federal Government Insurance Programs.

b. Medicare And Medicaid By 1982

Interestingly, President Lyndon B. Johnson signed into law legislation that established the Medicaid and Medicare Programs on July 30, 1965. As you may recall, I began my Anesthesia Residency Program in the Charity Hospital Anesthesia Training Program on June 1, 1965. The Hill-Burton Act was signed into law by President Harry Truman in 1946. These laws did not have an effect on slowing down or preventing the Flint-Goodridge Hospital of Dillard University's "Glory Years," from 1968 to 1980. The Wheels of Success of the Black Physicians at the hospital were rolling along without a single squeak, or most smoothly.

However, when the Civil Rights Movement gained its greatest momentum just before the Dr. Martin Luther King Jr assassination, things started to gradually change at FGHDU. Those years had a strong impact on the Black Physician Population. It was the growth area of Medicaid and Medicare, which were the Federal Government sponsored insurance for the poor, who were uninsured and the elderly. As a result of these Federal Government subsidized programs, most of the Black Physicians had to begin accepting and increased number of patients in order for them to survive with those insurance plans. That is, before Medicaid and Medicare, one patient of a Black Physician, who was insured, would potentially generate double or triple the income it would take four or five Medicare or Medicaid Patients to generate to treat similar ailments. In short, it was harder for the Black Physician to survive.

For example, Medicaid and Medicare reimbursement to the Black Physician was about 1/6% of their charges. Therefore, they had to have large numbers of patients to make ends meet. Many of the other groups of physicians, particularly White Ones, would not accept Medicaid or Medicare. The Hill-Burton Act impacted the Black Physicians Medical Practices, both at Flint-Goodridge Hospital of Dillard University and their private practices for the same reason I have already mentioned above. In addition, when the Medicaid and Medicare Bubble burst, many White Physicians pulled their Black Insured patients out of Flint-Goodridge Hospital of Dillard University, and provided them healthcare services at other hospitals, whose physicians were less reliant on subsidized Federal

Government Healthcare Programs. This left FGHDU "high and dry and dying by early 1982.

I. Flint-Goodridge Hospital Of Dillard University On "Life Support" By Early 1982

Usually, when a patient is placed on a "Life Support Machine," it is only a matter of time before death arrives. There are some few cases where a patient's health fortunes miraculously reverse itself, and the patient recovers and walks out of the hospital. Those patients can be called miracles! Flint-Goodridge Hospital of Dillard University did not come off of its Life Support, but an 11th hour attempt was made by some of the Black Physicians at the hospital, who tried to save it from imminent closure.

For a few months, some of the Black Physicians in New Orleans, LA thought they may have continued the "legend" of Flint-Goodridge Hospital of Dillard University. It was not feasible, or possible, because there were only about forty or fifty of them practicing in New Orleans, LA. That included the thirty that had been here approximately ten years, and roughly seventeen that had recently arrived. Of the thirty Black Physicians, half of them were beyond retirement age. Thus, the size of Flint-Goodridge Hospital of Dillard University could not be supported. And, as I have repeatedly said, due to Systemic Racism, and from the Louisiana Governor's Office on down, no one was running to put out a five-alarm burning fire such as the catastrophic collapse about to take place at Flint-Goodridge Hospital of Dillard University in just a matter of days.

Therefore, when the dust settled, and everything was taken into consideration possible, Dr. Samuel Dubois Cook stepped in to determine, like a County Coroner would do, to determine if there was any way to salvage the Flint-Goodridge Hospital of Dillard University.

J. Flint-Goodridge Hospital Of Dillard University Closed In Early 1982

After 90 years of growth of this hospital, which was oftentimes impeded by Systemic Racism, Jim Crow Laws, and De Facto Segregation, Kevin McQueeney substantiated this claim adding "despite assurances of nondiscrimination from hospital administrators in New Orleans, de facto segregation continued. Lawsuits for discrimination resulted in little change. A Department of Health, Education, and Welfare (HEW) study reported that between 1974 and 1977, up to 75 percent of all black patients in New Orleans used either Flint or Charity."[141] Many people, both Black and White with Flint-Goodridge Hospital of Dillard University may argue that segregation in the Healthcare Industry in New Orleans, LA did not have any bearing on the hospital's final demise-closure. Regardless of what anybody says, the historical record speak for itself. As such, McQueeney added "the [White] physicians played an active role in maintaining a two-tiered health-care system. White physicians would treat their black patients—especially poor black patients—only at Charity and their white patients at the private hospitals (a practice Flint forbade, which only contributed to the large number of resignations from Flint), which left a much smaller…staff at Flint."[142] In addition, this odorous practice cut White Physicians' affiliation with Flint-Goodridge Hospital of Dillard University by more than half! According to McQueeney, by May 1967, out of a total of 350 physicians, 236 had dropped their Flint Goodridge affiliation, which proved particularly devastating because they brought in most of the paying patients. Between 1965 and 1968, patient use overall dropped 36.2 percent…To make up for this loss, the board raised rates every year from 1964 to 1967, which had the effect of driving away paying patients."[143] Specifically, White Physicians' affiliation with Flint-Goodridge Hospital of Dillard University plunged 67.4 percent during this time. It did not get any better thereafter either. The exodus of Black Paying Patients was encouraged by White Physicians also.

It should be pointed-out here that the Flint-Goodridge Hospital of Dillard University's Board of Management was led by a White Female at the time. McQueeney stated "the new Flint board chair, [was] Rosa Keller, a leading white socialite…"[144] who was unable to soothe the "segregation fever" of White New Orleans, LA, or lay to rest their fear that financial

---

[141] McQueeney, Kevin, "Flint Goodridge Hospital and black Health Care in Twentieth Century New Orleans," The Journal of African American History, Volume 103, Number 4, https://www.journals.uchicago.edu/doi/full/10.1086/699952

[142] Ibid.

[143] Ibid.

[144] Ibid.

support of Flint-Goodridge Hospital of Dillard University would not threaten the viability of White Hospitals and its segregated staff.

a.   Financial Downfall Of Flint-Goodridge Hospital Of Dillard University In 1982

By mid-1965, the hospital was already running a deficit. McQueeney stated "in the month of September 1965 alone the hospital suffered a $17,000 deficit due to decreased income from patients...Old problems persisted into the 1960s. Unpaid bills continued to be a problem. For example, Flint turned over nearly $19,000 in bills from between February and October 1964 to the collections agency. The amount in unpaid bills grew even worse over the decade. Operating expenses continued to soar, as salaries were increased as the larger staff provided additional services in the hospital's new wing. As a result, the board raised rates 7–14 percent in 1964..."[145] The financial health of Flint-Goodridge Hospital of Dillard University did not recover but worsened. Moreover, McQueeney also stated "by 1981, the hospital reported that the government owed them $600,000 for unpaid or partially paid claims."[146] The Federal Government's Medicaid and Medicare Programs were a definite improvement in the healthcare indigent patients received; however, as it was then, the Federal government had a reputation of paying its bills slowly. This meant vendors often had to carry charges on their books, which became past due because Flint-Goodridge Hospital of Dillard University did not have the available funds to pay them.

When the financial record books of the hospital were examined by Dr. Samuel Dubois Cook in 1981, along with his top-level managers, he reported to the Board of Trustees that Flint-Goodridge Hospital of Dillard University had been a drain on Dillard University for some time. In fact, The New York Times reported the following on March 7, 1983: "Dr. Cook said the hospital had been a drain on Dillard, with $2 million in operating expenses in the last year and a half. He attributed its decline to ''tragic mismanagement,'' social change that desegregated hospitals, ''financial irregularities,'' the fact that 90 percent of the patients were on Medicare or

---

[145] Ibid.
[146] Ibid.

Medicaid..."[147] The first two reasons Dr. Cook gave for the tragic closing of Flint-Goodridge Hospital of Dillard University are likely closer to what caused the hospitals downfall than Medicare and Medicaid. With a diverse mix of customers, whereby some were insured by these programs, and, if there were among the patient population, a sizable number who could pay their own medical care cost, the hospital would likely be able to continue to operate. To the contrary, the death nail, or dagger that took Flint-Goodridge Hospital of Dillard University down were one, the "tragic mismanagement" of hospital affairs by the Board of Management, and two, the decision it made to begin performing complicated and sophisticated surgeries that were incompatible with the hospital's ability to perform them at the time without running up cost. Once all of the marrow was squeezed out of FGHDU, Dr. Samuel Dubois Cook had no choice left but to sell Flint-Goodridge Hospital of Dillard University. Appendices C and D contains a list of the names of the Black Physicians and Nurse Anesthetists who held Staff Positions at Flint-Goodridge Hospital of Dillard University, including the latter who were trained by the Charity Hospital's Anesthesia Program, before it closed in early 1982.

b. Flint-Goodridge Hospital Of Dillard University Sold In Early March 1983

During the beginning of the 1980s, private businesses were the catalyst underlying a trend that was sweeping across the nation, which involved the purchase of as many private and public hospitals as they could, for the primary purpose of obtaining an increasing share of the domestic healthcare market. Leading the way of this bonanza characterized mainly by the purchase of hospitals that could no longer operate in the "black," was namely, Hospital Corporation of America, which was, by far, the largest buyer of hospitals by 1980 and thereafter. In fact, according to The Wall Street Journal, "Hospital Corp., which operate[d] 158 hospitals...during the summer of 1980"[148] was prepared to buy more, and its competitors purchased any available and financially ailing hospitals left on the market

---

[147] BLACK-OWNED HOSPITAL SOLD IN NEW ORLEANS, New York Times, March 7, 1983, Section A, Page 13.
[148] "Hospital Corp. Sets $78 Million Merger With General Care," The Wall Street Journal, June 27, 1980, p. 8.

by the giants. It was similar to the Lions and Hyenas in the Serengeti in Tanzania, Africa. Once the Lions eat as much of the prey it killed, the Hyenas follow after they leave the area of the kill, and finish eating any parts of the caucus that remained.

Similarly, Dr. Samuel Dubois Cook sold its Flint-Goodridge Hospital of Dillard University during late February 1983. The New York Times reported "the hospital, in uptown New Orleans, was sold last week by Dillard University, a private black college…A group of black doctors had tried unsuccessfully to buy it. The buyer, National Medical Enterprises, which owns more than 40 general hospitals across the United States as well as other medical businesses, already owns five general hospitals in the New Orleans area and is building a medical center just north of the city."[149]

Thus, in a matter of a few days, what took the Black Community in New Orleans, LA 90 years to build into a viable Black-Owned Hospital, Flint-Goodridge Hospital of Dillard University disappeared unceremoniously and without any widespread media coverage in Louisiana. Since the "Glory Days" of the hospital, during the 1960s and 1970s, there has never been anything like it to come along since, which featured a Medical Staff of some of the best educated and trained Black Physicians in America and the world. I know in my heart this is true because I was one of them. I hope the younger generation of Medical Doctors learn something from the Flint-Goodridge Hospital of Dillard University Story. And, I am sure there is a roadmap in the "best of Times and the Worst of Times" that can be discerned to build another Medical Mecca similar to the one I was fortune to be a part of during my Professional Medical Practice and Career. I challenge this generation, and the next one, to find a way to, in the words of President Joe Biden, "Build Back Better."

I will always have a warm memory in my heart for this hospital; it helped me, and it helped all of my Black Physician Colleagues to serve the New Orleans, LA Community. Flint is still missed today, and I am sure when she closed her doors; served her last patient; and someone turned off the lights for the last time, while she took a moment to dry the tears from her eyes, I am sure those who had a fear of Flint felt relieved.

With the doors of Flint-Goodridge Hospital of Dillard University closed, and when the word spread throughout the New Orleans, LA

---

[149] Op. cit., The New York Times, Page 13.

Healthcare Industry, it sparked an interests in other local hospitals to bid on any available healthcare equipment left inside of Flint-Goodridge Hospital of Dillard University when it closed. The scene must have mimicked one when an animal dies; large, beautiful soaring vultures circle overhead, and at the precise moment the vultures register in their brains that the deceased prey is ready to be consumed, they descend on it and slowly devour it.

K. Local White Hospitals Absorbed Beds And Available Equipment In Obstetrics, Gynecology, And Pediatrics Among Others In 1983

Similar to the Lion-Hyenas Metaphor discussed earlier, when Flint-Goodridge Hospital of Dillard University closed its doors, some of the other local hospitals absorbed some of the beds, Obstetrics, Gynecology, and Pediatric Equipment among others. Some of its Medical Equipment was purchased by the Charity Hospital. Which Local White Hospitals were beneficiaries of the remainder of equipment and beds are not reported in the literature. However, it is known that National Medical Enterprises did not intend to reboot its former Flint-Goodridge Hospital property as a medical facility.

That being so, National Medical Enterprises likely sold the healthcare equipment to other local White Hospitals, and eventually its Flint-Goodridge Property was converted into an apartment complex for senior citizens 62 years old and over. Given the time Flint-Goodridge Hospital of Dillard University operated during the Jim Crow Era, it was allowed to do so like a healthcare island surrounded by less than favorable White Hospital Institutions. FGHDU operated for 90 years, and it enjoyed its best years during the 1960s and 1970s. It was only after the Civil Rights Movement pushed against Jim Crow Laws that the idea of Separate But Equal's grip, as a segregation practice, and adverse influence on Flint-Goodridge Hospital of Dillard University, loosened up.

L. Afro-American Hospital Closures Nationwide

Thus, the segregated Black Hospital served its purpose for 90 years as the only one, save Charity Hospital, where Black People could go to receive medical care. Similar to Grambling State University's Football Dynasty during the Eddie Robinson Era, which coincided with the Flint-Goodridge Hospital of Dillard University's "Glory Years," both of their reigns came to an end when the need for them to play the role of Separate but Equal in the community was no longer necessary. Overt Systemic Racism reinvented itself in many covert forms, which served, in principle, the same function as the old Separate But Equal Doctrine had done outright for many decades before.

Flint-Goodridge Hospital of Dillard University was not the only Black Hospital that closed during the 1980s. Sydenham Hospital in Harlem, NY closed in 1980. It was the first hospital that allowed African-American Doctors to treat their own patients there. Since 1990, there are only three or four Black Hospitals in the United States, namely, Howard University Hospital, Harlem Drew, Martin Luther King, and Hubbard Hospital. Some of them are also experiencing financial trouble, which could eventually result in their closure.

After the bitter pill of the closure of Flint-Goodridge Hospital of Dillard University, and similar to what my other Black Physician Colleagues were doing, I had to also undergo a re-organization of my Medical Practice.

CHAPTER XIX

BLACK PHYSICIANS REORGANIZATION OF THEIR MEDICAL PRACTICES

Unlike before the closure of Flint-Goodridge Hospital of Dillard University, Black Physicians could bring their patients to the hospital where they would administer a prescribed treatment. After the closure of the hospital took place, this was no longer an option. Because White Hospitals were reluctant to admit Black Patients at their facilities at the time, this meant the Black Physicians, including myself, had to rethink and reorganize our Medical Practices. Because of the changes in the medical community and the medical practice, some of us had to undergo reorganization. My Medical Practice was not immune.

A. Re-Organization Of Medical Practice Response To Flint-Goodridge Hospital of Dillard University Closure In Early 1982

Being a part of the Black Physicians' Medical Practice Climate I operated in at this time, my colleagues and I were suddenly confronted with increases in pay scales, increase in the cost of supplies, increase in the cost of insurance plans, and increase in all phases of having a *Solo Medical Practice*. There were many practitioners, that is, Black Physicians in particular, who began moving into group practice. In addition, there were those fellow practitioners, who gave up private practice and began working for private companies, hospitals, clinics and so forth. Recall, I stated earlier that giant hospital corporations were rapidly buying up hospitals and others at the beginning of the 1980s. This trend, coupled with the closure of Flint-Goodridge Hospital of Dillard University, increased the concentration of everything in the healthcare market in the hands of a few giant private businesses; and, as you have accurately imagined, this intended result meant, if anyone chose to practice in this changing healthcare environment, the practitioner would be faced with rising costs such as those I pointed-out earlier. Therefore, I correctly reasoned, if I plan to practice in this changing medical environment, I would need to incorporate my Solo Medical Practice.

a. Medical Practice Incorporated in 1972

My Solo Medical Practice was initially incorporated in 1972, and it had all of the entities that the big corporations had such as pension plans, medical insurance, mal-practice insurance, long-term care, life insurance, disability insurance, holidays, sick days, and education days and so forth. All of the above had a price, and the changes in the medical community made it difficult to continue as things were during the "Glorious Years" of Flint-Goodridge Hospital of Dillard University. Many of the healthcare costs the latter absorbed before the hospital closed, were passed down to my Medical Practice. Once I incorporated it, then I placed myself in a position to do what is famously known in the business community as *downsize*, or streamline cash-flow, and make changes in the overall delivery of healthcare services without adversely affecting the quality of care my patients received. As one can imagine, change of habits is oftentimes difficult to break! But, I knew if my Medical Practice was going to survive, then I had to make some tough decisions, which might not set well with some of my employees in the corporation. Nevertheless, I persevered hoping any resistance I met, regarding some downsizing changes that had to be made, would be minimal, or in the best case scenario, non-existent. During this time of downsizing my corporation, I was serving in the Louisiana Army National Guard. I was promoted to the rank of Lieutenant Colonel in 1981. If I had decided to go on full-time active duty, and serve during the Persian Gulf War, also called the Gulf War, which started on August 2, 1990, I would have been promoted to the rank of "General." I had a few battles I needed to fight at home, which were related to the re-organization of my Medical Practice, so I decided not to participate in this Foreign War.

b. Strategic Downsizing Steps Taken To Save Medical Practice

My Medical Practice gradually underwent re-organization. The "First Step" taken was the termination of the Defined Benefits Plan and the Defined Contribution Plan. Every member of the practice was given their shares in each plan. It was understood that each person would begin to manage their own funds, beginning on the date following the disbursement. By 1988-1989, I had four staff members. Then, the practice gradually began re-organization. That is, the "Second Step" involved the work day, and everyone's day in the practice were cut in half. Unlike before, everyone in the practice now worked a twenty-hour week. The "Third Step" was a discontinuation of the Health Insurance Plan, scaled down holidays, sick days, and education days. There was a discontinuation of disability insurance and life insurance. We continued Mal-Practice Insurance. The doctor's time was changed to one half day, and his other half day was spent working for other hospital institutions. By 1988, I began working part-time for the Charity Hospital Outpatient Medical Clinic. I worked for the latter to around 1996. As I pointed-out earlier, some people have a problem adjusting to change, and the downsizing strategy I implemented in my practice caused more internal turmoil than I anticipated. The philosophy that states "expect the unexpected" was applicable to my situation.

B. Turmoil In The Internal Organization Of Medical Practice By 1988

At this time, my wife, Angela Dixon Braud, was employed by the corporation. Everyone was impacted by my downsizing strategy, including myself. Everyone was affected equally because the staff members, who worked for my Medical Practice, ALL had to abide by the same rules. However, I was caught off guard by the fact my wife vehemently was opposed to her salary being cut in half like the rest of the members of the corporation. I tried to explain what was happening and why but Angela Dixon Braud remained steadfast and opposed to her salary being cut in half like the rest of us. My wife rebelled against this salary cut! I could not blame her for doing so, but if the downsizing plan I implemented was not put into practice, then, none of us would have a salary at all. Looking ahead, I knew the situation would not always be this way, but it is said on the Gravel Road by the older generation, that foresight is not common. The corporation had to survive so we could continue to meet the healthcare needs of our patients, and enjoy a comfortable life at the same time.

When I realized I could not make any headway, by getting Angela Dixon Braud to see this "Big Picture," I moved on; the tension caused by the rebellion simmered on a backburner; and I continued to deliver healthcare services to the community. Moreover, when fires start to breakout, the first sign of a developing problem is the proverbial "smoking gun." And, there was a new challenge that threatened the well-being of the corporation simultaneously. From 1988 to 1996, in spite of the backlash I received from Angela Dixon Braud, everything seemed to level-off in the corporation inasmuch as I was able, along with my staff, to move forward with the delivery of healthcare services to the New Orleans, LA Community.

However, during the latter part of 1996 and early 1997, there was a greater amount of turmoil in the practice. Members of the organization were trying to sue the company because of the twenty-hour work week, and other downsizing rules I put in place. The corporation had very good minutes and documents on all members. One person was trying to get unemployment compensation, but she had done many things that were not in her favor, and the same were documented. Specifically, on the morning of the meeting with the Louisiana Labor Board Officials, there were several workers present, who were going to serve as witnesses for the Plaintiff, but at the last minute, their participation was cancelled. The individual, who filed the suit, lost her case because of the timely documentation that I presented to the Labor Board. By 1998, all "hell" broke loose.

There was the continued re-organization of the Medical Practice in play; I became ill with Fatigue Syndrome and severe depression; and this coincided with the beginning of a domestic situation; and, in my estimation, there was nothing going right.

C. Change In Marital Status In 1997

Regarding my domestic situation, Angela Dixon Braud contacted a lawyer, and according to her wishes, she instructed him to serve me with divorce papers in 1997. At the time, we had four children. The oldest was 24 years old and the youngest was 16 years old. My Downsizing Strategy had remained alive in Angela and I's marriage for nearly ten years. Angela Dixon Braud's Financial Grievance, regarding the fact her salary, like every staff member who worked for the corporation, was cut in half, and it never went away. It was the *Elephant* in the room! Another factor that may have played a role in our marital breakup is Angela was younger than I was at the time, and this might have been partly the cause of our divergent expectations.

Because many identify themselves, or their personal identity and self-worth, so closely with how much money they have in their bank accounts, I imagine Angela Dixon Braud must have felt insecure, vulnerable, and afraid. And, consequently, to protect her assets, she chose to ask for a divorce so she would then have total control over her bank account. It is a rare thing to find people who are unafraid to share, and conduct their lives for the benefit of the group and less for the individual. The latter is ingrained in the minds of Americans, from the day we are born.

During the divorce proceedings, when all of my life-long assets were put on the table, I felt devastated; I did not know what to do; I felt afraid; and, it took me some time to understand why this divorce occurred, given the fact I had spent so much of my life helping people in my Braud Family Group; many I knew who lived on the Gravel Road; and those who I served when I became a Medical Doctor. I was, in fact, mentally troubled. I sought medical help from a psychiatrist; I was prescribed a medication, which I chose not to take. My prescription, for regaining my balance and personal well-being, was rooted in "Mother Earth." I called upon the teaching of my father and mother when I was growing up on the Gravel Road. They taught me to seek peace in good work, by creating life in the soil or dirt. This prescription worked for me; however, to regain my mental and emotional stability, eventually, I was forced to stop working and went on disability.

I applied for disability in 2001, and I was successful in getting accepted. For one year, I did not work but, instead, I received financial support from disability. This was a great help to me because it allowed me to recapture my energy and rebalance my emotional self. While on disability, I maintained my Medical Practice. One of the empowering events that occurred in 2002, which helped me to feel better, was our daughter-Shannon Braud-graduated with her Medical Degree from Meharry Medical School; she was the second of our children to earn this degree. Meantime, for three years, I was under Psychiatric Care. During this time, from 1996 to 1999, there were several physicians I hired to work in my Medical Practice part-time during my absence. They helped me the way Dr. Anthony Hackett did when he went on vacation for a month or so, and he left me in charge of the day-to-day management of his medical practice during the early 1960s. In addition, the other personnel were continued on a twenty-hour work week. Seemingly, everyone began to become less and less efficient. Things continued to go down and down.

D. Re-Organization Of Medical Practice By 2000

In order to halt this downward trend in my practice, I had to take another step to stop it by making a few more adjustment in its re-organization. At the end of December 1999, all of the personnel, who worked for the corporation, were given their severance pay and so forth, and they were told their services were no longer needed. The corporation continued to exist but I had to put it through some more re-organization to save it from collapse. Specifically, there was a matter of medical records, which had a life-span of forty or more years. There was a large office space; a large amount of medical office furniture; financial responsibilities related to accounts payable and receivables; a need to move from a large office space to a smaller office space. These were the primary changes I needed to make to further downsize my practice.

One of the biggest decisions I had to make was whether I would continue to practice medicine, or retire, since I was well over the age of retirement. For many months, I carried a big burden and could not decide on which direction to take. Eventually, I decided to finish the re-organization. The large office was closed down and the practice was moved into a Modular Building. That building was leased for five years. Sometimes I felt that I had downsized more than intended or necessary. We all have a tendency to "second guess" ourselves in a crisis moment, and I guess I was no different. My challenge was more related to "wondering' than self-doubt. Though implementation of my downsizing plan was influx, I took some comfort in the fact that my IRA, Roth IRA, and other personal accounts were in good standing. Regarding my children, four of them were still in school, and those with remaining education to complete, those funds could be shared by all of them.

Those five years I leased the Modular Building passed quite fast. Not very much had been accomplished because the practice had been downsized too severe, if there was such a thing. Anyway, the lease was up, and I spoke to the company about purchasing the Modular Building. The company wanted to sell the building for the same amount of money I had put into the lease. That was not a good option. So, I started leasing it month to month with the understanding that I would stop the lease whenever I decided with three months notification. Again, it was past retiring time for me.

In all, I entered the new Millennium in 2000 with many of the old problems I faced during the outgoing one. I wasn't dismayed and I knew if I remain "true to who I am and be myself" like I remembered myself from my days growing up on the Gravel Road, I would be alright. I never let a day past without reflecting on those memories, many of which I have already discussed in my Memoirs so far. After so many years have receded into the past since I started my life journey on the Gravel Road, I have realized that in spite of everything I been through up to the time I downsized my corporation, I am most proud of my children. Some of them became Medical Doctors in their own right. Others chose different paths to follow that fit their taste. Just when I thought my last major challenge was behind me, a natural disaster occurred in New Orleans, LA, which I will never forget, and I am sure all New Orleanians, and Americans as a whole, will remember it for centuries to come. I know I will do so!

CHAPTER XX

HURRICANE KATRINA STRUCK NEW ORLEANS, LA AND CHANGED THE CITY FOREVER

Before 2005, people from all over the United States came to New Orleans, LA to bask in its diverse culture, including food, jazz music (i.e. Jazz fest), art, fashion, Mardi Grau, sports, NFL Saints Football, NBA Basketball Pelicans, conventions such as the Essence Festival and more, which were all neatly connected to the French Quarters and its world-famous *Bourbon Street*. New Orleans, LA had soul, and everyone who visited became addicted to it. The man and woman from Washington State, New York City, Los Angeles, Chicago, Detroit, and all of the small cities, towns and villages in between, like Brookstown where I grew up in St. James Parish, had a desire to visit the "Big Easy." It was the place where Louisianians came to be a part of the on-going party, and in the French way of describing the feeling of it was: *Se le bon temp roules*!, or let the good times roll!

A. Hurricane Katrina Turned New Orleans, LA Upside Down On August 29, 2005

At the heart of the soul of New Orleans, LA was its local Afro-American Community, which included New Orleans East, Uptown Garden District, and Ponchatrain Park. The city's climate was hot and humid, and its diverse peoples were also "hot." It was a place where "Gala" was always in the air. That is, once anyone arrived in the Big Easy, and as soon as their airplane landed at the New Orleans, LA Louis Armstrong International Airport (MSY), and when they walked off it into the main terminal, the heart, feeling, and soul of the Big Easy greeted them with expectations of having a good time, which is why everyone comes to New Orleans, LA. For those who live and work in New Orleans, LA, and inclusive of those who schedule their conventions, balls, and others in the city, once their work day is done, everyone eases into the soul of the place and get "recharged and reinvigorated."

This was home to me. I considered New Orleans, LA my second home when I lived with my Aunts Leah and Mary Augustine on Olive Street near Xavier University in the Gert Town Section of the city. I knew all about the soul peoples came here to experience because I gave part of mine to keeping it alive like so many other Afro-Americans had done through the generations, from the American Institution of Slavery through time to 2005. No one could ever imagine the party, which had been going-on in New Orleans, LA for so long, would come to an end in 2004. I didn't but like most natives, we all knew we lived 6 feet below sea level in the "Bowl;" and yet, we felt the "out falling canals and big water pumps" would keep us relatively safe when it came to any catastrophic flooding. We felt, collectively speaking, that we were immune from any kind of weather event that would be powerful enough to put out the fire of the on-going party in New Orleans, LA. Like so many others, I thought it would go on forever. I thought it would be there for me when I felt my need to get back in touch with my soul, by going into the city and allowing "its soul" to wash over me, and soothe the nicks and bruises that I encountered during a days work in my Medical Practice.

Unfortunately, like thousands of other native New Orleanians, I was wrong. New Orleans, LA was not immune from climate change. And, like during years past, somehow, when the climate in the Gulf of Mexico, Caribbean, and the United States was not saturated with co2, or Carbon Dioxide, hurricanes usually fizzled-out before they got to New Orleans, LA, or they turned and went in another direction. This is what we native New Orleanians had gotten accustomed to. Thus, the party going-on in New Orleans, LA would continue indefinitely! This, of course was wishful thinking in the modern era, or new Millennium, which began in 2000. And, little did anyone know, the soul of New Orleans, LA, within the next four years, would be washed-out of the Big Easy, and the city, thereafter, would never be the same again. Oh no! Not like it was before 2005. I have walked the streets in the city where I use to walk before 2005, and the longer I walk and search for that soulful feeling, I have not been successful in finding it again. Do not get me wrong. One can still hear music, and see peoples moving about but, sad to say, the soul of New Orleans, LA is gone because it was scattered all over America similar to the way wind blows leaves and scatter them in all directions on a cold, gusty, and wintry day.

This is what happened to me in New Orleans, LA, when the soul of the city was scattered all over America, and part of it was drowned, and washed out into the waters of the Gulf of Mexico. The Perfect Storm changed my life too.

On the morning of August 29, 2005, Hurricane Katrina made landfall as a Category 4 Hurricane at Plaquemine Parish, Louisiana, which is roughly 45 miles southeast of New Orleans, LA. When Hurricane Katrina made landfall in Plaquemine Parish, it was about 400 miles wide, and its hurricane-force winds of 160 mph extended 90 miles in either direction from its center, or eye. Her eye was approximately 30 miles in diameter. Hurricane Katrina was a "Perfect Storm," and when she moved over the very warm waters in the Gulf of Mexico, namely, the Loop Current, she underwent rapid intensification, and when she made landfall her single eye changed into a double eye wall. Along the Louisiana and Mississippi Coasts, Hurricane Katrina pushed a 30 feet plus Storm Surge inland, and the devastation to property and loss of human life could, realistically speaking, be left to estimation and one's imagination.

As it was, New Orleans, LA was, to a large extent, left under at least 10 feet of water across the metropolitan area. Most of the flooding in the city was due to several serious failures in its protective levee walls. They were breached when Hurricane Katrina's Storm Surge roared inland through the Mississippi River Gulf Outlet, or MRGO, as many New Orleanians know it. When everything was taken into account, and some accounts are still outstanding because many properties that were either damaged or destroyed outright are still unaccounted for; the final damage and death toll, at best, remains estimates today.

Nevertheless, it is estimated that Hurricane Katrina caused $161 billion worth of property damage, and for New Orleans, LA only, the total number of deaths was 1,836. This is a conservative estimate because one cannot imagine the devastation a 30.0 feet or higher storm surge can cause, and when hurricane-force winds and tornadoes are added into the property damage and loss of life equation, the mentioned figures will remain questionable for years to come. That is, can a person be counted in the loss of life number, if one was swept out into the Gulf of Mexico when Hurricane Katrina's counterclockwise motion pushed her storm surge back out into its dangerous and churning waters?

At any rate, Hurricane Katrina touched the lives of thousands of New Orleanians, and although I evacuated out of the path of her fury, she nevertheless had a devastating impact on me emotionally, and my residence was visited by her unexpected and angry waters.

B. Modular Building That Housed The Corporation Flooded On August 29, 2005

The summer 2005 was not much different from the past one in 2004. There were the usual predictions made by the National Hurricane Center in Miami, FL, regarding the number of named tropical storms there might be. New Orleanians, like myself, were use to hearing about the predictions, and since none threatened us for more than a decade, we felt pretty secure that the summer of 2005 would be similar to those of the past. However, the summer 2005 broke the quiet pattern!

Several months after the beginning of the Hurricane Season on June 1, 2005, a tropical storm developed in the Atlantic Basin, and it was given the name-Katrina. As I have previously discussed, she became one of the most powerful hurricanes that ever made landfall in the United States. She was so powerful that her name has been retired for all times.

On August 29, 2005, Hurricane Katrina arrived in New Orleans, LA. Because the force of her storm surge, several levee walls failed, and the city's bowl rapidly filled up with saltwater. This event caused the Modular Building, in which I conducted my practice to become flooded. There was destruction of office furniture, equipment, supplies, medical records, and more. The leasing company was contacted several weeks later, and I notified a representative about the Katrina-induced flooding of the Modular Building. Eventually, I requested that the leasing company remove the Modular Building from the property, but it refused on the basis I was leasing the building when Hurricane Katrina flooded it. In short, I was told that I was responsible for their leased building. In other words, the company wanted me to pay for the building because I was leasing it at the time it was flooded. That is, the leasing company wanted me to pay $55,000 for the building!

Moreover, there was an endorsement on my office content and liability insurance policy for $55,000. The insurance company I had taken out the policy with was Fulton Insurance Agency located on St. Bernard Avenue. There was a "tug of war" because the office insurance company did not want to pay for replacement of the building because of its flooded condition, and the leasing company that owned the Modular Building did not want the building back because of mold and so forth. Imagine how frustrating this was for me? I had not missed a payment, for as long as I had my Fulton Insurance agency Policy, and, when I needed the latter to "honor" what I paid for years, I was told by a company representative that they could not help me at a time of my greatest need. I was so upset with the insurance company; this was the emotional devastation that Hurricane Katrina caused in her aftermath. There was no love or compassion; the insurance company clung to its money for dear life. I think more New Orleanians died an emotional death than those who purportedly died due to wind and flooding. The emotional Hurricane Katrina created an emotional storm inside of me, and inside of thousands of others like me, and it was very real, palatable, and life changing.

Two or three years later, the office liability insurance company worked-out a settlement with me, but it did not want to deal with the leasing company. Seemingly, the leasing company in Louisiana was purchased by a larger leasing company in Pennsylvania just before Hurricane Katrina occurred. So, I turned the matter over to my attorney that got the settlement for the office content and liability insurance company. Several years have passed and we have not heard anything! This was the awful dark-side of the situation; when I took out the insurance policy or lease for the Modular Building, everyone was smiling and shaking hands telling me that they will be there if I ever need them. When I needed their help, I could not get any satisfaction, and if I did get any, I had to get an attorney and end up paying more money. This is not satisfaction but the way sharks in the ocean behave; they are friendly until they get hungry; the insurance company was very friendly as long as I satisfied its hunger with money. On top of all of this drama, when New Orleans, LA was flooded by Hurricane

Katrina, the healthcare system shutdown save First Responder Medical Care and Triage. That is, real time decisions were being made about who would live or die based on the seriousness of one's injury.

Therefore, before Hurricane Katrina unleashed her fury on New Orleans, LA, I had begun to work part-time with a local pain clinic. I would work two or three hours a day for two or three days per week. It continued until Hurricane Katrina hit New Orleans, LA in late August 2005. The Pain Clinic I worked for was operated by Candice Dobbins; her clinic opened in 2003. And, after the medical community was shut-down in New Orleans, LA, the Pain Clinic relocated to Lafayette, LA in 2007. My return to New Orleans, LA, after Hurricane Katrina's floodwaters receded and streets in the city were passable again, I made my way back to my home and Medical Practice, and what I found is difficult even now to express in words.

C. Return To New Orleans, LA After Hurricane Katrina Moved North

I was in Nashville, TN when Katrina made landfall about 45 miles southeast of New Orleans, LA. I was not able to return to New Orleans, LA for almost a month because there were no airline flights available; no rental cars; no trains; and no buses were able to come into New Orleans, LA. Four or five weeks later, I was able to get a flight into Baton Rouge, LA, and from there, I got ground transportation to New Orleans, LA. When I arrived in the outskirts of New Orleans, LA, the Louisiana Highway Patrolmen, State, and City Police were only letting people with businesses into the city. I was able to gain entry, and once I got through the Police Checkpoint, I was able to go to my Medical Practice and inspect it. Looking around inside, I noticed, five weeks after Hurricane Katrina, there was minimal drainage of water from the Modular Building. I was shocked to see the destruction inside my Medical Practice! I felt powerless at the moment because the entire city was nearly totally devastated! The odor in the office was pungent and there was mold everywhere. I thought to myself "would the situation be the same at my home?"

a. Tudor Court Home Heavily Damaged By Katrina's Wind And Water

After leaving my practice, which was totally destroyed, I drove to my house in New Orleans, LA East at Tudor Court. When I arrived at my house, there was still large amounts of water draining from doors to the outside and driveway. Upon entrance into my house, I could see the water line, which was about 10 feet high on the walls. I surmised that the water covered the whole first floor, and it soaked through everything to the bottom of the second floor. The odor was pungent and there was mold and slime everywhere! It had been forming for days in the heat and humidity. For the most part, mostly large pieces of furniture were in the house. Such things as books, videos, tapes, silverware, records, china, plates, and pots were few in number. They all had floated through the house and carried by the floodwaters into Lake Willow behind the house. We were not able to find any, or a very few objects in the yard or street in front of the house. Since the house was constructed with more than 1/3 of glass for enclosure, things just floated out into oblivion. Furnishings such as chairs, benches, lamps, tapestries, art pieces, wall ornaments, pictures, and portraits, could not be found anywhere. A love chair was found caught between branches of a tree that was along the bulkhead of Lake Willow behind the house. One of the families on the opposite side of the lake found a bank with the address of my next door neighbor on their lawn.

According to the waterline around the walls of house on the First Floor, it indicated the water level was approximately 10 feet. Then, the moisture level on the sheet rock seemed to have been about two and one-half feet from the floor. Only large furniture items remained in my house, and all of the smaller pieces had been moved, by the water, into different rooms. There were eight Dining Room Chairs in other rooms, and it is difficult to imagine how one of them was found tangled in a tree by the lake, and another one was found several blocks away in a drainage canal with other debris. Moreover, on the driveway and lawn, there were items from other places, in addition to a 1999 Pontiac Grand Am (!), which had been, at some point during the flooding, covered by saltwater. There was discoloration of all of the trees, shrubbery, grass, and flowering plants due to the saltwater. Ninety percent of the grass, trees, shrubbery, and flowering plants were destroyed, or eventually died.

What happened to the vegetation at my house on a micro-level is exactly what happens to the vegetation along the Louisiana Gulf Coast. For example, when canals are dug by various oil companies to float their oil drilling rigs into the Gulf of Mexico, the excavated "channels," or water highways, allow saltwater from the Gulf to flow inland. And, when it interacts with freshwater vegetation, the latter dies the same way the vegetation around my house did. Worse, Coastal Vegetation dies, and because of continuous wave action, landloss results. Currently, Louisiana loses as much as a football field of land, along its coast, every three minutes. This means there was less Coastal Vegetation available to slow down Hurricane Katrina's 30 feet Storm Surge. Actually, scientists estimated that every 2.7 miles of Coastal Wetlands will reduce storm surge one foot.[150] In the absence of Coastal Wetlands, Katrina's storm surge made its way into New Orleans, LA; it broke through several levee walls; the water flooded the city; and my Tudor Court Home suffered major water damaged. Exacerbated by high temperatures and humidity, the odor in the atmosphere was nearly impossible to withstand. I was nearly overcome with grief! The devastation and destruction was nearly complete.

b. New Orleans East Became A Ghost Town After Hurricane Katrina Wreaked Havoc In the City

As the weeks passed, the odor in the atmosphere, smell of lawns, odor inside houses and destroyed buildings and so forth, became more pungent. I had to wear a mask to breathe, and so did many New Orleanians. Those who chose not to wear one likely contracted what became known after Katrina as the "New Orleans Cough." On top of all of this chaos and destruction, there was no electricity, water, gas, and other vital services for miles and miles in any direction. In addition, there were miles and miles of devastation and silence, foul-smelling odors, and a lack of life. There were no birds, no insects, no lizards, no fish in the lake, and the lake water had a black color. New Orleans East became totally black at nightfall. There was no adjusting of the eyesight in the absolute dark. Of all the destruction, and everything was bad across the board, one of the worse things I was

---

[150] Wetlands and Coastal Erosion-Southeastern Louisiana University, https://www2.southeastern.edu

most challenged by was the odor. It was impossible to escape because to live, I had to breathe, and with each breath I took, I could smell the rotten, sour, pungent odor everywhere.

Also, Hurricane Katrina was so powerful that whole houses, buildings, cars, boats, and many other heavyweight properties were literally moved off of their original foundations. For example, many houses, trailers, and so forth had moved from their customary foundations to other areas of the streets, lawns, canals either a few blocks away, or sometimes several miles from their original resting place. Other houses and buildings, in particular, just opened up and parts of the houses floated away with the water. That devastation was, or could be, seen for miles and miles. The only areas that could be traveled were the super highways such as I-10, I-610, and I-310. Most streets were closed because of the debris scattered all over them, for miles and miles. There were only a few people in the city because there was no place for them to stay in New Orleans, LA, or the suburbs, for miles and miles in any direction. In essence, the city was a ghost town! The trees were disfigured along the streets, highways, homes, and forests. They looked like grotesque statues where many branches were torn an shredded. Whole trees were uprooted and flung far in the distance. Some trees that remained standing had whole limbs ripped-off but they were nowhere in sight. On top of this, the saltwater, from the Gulf of Mexico, would inevitably form a white haze on the vegetation, and much of it was destined to die. There was no life, or at best, very little here and there.

If anyone ever been to war, or watched a war movie on television, then it is easier for someone to know I am not exaggerating when I say "New Orleans East, and other parts of the city, and the devastation I have described thus far, is similar to what one would expect to see in a war zone. New Orleans, LA, save the French Quarters and the Riverwalk Areas, and the catastrophic devastation that could be seen for miles and miles in any direction, was like a foreign nation had dropped a "bomb" in the city, which killed thousands and tore up entire neighborhoods. The Charity Hospital, where I did my Anesthesia Residency roughly 38 years before 2005, was so severely damaged that it was closed, by then Governor Kathleen Blanco, three weeks after Katrina devastated it in 2005. The Charity Hospital was classified as unusable.

As I said earlier, the "heart and soul" of New Orleans, LA was scattered by Hurricane Katrina's Winds and Waters. The city, especially for those people who knew her before 2005, already know that whatever goes on in it-Post-Katrina-is not truly the authentic New Orleans, LA of "Olden Days." The brothers and sisters of color, who cooked that food, sung those songs, played that jazz horn, and danced the second-line, like nobody else in the world can never duplicate, are gone! Like John Denver sung in his signature song "Rocky Mountain High," in which he sung "A man or woman is poor if they never saw an Eagle fly" (Paraphrase Mine). I feel the generations following Hurricane Katrina will never be able to feel the real experience of New Orleans, LA. This makes my heart heavy and sad to think about but it is true.

With the passage of time, the strangling odor became more pungent and profound. It was like the mercury in a barometer that goes up or down to measure a rise and fall in temperature, the pervasive odor, likewise, just kept on getting worse. And, no matter which way the wind blew, it did not make a difference, regarding blowing the pungent odor out of New Orleans East. Then, as people began to remove debris from their homes, one could see debris stacked up in growing piles, for miles and miles in either direction. The debris stacks got larger and larger, wider and wider, and higher and higher. There was so much devastation as you walked, or rode through passages called streets. There were lumps in all throats, tears streaming down faces, mental aberrations, people being numb and depressed, people needing treatment for allergies, depression, stress syndrome and many others. I was one of the people who felt this way. The situation in New Orleans, LA was horrible, and days and weeks after Hurricane Katrina drowned the city, many African-American Residents remained stranded on their roof tops in the "boiling sun" without any clean water to drink.

c. Mental Toll Caused By Katrina's Power Packed "One-Two" Punch

Katrina had swung a hard left hook and a stiff right cross, and it landed a solid blow to the mind and body of everyone, including myself. I was staggered like a boxer who is partially knocked-out, but somehow able to stay on his or her feet. If there is a place called "hell" that exist, what I observed and personally experienced at my house, and in my community, is the closest I will ever get to it. This is what I felt like; I felt I was in hell, and the fire got hotter every day that passed. Although this was the tip of the iceberg, there was no place for anyone to go for treatment, or general living. This was the lowest rung in Dante's Inferno.

All of that devastation, and its aftermath, whereby people were going into their grossly damaged houses, and having to carry-out debris, piece by piece, to the outside of the house, and with each handful of it, one remembered that those things were what they had accumulated as a result of many years of toils and tribulations. In all of those areas, which use to be communities before Katrina arrived, there was no electricity, no water, no gas, and other general services, for miles and miles. New Orleans East, and other areas, was a wasteland of tragic proportions. If I could count the number of tears that were shed by the people, mine included, I am sure it would be enough to fill up a swimming pool! The social media did not really have a clue of what was going-on with the people at the grassroot level. They were hurt; their pain was deep and chronic. Sometimes it became so great that the affected person just gave up and died. The "red tape" of the Federal, State, and Local Governments oftentimes moved at such a snail's pace that some people simple could not hold on any longer and gave up. I was a Medical Doctor so I knew what pain and disease are like because I studied it, and sought to cure it in my medical practice, many years before Katrina. Even though this was the case, the hardship still, nevertheless, fell on me like a ton of bricks because I had to remove my debris too, piece by piece, from my house, and battle my "doubts and fear" like everyone else had to. No one was left immune by Katrina save the Ruling Class. Adding to this emotional frustration I felt, including thousands of others like myself, there were no jobs. The New Orleans, LA Economy was completely shut down for months after Katrina.

d.   No Work In The City In Late 2005

There were no jobs; many people had no money or food; and most of us had to depend on what was given to us by Homeland Security, FEMA (Federal Emergency Management Agency), charities, and friends. This was the closest I ever came in my life to understanding what loneliness feels like. Everywhere I turned and looked, there was something that needed to be repaired, and there was not a whole lot of people running in my direction to assist me with them. It was decision-making time; that is, do I persevere and go forward, or do I say "this is too much for me to tackle and walk away. This was the so-called $64,000 question!

Like everybody else, when Hurricane Katrina shut down the New Orleans, LA Economy, my bills still needed to be paid. There was no temporary moratorium issued by Mayor Ray Nagin's Office telling us we did not have to pay our bills for one year or more. It is interesting how bill collectors can find people amid all of the devastation. Those people with obligations in other places, other than in the New Orleans area, had difficulty meeting those obligations. Some of the situations and people perished. The general area was plagued with mental aberrations and illness. Unfortunately, many people just withered away and disappeared.

For me, and having been strengthened by adversity I faced many years ago on the Gravel Road, and because I was taught how to face them by Joe Braud and Lillian Luellen Pierce Braud, my father and mother, rather than cave in and disappear like so many New Orleanians did, I decided to find employment in the midst of this aforementioned *haystack of devastation* and, simultaneously, clean out the debris inside and outside of my house, and then rebuild it. I had "shined shoes" in New Orleans, LA and "scrapped rice and potatoes" on the Gravel Road, and this experience prepared me early on to meet the challenges Hurricane Katrina left behind head-on.

D. Recovery And Rebuilding Process-Ordeal Of A Lifetime

The next step was to find employment and clearing of debris from my house, which included the daunting and painstaking task of removing mildew and slime from the walls and removal of water-soaked furniture and so forth. I was out of work for several months. In the meantime, I began removing debris from my house and yard. All of the wood floors, tile floors, rugs and so on had to be removed from the house. Everything was covered with mold and mildew and water-soaked. It was hot and humid and the pungent odor was nearly unbearable. I had to wear a special mask in order to work. If the Americans today had to remove mildew and mold from the houses they live in, there would be no questions raised, political or otherwise, whether wearing a mask takes away one's constitutional rights.

If one did not wear the required mask to remove mold, mildew, and slime for their houses, the latter would likely take away their lives. Social media never made this valuable connection related to some people's opposition to wearing a mask, regarding COVID-19 Protection. The recovery work ahead of me was extensive and dangerous to my health.

There was water damage to the ceiling of the first floor. Nails had to be removed as well as metal joints support for some of the rafters. In areas where there were rotten, or decayed rafters, those sills had to be removed. All windows and doors had to be removed. Throughout the first floor, mildew and mold covered everything, including the rafters, sills, iron beams, and supports. Once all of this damaged material were taken down, along with some that was laying on the floor randomly, it all had to be transported to the street by hand; a wheelbarrow was used to haul anything that could fit in it.

Thus, tons of debris and foul-smelling materials were placed in the streets beyond the sidewalks and drainage. One would never have imagined the amounts of materials that existed. All of the soaked sheetrock was increased in size, and with so many people "gutting out" their homes, the collective effort of stacking the debris on the streets in itself was breathtaking. At times, the ordeal would make me cry, and at others or simultaneously, I experienced a weakening feeling inside of myself. This was the real deal! It was like going to a funeral everyday and all day long that never came to an end. I was burying my things, which embodied a part of my labor that went into them. I felt awful for myself and my neighbors, and for the children. How must they have felt seeing all of the destruction everywhere they turned to look?! This situation was worse than an X-Box Video War Games. There were miles and miles of debris ten or twelve feet high as far as one could see!

Then, the time came when the heavy equipment was sent out to remove the mountains of debris from the streets. There were 18- Wheeler Dump Trucks of all sizes, Caterpillar Tractors, bulldozers, tractors, Billy Goats, Tree Cutters and Shredders and so on. The operators of this equipment were much appreciated by all, but they-too-were sickened by the devastation. One way their behavior was manifested was they cared nothing about the landscape, sidewalks, streets, barricades, and driveways among others. If the operators had to get on someone's lawn, they did not care; they just wanted to grab the debris and load it on the 18-wheelers and smaller Dump Trucks. It was nice to see the debris removed as well as the pungent odor, most of which left the area when the debris was transported out. I could put up with equipment tracks on the lawns far more than the mountains of debris that once rested uglily, foreboding, and menacing on them.

This debris removal activity lasted more than a year; it lasted even longer in areas where homes floated from one place to another, blocking streets, and thoroughfares. I often wondered what was done with all the debris that was collected in New Orleans East and elsewhere? It was brought to some unspecified sites where it was dumped, and after it was spread across an area, some equipment, of which I do not know the name, which has some of the biggest and widest wheels, rolled over the debris smashing it into smaller and smaller pieces; and, in this repetitive manner, the huge wheels drove the debris deeper and deeper into the land until it was no longer visible to the human eye.

While this burial of debris was going-on around the clock, the people in my neighborhood, and others, could only work on their homes, or others, during the day because there was no electricity, gas, or water for months. The electrical grid was destroyed by Katrina. Then, when the sunset, and the land was darker than black, large mosquitoes became overly active, and their bite was not like a regular mosquito bite that usually caused a little disquieting itching. Those mosquitoes that were blown in by Katrina, from places deep-down in the swamps, had a painful bite. That being so, the first line of defense against this dreaded mosquito was an insect repellant; the other defense was people made sure that he or she left the area near sundown, or run the risk of being attacked by what I named them-Katrina Mosquitoes. As time moved on, which seemed like it was in slow motion all of the time, eventually, the city supplied generator lights (Spotlights) in different areas where large thoroughfares intersected. With the help of the "Higher Power," I saw the light at the end of the tunnel but it still was way off in the distance.

E. Household Repairs, Chemical Treatments, And Home Insurance Struggles

a. Removing Mold And Mildew From My House

After all the debris was removed from my property, and other homes and shelters, the latter had to have a special treatment for mold and mildew. The special treatment was applied some three or four times over a six weeks to two month time period. Mold and mildew are difficult to kill due to an overabundance of moisture in my house. With just a little moisture, mold and mildew can multiply and spread. And, if it is not destroyed, it will make the inhabitants in an affected house very ill. If left undiagnosed, an affected person is at high risk of developing a catastrophic illness. So, I did not play around; I applied as much of the special treatment that was allowable.

In retrospect, it must have taken twelve to fourteen months to decrease the mountain of debris on my property. Then, it would take another year thereafter to have an appreciation of the total devastation. Four years later, or by 2009, there are still remnants of the devastation. Half of the homes are still awaiting the opportunity for their owners to get enough "money" to attempt to rebuild. Some New Orleanians, too many for that matter, never got enough money to do so, and many places where houses use to be before Katrina, have not been rebuilt by 2021! The only thing that exists on many sites like this today is a concrete slab foundation. Just thinking about this situation makes me feel terrible; yet, I wonder how people feel who are in the real jaws of the situation?!

Because I was one of the fortunate ones to have access to financial resources to rebuild, the next stage for me involved trying to treat rafters, sills, and beams for mildew. There was a special formula that one had to use. It was an application of Chlorox. We applied three or four coats of the material. Sometimes I wondered whether it was done well enough. In addition, there is one thing that has really bothered me in the whole Recovery Process; and that was, the condition of the brick on the outside of the house. With ten or more feet of saltwater on the bricks, for more than two weeks, how did it effect the mortar that kept the bricks in place? In the general area where my house was located, there were houses where the bricks came apart, or the structure crumbled to the ground. On the other hand, there were some houses where the bricks would leak, especially when there was a hard rain. I had good reason to be concerned because salt will eat up bricks and the mortar that holds them in place over time. How fast this deterioration occurs is dependent on how much salt is applied in a specified area.

With this thought occupying a portion of my mind, and each phase of the recovery process competed for its piece of my mind, all I could do was trust the process and hope for the best outcomes along the uncharted course. Several months past and another coat of Chlorox was applied to prevent the re-occurrence of the mildew. And, another coat was applied after the previous one. Nothing could be left to chance; mildew is like an untreated infection, and if it is allowed to reach Stage 4 or 5, it could multiply to the point that my house would become unsafe to live in. When the Chlorox Coat dried, the pest control company was called in to spray for any insects, or Anthropods, that eat mildew as part of their diets. Once my house was freed of mold and mildew, my next great hurdle was to bring in the carpenters to repair the house, both inside and outside.

b. House Repair Stage

As one can imagine, with ten feet of water swirling around on the inside and outside of my house for weeks and months, the damage to it was tremendous. Thus, I had to find licensed carpenters to come in and restore my house. They were not easy to find because everybody was trying to find the same carpenters, and, therefore, their availability was limited. At the outset, there were pros and cons to think about.

For beginners, the home owner insurance did not feel that the company should have to pay for coverage because it was water that caused the damage; yet Hurricane Katrina's winds started the damage in the first place. So, here we go again in the hair-splitting ring of the Three Ring Circus! In spite of the fact I had high coverage, the home owner insurance company did not honor the basic coverage. After all of the bickering, I was only awarded approximately one-half of the coverage I paid for years. This fact never gets reported during the 6 PM New Hour because the wolf is spoken about only as a sheep. I was struggling to survive; one of the most powerful hurricanes to ever make landfall in the United States did so about 45 miles from house. I was so angry and downtrodden in that moment when the home owner insurance representative told me the company would only honor 50.0 percent of my home owner insurance policy. Cursing would not do justice to the way I felt! In reality, I was going through another hurricane trying to get my house repaired. Sometimes I still wonder which one was worse?!

The flood insurance contract awarded the total coverage. Thank go-od-ness, there were no questions asked.

Then, next came the time to find a carpenter and other necessary repair technicians. I picked one that was unable to help me. Therefore, I suffered trying to get enough money to pay for the reconstruction.

For approximately one-and-one-half years, I lived in a FEMA Trailer. The trailer was housed on my front lawn. By that time, I had begun to work in Lafayette, LA. From all indications, I made a poor choice even though there was no employment in New Orleans, LA. I started working full-time at Maximum Urgent Care Clinic. There was no stress associated with the clinic. However, during that time, the clinic moved on three different occasions. I never became involved with the reasons for the moves of the clinic. Because I was desperate to get my house repaired, I probably kept my mouth closed fearing if I spoke out about the three moves the clinic made in its location, I might lose my job. At the time, the Medical Industry in New Orleans, LA was virtually shut down for the foreseeable future, and I needed a job! The sole purpose of working in the clinic was to assist me in getting my house back in use after Hurricanes Katrina and Rita. It was difficult to have my home reconstructed, while I simultaneously lived a few hundred miles away part-time in Lafayette, LA.

During that time, someone was undoubtedly going into the house and taking things out. There was a large size special made mattress and box spring that was difficult, at best, to remove out of my house, but it left and that was when the project was about one-half finished. The building contractor swore that it was not taken by his workers even though the theft occurred during, or after, the bed was dismantled to permit the painters to paint and make repairs in the Master Bedroom. There were many other items removed from the house. I should have known better to not have some kind of security check set up to watch the carpenters while they were doing their work in my house. The fact was people in New Orleans, LA, nearly all of them especially in New Orleans East, were desperate for everything. So, the vandalization of my house was, for the thieves, either a means to get an item to put in their house, or it was one that could be sold to get some money to repair their own or other. This was definitely an unusual time. There was nothing a person would not do to try to survive another day in a war zone of destruction caused by Hurricanes Katina and Rita.

On top of the vandalism, there was one section of my house that continued to have leakage from the roof. This was the area of the roof where a large branch, from a Pine Tree had fallen on the top of my house, during Hurricane Katrina. I had the feeling that the size of the branch, and wind from the hurricane, caused the roof to shift. That section of the roof was partially blown off during the hurricane. Thus, there have been several attempts to repair that section of the roof but nothing seems to work. In addition, I have continued to try and get the house back into its original splendor. When it is finished, it will have the look of the "million dollar house" of yesteryear. It may be able to be published in magazines and or other publications. During the repairs made on the inside of my house, I made a few structural changes.

F. Finished Product House More Elegant Than Before Hurricane Katrina And Rita

There have been multiple changes in the floor plan. The Living Room and Dining Room were changed into one large room. The Living Room is to the left and as one enters and straight ahead is a semi-panoramic view of the lake. It has several pieces of furniture from Europe, which gives somewhat of a classical look. There is an area with a formal table and chairs with another panoramic view of the lake and backyard. As you enter the house to the far right beyond the kitchen, is the Dining Room. It is elegantly furnished with some area for tapestry and or China Cabinet. To the right, one can enter the kitchen, breakfast nook, and the den. The lines are simple and furnishing are breathtaking. All counter tops have ebony marble that blend so elegantly with the soft white walls.

As one continues to the right through a short hallway, you enter the atrium and move toward hanging art pieces. It can be used for drawing, painting, and so forth. There is a butterfly throw rug on the floor as it leads one into the media room that has a big screen television and media arm chairs. The second floor is composed of the Master Bedroom that is large and luxurious with areas of padded walls and draperies. Its furnishings are mirrored somewhat sectional. In the Master Bathroom, there is an elevated bathtub with associated glass enclosed shower. The walls of the Master Bathroom are completely padded with olive green material. In addition to the special made drapes, seating and so forth, there is the Sauna lined with Cedar Wood and a spacious Master Bedroom Closet. The hallway on the second floor is L-Shaped and leads to the remaining three bedrooms, porch, and bath with multi-tiered drapes and art work. Furnishing in each bedroom is spectacular to say the least even though they are far from being completed.

The replacement of the house has been put on the back burner because of the situations that came to the forefront in late 2005. Some of the sources of monies for recovery from Hurricanes Katrina and Rita were stopped abruptly when I was working in a clinic in Lafayette, LA. A thorough, detail account of my actions while I worked for the Maximum Urgent Care Clinic in Lafayette, LA are included in the following Chapter.

G. "The Jackie Robinson Affect:" Brief Overview Of The Drug Enforcement Administration (DEA) Payback For Breaking Down The Closed Door Of The Charity Hospital Residency Anesthesia Training Program In 1966

Briefly, the Drug Enforcement Administration (DEA) alleged that I was in a "conspiracy" with the people that owned and operated the clinic. There was no truth in that false accusation. I continued to tell those DEA Investigators that I had nothing to do with the administration of that clinic, and I only saw and examined patients. From all indications, the people that owned the clinic are being slapped on the hand. In the same vein, I did not have the right attorney and when he was asked if there was anything else that could be done for me, and my own attorney told the court "no." That should have been my clue to get another attorney to represent me. Now, I am paying a "dear price."

In addition, my mind was in trouble. I could not think straight and went into a severe state of depression and suicidal ideations, or aberrations.

During the course of the court proceedings, I had a light left-sided stroke. I had to undergo psychiatric evaluation. I was placed on antidepressant medications. At the same time, a number of people tried to tell me that I was sitting around and not putting up a fight. I just could not. I felt paralyzed all over; it seemed like time had come to a standstill, yet everyone and everything around me seemed to be moving, and this was quite an unsettling experience that I had never had before in my life.

As mentioned earlier, I intend to set the record straight. This is my opportunity to do so. I would like to indulge everyone here to recall that when I arrived in New Orleans, LA in 1960, I was an educated Black Medical Doctor, who sought to set up my medical practice at a time when Jim Crow Laws were overtly practiced in the city, and Systemic Racism permeated every institution and had for generations, simultaneously conditioned the minds of White People, from one generation after the next, that Black People were inferior human beings, and they did not deserve justice of any kind. I had to interact in this unfriendly environment, and because I knocked the door down becoming the first Black Medical Doctor accepted in the Charity Hospital Anesthesia Residency Training Program in Louisiana in 1967, and although absolutely no social media coverage was ever given to the history changing breakthrough I made, many White People, in the Medical Profession and others, including politicians, were not excited about my achievement. They never forgot about I was the Black Medical Doctor, and to many, I was the "boy," who got out of his place. Years earlier at Charles H. Brown High School, I was told the day I left the school that I had "No Respect For Authority" This was not forgotten after all those years later. The only way this thought can live in one's mind is it has to become an individual's purpose for living.

Years later, and by late 2005, or 38 years after I broke through the racial door that had forbidden Black Physicians from being accepted into the Charity Hospital Anesthesia Residency Program, the DEA closed ranks on me with the sole intention of one, teaching me a lesson to not think I am their equal, as defined by White Supremacy, and two, to put me back in my place.

CHAPTER XXI

DRUG ENFORCEMENT ADMINISTRATION (DEA) CASE BASED ON "ALLEGATIONS" AND WOULD A TRIAL BY JURY REACH A GUILTY OR INNOCENT VERDICT?

During the course of my life journey, which I have written out on these pages thus far, there is one constant theme I have had to deal with, especially during that part of my journey, including much of my professional career while working as a Public-School Teacher and Medical Doctor. That is, before I became a trained educator and physician, I was not perceived by any of the "Powers That Be," that is, not to my knowledge, as being someone who was a threat to the "status quo," although I was a young Black Man on the rise during the Jim Crow Era. Nevertheless, as much as I flew under the radar, there were moments when I felt a tension in my "gut," regarding some statements that were made to me, which had racial implications. The constant theme I have had to deal with, throughout my Professional Years as a Medical Doctor, is I am an educated Black Man. This fact, as my life journey thus far attests, is undeniable, and my identity, no doubt, caused some people to keep a close eye on me; and, if the opportunity arises to "knock me back down on my knees," according to Sam Cooke, then I would be a target for action aimed at keeping me in check, or in my place.

A. Racial Climate Of The Time

For example, as I discussed earlier, the day I resigned my Biology Teaching Position at Charles H. Brown High School in Springhill, LA, and after

I told the principal I was leaving my teaching job because I had been accepted to study medicine at the Howard University Medical School in Washington, DC, the principal informed me, if I had not resigned, a decision had already been made, by the "Powers That Be" to transfer me to another public school somewhere in the "outback" of Webster Parish. I was feeling very good inside when he shared this news with me, and while holding back my excitement with my best Poker Face, and without any fanfare, I told the principal good day, and I started walking toward the door. Right before I placed my right hand on the door knob on the inside of the Principal Office, and while still seated behind his desk, he ask me "if I wanted to know why a decision was made to transfer me to another school?" I paused momentarily; took my right hand off of the door knob; and calmly turned around; looked the principal in his eyes for a brief moment; then, I answered "yes, I would like to know what prompted the decision to transfer me." The principal uttered these words that were shared with him: "You do not have respect for authority." I am proud of myself to this day, over a half century later, that I held my peace. I turned around and walked out of the Principal Office with my head "unbowed."

I held my peace because I was a thinking man on my feet. I had graduated from Southern University, and I had traveled around the world during World War II, risking my life for the protection of "freedom and liberty" in America for all of its peoples, so my justified self-restraint, to my mind, is what bothered the "Powers That Be." I was not behaving like the "low man on the Totem Pole." I was a young Black Man, who stood 6 feet tall with erect shoulders, and very articulate. Southern University President Felton Clark's Office Manager had prepared me to know how to handle myself in a situation like this one and others. Being a young man, and still, in many ways, holding onto the "innocence" I was taught by my parents on the Gravel Road, I, unknowingly at the time, did not fully realize I would encounter many more more serious challenges to my self-esteem later in my life, especially during my Professional Medical Career. It is necessary to remind everyone here that, from the mid-1950s to the beginning to the new Millennium in 2000 and thereafter, Jim Crow and Jim Crow Esq., its descendants, were alive and well; and, I might add, their purpose(s) was, generationally speaking, a carbon copy of its Antebellum past, both consciously and subconsciously. As I have noted all along, as long as I was perceived by most White People, who only knew me indirectly, or not at all, as a "good young Black Man," who would not be invited to dinner, but knew what side of the sidewalk I was suppose to travel down, then, I was alright with them. However, after I graduated with my Medical Degree, everyone began to take a second look at me to see where I was going, and if one could stop me from getting to my destination, they would try. Some working in the shadows and back channels, intentionally threw little roadblocks on my path and kept their hands hidden and a smile on their faces. They were subtly placed in my way to slow me down, or make me quit trying to excel. Every Black Person in America has a similar story he or she can tell the listener.

For instance, in my case, after working in my medical practice, and at Flint Goodridge Hospital of Dillard University for 15 years or more, I reached a point, at that time, when I felt I was ready to build my dream house. I was a young Black Medical Doctor with a proven track record, and I had collateral to spare, so I went to a Banking Institutions in New Orleans, LA to apply for a loan to build my dream house. I had a strong application but I was told by a bank representative that it could not provide me with a loan to build my dream house. Was this an uncommon occurrence that I was denied the loan I applied for, or was this another little subtle roadblock reminder that I should think smaller because Black People, during the mid-1970s, should not aspire to live in a good home in a neighborhood of their choice?

There are many other subtleties, or roadblocks I could divulge here, and rather than prolong my legal experience with the Drug Enforcement Administration, it is timely for me to proceed and explain what brought me to Lafayette, LA to work for the Maximum Urgent Care Clinic in 2005.

B. Climate Change

To avoid duplication of what I have already discussed about Hurricanes Katrina and Rita, I will repeat again that these two powerful storms completely shut down the Medical Industry in New Orleans, LA on August 29, 2005 and thereafter. My Medical Practice was destroyed; I had no way of earning an income. I needed to work because my Tudor Court Residence was also heavily damaged and uninhabitable. I was one step above being a vagabond. If it were not for my children, some of whom allowed me to stay with them, I would have been homeless like so many of my fellow New Orleanians, who were not as fortunate as I was to have a place to stay.

The weather climate had changed and produced a storm that tore up the "Big Easy." I had ten feet of water throughout the first floor of my residence. Snakes and alligators swam through it because my residence had become a part of the Gulf of Mexico. This was serious, a "Big Deal," and, by any psychological measurement, it was a crazy time. It was a time when the average New Orleanian, the people on Main Street, were devastated and suffering. Their social and economic condition can best be described as painful, heartbreaking, and impoverished.

Like them, I needed to work so I would be able to clean and restore my residence.

C. Work Climate Change

By the time Hurricane Katrina struck New Orleans, LA, I was ready to retire. Some people around town, both inside and outside of government, form a chorus and they sang one tune, which was "I worked too long." I would like to bring all of them to my Tudor Court Residence, and then ask "who among you will clean and restore my devastated home while I go to Jamaica and live on the beach?" Sadly, not one person would "step up" and take this monumental challenge. But, I had to "step up" because this was my home that had ten feet of water in it, including the mold, mildew, pungent odor, snakes, and alligators. Everything was in play. Nothing could be taken for granted. If I looked under a pile of wet clothes in my residence, or others, I might find a Black Moccasin ready to strike out with its deadly venom.

Worse, after paying my home owner insurances diligently through the years, and then when I called upon them at a time when I needed them the most desperately for help, invariably, I was told by a company representative that "we cannot help you because we do not insure water, or another told me we do not cover wind." Then, others told me they only cover water damage up to two feet, and not ten feet. This was nuts, and if you do not believe me, try to reason with these people for a period of time, and I am sure you might have felt like I did that they were driving me nuts. There was no work in my medical profession in water logged New Orleans, LA. However, sometime during the latter part of 2005, I was invited to interview for a pain management clinic located in Lafayette, LA, namely, Maximum Urgent Care, LLC. I did not want to take this job opportunity, but my New Orleans, LA home was in total destruction mode.

Some people say my decision to take this job was a poor decision. I ask them to put their feet in my shoes and walk in them for a day. I want them to walk inside my destroyed house, and then make a comment about whether I should or should not have taken the job I was offered by Maximum Urgent Care LLC?

Even after I began work, and after I found a licensed contractor to repair my house, the latter worked by day, and at night, some of the crew members returned to my house and stole everything I bought to restore my home to its former state. I could not call the police for help because the police were heavily impacted by Katrina and Rita also. It was like the "Wild Wild West," where anything goes!

In spite of all of my Katrina and Rita Troubles, unbeknownst me, I was being watched, or placed under surveillance, by the Drug Enforcement Administration (DEA) because, as I found out later, I was swept up in what it called a "Conspiracy to illegally distribute and dispense controlled substances, conspiracy to defraud Medicaid, and money laundering." I was totally devastated again when I was informed of this charge! I was trying to restore my Hurricane Katrina torn home, and in the midst of everything, then, unexpectedly, came a knock at my door, by a City Marshal, who served me papers that allegedly claimed that I was a part of some CONSPIRACY, which was equally amazing to me as it must have been for the DEA Officials that falsely claimed I knowingly and intentionally organized and participated in one. The only example that I can think of, which a majority of African-Americans, and other peoples of color can relate to, is when law enforcement want to remove one of us, a drug or weapon is planted at the scene to justify their action(s), and coverup a crime.

Therefore, in the following section, I will use the Drug Enforcement Administration's Criminal Docket 08-213, Sect. S MAG. 5 to show the DEA developed a number of allegations that were used to falsely claim that I "knowingly and intentionally" participated in the organization of a pain management clinic, for the purpose of distribution of illegal drugs to people, from 2005 to 2007.

D. Drug Enforcement Administration (DEA's) Unproven Allegations

On August 1, 2008, at 3:01 PM, the following document was filed in the Clerk of Court Office in the United States District Court in the Eastern District Of Louisiana, namely:

- Indictment For Conspiracy To Illegally Distribute And Dispense Controlled Substances, Illegal Distribution And Dispensation Of Controlled Substances, Conspiracy To Commit Health Care Fraud, Conspiracy To omit Money Laundering

The one word that stands out, among all others, is *conspiracy*. First, let me define the term. It means to devise a secret plan to do something unlawful or harmful. This definition suggests two or more people-a group-get together and work-out the details of a secret plan to do something unlawful and harmful. That being so, the central question here is was I ever a part of a group that developed a secret plan to do something unlawful or harmful? That is, did the Drug Enforcement Administration (DEA) include concrete data, either written or otherwise, in the above document, that link me to a group that devised a business, clinic, or other, that details my involvement in the establishment of such an entity? Before I answer this crucial question, there is one more term I must define, which is allegation.

An allegation is "a claim or assertion that someone has done something illegal or wrong, typically one made without proof."[151] Moreover, and more importantly, until the claims made by the DEA that participated in a group to develop a secret plan to do something unlawful and harmful is proven beyond a shadow of doubt, then its claim or assertion that I participated in a group to develop a secret plan is merely an allegation. The DEA's Conspiracy Theory was overthrown by its own inability to link me as part of the group of people, who it stated on Pages 1 and 2 of the above

---

[151] Oxfordlanguages.oup.com

Indictment Report, that organized and managed Maximum Urgent Care LLC that I worked for located in Lafayette, LA, from 2005 to 2007.

a. Non-Participation In A Conspiracy To Develop A Secret Plan To Organize And Manage Maximum Urgent Care LLC In Lafayette, LA-2005

As reported by the DEA Indictment Report mentioned above, several people, prior to January 2003, "...organized and managed...Maximum Urgent Care, LLC..."[152] My name is not mentioned anywhere in this regard. Before Hurricane Katrina, I worked roughly 1 or 2 hours per month for Maximum Pain Management LLC, which was located in New Orleans, LA; I imagined this clinic was shut down by Katrina's Floodwaters similar to the way it destroyed my Medical Practice. If I was a part of the DEA's Conspiracy Theory to reconstruct the Maximum Pain Management LLC as Maximum Urgent Care LLC in Lafayette, LA in 2005, wouldn't the DEA have documented evidence that I was a part of the mentioned group that the DEA says set up this clinic? Again, I am not mentioned anywhere in its Indictment Report that claims I was one of the Founders.

In addition, once again the DEA's Indictment Report stated several people "...organized and managed a company that operated a pharmacy in New Orleans, LA. The pharmacy was Southern Discount Drugs LLC."[153] I played no part in its formation or subsequent operation.

b. What Did I Know About The Organization Of The Two Entities?

Nothing. As I have maintained all along, my primary concern was getting my Tudor Court Property restored so I could live in it again. I had too many Hurricane Katrina Problems and insurance companies' to have any time to sit down an develop a secret plan to do something unlawful and harmful. I did not have a place to live. I was living out of a suitcase in a hotel room. Yet, throughout the DEA's Indictment Report, the latter alleges that even though my name was not linked to 98.0 percent of its 17 Indictments, I was, regardless, a Founding Member of the above clinics and pharmacy, although the DEA Officials did not have any concrete data, or other information, in any form, that linked me to their formation.

---

[152] See pp. 1 and 2.
[153] Ibid., p. 2.

All the DEA wrote down in its Indictment Report were unproven and unsubstantiated claims, which, in the absence of any proof, remained, from beginning to end, nothing but allegations.

Presently, I intend to highlight every allegation the DEA made against me without substantiated proof. To achieve their fictitious goals, the DEA needed me to go down with the Titanic to save their case based on a Trumpian-Like Conspiracy Theory. They needed me for this singular purpose but my innocence to them did not matter; I did not organize and manage any clinic or pharmacy-nothing at all!

E. DEA's Unproven Claims And Allegations

For easy comprehension, I placed the DEA's allegations, which are included in its 17 counts Indictment Report in Table 1.22 below. As it is, the allegations the DEA Officials purportedly wrote pertain to unlawful actions they thought I performed at the Maximum Urgent Care Clinic LLC in Lafayette, LA, during the time I worked there.

Table 1.22
Drug Enforcement Administration Allegations Related To Count 1 Unlawful Actions Purportedly Performed At The Maximum Urgent Care LLC, From 2005 To 2007

Year	Topic	Allegation	Result
2005-2007	The Doctors	Joseph Braud, MD "...while working at the clinic gave the public the perception of legitimacy to the clinic as he and *others* (Italics mine) signed dispensations orders and prescriptions for Schedule II, III, and IV controlled substances..." P. 2	Never Proven
2005-2007	Conspiracy	"...Joseph Braud, MD...knowingly and intentionally combine, conspire, confederate and agree with each other...to distribute and dispense quantities of Oxycodone...Schedule II, III, IV and V controlled substances..." P. 5	Never Proven
2005-2007	Manner And Means Of The Conspiracy	"During the course and in the furtherance of the conspiracy...Joseph Braud, M.D... organized and managed pain management clinics which were in essence "pill mills" which involved the defendants and *others* (Italic mine) ostensibly offering management" by doing little more than writing...prescriptions controlled substances...the patients requested..." P. 6	Never Proven
2005-2007	Same	"...organized and managed management clinics that only accepted cash for medical services." P.6	Never Proven
2005-2007	Same	"organized and managed clinics that did not offer appointments. Patients were scheduled to arrive at the clinic on a particular day." P.6	Never Proven
2005-2007	Same	"organized and managed clinics in which the medical staff assisting the doctors had no prior or formal medical training." P. 6	Never Proven
2005-2007	Same	"organized and managed clinics in which the cost of a doctor visit was determined by the type of controlled substances the patient wanted." P.6	Never Proven
2005-2007	Same	"organized and managed clinics in which patients regularly requested and paid for the type of drugs wanted before being seen by a doctor." P.7	Never Proven

2005-2007	Same	"organized and managed clinics that did not offer appointments. Patients were scheduled to arrive at the clinic on a particular day." P.6	Never Proven
2005-2007	Same	"organized and managed clinics in which the medical staff assisting the doctors had no prior or formal medical training." P. 6	Never Proven
2005-2007	Same	"organized and managed clinics in which the cost of a doctor visit was determined by the type of controlled substances the patient wanted." P.6	Never Proven
2005-2007	Same	"organized and managed clinics in which patients regularly requested and paid for the type of drugs wanted before being seen by a doctor." P.7	Never Proven
2005-2007	Same	"organized and managed clinics that provided seasonal coupons and free visits to those patients who brought in additional patients." P. 7	Never Proven
2005-2007	Same	"organized and managed clinics in which *doctors* (Italics Mine) continued to prescribe addictive controlled substances in the same manner notwithstanding notice of numerous patient overdoses, deaths, abuses of controlled substances…" P. 7	Never Proven
2005-2007	Same	"organized and managed clinics in which *doctors* (Italics Mine) would prescribe quantities and combinations of controlled substances…to patients that would cause patients to abuse, misuse…controlled substances." P.7	Never Proven
2005-2007	Same	"organized and managed clinics in which *doctors* (Italics Mine) would prescribe controlled substances without determining a sufficient medical necessity for the controlled substances." P.7	Never Proven
2005-2007	Same	"organized and managed clinics in which patients were not required to provide adequate histories nor were diagnostic tests ordered or performed." P.7	Never Proven
2005-2007	Same	"organized and managed clinics in which *doctors* (Italics Mine) did not communicate or maintain records of communication with prior physicians." P. 7	Never Proven

2005-2007	Same	"organized and managed clinics in which no alternative therapies were attempted beyond a very limited combination of highly addictive medications..." P. 8	Never Proven
2005-2007	Same	"organized and managed clinics in which there were no individualized treatment plans for patients." P.8	Never Proven
2005-2007	Same	"On or about November 21, 2006, in the Western District of Louisiana, the defendant, Joseph Braud, M.D., dispensed Oxycontin and Methadone, both Schedule II narcotic drug substances...outside of the scope of professional practice and not for a legitimate medical purpose." P. 11	Never Proven

Source: Author. Information taken from Court Document 08-213, SECT. S MAG.5 titled "Indictment For Conspiracy To Illegally Distribute And Dispense Controlled Substances, Illegal Distribution And Dispensation Of Controlled Substances, Conspiracy To Commit <u>Health Care Fraud, Conspiracy To Commit Money Laundering</u>, Loretta G. Whyte, Clerk, United States District Court Eastern District Of Louisiana, August 1, 2008. Page Numbers shown in the above Table.

Of all of the DEA Allegations shown above, which pertains to unlawful actions I "purported" performed at the Maximum Urgent Care LL in Lafayette, LA, from 2005 to 2007, everyone of them suggest a consistent pattern of contradictions due to the fact on one hand, the DEA indicated that I was a part of a conspiracy to *organize and manage* the mentioned clinic, and on the other, since the DEA did not list my name on Pages 1 and 2 of its Indictment Report, it is, therefore, impossible for DEA Officials to link me to the organization and management of the Maximum Urgent Care LLC as their series of allegations attempted to do. Another troubling problem with Count 1, where my name is mentioned most frequently, DEA Officials consistently mentioned that "other doctors" were involved in their allegations on Page 2, and they also mentioned "doctors" were involved in dispensation and prescription writing four times in their allegations. Interestingly, it was not lost on me that none of the doctors were ever identified in their Count 1 Indictment, nor was any other doctors identified by name throughout its entire 17 Count Indictment Report. *I was the only physician identified by name.* Was this a gross oversight on the DEA Officials part, or were their consistent omissions aimed at placing the total responsibility on me for all prescriptions written, although at least five other doctors worked at the Maximum Urgent Care LLC? A brief consideration of organizational management provides more evidence that the DEA's Allegations are troublesome and flawed.

F. Maximum Urgent Care LLC Top Level Management

As a part of Count 1 of its 17 Counts Indictment Report, the DEA failed, as I mentioned earlier, to link me with the alleged conspiracy it purported indicated I was a primary operator in setting up the clinic. Throughout private industry and Academia, the people who organize and manage these endeavors are part of what is commonly known as Top Level Management. Those individuals, who occupy this lofty position in a given organization have such titles as President, Vice-President, Chancellor, Chief Executive Officer (CEO), Provost, and Chief Financial Officer (CFO) among others. Beneath this management level, there are Deans, Chairs of Departments, Directors, and Contract Compliance Officers among others. This management tier is commonly known as Middle Level Managers.

Therefore, I was not a part of the Top Level Management, or the Middle Level Management, of the Maximum Urgent Care LLC. More importantly, this means, during the day-to-day operation of it, I did not participate in staff meetings where major policy matters were discussed, nor did I vote to approve policy(s), which affected the operation of the clinic in the short-term or long-term. Nevertheless, as the DEA's 17 Counts Indictment Report indicates, I was placed in the Top Level Management of the Maximum Secure Care LLC, which is a false allegation. The easiest thing for the DEA Officials to do was to list my name among the people they alleged were a part of a conspiracy to develop a secret plan to do something illegal and harmful. Although they did not name me a member of the alleged conspiracy, I was presented throughout its 17 Counts Indictment Report as if I was a part of its Top Level Management. A good lawyer could take this fact alone and show I was not a part of the organization and management of Maximum Urgent Care LLC, and based on the facts, the Presiding Judge would, based on the actual evidence, have no choice but to sever me from all of the DEA's alleged 17 Counts Indictment.

G. Motion To Sever Filed On November 18, 2008

After I explained to my lawyers, I had nothing to do with the organizing and management of the Maximum Urgent Care LLC Clinic in Lafayette, LA, nor one anywhere else, they collectively agreed the DEA's 17 Counts Indictments did not apply to me, and the United States District Court For The Eastern District Of Louisiana must sever, or remove me from its case. That being so, on November 18, 2008, my lawyers filed a Motion to Sever with this court.

The Motion to Sever clearly established that I did not know anything about the sale of controlled substances on the street, nor was I linked directly, by the DEA, to my actual participation of going on the street and making drug sales like a common "drug pusher." Given this fact, my lawyers stated on Page 10 of the Motion to Sever document "...Dr. Braud should be severed from the indictment." In addition, in the same Motion to Sever document, a request was made to Dismiss Count 1due to the fact the "manner and means" in Count 1and the "manner and means" in Counts 2 through 17 "...allegations are actually two separate conspiracies involving different legal issues, different factual issues, and different methods of proof. Accordingly, Count One should be dismissed as duplicitous" (See Page 1of Motion To Dismiss Count One As Duplicitous). For clarification, Count 1 "manner and Means" is, for example, Apples, and Counts 2 through 17 "manner and means" are Oranges. Thus, the DEA's Allegations in both situations would be very difficult to prove, and Count 1 should be dismissed because how could I be prosecuted for "manner and means" allegations that I had no involvement?

By late 2008, the train was rolling full steam down the railroad tracks, and nothing would be able to stop it short of me being sentenced. All of the DEA's Allegations were chimerical at best; reason and common sense became casualties in this struggle. Thus, on December 10, 2008, the Presiding Judge summarily denied my Motion to Sever and Motion to Dismiss Count One. By this date, I was near total exhaustion; I was under the care of a psychiatrist; and my overall energy level was low. I was tired and hurt. I felt like Sonny Liston must have felt when he sat on his stool, and refused to come out of his corner to face another round, during his Heavyweight Championship Fight with Muhammed Ali.

H. Drug Enforcement Administration (DEA) Knockout

I was on the ropes. I had taken countless body blows to my emotional stability. The more I fought with reason and determination, the more Medieval-Like Thinking kept evolving into something like a 10,000 Headed Monster. I was 82 years old, and I did not feel I had enough energy left to slay this beast, if I opted to have a court trial. I knew I could win my case but the main challenge was would I live long enough to see it through to the end? One part of me told me to fight like I had to growing up on the Gravel Road in St. James Parish, and for many years of my life, I fought a "hellava fight." "I Danced like a Falling Leaf and stung like a Hornet." I was quick enough to move out of the way of trouble many times.

I served my country in World War II; I nearly died when the Navy Ship-USS Randall was bombed by enemy airplanes only two hours after I disembarked. I went through a lot of changes in my life and I always bounced back stronger. But, this DEA Allegations Problem entered my life when I was much older, and my reflexes were not as keen as before. My mind was still pinpoint sharp but my body was tired. I needed some rest. Some around me thought I was not fighting hard enough saying "I was sitting around doing nothing." I was down on the canvass but I did not throw in the towel. Like the Buffalo Soldiers in my lineage, I planned to take the best way out available to me so I could live to fight another day. For many people, this is a foreign way of thinking to them.

I. Final Solution To The DEA Allegation Ordeal Designed To Silence

It should not be forgotten that on top of all of those allegations, I was going through the recovery and repair of my home destroyed by Hurricanes Rita and Katrina. For a period of time, my home was a part of the Gulf of Mexico, and it was so hard to handle this situation emotionally. I was 82 years old; many people do not live this long but I was fighting to get back on my feet, and like Sam Cooke sung in a "Change Is Gonna Come", when he went to his brother to ask for help, his brother knocked him back down on his knees again (Paraphrase is Mine). The DEA knocked me back down on my knees but I was not going to take the 8-Count.

Being guided by the Holy Spirit, I was led to the decision to "Plea Bargain." I did so at my sentencing hearing in 2009. In 1994, Former President Bill Clinton signed into law the Violent Crime and Law Enforcement Act of 1994. This law sent thousands of Black People, and others of color, to prison for commission of some of the most misdemeanor-like offenses. Today, the American Prison System is bulging at its midsection due to the large numbers of people of color, who were rounded up and sentenced to do prison time for the commission of menial offenses. This law was dusted off and applied to my Plea Bargain Decision. *Instead of me being sentenced to a mandatory minimum term of supervised release, I was, instead, sentenced to serve one year in a prison facility in Oakdale, LA.* Thanks to the Former President Bill Clinton, who millions of unwitting African-American Citizens voted for for President, and the United States Congress, which approved the Violent Crime and Law Enforcement Act of 1994, I did not get a mandatory minimum term of supervised release, but, instead I got a one year prison sentence. I added to the overrepresentation of African-Americans, and other peoples of color, in today's American Criminal Justice System.

I knew I was going to make a come-back, although I knew in my heart that the sentence I received was unfair because I was never proven by the DEA to be linked to the allegations it presented to the United States District Court For The Eastern District Of Louisiana. I am a stronger man today at 95 years old than I was when I was sentenced at 82 years old. I am doing just fine today. And, I am glad the Holy Spirit gave me this opportunity to set the record straight for my Pierce-Braud Family Group; my good friends and families on the Gravel Road; for the World Family; and for the many generations to come in which-ALL-people, all of those who are genuinely searching for the Truth, will have an opportunity to study my life story, so they can see for themselves that de facto Jim Crow is still very much alive today in all walks of life. I also hope the people will finally arrive at a verdict to make America, once and for all times, a place of social, economic, judicial, and political justice for all. Although we are currently living in the new Millennium, justice is still determined, to a large extent, based on economics and class.

CHAPTER XXII

CHARACTER IMPRESSIONS REMEMBERED BY MEDICAL COLLEAGUES, RELATIVES, AND FRIENDS

While it is most important to be a well-prepared Professional Medical Doctor in whatever one's chosen specialty might be such as Cardiology, Gynecology, Pediatrics, Optometry, and Pulmonary among many others, a physician must also develop a good bedside manner, and a positive relationship with his or her colleagues. In addition, the physician must, in the midst of the development of various treatment plans for patients, one must maintain a balance between his or her work and family life. In the event this delicate relationship becomes one-sided, in one direction or the other, this could eventually mean trouble inasmuch as the quality of medical care provided to patients will suffer. And, the affected physician may also begin to experience a negative fall-out inside of one's family, or in an intimate relationship, specifically. Personal friends are the third leg of the triangle, which is alive and fluid.

Friends are valuable because they offer the physician a third ear, who plays a role that is free from being invested in the medical practice, or family, both of whom are, to the contrary, invested in the quality of medical care delivered to patients. If the latter is moving along smoothly as possible, then friends offer outside support that could bolster the physicians' emotional well-being. All of the parts of the Triangle, that is, medical colleagues, family, and friends work together; and, each one is dependent on the type of Character the physician possess.

In short, a person's character is defined as the "mental and moral qualities distinct to an individual" (See Oxford Dictionary for more). Thus, of all the information previously mentioned in Dr. Joseph Pierce Braud's

Memoir, it is timely to ask this question: How was Dr. Braud's Character remembered by his medical colleagues, Relatives, and Friends? To answer this question, I developed three Character Surveys independent of Dr. Joseph P. Braud's input to protect objectivity. These surveys are found in the Appendix (E,F,and G) of this Memoir. Before I provide the results of the respondents, it is necessary to point-out here that the Character Survey is not meant to be a scientific exercise but, to the contrary, it is an activity that sought to glean some information about how Dr. Joseph P. Braud was remembered by some of his selected associates throughout his work, family, and social life. Toward this end, Table 1.23 shows the Character Results of those individuals, who responded to the survey. The Character Surveys used to collect data are included in Appendices E, F, and G.

Table 1.23 Character Survey Results

Medical Colleagues Variables	Never	Occasionally	Always
Need to be right all the time	X	X	X
Good listener			XXXXX
Motivator		XX	XX
Sense of humor			XXXXXXX
Problem solver		X	XXXX
Reliable			XXX
Selfish	XXXXX		
Flexible			XXXXX
Relatives Variables			
Good role model			XXXXXXXX
Generous with his time			XXXX
Good listener			XXX
Need to be right all the time	NNNNNNN	O	
Friends Variables			
Sense of humor		O	XX
Problem solver		OO	X
Good listener		O	XX
Selfish	NNN		
Reliable			XXX

	Motivator			XXX
	Flexible			XXX

Source: Author

Each alphabet represents one respondent's Character Survey. The alphabet N represents Never; O represents Occasionally; and X represents Always.

As the data shows, the vast majority of respondents indicated, based on the identified variables, that Dr. Joseph Pierce Braud presented a consistently moral point of view when he interacted with his medical colleagues, family, and friends. Overall, this is a strong indicator of the kind of man he was during his lifetime. This information also supports everything contained in Dr. Joseph Pierce Braud's Memoir. That is, it would be a major contradiction if the many good deeds mentioned throughout his Memoir are not corroborated by those people he worked with and lived with, who hold a front row seat as direct observers of Dr. Joseph Pierce Braud's Character, while he walked down the path on his journey through this life.

Lastly, the Character Survey has a place on it where a respondent could choose to write a comment about Dr. Joseph Pierce Braud's Character. Several did, and I present them below because they give more insight into the kind of man he is as seen through the eyes of another person.

- **Comment 1**: "Dr. Braud is someone that believes in Education to the max...My uncle always persisted to offer me the opportunity to pay for my Medical School fees, plus an apartment and spending money; if I would go...My uncle paid for his employees' children, to go to college and some received PhDs!"

- **Comment 2**: "Yes, Dr. Joseph P. Braud is a man and a very good person."

- **Comment 3**: "Dr. Joseph Braud is a true medical hero, healer, and physician par excellent. Who has ameliorated the lives of thousands of people in Louisiana directly through extraordinary patient care and vicariously via mentoring young and established physicians. The physicians fortunately embraced Dr. Braud's spirit of altruism, humanity, and love. In turn passed it forward to their patients and colleagues."

- **Comment 4**: "Upon meeting Mr. Braud, I was immediately impressed by his congenial manner and his level of self-confidence…I have found him to be the same quiet, confident and likeable person. This is the sentiment shared by our entire family. My two daughters are especially fond of their "Uncle Braud" and always look forward to his visits."

- **Comment 5**: "He was a good physician and surgeon, valued colleague of the Flint-[Goodridge] Hospital [of Dillard University] Medical Staff, an even-tempered, elegant, yet informal and a genuine Prince of a man. He was…very sociable, polite, caring person, who dated attractive, elegant, professional ladies. He was an active member of the Carnival Club. He was an extravert, informal, professional friend…All in all, I am most fortunate and grateful to have known Dr. Braud and I treasure the extraordinary friendship and I treasure the memory of times spent in his good company; he was friendly and open, gracious, kind."

- **Comment 6**: "Best Brother in the world. He [Dr. Joseph P. Braud] was the big boy in the family when my father died. He enlisted in the Navy so I could go to college. He got out of the Navy and Geraldine and Joe Braud graduated from southern University at the same time."

- **Comment 7**: "Dr. Joseph P. Braud was always a good and kind person, who went above and beyond to help others.

- **Comment 8**: "My father, Arthur S. Pierce, was Joseph's 1st cousin, and my father remembered vividly Joseph's mother, [Aunt] Lillian, of whom he was sacred as a little boy."

- **Comment 9**: At a time in my life when I was in the hospital, and my attending physicians were unclear about my longevity, Dr. Joseph P. Braud voluntarily drove from New Orleans, LA to

St. Louis, MO to give me moral support, and he added value to my determination that I needed to survive the health challenge I was going through at the time. In short, Dr. Joseph P. Braud is remembered by me as a man with immense compassion, empathy, dignity, and integrity. He inspired me to recover and excel in education.

- **Comment 10**: "Dr. Braud's life is an example of those African Americans who struggled and made sacrifices to make life better for their contemporaries and for those who would come later. They made progress in spite of systemic racism and long-standing racist policies…Dr. Braud's memoir and similar books should be included in high school curricula and other educational resources."

These few comments tell many things about Dr. Joseph Pierce Braud's Character. No doubt, he did endeavor, with every ounce of his energy, to make the world a better place for you and I to live. There is no dispute among us about this fact.

I have had the rare privilege to sit in Dr. Joseph Pierce Braud's home, at his favorite study table with him for hours, and absorb some of his wisdom and life experiences. Many will not have this rare opportunity to see inside of a great man as I had the occasion to do; however, my hope is you gained some knowledge of the growth and development of Dr. Braud's Wisdom after reading about it in his life journey contained in his Memoir.

CHAPTER XXIII

CONCLUSION

The overarching theme, which runs throughout my Memoir, is a variable, namely, changing times. Everything included in my Memoir is divided into two distinct time periods. The first consists of a span of time from 1632 to 1921, or 289 years, and the second time frame begins in 1926 and continues to 2022. This time period spans 96 years, which is exactly how old I am today. As you already know, I was born in 1926. The first time period is the foundation upon which the second one is built because, without it, the Pierce-Braud Family Group would not have come into existence and evolved into the magnificence that I am familiar with today.

That being so, I opened my discussion of my Memoir with a consideration of the social, economic, political, and physical environment in which the early Pierce and Braud Lineages evolved on the Louisiana River Road, which consists of several Parishes, namely, Ascension, St. James, St. John The Baptist, and St. Charles. This area, during the first time period, was dominated by the American Slavery Institution. Every available acre of land was a part of a series of plantations, from Natchez, MS to New Orleans, LA, which employed large numbers of African Slaves during the 19th Century. One of the plantations located on the West Bank of the Mississippi River was called the F. Braud Plantation. By 1850, the total African Slave Population in the mentioned River Road Parishes was 23,689. And, the ratio of the African Slave Population to the Free White Population was consistently 3 to 1. Illiteracy was greater than 50.0 percent among them by the time the American Civil War came to an end in 1865.

Interestingly, but not surprisingly, two-thirds of the millionaires in America resided on the Louisiana River Road by 1860.

The White Brault Family Group, which immigrated to Nova Scotia between 1605 and 1755, played an instrumental part in the establishment and maintenance of the African Slave Plantation System on the Louisiana River Road. Fleeing from the oppressive character of Feudalism, which was in existence 139 years before the French Revolution in 1789, some of Vincent Brault's White Family Group's offsprings migrated to St. James Parish from Nova Scotia. Alexis Breaux was the founder of the F. Braud Plantation (The plantation name was spelled Braud because this was the way White Breauxs were distinguished from Black Brauds). Particularly, Edouardo Breaux, Jr broke the normal trend of the day and married an African Slave Woman named Celestine. From this union, three children were born, who were Leontine Breaux, Theophile Breaux, and Marie Leontine Breaux. This crossover originated a Black Braud Family Lineage on the White Breaux Family Tree. Theophile Braud was born in 1842 and Louisa (Lise) Mulberry in 1851. Both were born during slavery.

Theophile Braud, aka Delpheo Braud, and Louisa (Lise) Mulberry married after the American Civil War, and they produced 10 children, one of whom was Albert Israel Braud, aka, Joe Braud. Concurrently, another family lineage was evolving alongside the Brauds known as the Pierces. Phillip Pierce married Suky Chapman Pierce, and they produced 12 children, and among them was Lillian Luellen Pierce. Joe Braud and Lillian Luellen Pierce Braud married on September 21, 1921, and shortly thereafter, I was born on September 11, 1926 in Brookstown.

By the time I was 5 years old, I saw a White Man in St. James Parish, who I later learned was a Medical Doctor. He immediately caught my attention because the fellow was dressed in white clothing, from head to toe every time I saw him. I later found out his name was Dr. Stephen Campbell. The moment I saw Dr. Campbell dressed in all-white clothing, I was inspired to become a Medical Doctor when I grew up. And, I did but I had many challenges to overcome.

First, my father died when I was 10 years old. My mother devised the Strategic Family Development Plan for her seven children to implement. It was simple but profound: That is, every one of her children would get an education of their choice in the midst of widespread illiteracy. Thus, every one of my siblings had to contribute to the fulfillment of this goal. We all pulled together, and we stayed together too. All of my sisters completed college except one; my younger brother decided he wanted to pursue a military career. And, since money was limited to the $18 per month my mother received from the Louisiana Social Service Department's Aid To Families With Dependent Children, my siblings and I *scrapped rice and potatoes* from the White Farmers Field after they harvested their crops, and I *shined shoes* near the baseball park where the New Orleans, LA Minor League Pelicans Baseball Team played their home games to make ends meet. This money helped, along with the wagon loads of potatoes and corn Evariste "Fray" Washington provided us until I graduated from Lowery High School.

I enrolled at Southern University in the Fall 1943, and after one year, I withdrew temporarily to join the Navy so I could send my mother an "Allotment of Money" to help with the education of my siblings. I re-enrolled in Southern in September 1948, and I graduated in Spring 1951. I was constantly aware of the educational teachings of my Aunt Leah Pierce Argieard, who taught me education is the key to success, and she predicted, when I was five years old, that men and women would be moving around in space before NASA was created by the Former President John F. Kennedy Administration in 1960.

After working briefly at Charles H. Brown High School, I was accepted in the Howard University Medical School in September 1954, and I graduated with my Medical Degree in May 1958. I had persevered and achieved my educational goal! My next challenge was to setup my medical practice. I set it up in New Orleans, LA, and I began working for Flint-Goodridge Hospital of Dillard University in 1960. At that time, the hospital did not have a Department of Anesthesia but there were several doctors and Nurse Anesthetists, who took care of putting patients to sleep during a scheduled surgery. I was chosen by Dr. Roy Boggs to be the first Black Physician to get accepted in the Charity Hospital Residency Training Program in 1965. No Black Physicians had been trained-beforehand-by the Charity Hospital in New Orleans, LA, in any specialty, since its inception.

I broke down its Segregation Door in 1965, and since 1967, Black Physicians and others of color, both male and female, have been steadily accepted into the Charity Hospital Internship and Residency Programs, including at other local White Hospitals. This change spurred an influx of admissions of people of color in formerly segregated White Hospitals and Universities across the South and nationwide.

In addition to this monumental social change, I was able to reverse an historical trend in education on the Louisiana River Road where for more than two centuries, Black People were classified as illiterate. And, from one generation to the next, my people prayed to God that one day their children would be able to get an education and live a better life than their parents did. When I graduated with my Medical Degree, I was the first Black Man from St. James Parish to do so. My educational achievement sent out a signal on the Gravel Road where I grew up that it is possible to not only go to school but excel in educational fields previously only White People were allowed to study.

Therefore, in Brookstown, St. James Parish, where the total population rarely exceeded 300 people, and Standing on the Shoulders of my Ancestral Giants, such as Theophile Braud, Louisa (Lise) Mulberry Braud, Celestine Breaux, Leontine Braud, Franklin Pierce, Suky Chapman Pierce, Joe Braud, Lillian Luellen Pierce Braud, Leah Pierce Argieard, African Priestess and Griot, and many others unknown, I was empowered to start an educational trend in this most tiny village where, surprisingly, *six Medical Doctors, one Juris Doctorate, one Doctor of Philosophy, four Master Degrees, and fourteen Bachelor of Science Degrees were earned by my Pierce-Braud Family Group since 1958 to date.* There are others marching toward obtaining an education now, who are holding the educational banner in their hands as I write these final words in my Memoir. No doubt, the numbers will continue to grow larger, and those of other family groups everywhere will do the same too.

Toward this end, more Black People from Brookstown, and other communities in St. James Parish, have obtained a college education since my Pierce-Braud Family broke through the Jim Crow and Separate But Equal Barriers set up to hinder us from excelling in education at the highest levels. I am very happy to know the part I played in breaking the chains of illiteracy in St. James Parish, and long the Louisiana River Road in general, has inspired a new generation of Black People to believe they-too-have the personal power within themselves to build a better life for their families. I am also excited that my grandchildren will have our educational experience to study and learn lessons from, which I believe, without a doubt, will also inspire them to become professionals in their chosen fields of study such as medical doctors, lawyers, nurses, teachers, engineers, farmers, computer scientists, physicists, chemists, bankers, musicians, and astronauts among many others. Table 1.24 includes a few examples of other Black People from St. James Parish, who have earned professional degrees in their chosen fields.

Table 1.24 New Generation of Educational Achievement In St. James Parish

Individuals	Occupation	Responsibility(s)	University	Degree
1	Apostle & Minister Medical Doctor	Television host of Activate Your Faith." Preach on Worldwide Television. First book published: Miracles On My Mind: Devotions to Last A Lifetime	St. Thomas Christian University, Dillard University	Medical Degree
1	Family Medicine	Family Practice	Meharry Medical School	Medical Degree
1	Professor at Xavier University Department of Physics	First Black Woman to receive PhD in Physics; Lectures and Research	Rensselaer Polytechnic Institute, Troy, NY	Doctoral Degree
1	Professor	Lecturer and Research	Springfield College, Boston, MA	Doctoral Degree
1	Board Certified R.N., West Jefferson Medical Center	Nurse	Nicholls State University	B.S.N.R.N.
1	Board Certified R.N.	Nurse	Dillard University	B.S. N. R. N.
1	Director of Performing Arts Center	Administrator	Southeastern Louisiana University & Nicholl State University	B S Degree and Masters Degree

1	Minister	Church Minister	Universal L.C.	Honorary Doctorate Degree
1	Apostle & Minister	Divine Deliverance International Outreach Ministries	World Christian Ministries	Honorary Doctorate Degree
1	Entergy	Business Administration 30 years Plus	Nicholl State University	BS Degree
1			Universal Life C.	Honorary Doctorate degree
12				Thirteen (13) Medical Doctors from St. James Parish
2				Two (2) Dentists from St. James Parish
1				One (1) Nurse Practitioner from St. James Parish
5				Five (5) Registered Nurses from St. James Parish
5				Five (5) Pharmacists from St. James Parish
6				Six (6) Doctors of Philosophy (PhD) from St. James Parish
6				Six (6) Attorneys from St. James Parish
1				One (1) Researcher at Mayo Clinic from St. James Parish

Source: Jones, Julie P., Doctorate of Divinity, St. Thomas Christian University and American Fellowship Center, IUHS School of Medicine. Dr. Jones provided the data contained in the first eleven rows in the above Table. Edwards, Monique, Attorney, Southern Uni- Law Center. Attorney Edwards provided the data contained in the last eight rows of the Table, February-March 2022.

As this information demonstrates, fifteen individuals, from St. James Parish where I was born and spent my childhood, earned their Medical Degrees, eleven Doctors of Philosophy, and six Juris Doctorates after I earned mine in 1958. Moreover, if I include the individuals, who earned Medical Degrees in my immediate Pierce-Braud Family Group, the total number is twenty-one! Although this educational achievement is not commonly known, St. James Parish has a rich legacy of producing highly trained professionals, which makes it one of the leaders in education today. No doubt, on a per capita basis, Brookstown, Lemonville, and Jones Road among others have the distinction of being the source where education was used to change illiteracy into literacy.

I am very proud of this educational legacy, including the people of St. James Parish, which is the place I still call home after my 95 years of living.

In summation, my life journey is, to me, worth all of the pain and suffering I had to go through to excel in my chosen educational field-Medicine. And, after 95 years of my life journey, I am happy to witness today many children of other St. James Family Groups are walking in the educational footprint my Pierce-Braud Family Group established several decades earlier. None of this would have been possible without the love of the great women in my life who stood by me when I was falling down and they held me up with their steady hands; and, after relieving my stress, they showed me the path and how to go on walking down it, for the people.

The most important lesson I learned during the 95 years of my journey is *education and knowledge is power*, and if one does not know how to handle it, he or she can become confused about their purpose, and effective service and living will, no doubt, suffer. My greatest hope for future generations is each will realize-sooner than later-that, the same power that is available to me is in unlimited abundance waiting for the brave to tap into it so they can accomplish even greater things than I have during my lifetime. Continuing Education is real because change is going-on all of the time. Without honest on-going self-examination, one's growth will be limited and wither away.

Lastly, I will always be grateful to those love ones, who saw the power and potential in me during times when, what they saw, seemed like a mystery to me. I now know power is the substance that makes mystery real.

APPENDIX

Appendix A: Braud Family Tree

Appendix B: Pierce Family Tree

Appendix C: Black Physicians At Flint-Goodridge Hospital of Dillard University

Appendix D: Black Nurse Anesthetists At Flint-Goodridge Hospital of Dillard University

Appendix E: Assessment Of Dr. Joseph Pierce Braud's Character From A Physicians And Medical Colleague Perspective Survey

Appendix F: Assessment of Dr. Joseph Pierce Braud's Character From A Relatives Perspective Survey

Appendix G: Assessment Of Dr. Joseph Pierce Braud's Character From A Friends Perspective Survey

APPENDIX A

BRAUD FAMILY TREE

NOTE: To get a clear understanding of the following Braud and Pierce Family Trees, I suggest the reader first make a zerox of each page, and second, tape them together according to the provided numbers and alphabets on each page.

1

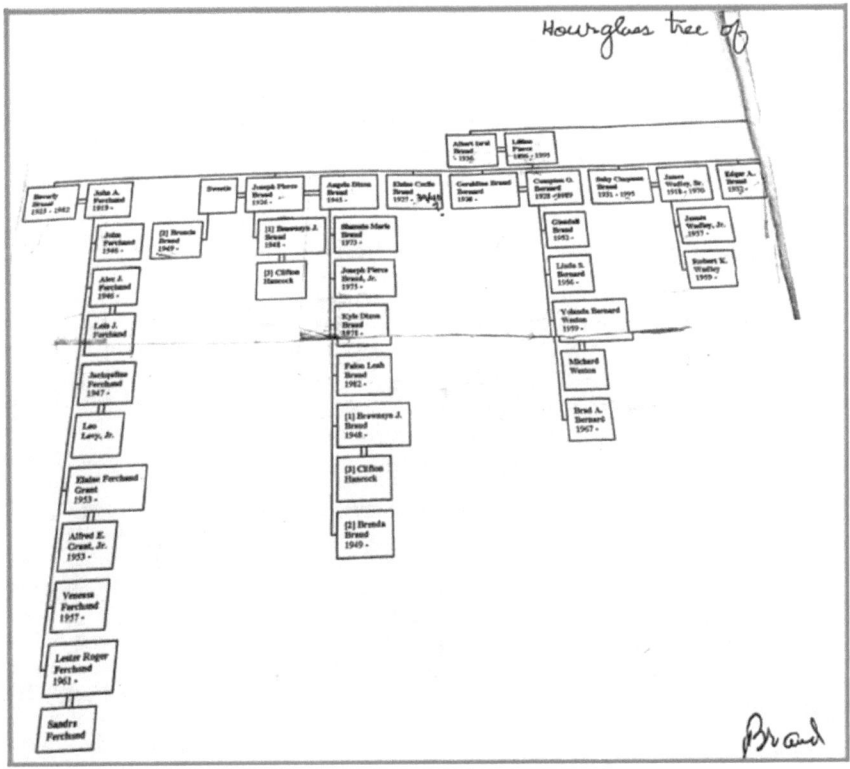

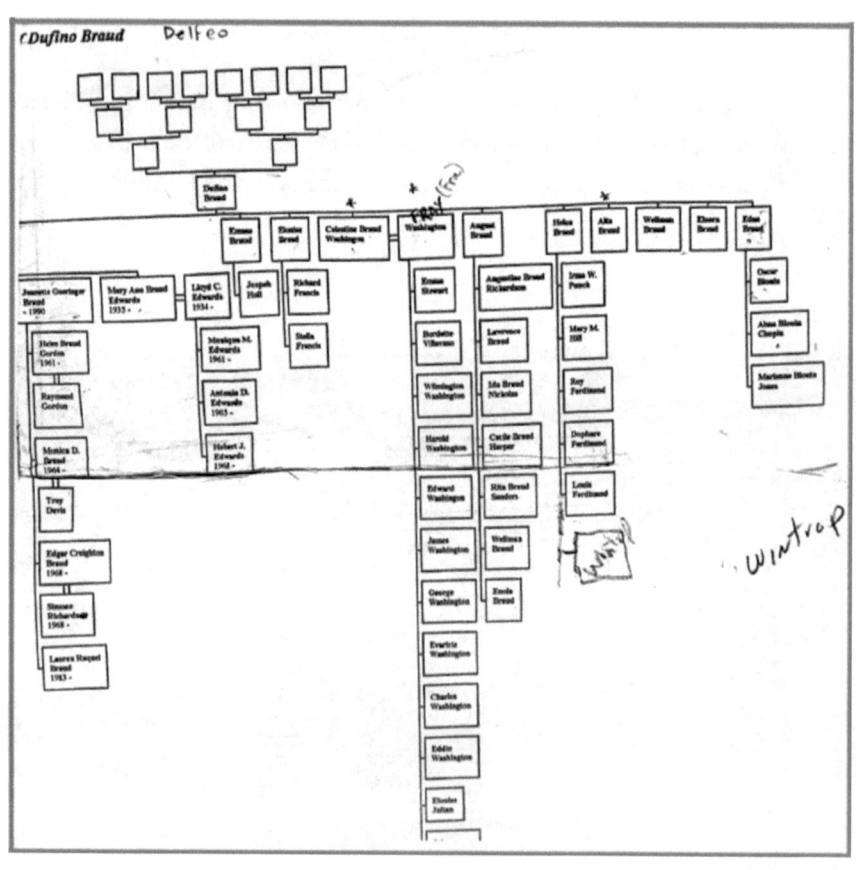

APPENDIX B

PIERCE FAMILY TREE

A

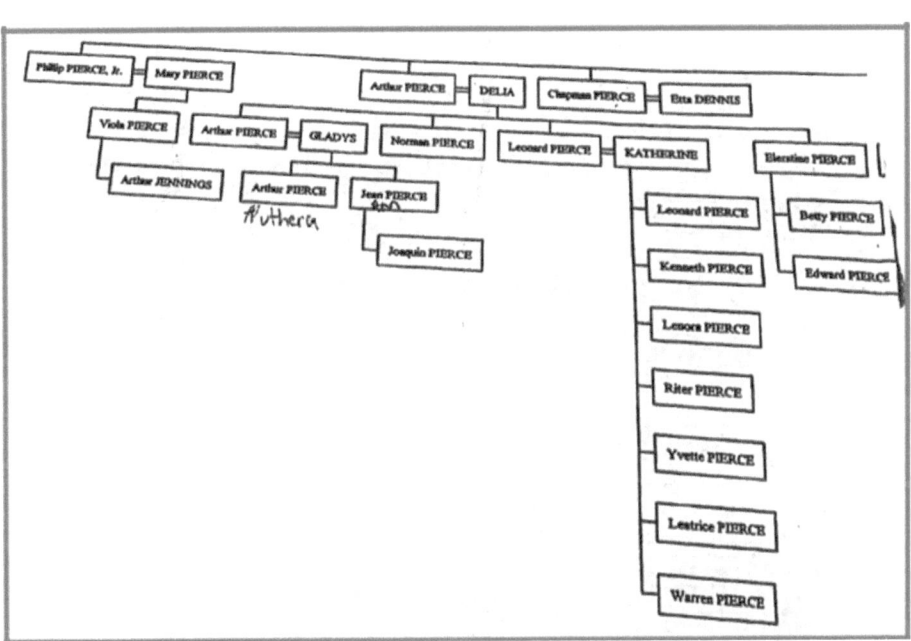

B

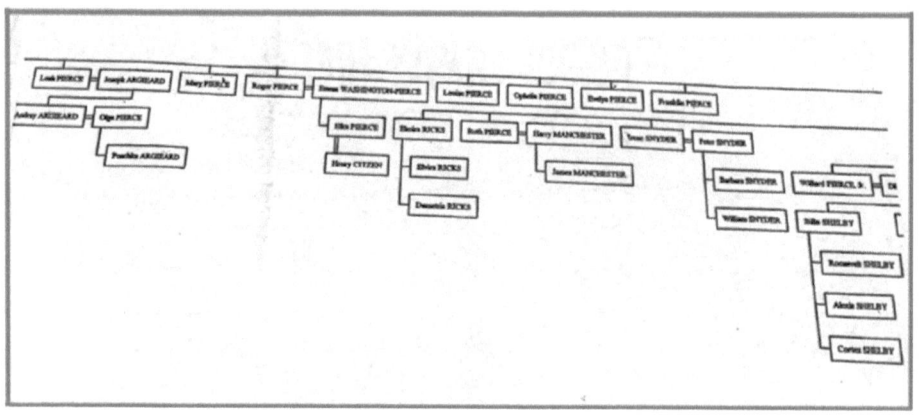

C

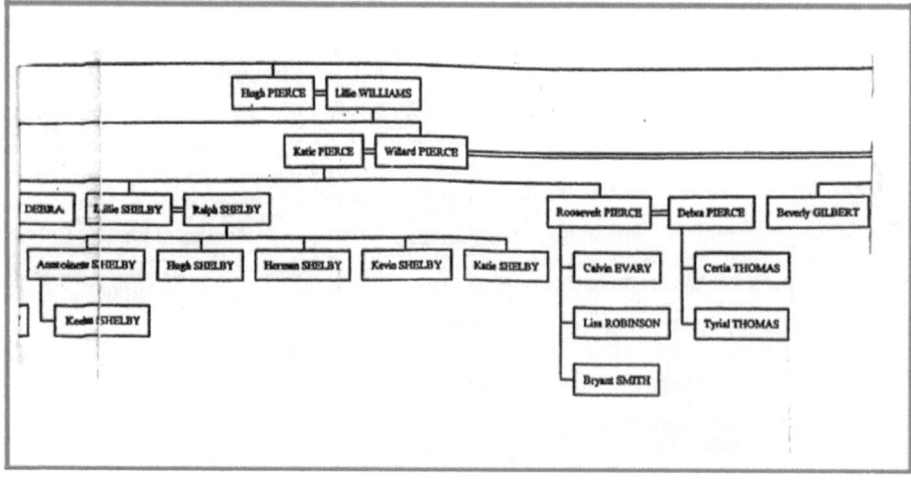

D

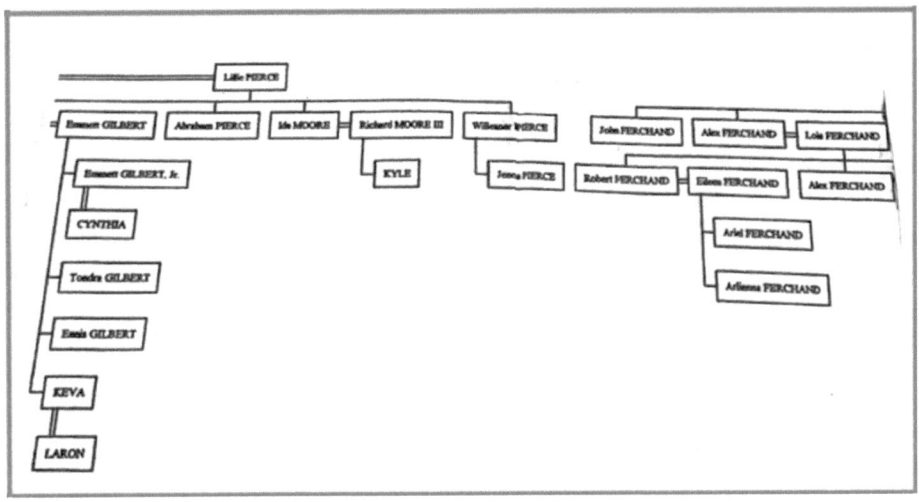

E

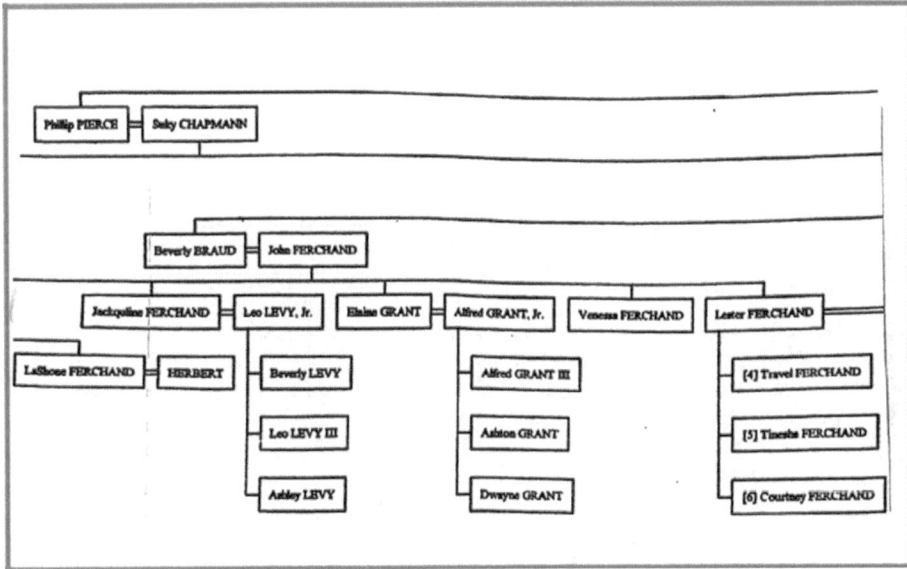

F

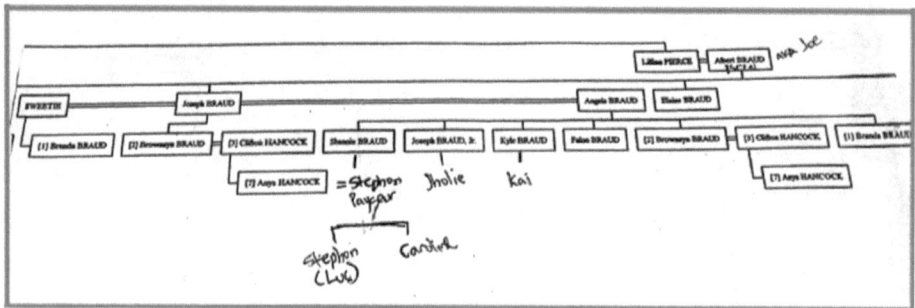

G

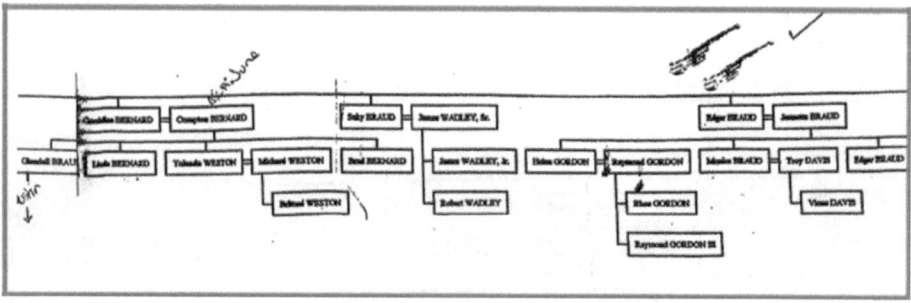

H

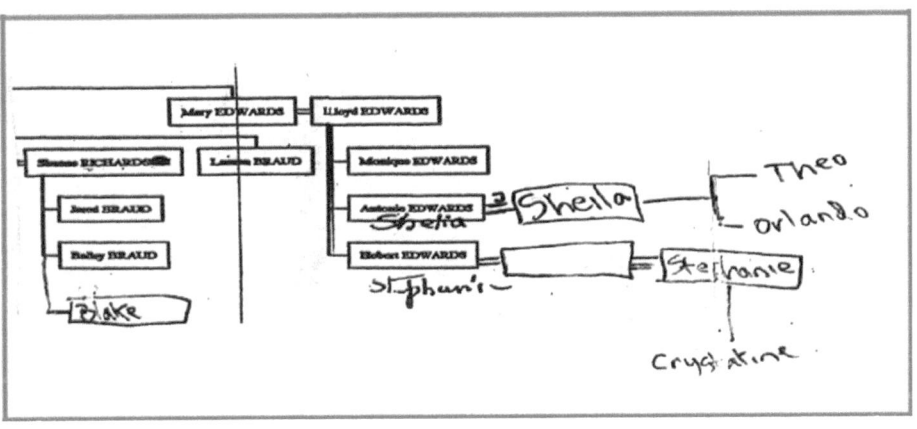

APPENDIX C

BLACK PHYSICIANS AT FLINT-GOODRIDGE HOSPITAL OF DILLARD UNIVERSITY

The following is a list of names of Black Physicians, who were on staff at Flint-Goodridge Hospital of Dillard University, between 1960 and 1982. Each person on the list worked varying years, depending on when they accepted a Staff Position.

1. Joseph Labat, MD, Surgeon
2. Leonard Weather, MD, Obs-gyn
3. Henry Evans, MD, General Practice
4. William R. Adams, MD, Gynecology, Surgery
5. Barrial, W., MD, Surgery
6. Bernard, MD, Med, Internal Medicine
7. Boggs, Roy E., MD, Anesthesia
8. Boutte', MD, OB Gynecology
9. Braden, H.E., MD, Surgery
10. Braud, Joseph P., Surgery, Anesthesia
11. Cherries, Ernest, Sr, MD, Radiology
12. Cherrie, Earnest, Jr, MD, OB Gynecology
13. Clanton, MD, Ear, Nose, Throat
14. Dean, MD, OB Gynecology
15. Darenburg, MD, OB Gynecology
16. Davidson, MD, OB Gynecology
17. Haydel, MD, Ear, Nose, Throat
18. Hackett, Anthony, MD, OB Gynecology
19. Jones, MD, Surgery

20. Pratt, A., MD, Surgery
21. Epps, J. M., Sr, MD, Surgery
22. Riordan, MD (White), Hand Surgery
23. Roberts, MD, Anesthesia
24. Robinson, H.E., MD, OB Gynecology
25. Segre', MD, OB Gynecology, Pediatics
26. Timpton, MD, Radiology
27. Thomas, MD, Urology
28. Unkauf, MD, Ortho.
29. Woods, MD, Anesthesia
30. Gibson, Johnny, MD, Surgery
31. Abrams, Matthew, MD, Obs-gyn (Baton Rouge, LA)
32. Bryant, D'Arcy, MD, Obs-gyn (Baton Rouge, LA)
33. Quintal, Errol, MD, Dermatologist
34. Ferdinand, Keith, MD, Cardiology
35. Medley, Jerome, MD, Ophthalmology
36. McKenna, Warren, MD, Ophthalmology
37. Branch, Lionel, MD
38. Nunnery, Charles, MD, General Practice
39. Ames, MD, Internal Medicine
40. Walker, George, MD, Ear, Nose, and Throat
41. McKenna, Dwight, MD, Surgery

APPENDIX D

BLACK NURSE ANESTHETISTS AT FLINT-GOODRIDGE HOSPITAL OF DILLARD UNIVERSITY

The following is a list of Certified Registered Nurse Anesthetists (CRNA), who worked for Flint-Goodridge Hospital of Dillard University, or received their Anesthesia Training at Charity Hospital, at some point between 1960 and 1982.

1. McLean, Avery, Washington, DC
2. Myrtle Ball Garrison, Houston, TX
3. Violet Burns, New Orleans, LA
4. Frankie Downs Dillard, Houston, TX
5. Carrie B. Coleman, Mound Bayou, MS
6. Sally Flanders, Melbourne, FL
7. Mattie Hansberry, New Iberia, LA
8. Dorothy Jones, Dallas, TX
9. Earnestine Jones, TX
10. Lewis Ruth, New Bern, NC
11. Doris Nearror Montgomery, AL
12. Shirley Patterson Theodore, New Orleans, LA
13. Stella Johnson, GA
14. Naomi Duvernay, RN-OR Supervisor
15. Georgetta Yellock, Asheville, NC
16. Barbara Bishop, BSN (Operating Room Nurse, Dillard University)
17. Delores Jordan, BSN (Operating Room Nurse, Dillard University)
18. Juanita Slater, BSN (Operating Room Nurse, Dillard University)
19. Carrie B. Coleman, BSN (Operating Room Nurse, Dillard University)

APPENDIX E

ASSESSMENT OF DR. JOSEPH PIERCE BRAUD'S CHARACTER FROM A PHYSICIAN AND MEDICAL COLLEAGUE'S PERSPECTIVE SURVEY

Directions: Please save this survey in the Inbox of your e-mail. Next, open it on your computer and place an (X) in the blank that best fit your answer to each question. Once you have completed the survey, save it with your selected answers and return the survey to the following e-mail address as soon as possible: lionellyles9009@gmail.com as an attachment (Any written comments you may wish to write can be placed in the comments section provided at the end of this survey).

Note: Please respond to each of the questions below within the context in which you had an opportunity to be associated with Dr. Joseph P. Braud.

1. Is Dr. Joseph P. Braud someone who needs to be right all of the time?
   Never_____ Occasionally_____ Always_____

2. Is Dr. Joseph P. Braud someone who is flexible and able to change to accommodate new medical trends?
   Never_____ Occasionally_____ Always_____

3. Did Dr. Braud make you feel lighthearted and cheer you up at work, or in another social setting?
   Never_____ Occasionally_____ Always_____

4. Is Dr. Joseph P. Braud someone who encouraged or motivated you to improve your treatment plan, or a medical technique?
Never_____ Occasionally_____ Always_____

5. Is Dr. Joseph P. Braud someone who enjoyed other people's company, and had a good time sharing his experiences and listening to those of others' during a conversation?
Never_____ Occasionally_____ Always_____

6. Do you consider Dr. Joseph P. Braud reliable?
Never_____ Occasionally_____ Always_____

7. Do you consider Dr. Joseph P. Braud selfish?
Never_____ Occasionally_____ Always_____

8. Is Dr. Joseph P. Braud someone you could talk with in confidence?
Never_____ Occasionally_____ Always_____

9. Is Dr. Joseph P. Braud someone who was able to put his needs aside and give yours' his undivided attention?
Never_____ Occasionally_____ Always_____

10. Was Dr. Joseph P. Braud willing to make time to listen to your medical practice concerns?
Never_____ Occasionally_____ Always_____

11. Did Dr. Joseph P. Braud discuss his non-work-related hobbies with you?
Never_____ Occasionally_____ Always_____

12. Did Dr. Joseph P. Braud have a sense of humor during difficult times?
Never_____ Occasionally_____ Always_____

13. Was Dr. Joseph P. Braud a good Team-Player and problem-solver?
Never_____ Occasionally_____ Always_____

14. When you were faced with a problem in your medical practice, did Dr. Braud offer you a creative solution, or helpful advice?
Never_____ Occasionally_____ Always_____

15. Did Dr. Joseph P. Braud make himself vulnerable by self-disclosing some of his past or current challenges he experienced in his life?
Never_____ Occasionally_____ Always_____

Comments (Optional):

APPENDIX F

ASSESSMENT OF DR. JOSEPH PIERCE BRAUD'S CHARACTER FROM A RELATIVE'S PERSPECTIVE SURVEY

Directions: Please save this survey in the Inbox of your e-mail. Next, open it on your computer and place an (X) in the blank that best fit your answer to each question. Once you have completed the survey, save it with your selected answers and return the survey to the following e-mail address as soon as possible: lionellyles9009@gmail.com as an attachment (Any written comments you may wish to write can be placed in the comments section provided at the end of this survey).

1. Did Dr. Joseph P. Braud read a nighttime book to you before you went to sleep, or on another occasion?
   Never_____ Occasionally_____ Always_____

2. Did Dr. Joseph P. Braud Play with his siblings, children, grandchildren nieces and nephews indoors?
   Never_____ Occasionally_____ Always_____

3. Did Dr. Joseph P. Braud take his children, and other relatives, on outings to the park during holidays and other times?
   Never_____ Occasionally_____ Always_____

4. Was Dr. Joseph P. Braud available to help his siblings, children, and other relatives with schoolwork, or other projects?
   Never_____ Occasionally_____ Always_____

5. Did Dr. Joseph P. Braud include grandchildren, nieces and nephews in holiday outings?
   Never_____ Occasionally_____ Always_____

6. Did Dr. Joseph P. Braud take his children to visit their grandparents and aunts?
   Never_____ Occasionally_____ Always_____

7. Did you feel safe in the world knowing Dr. Joseph P. Braud loved you?
   Never_____ Occasionally_____ Always_____

8. Was Dr. Joseph P. Braud a good role model?
   Never_____ Occasionally_____ Always_____

9. Was Dr. Joseph P. Braud generous with spending time with you during the holidays?
   Never_____ Occasionally_____ Always_____

10. Did Dr. Joseph P. Braud take you on family vacations?
    Never_____ Occasionally_____ Always_____

11. Did Dr. Joseph P. Braud help his siblings' children with items they needed for school and other occasions?
    Never_____ Occasionally_____ Always_____

12. Did Joseph P. Braud attend parent-teacher conferences when you were enrolled in K-12?
    Never_____ Occasionally_____ Always_____

13. Is Dr. Joseph P. Braud Someone who needed to be right all of the time?
    Never_____ Occasionally_____ Always_____

14. Did Dr. Joseph P. Braud host Thanksgiving Dinners at his home for his and extended family members?
    Never_____ Occasionally_____ Always_____

15. Is Dr. Joseph P. Braud a good listener?
    Never_____ Occasionally_____ Always_____

Comments (Optional):

APPENDIX G

ASSESSMENT OF DR. JOSEPH PIERCE BRAUD'S CHARACTER FROM A FRIEND'S PERSPECTIVE SURVEY

Directions: Please save this survey in the Inbox of your e-mail. Next, open it on your computer and place an (X) in the blank that best fit your answer to each question. Once you have completed the survey, save it with your selected answers and return the survey to the following e-mail address as soon as possible: lionellyles9009@gmail.com as an attachment (Any written comments you may wish to write can be placed in the comments section provided at the end of this survey).

Note: Please respond to each of the questions below within the context in which you had an Opportunity to be associated with Dr. Joseph P. Braud.

1. Did Dr. Joseph P. Braud enjoy making his friends laugh?
   Never_____ Occasionally_____ Always_____

2. Was Dr. Joseph P. Braud a trustworthy friend?
   Never_____ Occasionally_____ Always_____

3. When you needed a favor, did Dr. Joseph P. Braud help?
   Never_____ Occasionally_____ Always_____

4. When you had a problem, did Dr. Joseph P. Braud offer you positive advice?
   Never_____ Occasionally_____ Always_____

5. Did Dr. Joseph P. Braud share his hobbies with you?
   Never_____ Occasionally_____ Always_____

6. Was Dr. Joseph P. Braud willing to take time to listen to your concerns?
   Never_____ Occasionally_____ Always_____

7. Was Dr. Joseph P. Braud able to put his needs aside and give your's undivided attention?
   Never_____ Occasionally_____ Always_____

8. Was Dr. Joseph P. Braud someone you could talk with in confidence?
   Never_____ Occasionally_____ Always_____

9. Was Dr. Joseph P. Braud arrogant and self-important?
   Never_____ Occasionally_____ Always_____

10. Do you consider Dr. Joseph P. Braud selfish?
    Never_____ Occasionally_____ Always_____

11. Do you consider Dr. Joseph P. Braud a reliable friend?
    Never_____ Occasionally_____ Always_____

12. Was Dr. Joseph P. Braud easy to get along with?
    Never_____ Occasionally_____ Always_____

13. Is Dr. Joseph P. Braud someone who liked to relax and have a good time?
    Never_____ Occasionally_____ Always_____

14. Is Dr. Joseph P. Braud someone who encouraged or motivated you to improve yourself?
Never_____ Occasionally_____ Always_____

15. Is Dr. Joseph P. Braud someone who is flexible and able to change?
Never_____ Occasionally_____ Always_____

Comments (Optional):

BIBLIOGRAPHY

Chapter I: Introduction

Chapter II: Geography Of The Louisiana River Road, Plantations, And The Mississippi River

1. Klinkenberg, Dean, "The 70 Million-Year-Old History of the Mississippi River," Smithsonian Magazine, smithsonianmag.com, September 2020.
2. Ibid.
3. Ibid.
4. Ibid.
5. _____Mississippi River Facts, National Park Service, nps.gov.
6. Ibid.
7. Louisiana Division of Historic Preservation, The River Road, National Park Service, U.S. Department of the Interior, nps.gov.
8. _____Road Atlas, Large Scale, Rand Mcnally, 2021.
9. Brewington, Jordan, "Dismantling the Master's House: Reparations on the American Plantation," The Yale Law Journal, Vol. 130: 2160, yalelawjournal.org, 2021, p. 2167.
10. _____"Plantations of the Mississippi River from Natchez to New Orleans, 1858," 1931, TSLA Map Collection, 42389, Tennessee State Library and Archives, Tennessee Virtual Archive, https://teva.contentdm.oclc.org/digital/collection/p15138accessed 2021-07-11.
11. Louisiana Division of Historic Preservation, The River Road, National Park Service, U.S. Department of the Interior, nps.org.
12. Timmons, Greg, "How Slavery Became the Economic Engine of the South," History, https://www.history.com/.amp/news/slavery-profitable-southern-economy, September 2, 2020, (Original: March 6, 2018).
13. Ibid.
14. Ibid.
15. Clark, Maria, "River Road plantations wrestle with selling slavery," New Orleans City Business, https://neworleanscitybusiness.com/blog/2014/12/11/river-road-plantations-wrestle-with-selling-slavery/, December 11, 2014.

16 Mires, Peter Bingham, "Predicting the Past: The Geography of Settlement in Louisiana, 1699-1890, and Its Application to Historic Preservation." (1988). LSU Historical Dissertation and Theses. 4661. Https://digitalcommons.lsu.edu/ gradschool disstheses/4661

17 Ibid., p. 153.

Chapter III: Selected Demographic Characteristics Of The White And African Slave Population For River Road Parishes-1850 To 1950

18 Ibid., p. 157.

19 United States Census of Population, 1940, Sixteenth Census, Characteristics Of The Population, Composition Of The Population, By Parishes: 940, pp. 362 and 364.

Chapter IV: Thirteenth Amendment To The U.S. Constitution, Freedman Bureau Bill, 1865, Sharecropping System And Out-Migration On The River Road

20 Lyles, Lionel D., Ph. D., <u>Neoliberalism Economic Policy And The Collapse Of The Public Sector: How the Jindal Administration Allowed It to Happen-2008 to 2016</u>, iUniverse, Bloomington, IN, 2018, p. 309.

21 Ibid., p. 310.

22 Blackmon, Douglas, A., *Slavery By Another Name*, Doubleday, 2008, p. 53.

23 Lyles, op. cit., p. 309.

24 The New Capitalist had an inexhaustible demand for raw cotton, and they urged the U.S. Congress to pass the Freedmen Bureau Bill in 1865.

25 Lyles, Lionel D., PhD, Historical Development of Capitalism In The United States And Its Affects On The American Family: From Colonial Times to 1920, Volume One, iUniverse, Inc., New York, 2003, p. 107.

26 Reonas, Matthew, "Sharecropping," 64parishes.org, February 15, 2019.

27 Ibid.

28 Ibid.

29 "Sharecropping in Mississippi," American Experience, pbs.org

30 Ibid.

31 Boonstra, C A., "Rough rice marketing in Louisiana" (1942). *LSU Agricultural Experiment Station Reports*. 595. http://digitalcommons.lsu.edu/agexp/595, March, 1942, p. 3.

32 Bolano, Alex, "How Many Feet Are In 1 Acre?" Science Trends, https://sciencetrends.com, January 5, 2019.

33 Boonstra, op. cit., p. 4.

Chapter V: Domestic Terrorism, Ku Klux Klan, And Jim Crow Restrictions Put In Place To Stop Negro Progress

34 Morris, Jr, Roy, <u>Fraud Of The Century: Rutherford B. Hayes, Samuel Tilden, and the Stolen Election of 1876</u>, Simon & Schuster, New York, 2003, p. 1.
35 Ibid., p. 1.
36 Ibid., p. 3.
37 Ibid., p. 63.
38 Ibid., p. 63.
39 Ibid., p. 44.
40 Ibid., p. 249.
41 Ibid., p. 119.
42 Ibid., p. 133.
43 Ibid., p. 247.
44 Ibid., p. 246.
45 Ibid., pp. 247 and 248.
46 Ibid., p. 248.
47 Ibid., p. 248.
48 Ibid., p. 248.
49 Ibid., p. 248.
50 Ibid., p. 248.
51 Ibid., p. 250.
52 History.com Editors, "Plessey v. Ferguson, https://www.history.com/.amp/topics/ black-history/plessy-v-ferguson, January 20, 2021.
53 Ibid.
54 Morris, op. cit., p. 33.
55 Ibid. p. 33.
56 Ibid., p. 37.
57 "Lynching in America: Confronting the Legacy of Racial Terror, Supplement: Lynchings by County," www.eji.org, 1877-1950, p. 3.
58 Ibid., Report Summary, pp. 2 and 3.
59 Ibid., p. 3.
60 United States Census of 1940, Sixteenth Census of Population: Internal Migration, 1935 to 1940, p. 98. This was the first census to compile statistics on the subject.

Chapter VI: Origin Of The Pierce-Braud Family Group From Pre-Civil War To 1921

61 "The family name comes from either an ancient Gaulish word, "Brolii" meaning small woods surrounded by a wall; or a town named Broilum, about year 1142 in

Department of Seine-et-Marne...Brault, a word derived from Gallo-Germanic Beroaldus, is a very old name borne by many French families in and around France." Breauxfamily.files.wordpress.com/2017/03/vincentbreaux article.pdf, p. 1.
62. Duncan, Janet Wood and Duncan, Stephen Joseph, "On The Shoulders Of Giants: Addendum To The Allendom Papers," www.safero.org, Acadia, June 1995.
63. Op. cit., See Footnote 61.
64. Ibid., See Footnote 61, p. 2.
65. Ibid., p. 2.
66. Ibid., p.2.
67. Op. cit., See Footnote 62.
68. Ibid., See Footnote 62.
69. Op. cit., See Footnote 61, p. 2.
70. Ibid. Part 2.
71. Op. cit., see Footnote 61, p. 2.
72. Marsh, Jordan H., "Acadian Expulsion (the Great Upheaval)," the canadianencyclopedia.ca, July 15, 2015.
73. Op. cit., See Footnote 61, Part 1.
74. Ibid.
75. Ibid., See Footnote 61, Part 3.
76. Op. cit., see Footnote 62, Part 2.
77. Ibid.
78. Ibid.
79. Ibid., Part 3.
80. Marsh, op. cit.
81. Duncan and Duncan, op. cit., See Footnote 62, Part 4.
82. Ibid., Part 4.
83. Ibid., Part 4.
84. Ibid., Part 1.
85. Ibid., Part 4.
86. Ibid., Part 4.
87. Ibid., Part 4.
88. Honore Breaux had another female companion name Anne Trahan.
89. Op. cit., See Footnote 62, Part 4, June 1995.
90. Ibid., Part 5.
91. Ibid., Part 5.
92. Ibid., Part 6.
93. Ibid., Part 6.
94. Ibid., Part 6.
95. To avoid any confusion, the White Brault Family Group goes back in time at least seven generations, beginning in Loudun, France. Thus, the Black Braud Family Group only came into existence when Edouardo Breaux, Jr and Celestine

(Former African Slave) got married. Although their only son, Theophile Braud was born in 1842, the generation count did not begin until he married Louisa (Lise) Mulberry, and they started producing children. Then, the Generation clock began to tick.

96 Theophile Braud appears in the 1850 and 1860 Census with his name recorded as shown. However, there are several other ways Theophile Braud's name has been written through the generations. They are: Defeo, Dufino, and so forth.

97 Wellman Braud was a famous musician, and during his professional career, he played with the Cab Calloway Band, Duke Ellington Orchestra, and Borne Brigard.

Chapter VII: Joe Braud And Lillian Luellan Pierce-Braud Household

98 Maxwell, Kelena Reid, "Birth Behind the Veil: African American Midwives and Mothers in the Rural South, 1921-1962," Dissertation, Rutgers, The State University of New Jersey, New Brunswick, New Jersey, 2009, p. ii.

Chapter VIII: Social Life In Brooktown And Surrounding Villages

99 When a person is baptized with water, it is an act in which the one baptized commit oneself to be an obedient believer in God's Teachings in the Bible. During the Pre-Baptism Ritual Process, the seeker aims to repent his or her sins, and make a change to live a spiritual life. Selfishness, pride, and ego are placed before the Lord.

Chapter IX: Joseph Pierce Braud's Childhood World Turned Upside Down In 1936

100 Sometime between 1915 and 1918, which was three years before my parents got married, Joe Braud was accidentally struck in the head by a falling can of grease on a dredge boat. He was employed at the time engaged in Mississippi River Levee work. After this accident, I was told my father was unconscious for several months. Joe Braud recovered from this accident, and by 1921, he married Lillian Luellen Pierce, and they raised seven children together in Brookstown before his death.

Chapter X: Southern University Education Temporarily Put On Hold To Join The Military To Advance The Pierce-Braud Strategic Family development Plan

101   The allotment I received from the Navy was between $200 and $300 per month. No doubt, this sum was far more than the $18 per month we received from the Louisiana Welfare Department's Aid To Dependent children Program.

Chapter XII: Post-Southern University And The Beginning Of My Professional Career In 1951

102   _____ "Dozens gather to remember historic sit-in," www.wafb.com Mar. 29, 2013.

Chapter XIII: Marriage To Swedie Weary Brown In 1952

103   According to Stephen Altrogge, "People prefer to carry on behaving as they have always done even when the circumstances that might influence their decisions change…Default behaviors are the actions you take without thinking. They're your *habits, routines,* and compulsions. With more than 40% of our daily actions controlled by our defaults, they're powerful tools for helping (or hurting)…," "What to change your life? Start with changing your default behavior," www.rescuetime.com, September 26, 2019.

Chapter XIV: Howard University Medical School In Washington, DC From 1954 To 1958

104   Morais, Herbert M., THE HISTORY OF THE AFRO-AMERICAN IN MEDICINE, The Publishers Agency, Inc., Cornwells Heights, Pennsylvania, 1978, p. 138.
105   Washington Area Spark, "White students terrorize Anacostia black students: 1954," www.flickr.com. For more information, go to www.flickr.com/gp/washington area spark/564wW3
106   Ibid.

Chapter XV: Post-Howard University Medical School Internship Decision And Family Matters

107   Swedie Braud was under the influence of her biological family regarding her aversion to adoption of my two children, namely, Bronsyn Baud and Glenn Braud. She was likely coached by her brother-James Weary. He may have planted the thought in her mind related to inheritance. My two children would become heirs

to Swedie Braud's Estate if something happened to her. By not adopting my two children, this fact would never come to pass, or become a reality.

Chapter XVI: Louisiana Homecoming And Returned As A Medical Doctor

108 Wilson, Michael L., Secretary, "Dr. John Lowery, Louisiana Activist born," John Harvey Foundation, 509 Lessard Street, Donaldsonville, Louisiana, www.aaregistry.org
109 Ibid.
110 Ibid.
111 "African American Physicians and Organized Medicine, 1846-1968, Medico-Historical Events, https://www.ama-assn.org/media/14066/download, p. 7.
112 Besides Dr. Anthony Hackett, a few of the other Black Medical Doctors I had the privilege to meet were Dr. Joseph Epps, Sr, Dr. Thelma Boute, Dr. George Thomas, Dr. William Adams, Dr. Alvin Smith, Dr. Henry Braden, and Dr. Norbert Davidson among others.

Chapter XVII: Flint Goodridge Hospital Of Dillard University Glory Years From 1959 To 1983

113 Tanner, Lindsey, "AMA meets amid backlash over racial equity plan," Associated Press, June 13, 2021.
114 Ibid.
115 "THE HISTORY OF FLINT-GOODRIDGE HOSPITAL OF DILLARD UNIVERSITY, Journal OF The National Medical Association, Vol. 61, No. 6, November 1969, p. 533.
116 Ibid., p. 533.
117 Ibid., p. 533.
118 Ibid., p. 533. This data is taken from Cobb, W. M., Progress and Portents for the Negro in Medicine, NAACP, N.Y., 1948, p. 12.
119 Ibid., p. 534.
120 Ibid., p. 534.
121 Ibid., p. 534.
122 Ibid., p. 534. Prior to 1958, Flint-Goodridge Hospital was a four-story building with a separate building that had a small living quarters for nurses, and a house that was for the administrator. It was a hospital where the nursing students from Dillard University did some of their clinical training. There was also a Nurse Anesthesia Program that trained Black Nurse Anesthetists from all around the United States.
123 Ibid., pp. 534 and 535.

124 Richardson, Joe M., "Albert W. Dent: A Black New Orleans Hospital and University Administrator," The Journal of the Louisiana Historical Association, vol. 37, No.3, (Summer, 1996), p. 309.
125 op. cit., Journal of the National Medical Association, p. 535.
126 Ibid., p. 535.
127 Ibid., p. 535.
128 Ibid., p. 535.
129 Ibid.. p. 535.
130 Ibid., p. 535. There was only one set back, New Orleans, LA only had roughly 30 Black Physicians to utilize. The 96 bed hospital, therefore, had to depend other ethnic physicians, particularly White Ones.
131 A Nurse Anesthetist is a person who is a registered nurse, who has completed two or more years of additional specialized training and education and is a certified to administer anesthetics. This person is a Certified Registered Nurse Anesthetist (CRNA). He or she is qualified to administer Anesthesia required to put a patient to sleep; monitor their vitals during a surgical operation; and assist the patient's return to an awake state after a given surgery is completed. The CRNA is a highly skilled medical professional.
132 According to Mrs. Myrtle Garrison, "Mrs. Baker was a graduate of Flint-Goodridge School of Nursing, which was no longer in existence in 1960. Miss Shirley Patterson Theodore was a graduate of Dillard University School of Nursing and Flint-Goodridge Hospital of Dillard University School of Anesthesia. There was no Physician Anesthesiology Resident Program at Flint."
133 Morais, op. cit., p. 177.
134 Ibid., p. 177.

Chapter XVIII: Flint Goodridge Hospital Of Dillard University Rise And Untimely Fall From 1960 To 1983

135 Schumann, John Henning, "A Bygone ERA: When Bipartisanship Led To Health Care Transformation," Shots, https://www.npr.org/sections/health-shots/2016/10/02/495775518/a-bygone-era-when-bipartisanship-led-to-health-care-transformation, October 2, 2016.
136 Ibid.
137 Ibid.
138 Ibid.
139 _____ "Free healthcare from the Hill-Burton federal program," https://www.needhelppayingbills.com/html/hill-burton_act_free_healthcar.html
140 Ibid.

141 Largent, Emily A. PhD, JD, RN, "Public Health, Racism, and the Lasting Impact of Hospital Segregation," Public Health Report, 133(6): September 17, 2018, PP. 715-720.
142 McQueeney, Kevin, "Flint Goodridge Hospital and black Health Care in Twentieth Century New Orleans," The Journal of African American History, Volume 103, Number 4, https://www.journals.uchicago.edu/doi/full/10.1086/699952
143 Ibid.
144 Ibid.
145 Ibid.
146 Ibid.
147 Ibid.
148 _____ BLACK-OWNED HOSPITAL SOLD IN NEW ORLEANS, New York Times, March 7, 1983, Section A, Page 13.
149 _____ "Hospital Corp. Sets $78 Million Merger With General Care," The Wall Street Journal, June 27, 1980, p. 8.
150 Op. cit., The New York Times, Page 13.

Chapter XX: Hurricane Katrina Struck New Orleans, LA And Changed The City Forever

151 _____ Wetlands and Coastal Erosion-Southeastern Louisiana University, https://www2.southeastern.edu

Chapter XXI: Drug Enforcement Administration (DEA) Case Based On Allegations And Would A Trial By Jury Reach A Guilty Or Innocent Verdict?

152 Oxfordlanguages.oup.com
153 See pp. 1 and 2.
154 Ibid., p. 2.

www.ingramcontent.com/pod-product-compliance
Lightning Source LLC
LaVergne TN
LVHW042251070526
838201LV00089B/106